STUDIES IN THE HISTORY OF OLD ENGLISH LITERATURE

STUDIES IN THE HISTORY OF OLD ENGLISH LITERATURE

BY

KENNETH SISAM

OXFORD
AT THE CLARENDON PRESS

Oxford University Press, Great Clarendon Street, Oxford OX2 6DP
Oxford New York
Athens Auckland Bangkok Bogota Buenos Aires Calcutta
Cape Town Chennai Dar es Salaam Delhi Florence Hong Kong Istanbul
Karachi Kuala Lumpur Madrid Melbourne Mexico City Mumbai
Nairobi Paris São Paolo Singapore Taipei Tokyo Toronto Warsaw
and associated companies in
Berlin Ibadan

Oxford is a registered trade mark of Oxford University Press

Published in the United States by
Oxford University Press Inc., New York

British Library Cataloguing in Publication Data
Data available

ISBN 0-19-811392-7

1 3 5 7 9 10 8 6 4 2

Printed in Great Britain
on acid-free paper by
Bookcraft (Bath) Ltd.,
Midsomer Norton

PREFACE

APART from their general subject, these papers have a certain unity in that most of them are concerned with problems of textual transmission. In the Anglo-Saxon period this field has not had much attention. It does not promise quick, regular, or wholly satisfactory results. Yet, until it is better explored, writers on Old English literary history or textual criticism or language must often do without significant facts that are discoverable.

I foresee two just criticisms. One is that insufficient account has been taken of recent work on Old English. In a technical subject which has been intensively studied in many countries, the knowledge of what has been done is an essential part of the equipment of a professional scholar. But for more than thirty unquiet years of administrative work, I have not been able to watch the flow of articles and monographs, or to keep in touch with specialists at home and abroad. So I have not attempted to revise the pieces that have been published already, beyond correcting a slip here and there and adding in brackets an occasional reference or clarification. The other fault—the rambling nature of many of these studies and their notes—is partly due to the same cause. They are not systematic studies, but the result of following some idea or observation wherever it might lead, with the books and materials that were at hand. For such weaknesses I hope to have the grace that is allowed to amateurs. I would even claim that the amateur, working outside the main trend, has still a certain usefulness. He is less likely to be over-influenced by current fashions, especially those simplifying assumptions and generalizations which, in an historical subject, are convenient for teaching but unfavourable to research.

My acknowledgements of help that cannot be specified include some very old debts: to my master Arthur Napier, whose knowledge of Early English was exquisite; to Henry Bradley; to Sir William Craigie, happily still with us. For guidance in subjects outside my competence I owe a great deal to Edmund Bishop, André Wilmart, and, latterly, to Professor Paul Maas. Mrs. J. E.

Heseltine, Miss Celia Sisam, and Mr. Neil Ker have reported on books and manuscripts that are beyond my reach. Miss Dorothy Whitelock and Professor Norman Davis have helped generously in the proof stages. Finally my thanks are due to the Delegates of the Clarendon Press and my former colleagues of their staff who have made this book practicable.

K.S.

St. Mary's,
Scilly Isles

CONTENTS

1

CYNEWULF AND HIS POETRY[1]

IT is common ground that Cynewulf was a pre-Conquest poet whose name is found in runic letters at the end of an Old English poem on *St. Juliana* in the Exeter Book; at the end of a poem on the Finding of the Cross by St. Helena (*Elĕne*) in the Vercelli Book; and, again in association with English verse, on f. 19 of the Exeter Book and f. 54 of the Vercelli Book. That may seem a slender basis of agreed fact on which to speak the hour-glass out, especially as I hope to eschew the colours of romance. There is a legend of Cynewulf built up not in the Middle Ages, which have left no record of him outside his own work, but in the last hundred years. Some half-century ago a staid critic could create for him a wife Cyneburh, without even a rib to build on. These were the excesses of an age of great discoveries, and should be passed lightly. But a stricter view of the evidence must make claims on your patience. It will be disjointed like the evidence itself, and full of argument.

I begin with the question: To what part of England did Cynewulf belong? Like nearly all the rest of Old English poetry, his poems are found in copies made in the South of England. These copies exhibit a mixed dialect, which indicates either that the poems were not originally composed in West Saxon—the literary dialect from Alfred's time—or that they have passed through other dialects in the course of transmission. The only clear evidence of provenance is a passage of rhyme and assonance which introduces the runic signature to *Elene*. It is remarkable because rhyme is not native to English verse. There is no sequence of rhyming verses in *Beowulf* or in religious poems like *Genesis* which are

[1] The Sir Israel Gollancz Memorial Lecture, read 8 March 1933, *Proc. British Academy* xviii. A convenient bibliography and account of Cynewulf studies up to 1907 is Karl Jansen's *Die Cynewulf-Forschung*, Bonner Beiträge zur Anglistik xxiv, Bonn 1908.

agreed to be early. A sustained passage of fifteen lines of the regular type,

> Þus ic frōd ond fūs þurh þæt fǣcne hūs,

with rhymes of one, two, or three syllables at the end of each half-line, can only be explained by a strong influence of Christian Latin verse. Now in the passage from *Elene* there are verses like

> þurh ðā mǣran *miht* on mōdes *eaht*,

where the West Saxon forms of the manuscript, *miht*: *eaht*, do not rhyme. Yet the rhyme is perfect if we substitute the forms usual north of the Thames: *mæht* : *æht*. It is, then, a fair deduction that Cynewulf wrote in the Anglian dialect—in Northumbrian or in Mercian. A number of special reasons derived from the Cynewulf legend, and the literary prestige of Northumbria, have inclined most critics in that direction; but there is no ponderable evidence for the one kingdom or the other.[1]

The question when Cynewulf wrote is not less obscure. Obviously his poems are older than the Exeter Book and the Vercelli Book in which they are preserved, and both these manuscripts belong to the latter part of the tenth century. Allowing the minimum time for translation from Anglian into their present form, we may fix the middle of the tenth century as the extreme later limit for the date of composition.

The safe earlier limit is a long way back. In *Juliana* and *Elene* the runes spell CYNEWULF. The third signature, which is in the Exeter Book, reads CYNWULF without the *E*, and it used to be thought that a verse containing *E* had dropped out of the text. Then in 1888 Napier[2] discovered a fourth signature on a blotted page of the Vercelli Book, and could see no rune for *E*. In 1891 Sievers examined the new evidence in a classic article,[3] and con-

[1] Sievers *Die neueren Sprachen* 6. Beiheft (1925), p. 65 states that his new method of 'Schallanalyse' enables him to decide for Northumbrian. I leave aside rather than neglect his recent work on Cynewulf. No one has better claims to the trust of students of Old English; but the method avowedly depends on a rare special faculty of perception, and those who do not possess that faculty are in no position either to criticize the results or to accept them. [For an indication favouring Mercia see below, p. 134.]

[2] *The Academy*, 8 Sept. 1888, p. 153; and *Zeitschrift für deutsches Altertum* xxxiii (1889), p. 66 ff.

[3] *Anglia* xiii (1891), p. 1 ff.

cluded that Cynewulf spelt his name both ways. In a Middle English or Elizabethan writer an *e* more or less would not matter, but in Cynewulf's day two spellings recorded with such deliberate care indicate alternative pronunciations. So Sievers investigated the history of the name.

In Bede, who died in 735, the first element of such names is regularly *Cyni-*, never *Cyne-*. Forms with *e* are not recorded in Southern documents before 740,[1] or in South Midland documents before 770; and there are indications that *i* spellings remained longest in the North. Since the runes leave no doubt that *e* and not *i* is original, the indication is that Cynewulf wrote after the middle of the eighth century. The second form, CYNWULF without *E*, carries us no farther because it is found beside CYNEWULF throughout Old English.[2] So far Sievers, whose investigations covered all comparable words, and whose results have been generally accepted.

But what is the evidence after Bede for the spelling in Northumbria, which most critics think of as Cynewulf's home? The *Liber*

[1] The dates given here apply to the texts of charters, not to the extant copies which are our witnesses for spelling. It is usually impossible to say that an early MS. of a genuine charter is original or strictly contemporary. Thus the charter of 740 (Augustus II. 101), which shows some *e* forms, is so dated by a conjecture of Kemble's. On its face it bears the date A.D. 741, Indiction iii, and the Indiction fits neither 741 (ix) nor 740 (viii): the double error could hardly be made unless the copy is later than the year of signature. Similarly, the first charter to show *e* forms consistently (Sweet's *Oldest English Texts*, p. 432) bears the date 742; but the investigation of the signatures in Haddan and Stubbs, *Councils* iii. 342, note *d*, shows that the early copy from which Sweet prints gives a sophisticated text of later date. In the South and South Midlands the second half of the eighth century is the period of transition. One charter, as Sievers noted, seems to show *e* forms much earlier: it is the Essex charter MS. Augustus II. 29, which is accepted as an original of the years 692–3 in *Facsimiles of Ancient Charters in the British Museum*, 1873. But I think palaeographers would now agree that a charter in these stiff imitative uncials is not an original of the late seventh, but a copy of the late eighth century. Thus we have welcome confirmation that the criterion is sound.

[2] The sequence *Cyni-* ⟩ *Cyne-* ⟩ *Cyn-* is sometimes assumed and used to establish the chronological order of Cynewulf's poems. In fact, *Cynuise* occurs in Bede, who has no *Cyne-* forms; and *Cyn-heard*, *Cyn-helm* occur in the *Liber Vitae* which has no *Cyne-* forms. In theory, there seems to be no objection to the alternative developments *Cyni-* ⟩ *Cyn-*, and *Cyni-* ⟩ *Cyne-* ⟩ *Cyn-*.

Vitae, which records the names of those who were remembered in the prayers of the community at Lindisfarne, is shown by the names to be of the early ninth century, and, if some likely identifications hold good, may be as late as 830 or even 840.[1] It has over a hundred examples of the spelling *Cyni-* and no single instance of *Cyne-*. This evidence from Lindisfarne itself is awkward for those who have identified our poet with Cynewulf, the bishop of Lindisfarne, who died after a stormy life in 783.

Sievers relied on another document which can be certainly dated within a year or two of 812, and which shows both *e* and *i* forms. It is the so-called 'Northumbrian Genealogies' in MS. Vespasian B VI. These are really lists of bishops for the whole country and royal genealogies for Northumbria, Mercia, and Kent. The unfortunate title is due to Henry Sweet, who heads the lists 'Genealogies: Northumbrian (?)' in his corpus of the Oldest English Texts. But Sweet, perhaps the greatest master of linguistic science that this country has produced, was unhappy when he ventured on the history of manuscripts bearing the pressmark Vespasian.[2] The British Museum palaeographers, after a careful study of the writing and the contents, had described Vespasian B VI as Mercian.[3] Sweet preferred Northumbria for reasons that will not bear

[1] See *Catalogue of Ancient MSS. in the British Museum*, Pt. II Latin, 1884, p. 81 ff. The Introduction to the facsimile edition by the Surtees Society (1923) is not yet available.

[2] Similarly, in his edition of the Vespasian Psalter, which by reason of its interlinear gloss is the main authority for early Mercian, Sweet rejects Wanley's statement that a MS. of identical content was described by Thomas of Elmham in the early fifteenth century as an ancient treasure of St. Augustine's, Canterbury. So he obscured the importance of the Vespasian Psalter as a witness of Mercian learning at Canterbury in the ninth century, probably in the time of the Mercian archbishop Plegmund. That the early-eighth-century Latin text is a Canterbury production is not established; but certainly the ninth-century Mercian gloss was copied into it from another book. The clearest of a number of indications is Ps. lxvii. 31: *Increpa feras* glossed *ðu ðreades* as if *increpaueras*. In the uncials of the Vespasian Psalter the two Latin words are distinct; but the mid-tenth-century MS. Royal 2 B V preserves the reading *increpaferas*, without division, and has the marginal gloss *i. increpaueras*. The Vespasian gloss must have been made for a text with this peculiar reading.

[3] See *Catalogue of Ancient MSS. in the British Museum*, Pt. II Latin, 1884, p. 79 ff.

examination; and philologists can hardly be blamed for following his authority. But the case for Mercia seems to be overwhelming; and I find evidence that the lists come from Lichfield, the ecclesiastical centre of the old Mercian kingdom. The lists for the Northern sees remain almost as they were first written: the Lindisfarne list, for instance, is continued by one name, Eadmund, who is unknown to history.[1] But the bishops of Lichfield alone have

[1] The argument would be weakened if, as W. G. Searle *Anglo-Saxon Bishops, Kings and Nobles*, 1899, p. 190, supposes, the Eadmund in the Lindisfarne list of MS. Vespasian B VI is the bishop of Durham (1020–42); but the entry was made two centuries before his accession. The matter stands thus:

(i) Stubbs *Registrum Sacrum*, 1897, and Searle accept Heathured at this point in the Lindisfarne list, the succession being 'Ecgberht, Heathured, Ecgred, Eanberht, Eardwulf'. This order is supported by the Lindisfarne Annals (*Mon. Germ. Hist. Scriptores* xix. 502 ff. from a twelfth-century MS.) except that they point to a lacuna before Eardwulf; by Simeon of Durham (Rolls Series i. 52); and by the interpolations in Florence of Worcester (for Heathured see MS. CCC Oxford CLVII, pp. 282, 284). These three witnesses are dependent on a single source of information; and the same Durham source seems to be followed in the list of bishops of Lindisfarne and Durham which was added to MS. CCCC 190 at Canterbury about 1100 (A. Whelock *Bede* &c., 1644, p. 569).

(ii) The list of Bishops of Lindisfarne attached to Florence of Worcester's Chronicle has 'Ecgbert, Eardulf', i.e. it skips at the critical point; and this is the tradition followed by William of Malmesbury (*Gesta Pontificum*, Rolls Series, p. 269).

(iii) Eadmund seems to be found only as an almost contemporary addition to MS. Vespasian B VI.

(iv) But in the same MS., in what appears to be the same hand, Heathured is added to the list of the bishops of Whitern or Candida Casa in Galloway. The catalogue of the bishops of Whitern attached to Florence's Chronicle also has Heathured after Baldwulf (MS. CCC Oxford CLVII, p. 45).

The contemporary MS. Vespasian B VI is good evidence that there was at least one bishop of Whitern after Baldwulf, who is last heard of in 805. That the Whitern line ended with Baldwulf is an inference *ex silentio*: William of Malmesbury says (*Gesta Pontificum*, p. 257) 'nec praeterea plures alicubi reperio'. He was probably relying on a copy of the lists of MS. Vespasian B VI made before they were added to. The existence of such a copy in the South is attested by MS. Tiberius B V. This Christ Church compilation of the time of Archbishop Sigeric (990–4) contains, in corrupted form, the same lists of bishops and royal genealogies, the Lindisfarne line stopping at Ecgberht and that of Whitern at Baldwulf,

been brought up to date, once between 828 and 836, and again at the end of the twelfth century; and where the manuscript shows by two columns the division of the see into Lichfield and Leicester, a twelfth-century hand also continues the list of bishops of Leicester until that see was removed to Dorchester. This document, which shows both *e* and *i* about the year 812, is of the central Midlands.[1] It is not a witness for *e* in Northumbrian usage; and there is nothing else to discount the testimony of the *Liber Vitae* that the Northumbrian spelling in the early years of the ninth century is *Cyni-*.

On this evidence, the many critics who believe that Cynewulf was a Northumbrian can hardly assign his work to a date earlier than the ninth century. The few who think he was a Mercian may still cling to the late eighth century, though why they should prefer the earliest conceivable date is not clear. Elaborate linguistic and metrical tests have been applied to establish the chronological order of Old English poems. Because these tests leave out of account differences of authorship, of locality, of subject, and of textual tradition, the detailed results, whether of relative order or absolute date, are little better than guess-work hampered by statistics. Still, they point to one broad conclusion: that Cynewulf's poetry, though it does not show the failing technique of poems known to belong to the tenth century, is later than poems like

as they do in the original script of MS. Vespasian B vi (see Wright and Halliwell *Reliquiae Antiquae* ii. 170).

The conflict between the contemporary Mercian record and the Durham tradition as reported early in the twelfth century might be explained by supposing that Eadmund was really the contemporary bishop of Whitern, and that the scribe by mistake entered his name in the Lindisfarne list and Heathured's in the Whitern list. But it is enough to have stated the problem.

[1] A good text from Lichfield would be valuable to philologists, because at this period there is no other documentary evidence for the language of the Central and North Midlands. But a collection of names of varying dates, gathered from all parts of the country, is treacherous material: it is impossible to say how far the names were modernized in each of the lists that lay before the compiler, and how far he adapted these lists to his own usage. In MS. Vespasian B vi spellings with *i* are a minority in all but the Northumbrian lists, and there are none in the additions to the original script. In the Northumbrian names, forms with *i* predominate.

Genesis, *Exodus*, and *Beowulf*, which have the best claims to be considered early. We shall have occasion to notice other indications, and their trend is the same. Reviewing them all, and granting that their strength is largely in the absence of conflicting indications, I should assign Cynewulf, whether Mercian or Northumbrian, to the ninth century.

And lest it should be said that the ninth century in England was one in which a cultured poet could not live because the Danes had wiped out all culture, let me recall a few dates. Alcuin was still alive when the century began. As late as 850 Lupus, abbot of Ferrières, wrote to York for Quintilian's *Institutes* and other books, so the great library was still famous. In the first half of the century the community at Lindisfarne produced their *Liber Vitae*, not meanly or hurriedly but in stately letters of gold and silver; and it was not till 875 that they were forced to abandon the monastery. Peterborough stood till 870; and when Alfred came to restore learning in the South, there was still learning in Mercia; for besides Asser of Wales, Grimbold of Flanders, John the Old Saxon, he found two Mercian scholars to help him in the task—Wærferth, bishop of Worcester, and Plegmund whom he made archbishop of Canterbury. The stream of literature and learning certainly dwindled in the first three quarters of the ninth century, but it is dangerous to treat that period as a void between the glories of eighth-century Northumbria and the revival under King Alfred.

The canon of Cynewulf's work is also disputed. At one time or another the bulk of Old English poetry has been attracted to his name. Nowadays more conservative views prevail, and I need do little more than inquire what poems he signed, for even that is in question.

There is no doubt about *St. Juliana.* Here Cynewulf follows the once popular Latin prose legend that may be found in the *Acta Sanctorum* at 16 February. To a modern taste the subject is a poor one: the stock torments—imprisonment, hanging by the hair, scourging, a wheel set with swords, fire, molten lead—are eked out by St. Juliana's long dispute with a fiend who is too miserable to be interesting. Critics have not found much merit in Cynewulf's rendering, but it is fair to say that there are two big gaps in the text where leaves have been lost in the Exeter Book.

Elene in the Vercelli Book is also an undoubted work. Again Cynewulf follows a Latin prose romance which is itself translated from the Greek.[1] But here he is more fortunate in his original. The mustering of the barbarian invaders, the vision of Constantine, the battle of the Milvian Bridge, Helena's sea-voyage to Jerusalem, the memories of Judas Quiriacus, the triumphant discovery first of the Cross and then of the Nails, offer a variety of opportunities which he turns to account; and the Epilogue written round his runic signature is of unusual interest. I rank *Elene* as the most pleasing, though not the most vigorous or original, of the translations from Latin which form the bulk of Old English poetry.

The signature discovered by Napier in the Vercelli Book follows a short poem of eighty-seven lines on the places where the Twelve Apostles preached and died, and the proper names show that this poem is based on Latin sources. Such short lists in Latin are not uncommon, and though none has been found corresponding exactly to Cynewulf's text, his *Fates of the Apostles* has no claims to originality or poetic merit. It belongs to the class of memorial verse.[2]

[1] Ed. A. Holder *Inventio Sanctae Crucis*, Leipzig 1889.

[2] The text of *The Fates of the Apostles* raises two points of interest:

(i) The ending is disproportionately long and repetitive. The list of the Apostles is completed; there is a prayer for the author (ll. 88–95); then the runic signature (ll. 96–106); then a prayer for the author (ll. 107–14) in almost the same words as before; and the final close. Sievers at first (*Anglia* xiii, p. 22 ff.) thought that the runic signature and the lines that follow it have nothing to do with the poem on the Apostles; but later (*Die neueren Sprachen* 6. Beiheft, 1925, p. 66 ff.) he seems to have approached the view, set out by Skeat in *An Old English Miscellany presented to Dr. Furnivall*, 1901, p. 419 f., that an alternative ending has been preserved by accident. Such a scribal error is not unexampled; I have given an instance from Ælfric's *Catholic Homilies* in *Review of English Studies* [see p. 175 below]: but it could hardly escape Cynewulf's notice. The whole text may be accepted if allowance is made for the structural looseness of Old English poems, which is mentioned at p. 14 below. Cynewulf always adds something after his signature, probably to attain the quiet close which Old English poetry derived from the sermon tradition. Without the second ending, this serious poem would close like a riddle, whereas usage demanded a prayer or its equivalent.

In the manuscript it comes immediately after *Andreas*, the story of the adventures of St. Andrew and St. Matthias among the cannibal Mermedonians; and many critics think that it is not an independent poem but the epilogue to *Andreas*, which then becomes a signed work of Cynewulf. On a full examination, the manuscript arrangement seems to me to tell neither for nor against this view. But complete translations from two distinct sources can hardly be

(ii) The order of the Apostles is not likely to be random, because an ecclesiastic had constantly to repeat the names in prayers and litanies, and they are an integral part of the Canon of the Mass. The late Edmund Bishop showed (*Journal of Theological Studies* vii (1905), p. 124 f. and p. 135 f.) that, besides the order of the Roman Canon which is likely to occur everywhere, early documents of Irish and English origin, such as the archaic diptychs of the Stowe Missal, have an unusual order derived from St. Matthew's Gospel x. 2–4. Cynewulf's poem has the order of the Stowe Missal except in one point: instead of Peter, Paul, Andrew, *James*, *John*, Philip, Bartholomew, &c., it has Peter, Paul, Andrew, *John*, *James*, Philip, Bartholomew, &c. The text is proof against derangement at this point; there is no metrical reason for putting John before James; and the Roman Canon supports the usual order 'James, John'. Now in Irish and English documents before 800, at which date his survey ceased to be complete, Bishop found no instance of the order 'Andrew, John, James, Philip, Bartholomew'. Yet that order occurs in several late Old English litanies of varied provenance, e.g. the Paris Psalter, MS. Bibl. Nat. Lat. 8824; the *Liber Vitae of Newminster*, Winchester (ed. W. de Gray Birch, 1892, p. 154); the Missal of Robert of Jumièges (Henry Bradshaw Society, 1896, pp. 287–8)—all three South-Western books written about 1020; and Bodleian MS. Douce 296 from Croyland about 1050. I had the privilege of discussing these litanies with Edmund Bishop in 1913, and where he would not hazard an explanation, am content merely to note that Cynewulf's order is not found in Insular documents before 800 and is found in several late Old English MSS.

The order of the Apostles in *The Fates* has been discussed by G. L. Hamilton in *Modern Language Notes* xxxv (1920), p. 385 ff., on the basis of Bishop's article and the less critical collection of material in T. Schermann's *Propheten- und Apostellegenden*, 1907, p. 216 ff. Mr. Hamilton, who was not aware of the later English examples, thinks (p. 393) that the order 'John, James' in *The Fates* is easily explained by reference to an early prayer (*Book of Cerne*, ed. Kuypers, p. 104) and a list in the Syriac *Book of the Bee*, ed. A. Wallis Budge, 1886, p. 104 ff. The first may well have been known to Cynewulf, but its order 'Petrus et Paulus, Johannes et Andreas, tres Iacobi' is not to the point. The second has the different order 'Peter, Andrew, John, James, Philip, Thomas, Matthew, Bartholomew'; and a thirteenth-century Syriac list, even if its order reflects earlier sources, is not prima facie evidence for ninth-century England.

regarded as one poem unless the translator supplies something that binds them together. Nobody suggests that the Latin Acts of Andrew and Matthias had any special connexion with Latin lists of apostles. When Andrew is mentioned in *The Fates of the Apostles*, there is no backward reference to *Andreas* such as one would expect in its epilogue. The only apparent link is the mention of the dispersion of the Twelve Apostles in the first few lines of *Andreas*, which might seem to be resumed at the end in the *Fates* of the Twelve. But the reference to the dispersion is inevitable at the beginning of *Andreas*, because it occurred at the beginning of the Latin source: it appears in the same place in the Anglo-Saxon prose legend of St. Andrew which makes no further mention of the Twelve. Since there is no evidence of a designed linking by the author, I conclude that the poems are separate works and that *Andreas* is not covered by Cynewulf's signature. It might still be an unsigned work of Cynewulf. But the most one can claim for this attribution is that it has not been conclusively disproved. If a personal impression has any value, I should say that *Andreas* is at once cruder and more vigorous than the certain work of Cynewulf.

We come now to the problem of the first 1,664 lines in the Exeter Book. They deal in three divisions with Advent, Ascension, and Judgement Day, and, taken together, have been given the title *Christ*. Which of these divisions bears Cynewulf's signature? Are they three poems or two or one? Did Cynewulf write all three?

Wanley in 1705 reported the manuscript divisions, according to which Cynewulf's signature belongs to the close of *The Ascension*. Unfortunately, in Thorpe's edition of 1842 the signature was mistakenly attached to the beginning of the third division on *Judgement Day*. It was the service of Sir Israel Gollancz to re-establish the true division in his edition of 1892, and to confirm it by reference to the Latin source. So *Judgement Day* is not covered by Cynewulf's signature unless it can be shown to make one poem with *The Ascension* which precedes it.

As early as 1853 Dietrich observed that the end of a famous homily by Gregory is the source of Cynewulf's *Ascension*.[1] Cyne-

[1] *Zeitschrift für deutsches Altertum* ix (1853), p. 204 ff. For the sermon (II. xxix) see Migne, *Patrologia Latina* lxxvi, col. 1218.

wulf can hardly be said to translate Gregory: he adapts and expands his original freely and with real art. But from beginning to end the Latin homily guides his thought; and its influence does not extend to *Judgement Day*. Hence *The Ascension* should be regarded as a separate poem unless the author linked it closely with *Judgement Day*.

At first sight this condition is fulfilled. The lines that contain Cynewulf's signature to *The Ascension*, and those that follow it, do treat of Judgement Day. But the subject is dealt with in the corresponding part of the Latin homily; and, besides, meditations on the Judgement are a regular accompaniment of his signature. The link may therefore be accidental; and we are free to give full weight to the evidence derived from metre, language, and style, which seems to be decisive against Cynewulf's authorship of *Judgement Day*. The occurrence of this poem immediately after *The Ascension* in the Exeter Book can be explained by a modest power of arrangement in a compiler.

It remains to inquire into the relation of *The Ascension* to *The Advent* which precedes it. Again there is an apparent link: *The Ascension* sets out to tell 'how it came about when the Almighty was born into the world in purity and after he had chosen Mary as his protectress, that there appeared not angels arrayed in white'. But this is the point Gregory sets out to explain, and it is therefore inevitable whether an Advent poem precedes or not. *The Ascension*, which is a complete rendering of a single source and is expository in tone, should be regarded as a poem separate from *The Advent*, which is a lyrical outpouring inspired by the services of the Church and comes to a full close with no hint of a sequel.

Perhaps the best reason for keeping an open mind about Cynewulf's authorship of *The Advent* is that its beginning is lost. *The Ascension*, which follows it, begins 'Now, renowned man, in spiritual meditation seek with thy mind to know the truth'. *The Ascension*, then, was written for the instruction, and perhaps at the request, of some great man. There is no means of knowing who Cynewulf's patron was; and there is just the chance that the lost opening of *The Advent* referred to him again.[1]

[1] Linguistic differences between *The Advent* and Cynewulf's signed

On a strict reckoning Cynewulf is still left—in *Juliana*, *Elene*, *The Fates of the Apostles*, and *The Ascension*—with roundly 2,600 lines of verse;[1] while of the rest of English poetry written before Alfred's

poems have been assembled, particularly by A. J. Barnouw *Textkritische Untersuchungen* &c., Leiden 1902, p. 150 ff., and C. Richter *Chronologische Studien zur angelsächsischen Literatur*, Halle 1910, p. 48 ff. and 93 f. Both are inclined to emphasize these differences, which are much less striking than those observed in *Judgement Day*. For instance, only the third of Richter's four tests yields much evidence against Cynewulf's authorship, and it shows merely a higher proportion of monosyllabic forms like *wuldr* in *The Advent* (4:6) than in *Elene* (6:28). Against this it might be urged that the undoubted works, *Juliana*, *The Ascension*, and *Elene*, are by no means uniform. But neither critic mentions the special significance of the comparison between *The Advent* and *The Ascension*. If these are one poem, or two intimately connected poems by Cynewulf, then they are presumably close together in date, whereas *Juliana*, *The Ascension*, and *Elene* may belong to different periods of his life; and they would pretty certainly have the same textual history, since they appear side by side in the Exeter Book, whereas *Juliana*, which is separated from them by non-Cynewulfian work in the Exeter Book, may not have an identical tradition, and *Elene* comes from another MS. When these ways of accounting for discrepancies of usage are eliminated, there remain only such explanations as may be derived from differences of the author's mood and subject, and I doubt whether they are sufficient.

[1] It is remarkable that two signed works of Cynewulf should be preserved in the Exeter Book and two more in the Vercelli Book. The extant codices of Old English poetry, though some of them are miscellaneous in content, hardly overlap at all; whence it may be inferred that they contain a small part of the verse known at the end of the tenth century [but see p. 100 below]. Of all the works of Cædmon, none certainly survives except the short Hymn, which owes its preservation to Bede's reference. That a ninth-century Anglian poet should be represented by four poems and that four elaborate signatures should be handed down intact, points to some special favouring condition. Most likely a codex of Cynewulf's poems found its way to the South in the critical period that began with Alfred and ended with Athelstan. A written, not an oral or partly oral tradition, would account for the retention of the signatures and the correct transmission of such details as the elaborate dating (A.D. 233) with which *Elene* begins. Such an unpretentious and even unattractive beginning would suit a collection made for the use of men who had learned interests; and the opening lines of *The Ascension* (p. 11 above), if they do not refer to something in the lost beginning of *The Advent*, could hardly be explained unless *The Ascension* was one of a series or collection of Cynewulf's works.

If we postulate the comparatively late transfer of a codex to the South

time, only nine lines by Cædmon and five lines by Bede can be attached to an author's name.

Surveying his subjects, we see that none of the signed poems deals with Bible story, which first claims the attention of Christian poets in the vernacular. The lost works of Cædmon, the extant Old English poems on *Genesis*, *Exodus*, and *Daniel*, the ninth-century Old Saxon *Heliand*, the ninth-century Gospel versions of Otfrid in Old High German, all aimed at making essential parts of the Bible available to men who could not read Latin. Cynewulf's themes belong to a later stage, when the foundations are laid, and the demand is for works of devotional interest: for legends of saints and special expositions. To the latter class belongs *The Ascension*. The other three poems might be called martyrological. The standard martyrology[1] of the time begins with summary lists of Apostles, on which Cynewulf modelled his *Fates*. St. Juliana's martyrdom is celebrated at 16 February, and appears in English calendars from the time of Willibrord. The Feast of the Invention

in order to account for the unusual number of Cynewulf's poems that survive, that postulate does not entitle us to claim for him still more of the extant poetry. In style and phrasing *Juliana*, *The Ascension*, and *Elene* seem to me to form a close group as against all other surviving poems that are long enough to make comparison safe. Perhaps *Guthlac B*, which is presumptively a Mercian composition, comes nearest to this group. But the likeness falls far short of what is necessary to establish that it is by the same author. Resemblances that are striking when attention is concentrated on the small corpus of extant verse would probably appear less significant if they could be studied against their proper background, which is the whole body of Old English verse that once existed.

Again, if Cynewulf's four signed poems are to be regarded as chance survivors from a larger collection of his works, certain arguments become unsafe which would be legitimate if the whole or the bulk of his verse were extant. We know that he thought it worth while to write about St. Juliana, but do not know that he preferred her story to that of St. Agnes or St. Agatha, and so cannot usefully speculate on the possibility that *Juliana* was written for some special occasion. All that can safely be said is that his subjects are suggested by the calendar and the services of the Church.

[1] *Martyrologium Hieronymianum* in *Acta Sanctorum* for November, II. ii (1931). The oldest (Epternach) MS. is in Anglo-Saxon script of the early eighth century and may have belonged to St. Willibrord, with whose Calendar it is now bound up in MS. Bibl. Nat. Lat. 10837.

of the Cross on 3 May[1] comes from France, and seems to have been established in England on that day before the close of the eighth century. Thus all Cynewulf's signed poems are associated with and explain special occasions in the Church calendar.

All are based on Latin sources, and the rendering shows that he was competent in Latin, though quite uncritical in matters of history. That the sixth year of Constantine should fall in A.D. 233; that Judas Quiriacus, the helper of Constantine's mother, should be the brother of St. Stephen, troubled him no more than it did the average medieval reader, who kept no order in the distant past. He was concerned only with the story as the Latin text presented it, or, as he says with a note of pride, 'as I found it in books'.

He owes more than the matter of the story to his originals. Any merit in the structure of his poems seems to be due to them. The formlessness of Old English religious poetry has already been exemplified in the so-called *Christ*, for only where standards of form are low could such questions of unity or division be debatable. And if *Beowulf* is a fair specimen of the longer secular poems, the Anglo-Saxons were poor story-tellers, weak in proportion and too ready to be distracted from the regular sequence of events. The appearance in Old English of a well-balanced, smooth-jointed narrative, such as *Elene*, is a sign that a Latin source is followed closely.

I do not mean that Cynewulf is a slavish paraphraser. He is always ready to develop a hint when he can do it effectively. A well-known example is his description of Elene's voyage, which is barely mentioned in the Latin.

At once a band of warriors hastened down to the sea. The ships stood ready by the shore, afloat and anchored. Then all might see the Queen's journeying, when she sought the surging waves with her retinue. There on the Mediterranean shore stood many a proud man. Troop after troop

[1] See *Elene*, ll. 1227–9:

Wæs þa lencten agan
butan VI nihtum ær sumeres cyme
on Maias Kł. (*so MS.*)

Summer began on 9 May. The editors read *kālend* as an Old English word, but *Māius mōnað* should be substituted for the Latin forms of the date.

in turn marched over the ways and loaded the vessels with mailcoats, shields, and spears, with armed warriors, men, and women. Then they loosed the tall ships to go foaming over the sea-monsters' home. Their sides took many buffets from the waves; the sea made music. Never, before or since, have I heard of a lady leading on the ocean-ways a fairer company. One who watched their passage might see the ships breaking through the waters, speeding along under swelling sails: the sea-steeds danced as they went. The brave warriors were glad and the Queen rejoiced in her voyage, when the ringed-prowed ships had passed over the ocean-strongholds to their haven in the land of the Greeks. They left their wave-beaten vessels anchored at the shore to await the result of their mission. (l. 225 ff.)

In its context this description of a fair-weather voyage is apt and decorative. But, like the voyages in *Beowulf*, it is written from the landsman's point of view: there is an elaborate embarkation, a picture of dancing ships with sails set to a fair breeze, as seen by a watcher from the shore; and then suddenly the long voyage is over, the anchors are down, and the pageant of an army marching begins again. The sea-piece is pretty, but slight and obvious. No doubt Cynewulf could have managed as gracefully the conventional Old English storm, with leaping porpoises, gulls screaming, and (even in mid-ocean) the beat of the waves on the shore. No doubt his subject and style exclude the humbler side of sea-faring, as it appears in the description of a sailor's home-coming by an Old English poet of another school, who seems bent on bringing us down from epic heights: 'The sailor is welcome to his Frisian wife, when his vessel anchors. The ship is arrived and her man home, her own breadwinner; and she bids him in, and washes his dirty clothes and gives him a change.'[1] But there is a touch of reality in the matter-of-fact statement. I cannot trace in the passage from *Elene* or elsewhere in Cynewulf's poetry any first-hand experience of sea-going; still less that passion for the sea which has been attributed to him, and which in fact finds expression only once in Old English, in the cryptic piece called *Seafarer*.

His descriptions of war have the same character; they are decorative and finished, and yet conventional. His distinction lies

[1] Gnomic Verses from the *Exeter Book*, ed. Grein-Wülker, i. 346, l. 95 ff.

not so much in these purple passages borrowed from the epic tradition as in the plain staple of his verse, in comparison with which the Old English *Genesis* is rough and the *Exodus* obscure.

Certainly the earliest English religious poets had the more difficult task. They had neither a stock of ready-made phrases for expressing Christian ideas, nor the traditional experience necessary for their easy manipulation in alliterative verse. One reason why our first Christian poets made the most of warlike occasions is that it was easy to write well about them in the native style, in which there were plenty of good models. When the material offered no such opportunities, some did not hesitate to arm the saints. The author of *Andreas*, who is only half weaned from the heathen epic forms, begins:

> Lo, we have heard of twelve glorious warriors, thanes of the Lord, who lived in old days beneath the stars. Never did their prowess fail in battle, when standards clashed, after they had separated as the Lord himself, the high King of Heaven, appointed their lots. They were famous men upon earth, brave leaders and keen in war, doughty warriors when shield and hand guarded the helm on the battlefield.

I doubt if he had in mind the Church militant, or that he thought solely of the martial tastes of his audience: rather he felt that in alliterative verse he could not make the apostles live and move except to the clank of arms. That is what the late Poet Laureate meant when he wrote:

> Time was when good St. Andrew strode forth in platemail.

Without such means of casting their matter in the traditional moulds, the struggle with the mechanism of alliteration becomes too obvious, and the flow of the verse tends to be clogged with synonyms. Synonyms, the ornaments of the alliterative style, had special functions in the economy of preliterary verse. They helped a primitive audience by diluting the sense and hammering it in with varied repetition. They also gave an improviser an easy way of introducing words and ideas into the alliterative frame.[1] But in

[1] In the best verse synonyms are too often used to introduce a new alliterative sequence, so that in the first half of the line the poet seems to mark time in order to change feet and take a step forward in the second half. Here is an example from *Beowulf*, l. 344 ff.:

the more deliberate literary forms this facility became a source of weakness, and synonyms are often multiplied mechanically, like the rhyming tags of a later age. Cædmon's famous Hymn is nine lines long, and nearly half of it is taken up with synonyms for 'God', of which there are no less than eight. The opening of *Exodus* is equally embarrassed. Now set beside them a few inconspicuous lines from *Elene*, where Cynewulf has to translate the place in Isaiah: 'The ox knoweth his owner and the ass his master's crib; but Israel doth not know, my people doth not consider.' Cynewulf's version has not the strength and reticence of our Bible, but, literally translated, it makes modern prose:

> The wretched oxen, that are daily driven and beaten, know their benefactors, and do not maliciously hate their friends who give them fodder; and me the people of Israel would never acknowledge, although in my time I have worked many miracles for them. (l. 357 ff.)

The paraphrase is clear and runs smoothly. Compared with the earliest English Christian poetry it is classic, in the sense that Ælfric's prose is classic beside Alfred's; and for similar reasons. Cynewulf's natural good taste played a part. Practice played a part, for by his time English Christian poetry had its own traditions. But there is something more. This is the style of a man trained to read and write Latin, to admire the orderly progress of a Latin sentence, and to prefer its clarity to the tangled profusion of the native style. We have seen that Cynewulf took the matter and

---

'Wille ic asecgan sunu Healfdenes,
mærum þeodne, min ærende,
aldre þinum, gif he us geunnan wile,
þæt we hine *swa godne* gretan moton.'
Wulfgar maþelode, þæt wæs Wendla leod,
wæs his modsefa manegum gecyðed,
wig ond wisdom: 'Ic þæs wine Deniga,
frean Scyldinga, frinan wille,
beaga bryttan, swa þu bena eart,
þeoden mærne, ymb þinne sið' . . .

Cynewulf's poems are not free from this fault: for instance, there is excessive repetition and padding in *Elene*, l. 1286 ff. But his average standard is high. The few lines that Bede made on his death-bed are the only certain specimen of Anglo-Saxon verse composed by an expert writer of Latin prose; and though they move stiffly, they are free from the doublings and circumlocutions of the native style.

arrangement of his poems from Latin, and borrowed the new ornament of rhyme from Latin. The same great influence guided his treatment of alliterative verse, which in his best passages reaches its highest level of ease, refinement, and adaptability.

The briefest survey would be incomplete without some attempt on the riddle of the runic signatures. Facsimiles of the two signatures in the Exeter Book appeared in Hickes's *Thesaurus* in 1703;[1] but it was not till 1840 that Kemble and Jacob Grimm almost simultaneously announced the poet's name; and from that time the signatures have been a centre of controversy.

Every rune had a name of which it was the first letter: for example, *wyn* was the name for the runic *W*. The English names are recorded from three Old English manuscripts, Domitian A IX, Galba A II, and St. John's College, Oxford, 17.

The runic alphabet in Domitian A IX is written on the back of a single leaf torn from the end of a manuscript of Alfred's time. The runes and the names of a few special letters were written about the middle of the tenth century. The names of the ordinary runes were added early in the twelfth century, and from the forms one would judge that the manuscript was then in Kent. There are also Latin equivalents of the English rune-names, which have hitherto passed as medieval: in fact they are the work of an ill-informed Elizabethan antiquary.[2]

Two fires have left nothing of Galba A II; but Wanley, who in his young days planned a comprehensive work on alphabets, gave

[1] Plates IIII, C and V, D of the *Icelandic Grammar* (1703). It is strange that Hickes did not read the poet's name, but had he done so he could hardly have failed to mention it at p. 5 of his text.

[2] For facsimiles of the alphabet in MS. Domitian A IX see Hickes's *Thesaurus*, p. 136 of the Anglo-Saxon Grammar (1703); and G. Hempl *Modern Philology* i (1903) at p. 135. Note that the tenth-century scribe who wrote the runic letters transliterated the symbols for M and D correctly by *m* and *d* written below. The early-twelfth-century scribe who inserted the names wrote *deg* above the rune for M and *mann* above the rune for D. Following his error, the sixteenth-century antiquary wrote *d* above the tenth-century *m*, and *m* above the tenth-century *d*. The error was thence transferred to Hickes's print of the *Runic Poem* (Anglo-Saxon Grammar, p. 135).

facsimiles of the runes to Hickes for publication in his *Thesaurus.*[1] The names seem to have been written early in the twelfth century. This manuscript was said to have been St. Anselm's,[2] and, if that tradition is good, it probably came from Christ Church, Canterbury.

The runic letters from St. John's MS. 17 were also reproduced in Hickes's *Thesaurus*, but their names have only lately been published.[3] The manuscript appears to have been written in the year 1110, and several slight but independent indications again connect it with Christ Church, Canterbury.[4]

[1] Plate VI of the *Icelandic Grammar* (1703).

[2] M. R. James *The Ancient Libraries of Canterbury and Dover*, p. xxvi, refers to Thomas Smith who, in his Catalogue of the Cottonian MSS. (1696), says that the lost Galba A III was the second volume of Galba A II, and that Galba A III belonged to Fountains Abbey. Wanley is not likely to have overlooked this evidence. It is possible that Galba A III, like so many of Cotton's MSS., was a comparatively recent composite, and that only its last part, Stephen's case against Matilda, is covered by Smith's attribution to Fountains Abbey.

[3] By C. L. Wrenn in *Medium Ævum* i (1932), p. 24 ff. But Hickes does not say that the names of the runes are absent from the MS. By '*In codice litterarum potestates desiderantur*' he means that the roman-letter equivalents of the runes, which appear in plate A. II of his *Icelandic Grammar*, are not in the MS. The names from Domitian A IX are similarly omitted in this plate.

[4] (i) A pencil note by the late W. H. Stevenson identifies St. John's MS. 17 with the codex described in detail by Leland, *Collectanea*, 1715, iii, p. 97. It was then in the possession of Robert Talbot, prebendary of Norwich (d. 1558), a diligent collector of MSS., who had access to the library of Christ Church, Canterbury: see W. de Gray Birch *The Utrecht Psalter*, 1876, p. 104 ff.

(ii) It contains an elaborate acrostic addressed to Dunstan by Abbo of Fleury, which Stubbs prints from another MS. at p. 410 of his *Memorials of St. Dunstan* (Rolls Series).

(iii) In the calendar, of which the original script shows little trace of local usage, only two later English saints are added, Dunstan and Ælfeah, both of Canterbury.

(iv) There seems to be a relation between this MS. and the lost Galba A II. They contain the same Norse alphabet with East Norse rune-names. In the English alphabet, St. John's 17 has *hægel* altered to *hægil*, an unusual late spelling; and Galba A II reads *hegil*. Forms like *feh* for *feoh*, *coen* glossed *cen*, *oeþel* glossed *eþel*, *geofu* glossed *gyfu*, indicate that the rune-names in the St. John's MS. derive from a Northern or Midland original.

The agreement of three early-twelfth-century lists, all probably from Kent, may seem to be insufficient witness for Cynewulf's usage. Still, their testimony is stronger than it looks: the absence of earlier lists of names for the ordinary runes (for instance, in the tenth-century script of Domitian A IX and in the lost manuscript of the *Runic Poem*) is only part of the evidence that up to the time of the Conquest these names were familiar and certain in England. And fortunately there is a witness on the Continent just when we need it. Alcuin's closest friend was Arno, archbishop of Salzburg, to whose care is due the preservation of so many of Alcuin's letters. In the year 798, and perhaps under Arno's personal direction, was compiled the manuscript formerly called Salzburg 140.[1] It contains, in association with letters from Alcuin, an English runic alphabet and the English rune-names. On the letters of Cynewulf's name it agrees exactly with the three twelfth-century English documents: the runes for C, Y, N, E, W, U, L, F were called *cēn*, *ȳr*, *nēd*, *eoh*, *wyn*, *ūr*, *lagu*, *feoh*. There is no evidence (unless it be in Cynewulf's signatures) that any other names for these runes were used in Old English.

Five of the names, *nēd*, *eoh*, *wyn*, *lagu*, *feoh*, were used as ordinary Old English words. The other three, *cēn*, *ȳr*, *ūr*, are found only as rune-names; and for their meanings we rely on the cognate languages and on the *Runic Poem*, which gives first the runic letter and then a brief explanation in verse. The sources concur in the meanings: *cēn* 'torch', *ȳr* 'bow', *nēd* 'necessity', *eoh* 'horse', *wyn* 'joy', *ūr* 'bison', *lagu* 'sea', *feoh* 'wealth'; and there is no evidence (unless it be in Cynewulf's signatures) that any other meanings were known in Old English.

[1] Now Vienna Hofbibliothek MS. 795. On the date of the runes see Th. Sickel *Alcuinstudien*, in Sitzungsberichte der phil.-hist. Klasse der Kais. Akad. der Wissenschaften, Wien, vol. lxxix (1875), p. 476, n. 2. On the MS. generally see A. Chroust *Monumenta Palaeographica*, I. i, Lief. vii, pl. 3. The runes and names may be seen in L. F. A. Wimmer's *Die Runenschrift*, Berlin 1887, p. 85. This old-fashioned facsimile is substantially correct, except that *sygil* should be read *sigil* (the first *i* corrected from *y*), and in the manuscript the name of the æ rune is clearly *æs* not *ær*. There are useful tables of runic alphabets in Continental MSS. in an article by T. von Grienberger *Arkiv för Nordisk Filologi* xv (1899), p. 1 ff.

I take first the signature to *Juliana*, which is different in method from the other three. It runs:

My soul shall go forth from the body on its journey, I know not whither, to what unknown land. I must go hence to seek another place according to my deeds in the past. Sadly will journey *Cēn*, *Ȳr* and *Nēd*; the King of Heaven, the Giver of Victory, will be stern when *Eoh*, *Wyn* and *Ūr*, sin-stained and trembling, await what will be adjudged them according to their deeds, as the earning of life on earth. *Lagu*, *Feoh* shall stand and quake in misery. I shall remember all the pain, all the wounds of sin I wrought in the world, &c.

Here the runes are in three groups: C, Y, N; E, W, U; and L, F. And *cyn* is a word meaning 'race' which can be made to yield some kind of sense in the context, such as 'the race of men will journey sadly'. *Ewu* could be a dialect form of a plural which has been translated 'sheep': 'the sheep trembling await judgement';[1] and though *lf* is not a word, and *lagu feoh* is nonsense, various substitutes have been suggested. Before considering these substitutes I shall interpolate a rule of criticism: in a matter fully within his grasp an Anglo-Saxon writer may be expected to show common sense. Now *ewu* does not really mean 'sheep': it means 'female sheep'; and that Cynewulf should picture himself on the Day of Judgement as a ewe is plainly ridiculous. Since *cyn* also had to be twisted from its natural meaning to make sense, we need not speculate about the third group *L*, *F*. The runes have only their value as letters spelling his name.[2] Immediately before and

[1] M. Trautmann: *Kynewulf, der Bischof und Dichter*, Bonner Beiträge zur Anglistik i, 1898, p. 49; W. J. Strunk *Juliana*, 1904, p. 60; K. Jansen *Die Cynewulf-Forschung*, 1908, p. 123; Carleton Brown *Englische Studien* xxxviii (1907), p. 199; and others.

[2] Trautmann, and those who believe with him that the rune-groups of *Juliana* form words, find evidence in the syntax: the singular before 'C, Y, and N', the plural after 'E, W, and U', the singular after 'L, F'. But if the runes taken severally stand for letter-names and taken in groups stand for 'Cynewulf', some uncertainty of concord in the original might be expected, and there would also be a risk of inaccurate transmission: Trautmann himself assumes corruption in one place (l. 705), reading *fā* pl. for MS. *fāh*. Even if the runes were construed as letter-names only, the syntax of the manuscript would not be impossible. The singular preceding a group of subjects like 'C, Y, and N' is not uncommon. The singular adjective *fāh* preceding the group 'E, W, and U' might be explained in the same way, whereas the adjective and verb following such

immediately after them Cynewulf speaks in his own person; and good sense is obtained if each group of letters is taken to stand for his full name.

The signature to *The Fates of the Apostles* is the only one in which the runes are not set out in their right order; and Cynewulf is careful to say so. He begins:

> Here a man of good wit who takes pleasure in verse may discover who made this poem: *Feoh* stands last; high men enjoy it on earth, but dwellers in this world cannot have it for ever.

He continues with W, U, L to complete *wulf*; then C, Y, N to give the first part of the name in the short form *Cynwulf*; and then announces that the signature is finished: 'Now you may know who is revealed to men in these words.' Notice that *feoh* here is no mere letter-name, but has its ordinary meaning 'wealth': 'high men enjoy *wealth* on earth, but cannot have worldly *wealth* eternally.' This principle is used also in the signatures to *The Ascension* and *Elene*.

As the runes in *The Ascension* present no special feature, I pass on to the famous passage in *Elene* which begins in rhyme,

> Þus ic frod and fus   þurh þæt fæcne hus:—

> Thus I, old and near my death through the body's frailty, have woven with skill in words and gathered wondrously, often pondering and arranging my thoughts with travail in the night. I knew not fully the truth about the Cross, until, through illustrious power, God disclosed wisdom to the counsels of my heart, a deeper understanding. I was sullied by my deeds, fettered in sins, afflicted by sorrows, bound in bitterness, oppressed by cares, until in glorious wise the radiant King of Might gave me knowledge, a perfect gift, as a comfort to my age, bestowed it upon me and set it in my mind, revealed it and from time to time amplified it. He unbound my body, unfettered my heart, unlocked the power of song, which I have gladly and joyously used in the world. Not once but often I had thoughts of the Tree of Glory before I discovered the wonder of the bright Cross, as, in the course of things, I found it written in books about the Sign of Victory. Till then the man was buffeted by cares, *Cēn* was losing his strength, although he received precious gifts of bossed gold in the mead-hall. *Ȳr* mourned, the *Nēd*-journeyer (?) suffered anxiety, an oppressive secret, where before his

---

a group are regularly plural. The verbs following *Lagu, Feoh* without a conjunction are naturally singular.

eyes *Eoh* strode over the mile-paths and galloped in its pride, decked with woven metal. *Wyn* and delight are vanished with the years; youth is changed and former pride. *Ūr* was once the radiance of youth. Now after a little while the old days are gone; the joys of life have departed, as *Lagu* glides away—the driven floods. For every man worldly *Feoh* is transitory; the ornaments of earth pass away beneath the heavens most like the wind, when in the sight of men it rises loud-roaring, and roves in the clouds, and travels raging; and again of a sudden it becomes still, closely pent up in its prison, straitly suppressed.

If in this rendering 'by necessity' is substituted for *nēd* as the first element of a compound; 'horse' for *eoh*; 'joy' for *wyn*; 'sea' or 'water' for *lagu*; 'wealth' for *feoh*, the context is satisfied; and these are the five rune-names that are also current words in Old English. But 'torch' for *cēn* is not happy; 'bow' will not do for *ȳr*; and there is no means of accommodating a 'bison' for *ūr*. The known meanings of the three words that are only rune-names fail in *Elene*; they fail equally in *The Ascension* and *The Fates of the Apostles*. The expectation that the acrostic will be symmetrical is disappointed. Did Cynewulf, then, for these three letters, use names otherwise unknown, or meanings otherwise unknown?

Without some fresh clue we shall be lost in a maze of ingenuities, so I prefer an easier question. How came it that Cynewulf, alone among Old English poets and in the face of a long tradition of anonymity, took such pains to record his name?

The desire that moved him appears everywhere in the Latin letters of his time; it gives us the names of scribes and authors in the colophons of Latin manuscripts, and fills confraternity books like the Lindisfarne *Liber Vitae*: it is the desire to be remembered by name in the prayers of others. This does not depend on interpretation, for Cynewulf says so expressly, twice in *The Fates of the Apostles* and again in *Juliana*: 'I beg every man who repeats this poem to remember me *by name* in my need.'

Once his purpose is clear, it is easy to see why the thought of Judgement Day recurs with each signature: it is against that Day he begs for the help of prayers. But it would not be safe to interpret his lively fear for his soul either as a morbid obsession or a sign that he had been an exceptional sinner. The same anxiety is expressed many times in the letters Alcuin wrote in his last days.[1] Cynewulf, writing in English, is less restrained in expression; but not different in spirit from other good and well-balanced men of his day when they come to review their lives in old age.

It is true he makes a heavy count of his sins and miseries in the Epilogue to *Elene*, but one must not forget the forms of humility that were then current, or miss in the same passage an oddly contrasting undertone of self-satisfaction. One of the best early critics remarked it, and interpreted it as a note of authority suitable to a bishop. It is not easy to distinguish the voice of a bishop across a thousand years, especially in times when a churchman so great as Alcuin remained to the end of his life in deacon's orders. And there is a different explanation. Deep down in the heart of the Anglo-Saxon is a consciousness of merit which makes uneasy to him the formulas of self-abasement that are natural enough in Celtic piety. It is not that he uses these forms insincerely, but he feels they need balancing. A good example occurs in the colophon to the Lindisfarne Gospels, where the glossator, Aldred, begins in regular form 'I Aldred, *presbyter indignus et miserrimus*', and adds in the margin the information that he is 'the excellent son of Tilwyn, a good woman'. In Cynewulf it is perhaps no more than an artist's pride which naturally comes to the surface when he asks for prayers as the reward of his finished work: 'This poem', he seems to say, 'is a work of research, piety, and art, which deserves your prayers.'

Now we may return to the runes with a clue. A man of common sense, thinking anxiously as Cynewulf did of his future lot, and believing as he did that the fate of his soul could be swayed by the

[1] Compare, for example, with the trend of thought in Cynewulf's signatures *Mon. Germ. Hist. Epist. Karol. Aevi* ii, p. 370:

> Ideo diligentius iubeatis orare pro nobis. Quia tempus adpropinquat quo hoc hospicium deserendum est et ignota appetenda, &c.

and p. 383:

> Omnis igitur corporis mei, ut vere fateor, dignitas et fortitudo recessit, abiit et cotidie fugiet . . . ut si quoquo modo, deo Iesu miserante, metuendas antiqui hostis accusationes evadere valeam, et aliquem sanctorum habere adiutorem merear, mecum stantem, pro meaque intercedentem fragilitate; ne tradar in manus inimicorum meorum. O quam timendus est omni homini dies ille! &c.

commendation of his name in prayers, would surely not take the risk of losing one single prayer. He might miss his purpose, which was no less than his own salvation, if he puzzled the simplest mind about his name. If, then, very acute modern critics are baffled by his signatures, it is likely that the puzzle is of their own making.

Let us see what his problem was. Runes are not used in the Latin signatures he imitated. A ninth-century English example of the usual Latin acrostic may be seen in Bishop Æthelwald of Lichfield's verses in the Book of Cerne:[1] the initial capital letters of the Latin verses, taken in order, spell out his name.

But this method would not serve Cynewulf. It depended on each verse beginning a new line, and Old English verse was written continuously, like prose. More important still, it was intended for the eye of a reader, whereas a vernacular poet addressed himself primarily to the ear of a listener. It is doubtful whether any listener could follow the Latin method. Cynewulf used runes because, while they were obvious to a reader, they made possible the communication of his name to an audience in a way at once memorable and sure. An Anglo-Saxon hearing *cēn*, *ȳr*, would know at once that he was dealing with runes; his attention would be directed at once to the task of solution because runes sometimes played a part in Old English riddles; and he would listen closely for the succession.

When the rune-names were ordinary words, such as *feoh* and *wyn*, it was fairly easy for the poet to work their meanings into his verse. But what was he to do with *cēn*, *ȳr*, *ūr*, which had no currency as words in Old English? Assume for a moment that he thought of two favourite modern solutions, substituting for *cēn* the common adjective *cēne* 'bold', and for *ȳr* the common word *yfel* 'evil'. How was he to write them? If he wrote the runes for

[1] *The Book of Cerne*, ed. A. B. Kuypers, 1902, p. 41. The consideration of the spelling of Cynewulf's name (above, p. 3 f.) makes it possible to decide, against the great authority of E. Bishop *Liturgica Historica*, 1916, p. 192 ff., that this *Ædelvald* was the bishop of Lichfield (818–30), and not the bishop of Lindisfarne (721–40), who would certainly have signed himself *Ædil-*. [For a full discussion see W. Levison *England and the Continent in the Eighth Century*, 1946, p. 295 ff.]

C and Y, who could know that they stood for *cēne* and *yfel*? If he wrote *cēne* and *yfel*, who could know that they stood for the runes C and Y?

Even if he was able to get out of this dilemma by some device in his manuscript that has not been preserved in the extant copies, he must still face the major problem of the listener, whom modern critics in their libraries are inclined to forget. In *The Fates of the Apostles*, where the runes begin with the common word *feoh*, he is careful to say that the signature is beginning, that *feoh* is its last letter, that the signature has ended. But there is no warning before the runes begin in *The Ascension* or in *Elene*, though the rhyming lines of *Elene* were presumably designed to heighten attention.[1] Without warning, no audience when they heard the common words *cēne* and *yfel* in their common meanings could be expected to guess that *cēne* and *yfel* stood for the runes *cēn* and *ȳr*. Yet unless they guessed right very quickly their chances of detecting the name were gone, and Cynewulf lost their prayers.

I conclude that with Anglo-Saxon common sense he was content to let *cēn* and *ȳr* be what they are—simple letter-names that would serve as warnings of less obvious letter-names to follow. So far from regretting that *cēn* and *ȳr* were not ordinary words, he probably blessed his luck in having a name that began so unambiguously in runes. To critics who say the acrostic is imperfect or too easy for a reader, he would answer that it was only a means of communicating his name; and his amazing success must be allowed.

Of course he had to give these letter-names some function in the sentence: when *cēn* and *ȳr* stand alone, or form part of a group of runes, the single letter or group stands for the whole name 'Cynewulf', as in the *Juliana* signature. *Ūr*, however, is exceptional because to a listener it is identical with the pronoun meaning 'our', and perhaps Cynewulf intended it to bear that meaning in *The Fates*, *The Ascension*, and *Elene*. Then the *Elene* passage gives a sense tolerable in this kind of composition:

[1] Cp. Boniface's letter to Nithard in *Mon. Germ. Hist. Epist.* iii, p. 251. At the end of this letter Boniface breaks into rhymed Latin verse and introduces the name NITHARDVS in the initial letters of lines 15–23.

Till then, I, Cynewulf,[1] was buffeted with cares, I was failing in strength, although I received precious gifts of bossed gold in the mead-hall. I was sad; a journeyer perforce, I suffered anxiety, an oppressive secret, where before my eyes the horse strode over the mile-paths, and galloped in its pride, decked with woven metal. Joy and delight are vanished with the years; my youth is changed, my former pride. Ours was once the radiance of youth. Now after a little while the old days are gone; the joys of life have departed, as water glides away, the driven floods. For every man worldly wealth is transitory, &c.

I have said nothing of Cynewulf in the various romantic capacities that Henry Bradley scotched when he declared in 1888 that the 'First Riddle' of the Exeter Book was not a riddle at all.[2] The interpretation just given, which associates him with gold in the mead-hall and a galloping horse, might suggest a worldly state from which he was converted by the spiritual experience described earlier in the passage. But, particularly in Cynewulf's day, English ecclesiastics were not recluses. They were often men of affairs with worldly tastes. They were no strangers to horses, and Cynewulf could not avoid a horse when he spelt his name in runes with an *E*. The reference to gifts of gold in the mead-hall is an epic way of saying that he enjoyed a great man's favour, and we know that he wrote *The Ascension* for a great man's instruction. His spiritual illumination is curiously bound up with his discovery and understanding of the apocryphal tract on the Finding of the Cross, which for him was not a legend riddled by historical criticism, but the true account of a great feast of the Church, bearing associations that we can hardly recover.

This difficult fragment of autobiography does not disturb the evidence of the rest of his work: that he was a ninth-century

[1] Reading *secg* 'man' for MS. *sæcc*, with most editors. Professor Carleton Brown (*Englische Studien* xxxviii, 1907, p. 196 ff.), who argues that there is no autobiographical element in this runic passage, retains *sæcc* 'strife'; but the construction of *drusende* is then hardly tolerable. There is good reason to believe that Cynewulf was thinking of himself when he signed his name. That his statements are vague and general is explained by the conditions of his task: in a limited space he had to introduce words of meaning so heterogeneous as 'necessity', 'horse', 'joy', 'water', 'wealth'; and since it was desirable that the rune-names should not be disguised by inflexion, they must usually serve as subjects.

[2] *The Academy*, 24 Mar. 1888, p. 197.

ecclesiastic of cultured taste; very devout in his old age and probably always of a devotional cast of mind; not a great scholar like Bede, but well versed in the Latin works that the educated clergy of those days used; not boldly original, but unusually sensitive and pliant to the influence of Christian Latin models; and, perhaps one may say, a man of letters, the first in English whose name and works are known.

2

THE AUTHORITY OF OLD ENGLISH POETICAL MANUSCRIPTS[1]

I

Genesis B 313–17 (MS. Junius 11)

þær hæbbað heo on æfyn   ungemet lange
ealra feonda gehwilc   fyr edneowe;
þonne cymð on uhtan   easterne wind,
forst fyrnum cald;   symble fyr oððe gar,
sum heard gewrinc   habban sceoldon;

For manuscript *gewrinc*, modern editors accept Grein's *geswinc*, which renders *tribulatio* in some Biblical texts. But, whatever the explanation of *gar* in *fyr oððe gar*, these words indicate violent tortures, so that *geswinc* gives a weak effect. Read *geþwinc* = *geþwing*, Old Saxon *gethuing* 'torment' as in *Heliand* 2144 f.:

Thar ist gristgrimmo   endi gradag fiur,
hard helleo gethuing,   het endi thiustri.

In the only other English example, *Genesis B* 696 *hellgeþwin*, the erasure of final *g* in the manuscript indicates that the word was unfamiliar; and at line 802, for which the Old Saxon source is available, the verb *thuingan* is translated by OE. *slitan*.

Genesis B 327–9

hie hyra gal beswac,
engles oferhygd,   noldon Alwaldan
word weorþian;   hæfdon wite micel: &c.

The use of *engel* after their Fall deserves notice, though it is easier to explain than the singular *engles* in a plural context. Certainly Lucifer's arrogance has been referred to earlier in the poem (262, 272); but that does not justify the interpretation *engles* = 'Lucifer's' in this passage, where it is emphasized that arrogance is the fault of all the fallen angels (332, 337), and where *engles oferhygd* is naturally taken as a variant of *hyra gal*. Nor does Old English

[1] From *The Review of English Studies* xxii (1946), p. 257 ff.

usage allow us to take the singular as generic, translating 'angelic arrogance'.

Must we be content with the manuscript reading even though it involves such difficulties? Recent practice favours that choice: an editor's reputation for soundness would gain rather than lose by his tenacious defence of the manuscript, unless its reading were as patently wrong as *gewrinc* in the previous passage. If this attitude has a basis in reason, it implies that the extant manuscripts of Old English poetry represent the original compositions with a high degree of accuracy. Yet there seems to be no modern work which attempts to establish a thesis so fundamental. To say that 'an accurate scribe did not as a rule depart from the *wording* of his original except as a result of oversight'[1] is begging the question, unless the editor goes on to inquire whether the scribes with whom he is concerned were accurate in this sense, and whether, since the assumed date of composition, the transmission of the text has been entirely in the hands of scribes who aimed at copying what was before them. A following section deals mainly with the first of these questions; and in anticipation of the argument, I propose to read here *egle oferhygd* '(their) pernicious arrogance'. *Oferhyd egle* occurs in *Daniel* 679. In *Guthlac* 935 (= 962) the manuscript has *engle* for *egle*, in *Christ* 762 *englum* for *eglum*.

[1] R. W. Chambers's Preface to *Beowulf*, 1914, p. xxvi. There is much that should be common ground in this persuasive manifesto of the school which makes the defence or conservation of the MS. readings its ruling principle, and is therefore called 'conservative'. The term does not imply a generally conservative attitude in criticism.

The history of opinion has its interest. The headship of this school in Old English poetry belongs to R. P. Wülker, who succeeded Grein as editor of the *Bibliothek der angelsächsischen Poesie*. In the Preface to his first volume (1883) he announced: 'In bezug auf die textherstellung habe ich mich . . . bemüht möglichst die lesungen der handschrift zu wahren.' The best textual critics of that brilliant time were grateful for the materials he provided, which were then not so accessible as they are now; but they joked at his obtuseness: Cosijn pencilled *unsinnigen* before *lesungen* in his copy of the volume. In 1894, when Wyatt declared in his Preface to *Beowulf* that anyone who himself proposed emendations suffered from 'the greatest disqualification for discharging duly the functions of an editor', he drew a protest from Zupitza, who excelled in editorial judgement. In 1914 Chambers could fairly say that the battle for conservatism was won.

II

Was the poetry accurately transmitted?

This subject could well occupy a monograph, and even a selective treatment requires many illustrative examples. One might start from the considerable number of gross errors that appear in the principal manuscripts; but single lapses are not necessarily inconsistent with a high general level of accuracy, and that is the quality to be discussed.

Nearly all the poetical texts depend on a single manuscript; but the contents of three out of the four great codices show a very small overlap. Thus both the Exeter Book and the Vercelli Book contain a poem on the Soul and the Body. The following specimen is set out in short or half lines for convenience of comparison, and substantial differences are italicized in both texts:

A

Exeter Book	Vercelli Book
Sceal se gæst cuman	Sceal se gast cuman
gehþum hremig	geohðum hremig
symle ymb seofon niht	symble ymbe seofon niht
sawle findan	sawle findan
þone lichoman	þone lichoman
þe heo ær longe wæg	þe hie ær lange wæg
þreo hund wintra	þreo hund wintra
butan ær *wyrce*	butan ær *þeodcyning*
ece dryhten	
ælmihtig god	ælmihtig god
ende worlde	ende worulde
	wyrcan wille
	weoruda dryhten
Cleopað þonne swa cearful	Cleopað þonne swa cearful
caldan reorde	cealdan reorde
spriceð grimlice	spreceð grimlice
gæst to þam duste	*se* gast to þam duste
hwæt drug*u* þu dreorga	hwæt dru*h* ðu dreorega
to hwon dreahtest þu me	to hwan drehtest ðu me
eorþan f*y*lnes	eorðan f*u*lnes
eal for*weornast*	eal for*wisnad*
lames gelicnes	lames gelicnes
lyt þu ge*þohtes*	lyt ðu ge*mundest*

to won þinre sawle *sið*	to hwan þinre sawle *þing*
siþþan wurde	siðþan wurde
siþþan *heo* of lichoman	syððan of lichoman
læded wære.	læded wære.

The next specimen from the *Daniel-Azarias* verses allows a comparison of the Exeter Book with MS. Junius 11. It does not show the widest divergencies of content, but evidently contains a deep-seated corruption:

B Exeter Book (*Azarias*)	MS. Junius 11 (*Daniel*)
þu him gehete	þu him *þæt* gehete·
þurh hleoþorcwid*as*	þurh hleoðorcwyd*e*·
þæt þu hyra fr*o*mcynn	þæt þu hyra fr*u*mcyn·
on fyrndagum	*in* fyrndagum·
ycan wolde	ican wolde·
þæt hit after him	*þætte* æfter him·
on *cyneryce*	on *cneorissum*·
cenned wurde	cenned wurde·
yced on eorþan	*and seo mænigeo*
þæt swa unrime	*mære wære*·
had to hebban	*hat* to hebban*ne*·
swa heofonsteorran	swa heofonsteorran·
bugað bradne hw*ea*rft	*be*bugað bradne hw*y*rft·
oð brimflodas	oð *þæt* brim*faro*· *þæs*
swa w*a*roþa sond	*sæf*aroða sand·
ymb sealt *wæter*	*geond* sealt*ne wæg*·
yþe geond eargrund	*me are gryndeð*·
þæt *swa* unrim*e*	þæt *his* unrim *a*·
ymb wintra *hwearft*	*in* wintra *worn*·
weorðan sceolde.	wurðan sceolde.

Two manuscripts are available for lines 30–94 of *Salomon and Saturn*, MS. CCCC 422 of the second half of the tenth century and a fragment in the margin of CCCC 41 which may be a century later.[1] Lines 75–84 will serve as a sample:

[1] I have not seen this MS., but have noted (*Medium Ævum* xiii (1944), p. 35) that it was nearer to the original than the earlier MS. in omitting the runes for PATERNOSTER. The latest editor, Robert Menner, whose readings I follow, dates the hand 'at the end of the eleventh or beginning of the twelfth century'. Mr. Neil Ker tells me he would place it considerably earlier. It is disadvantageous to use such a late copy, because the

C

MS. CCCC 422	*MS. CCCC 41*
He is modigra	He is modigra
middangeard*e*	middangeard*es*
staðole strengra	staðole *he is* strengra
ðonne eal*ra* stana gripe	þone eall*e* stana gripe
lamena he is læce	lamana he is læce
leoht wincendra	leoht winciendra
swilce he is deafra duru	swilce he his deafra duru
dumbra tunge	*deadra* tunge
scyldigra scyld	scildigra scild
scyppendes seld	scippendes seld
flodes ferigend	flodes feriend
folces nerigend	folces neriend
yða yrfeweard	yða yrfeweard
earm*ra* fisca	earm*a* fixa
and wyrma *welm*	wyrma *wlenco*
wildeora holt	wildeora holt
on westenn*e* weard	westen*es* weard
weorðmynda geard.	weorðmynta geard.

I am concerned only with the amount of variation and the nature of the variants, not with their merits. There are differences of inflexion, e.g. **B** *hleoþorcwidas: hleoþorcwyde*, sometimes with other modifications, as **C** *on westenne weard: westenes weard*, or **A** *forweornast: forwisnad*. Minor words are added or omitted, e.g. **C** *staðole* [*he is*] *strengra*, or **A** [*se*] *gast*. Prepositions are varied, e.g. **B** *ymb wintra hwearft: in wintra worn*. Substitution of one word for another is common: sometimes the forms are similar, e.g. **C** *welm: wlenco*; and, with inferior alliteration in the first reading, **B** *swa waroþa: sæfaroða*. Sometimes the words have the same alliteration and rough sense, as **B** *ymb sealt wæter: geond sealtne wæg*; sometimes only the alliteration is the same, as **B** *cynerice: cneorissum*; sometimes only the meaning and syllabic weight, as **A** *geþohtes: gemundest*. Omissions or additions with considerable

great bulk of the poetry is contained in MSS. of the second half of the tenth century—Exeter Book, Vercelli Book, Junius 'Cædmon' (original part), Beowulf MS., MS. CCCC 422 of *Salcmon and Saturn*; and new factors affecting transmission may arise in MSS. written much after that time. I have excluded the poems contained in the Chronicle partly for this reason, partly because they are all late compositions transmitted in an unusual way. Similarly *Be Domes Dæge* is left out of account.

rearrangement occur at **A** 13 f. There is a new composition at **B** 320, and *þæt swa unrime* in the *Azarias* text recurs below. **B** *yþe geond eargrund: me are gryndeð* shows the making of a crux. At **B** 322 the *Daniel* scribe fails to recognize *brimfaroþes*, and points the verse before the last syllable, which he takes to be the word *þæs*. At **A** 17 both copies bungle the formula *Hwæt druge þu?* (*Genesis* 888, *Juliana* 247), so creating, even for Bosworth-Toller's Supplement and the latest editors,[1] a noun variously identified as *druh*, *drug*, *druhþu*, *druguþu*, and supposed to mean 'dust'.

In sum, the number of variants is very large. Though they are of a pedestrian kind,[2] many of them cannot be accounted for by simple errors of a scribe's eye or ear. More often than not they make metre and some sense: even **C** *deadra tunge* might be defended if there were no second manuscript to support *dumbra*. But as compared with the variants in classical texts, they show a laxity in reproduction and an aimlessness in variation which are more in keeping with the oral transmission of verse. An editor who has these passages in mind will not regard the integrity of a late manuscript as axiomatic.

All the major manuscripts already sampled were written within one half-century, and all come from the South or South Midlands, an area which was fairly homogeneous in literary language and culture at that time. It is possible to reach back into earlier times and different conditions because three short pieces, recorded in the eighth or ninth centuries, are also found in late-tenth-century copies: they are Cædmon's *Hymn*, the *Leiden Riddle*, and the Ruthwell Cross runic inscriptions.

The Ruthwell Cross runes, which are not necessarily as old as the Cross itself, give four groups of verses that can be identified in the Vercelli Book between lines 38 and 64 of the *Dream of the Rood*. The latter poem is so different in bulk, and so uneven in quality,

[1] Krapp *Vercelli Book*, 1932, p. 126; Krapp and Dobbie *Exeter Book*, 1936, pp. 175, 317; Mackie *Exeter Book* (E.E.T.S. 1934), p. 74 f.

[2] A variant is exceptionally preserved in the MS. at *Christ* 1653: 'ðær is leofra lufu, lif butan ende deaðe'; where *ende* makes an almost inevitable phrase, and the alternative *deaðe* matches the group of opposites that follows.

that a comparison could not favour the hypothesis of accurate transmission; and the first inscription differs remarkably from the corresponding lines in the Vercelli Book:[1]

(on)geredæ hinæ god almegttig   þa he walde on galgu gistiga
modig f(ore allæ) men   bug . . .

Ongyrede hine þa geong hæleð,   þæt wæs God ælmihtig,
strang and stiðmod.   Gestah he on gealgan heanne,
modig on manigra gesyhðe,   þa he wolde mancyn lysan.
Bifode ic þa me se beorn ymbclypte;   ne dorste ic hwæðre bugan to eorðan . . .

The absence of any probable alliteration in the second runic line is evidence of adaptation to the special purpose, and it would be unsafe to make much of the detailed variants where the conditions of recording are so abnormal.

The exceptional character of Cædmon's *Hymn* is marked by the many copies in which it appears.[2] If manuscripts later than the tenth century are excluded, the reproduction of the original words is good, with five variants, four minor and one major, of which only the last, *eorðan* (*bearnum*) for *aelda*, can be traced back to the ninth century. But it is a very short piece of miraculous origin, and it has been preserved as a quotation in historical prose texts, either the Latin of Bede's *History* or the late-ninth-century English translation from it. Here the conditions of transmission are abnormal, and again it is unsafe to rely on the evidence.

There remains the *Leiden Riddle*, found in a ninth-century Continental manuscript and in the Exeter Book. A specimen is unnecessary because the two manuscripts have often been printed side by side.[3] Apart from details of inflexion and uncertainties of reading in the Leiden manuscript, there are half a dozen variants

[1] See *The Dream of the Rood*, ed. Bruce Dickins and A. S. C. Ross, 1945.

[2] See *The Manuscripts of Cædmon's Hymn and Bede's Death Song* by E. van K. Dobbie (New York 1937). I omit *Bede's Death Song*: the Northumbrian text is preserved in Continental MSS. from the ninth century onwards; but, for comparison, there is only a very late West Saxon text, equally uniform, preserved in MSS. from the twelfth century onwards. Its four variants from the Northumbrian text have no claim to authority.

[3] See especially *Three Northumbrian Poems*, ed. A. H. Smith, 1933.

of some importance in sixteen corresponding lines, and the last two lines of the Leiden version, which are supported by the Latin original, have been replaced by a conventional riddle-ending in the Exeter Book. The degree of variation is not very different from that exhibited in the much shorter Riddle 31, of which two copies survive by an exceptional chance in the Exeter Book.

In these three pieces the tenth-century texts show no attempt to reproduce the archaic or dialectal forms and spellings of the earlier copies: Bodleian MS. Tanner 10 of Cædmon's *Hymn* and the early-eighth-century Moore MS. are identical only in a few invariable words. Ample evidence from other sources confirms that copyists of Old English texts were not expected to reproduce their originals letter for letter, as they were when copying Latin and especially Biblical texts. Modernization of forms in the course of transmission was allowed and even required by the use for which Old English works were intended,[1] and the practice was obviously dangerous for the wording.

A defender of the manuscript readings might well say that the evidence so far adduced is not ample or varied enough, and might argue that the scribes were well trained, and that they knew more

[1] This has a bearing on attempts to defend the MS. reading *wundini golde* in *Beowulf* 1382, where the slight emendation *wundnū* = *wundnum* had become established. It is not quite certain that *wundini* is the reading of the MS., and it is very doubtful whether a form *wundini* ever existed: in the recorded *-numini*, all the examples of which may go back to a single late-seventh-century gloss, the stem is short. But if there were no such doubts, it is most unlikely that this extraordinary ending would survive for three centuries, in a common word and phrase, to appear in the Beowulf MS. It would require, in this one place only, a suspension of the normalizing practice of scribes, and minutely accurate unintelligent copying throughout the whole long chain of transmission. That the acceptance of this reading leads to startling conclusions about the written tradition of *Beowulf* is another reason for preferring the simpler solution *wundnum*.

The habit of normalizing helps to explain some corrupt readings. In the Paris Psalter LXII. 11 *sine causa* (*justificavi cor meum*) is rendered, according to modern editors: 'þeah þe ic on [me] ingcan ænigne [ne] wiste &c.' It is more likely that *ic intingcan* was the original reading, that *t* dropped out leaving *ic in ingcan*, and a scribe changed *in* to *on*, as he would the preposition. The only other place where *causa* has to be translated is Ps. LXIII. 21 *iudica causam tuam*: 'dem þine nu ealde intingan'.

about Old English usage, thought, and tradition than a modern critic can. I doubt if this holds good for the earlier poetry. In *Beowulf*, recent editors agree that the first scribe writes *gara* (*cyn*) 461 clearly and boldly for *Wedera* (*cyn*), without sense or alliteration, with no likeness in script or sound, or anything in the surrounding verses to mislead him; and the aberration is passed over in their commentaries. For *Cain* 1261 (misread as *cam*) he writes *camp* 'battle', just as in *Genesis* 1938, 2400, *Loth* becomes *leoht* with no glimmering of sense. At a critical point in the Finn episode (1127 ff.), he leaves us the meaningless 'Hengest . . . wunode mid finnel unhlitme'. Rather different is 1960 f.: 'þonon geomor woc hæleðum to helpe', where, misled by a possible spelling or pronunciation of the initial diphthong, he has taken the proper name *Eomær* for the common adjective *geomor* 'sad'.[1] I have previously noted[2] a similar instance in the Exeter Book, where *onsyne beorg* appears in *Christ* 876, 900 for *on Sione beorg*, because the scribe mistook *onsione* for the common noun meaning 'face', &c.; and MS. Junius 11 shows the same misunderstanding in *Exodus* 386 *onseone* (*beorh*) for *on Sione*. All these are proper names, which I have preferred because there can be little doubt about the true reading when a name is miswritten. To show that the scribe misunderstood the meaning of common words we must use conjectural emendations, and, though I shall indulge in conjecture

[1] The MS. reading *geomor* has been defended, e.g. *Mod. Phil.* ii. 54 ff. Faith in the accuracy of this scribe, or his kind, underlies the doctrine that, in one poem or tradition, the same person sometimes has two authentic names, metrically equivalent and similar in script, but etymologically different in the significant first element: e.g. *Beow.* 467 *Heregar* beside *Heorogar* 61 and *Hiorogar* (second scribe) 2158; or *Oslaf* 1148 beside *Ordlaf* in the Finnsburh fragment. That two names, having such practical inconveniences and no technical purpose, should be maintained for centuries within a single poem or tradition seems to me to be a major improbability, which is not much lessened by evidence (e.g. in Klaeber's *Beowulf*, 1936, p. xxxii, n. 5) that some persons who can be identified in both literatures have Old English names differing in formation from their Scandinavian names. It is more likely that a scribe has slipped again, where he should have written *Heorogar*, *Or*(*d*)*laf*.

[2] *R.E.S.* x. 340. [The confusion occurs in psalter glosses: XIII. 7 *ex Sion* = Vitellius E XVIII (G) *on seone*; Tiberius C VI (H) *ansyne*; Arundel 60 (J) *ansine*.]

from this point, there is a risk of arguing in a circle. But in *Juliana* 482 the bad form *hyradreorge* (for *heoru-*) arose because the first element was mistaken for the pronoun *heora*, which usually has the form *hyra* in the Exeter Book.[1] In *Genesis* 2174 f.

> Hwæt gifest þu me, gasta waldend,
> freomanna to frofre, nu ic þus feasceaft eom?

it can hardly be doubted that a scribe has lost the sense by substituting *freomanna*, a legal not a poetical word, for *fremena* gen. pl. 'benefits' depending on *hwæt*. And because one can seldom prove that the scribe was alert when he wrote something wrong, it is worth noting a scrap of evidence at *Beowulf* 1981: 'hwearf | geond þæt (side) reced Hæreðes dohtor.' Here the copyist has added *side* as a correction above the line, which shows that his attention was directed to an error; and, for the sake of the alliteration, the editors must either reject his correction, or assume a lacuna after *reced* which escaped him. But there is no need to multiply indications that the scribes were often ignorant, or inattentive to the meaning.

As a last resort, it might be argued in defence of the poetical manuscripts that their authority is confirmed because they have passed the scrutiny of Anglo-Saxon readers, who knew things unknown to us. In fact there is hardly a trace of intelligent scrutiny. It is a curious feature of the great poetical codices that no early reader seems to have noticed the most glaring errors left by the scribe.

My argument has been directed against the assumption that Anglo-Saxon poetical manuscripts are generally good, in the sense that, except for an inevitable sprinkling of errors, they faithfully

[1] *R.E.S.* x. 340. Should not *Exodus* 218 *habban heora hlencan* be read *habban heorahlencan* (Sievers's expanded D-type, with extra alliteration which is not objectionable in the context)? In MS. Junius 11 the elements of a compound are often separated, and the MS. arrangement here is the same as in *Exodus* 181 *heorawulfas*. *Hioroserce* occurs in *Beow.* 2539; *wælhlence* in *Exodus* 176; but *hlence* by itself nowhere means 'coat of chain-mail', and such a meaning for the simplex is not likely. The passage has been used to emend *Finnsburh* 11 *habbað eowre landa*, which has a modern ring. Here we have to do with what Hickes and his printer made of the lost MS., and perhaps *habbað* (*h*)*eorelinda* is worth considering, though that compound is not recorded.

reproduce the words of much older originals. It does not attempt to establish that all the poems have survived in bad texts: three such pieces as *Widsith*, *Juliana*, and the *Gnomic Verses*, all preserved in the Exeter Book, may well have been subjected to different chances in their earlier transmission, and there may be reasons for believing that some poems were lucky.

Nor should acceptance of this argument discourage the habit of constant recourse to the manuscripts. Long after all the letters that can be read in them are settled in cold print (and not many finds like Mr. J. C. Pope's *Geatisc meowle*[1] at *Beow.* 3150 can now be expected) they will repay close study, because they are the primary witnesses. If there were enough of them, all the facts about the written transmission would be in evidence.

But when, as is usual for Old English poetry, only one late witness is available, there is no safety in following its testimony. The difference between a better reading and a worse is, after all, a matter of judgement; and however fallible that faculty may be, the judge must not surrender it to the witness. To support a bad manuscript reading is in no way more meritorious than to support a bad conjecture, and so far from being safer, it is more insidious as a source of error. For, in good practice, a conjecture is printed with some distinguishing mark which attracts doubt; but a bad manuscript reading, if it is defended, looks like solid ground for the defence of other readings. So intensive study with a strong bias towards the manuscript reading blunts the sense of style, and works in a vicious circle of debasement.[2]

[1] *The Rhythm of Beowulf*, 1942, p. 233.

[2] The process extends to grammar. It is enough to quote the most distinguished English commentator of the conservative school, R. W. Chambers, defending the MS. reading *licað leng swa wel* at *Beow.* 1854 against Grein's conjecture *sel*: 'If one finds gross anomalies in accidence in the *Beowulf*, why should one look for a flawless syntax?' (Here, it should be noticed, there is confusion between the late MS. of *Beowulf*, to which the *if* clause must refer, and the text to be derived from it by critical methods, to which the apodosis refers.) The principles of phonology must also yield: in Boethius *Metra* xxxi. 11 the editors and modern dictionaries accept *fierfete* 'four-footed' on the evidence of Junius's transcript of a leaf since destroyed, though *fier-* is against all rules, and the regular word is *fiðerfete*.

As a simple example, the Vercelli MS. reading *Hwæt, druh ðu dreorega* in *Soul and Body* 17, already mentioned, provides not only a ghost-word *druh*, &c., but a form of apostrophe new to Old English verse in its word order. A more complex example comes from the narrative passage in *Genesis A* which describes the flight of the raven and the dove from the Ark, lines 1443 ff.:[1]

Noe tealde, þæt he on neod hine,
gif he on þære lade land ne funde,
ofer sid wæter secan wolde
on wægþele; eft him seo wen geleah;
ac se feond[e] gespearn fleotende hreaw:
salwigfeðera secan nolde.
He (*sc.* Noe) þa ymb seofon niht &c.

The last two complete lines are interpreted 'but he (the raven), rejoicing, alighted on a floating corpse: the dark-feathered (bird) would not seek.' I find them ungrammatical, for *secan* is never left in the air like this in a sound text, and it is the more intolerable with *secan wolde* just above, and *sohte*, *secan* in the following lines, all with the regular object. The abruptness of the expression is equally disturbing, because the narrative in the whole passage is full and easy, and the poet has gone to a commentary for more about the raven than the Bible tells. The indications are that at least a line is missing, probably after *hreaw*, which contained the object of *secan*. But if such a manuscript text is regarded as sound, the chances are small that any lacuna of a line or more will be admitted on internal evidence. In fact, few are admitted by modern editors.[2]

[1] The text is that of Holthausen (1914) and Krapp (1931).

[2] When there is only one MS., gaps other than those due to its physical condition may sometimes be established from our knowledge of the subject-matter. But generally lacunae are conjectural. The weakness of such conjectures is that they are vaguer than specified readings, and therefore easy. Still, they should be considered on the balance of probability. Note:

(i) The mechanical dropping of one or more verse lines, which is common in MSS. of Latin poetry, is not so likely in Old English MSS., because in them the written line rarely corresponds with the verse. If the copyist dropped a line or more of his pattern MS., the ragged parts of two verses would usually be brought together, and metre as well as sense

There is, then, no escape from the task of questioning our single witness, beginning with tests of general credibility like those I have suggested already. If the results are not satisfying, we must examine and cross-examine on every sign of weakness in particular places. Thus in line 1446 of the passage just quoted, how is *eft* to be accounted for in the second half-verse? Noah has not been disappointed before, and the formula *him seo wen geleah* is elsewhere a complete half-verse (*Gen.* 49, *Beow.* 2323, *Andr.* 1074). Here the manuscript pointing of the verse is at fault. In the next line *feonde* 'rejoicing' for manuscript *feond* was suggested by Grein and confirmed by Cosijn; but there is no good evidence for a simple verb *feon* beside regular *gefeon*, and it is especially awkward in the present participle. Then again, a demonstrative pronoun *se* 'he' so clumsily separated from its noun *hrefn* is hardly possible:

would show up the fault. If the omission escaped the copyist, subsequent patching up is likely.

(ii) But one would expect a kind of omission to which Latin verse is not subject: the feeling for alliteration was strong, and when the scribe had written part of a verse, his eye might drop to a verse below with the same alliteration. So a lacuna could occur with no break in the alliteration. This possibility should be taken into account in such places as *Beow.* 1931, where Old English usage gives the clear indication that *modþryðo* is a compound abstract noun, object of *wæg* (*Gen.* 2238 *higeþryðe wæg*; *Guthlac* 982 *hygesorge wæg*, 1309 *gnornsorge wæg*; *Elene* 61 *modsorge wæg*, 655 *gnornsorge wæg*; *Beow.* 152 *heteniðas wæg*, 2780 *ligegesan wæg*: all second half-lines). See also Craigie 'Interpolations and Omissions in Anglo-Saxon Poetic Texts' *Philologica* ii (1923–4). [There is another reason for suspecting a lacuna here: the name of a new and important character, especially where it is suddenly introduced, should be emphasized by the alliteration; cf. *Sigemund* 875, *Heremod* 901, 1709.]

In *Azarias* 109 ff.

þu þæs geornlice
wyrcest wuldorcyning wæstmum herge
bletsien bledum, &c.

pretty clearly a subject has been lost before *wæstmum* or after *herge*, and the Latin *benedicat* terra *Dominum* confirms it. But rather than admit a lacuna, modern editors (Grein-Wülker and Krapp-Dobbie) assume an unknown fem. pl. *herge*, a meaning 'groves' otherwise unrecorded in Old English, and the free choice in this context of a word with peculiarly heathen associations; although *hergen* 'let them praise' occurs six times elsewhere in this paraphrase of the *Canticum Trium Puerorum*, thrice in association with *bletsien*. It is an example of the speculation which is induced by too much faith in the MS.

it is better to take *se* as a consequence of the misreading *feond*, and to substitute *he* as a necessary part of Grein's proposed emendation.

The cluster of difficulties in these few lines shows how complicated corruption may be. If the average text offered by the manuscripts were open to so many doubts, a critic's work would be hopeless. But long stretches have no such obvious faults: whether or not they represent the exact words of the original composer, they make good sense, grammar, and metre by the standards at present available. So a proper respect for the manuscripts is consistent with a critical and independent attitude towards their evidence. Nothing is to be gained by judging them with a hostile bias; and occasionally they still offer readings which modern editors have rejected, and which deserve to be restored.[1]

Because our means of criticizing the manuscripts are still so small, and some of them are weak from disuse, the change of approach which I suggest would not produce texts very different

[1] In *Elene* 925 'Gen ic findan can . . . wiðercyr wiððan', the editors since Grein read *siððan* with feeble sense. In *Guthlac* 465 'Ic eow soð wiððon secgan wille', they again alter to *siððon*. In *Menology* 146 'hæfð nu lif wið þan', the alteration is not possible. The meaning in *Elene* and *Guthlac* is 'Still I can devise a counter-stroke *against that*', &c., and the MS. readings are sound. *Wið þan* fills a similar place in the verse in Paris Psalter CXVIII. 158: 'and ic þand wið þan þe hi teala noldan | þinre spræce sped gehealdan', where *þriste* should be read for MS. *teala*.

Again, in his edition of *Genesis A*, Holthausen has the courage to say that he does not understand line 1400 in the account of the Flood:

Fiftena stod
deop ofer dunum se drenceflod
monnes elna. þæt is mæro wyrd:
þam æt niehstan wæs nan to gedale,
nymþe heo[f] wæs ahafen on þa hean lyft, &c.

Bouterwek, who established this punctuation in 1849, described the passage as 'sehr dunkel', and it troubled Cosijn and Sievers (Paul and Braune's *Beiträge* xix. 448 f.). If MS. *heo* is restored instead of Sievers's suggestion *heof* 'lamentation', and if *þæt is mæro wyrd* is bracketed as a parenthesis, for which there is an exact parallel at *Gen.* 2566, the MS. reading makes grammar and sense: 'Fifteen of our (*monnes*) ells above the mountains stood the whelming flood (that was a great marvel!); and at last there was none to divide the flood (*þam . . . to gedale*) unless it (sc. *seo dun*) rose up to the high firmament.' This is not far from the Latin: 'opertique sunt omnes montes excelsi sub universo caelo. Quindecim cubitis altior fuit aqua super montes quos operuerat.'

from those that are now reckoned good. Editors would less often write as if they were presenting a distant original exactly, except for its archaic and dialectal forms. They would also be less ready to cumber the text with palaeographical features or linguistic oddities from the late manuscript: the first are useless in an age of cheap and good photography, for palaeography cannot be learnt from type; the second raise more delicate problems, but the retention, for example, of the normal nominative plural form *yrfeweardas* at *Beow.* 2453, where it stands for the normal genitive singular *yrfeweardes*, is a nuisance to the reader.[1]

One might expect a considerable increase in the number of places marked as cruces, i.e. places where the manuscript reading is

[1] The historical grammar of Late West Saxon is a neglected subject, but poetical MSS. and commentaries on poetry are not the places in which it can best be studied, and the editors are far from consistent. Thus the Beowulf MS. has *Ecgþeow* fourteen times, but *Ecþeow* 263 with *g* added later by the scribe, and *Ecþeow* unaltered 957; *Ecglaf* four times, but *Eclaf* 980; and *sec* 2863. Chambers follows the MS. at 957, 980; 'corrects' *sec* to *secg*; and fails to note that *Ecþeow* was originally written at 263. Klaeber, who assembles the facts, regularizes throughout. But instead of normalizing MS. *siexbennum* 2904 to *seax*-, Klaeber reads *sex*-, which is a conjectural form based on an assumed confusion with the numeral. In the Beowulf MS. *siex*- would be an exceptional form of 'six', and an alternative explanation is possible. There is a late *ie* for *ea* which has escaped Sievers's Grammar. It is common in the mid-eleventh-century Cambridge Psalter (ed. Wildhagen, 1910), which has *ie* not only in *wiex* = *weax* n., *geþieht*, *iec* = *eac*, and in *ciestyr* = *ceaster*, but also in *iert* = *eart*, *sielm* = *sealm*, *lies* = *leas*, &c. This MS. has Canterbury connexions, and the second hand of the Beowulf MS. shows South-Eastern forms; but as some other examples of late *ie* = *ea* are not clearly South-Eastern, I merely note the alternative explanation. An inclination towards standard spellings in the printed text has a further advantage, because in these details too scribes make mistakes, not all of which can be accounted for. Beside *missere*, editors and dictionaries accept a form *missare*, which is a possible alternative in Old Norse but not in Old English. It is inferred from the dat. pl. *missarum* in *Gen.* 2345, where I have little doubt that the scribe thought of *missarum*, gen. pl. of the familiar Church Latin *missa*. In Old English there are such errors due to the religious preoccupations of the copyists. Thus *heofon* for *geofon* 'ocean' occurs in the MS. of *Andreas* 393, 1508, and 1585, where the corrections were made by Kemble (1843). And *amen* for *agmen*, *angelo* for *angulo* in classical MSS. (see L. Havet *Manuel de critique verbale*, 1911, p. 263 f.) are in the same kind as *engle* for *egle*, which was our starting-point.

judged to be unsound and there is no convincing conjecture to replace it. Klaeber in his standard edition of *Beowulf* (1936) marks only one crux (*mwatide* 2226) and one lacuna of a few words at line 62; Chambers marks the lacuna but not the crux; Sedgefield admits neither. For a text of the form and content of *Beowulf*, subject, according to these editors, to the vicissitudes of three centuries, this residue of faults detected and not made good is incredibly small. It indicates that comfortable conventions have become established, so that healthy doubts have been stilled.

An increase in the number of recognized cruces would cause some conjectural readings to disappear from the text. But, in compensation, some others would replace manuscript readings which are now retained on the assumption that a single late manuscript has extraordinary authority; and there would be a real gain if conjecture, instead of being reserved for the useful but disheartening task of dealing with obvious or desperate faults, were restored to its true functions, which include probing as well as healing.

3

'SEASONS OF FASTING'

FOR Anglo-Saxonists of the twentieth century a new piece of verse is a rare thing. We are accustomed to deal, not with texts in the raw as they appeared to their first discoverers, but with printed texts that owe their finish to the work of several generations of editors and commentators, above all, to men like Grein and Cosijn who ranged familiarly over the whole corpus of verse and explained or emended difficult places with a feeling for Anglo-Saxon expression which is the best gift a textual critic can have. The constant use of their work contributes to the impression that Anglo-Saxon poems, as transmitted by the manuscripts, are on the whole well transmitted.

When he was examining the transcripts by Laurence Nowell which Lord Howard de Walden gave to the British Museum, the late Robin Flower[1] found in MS. Addit. 43703, transcribed by Nowell in 1562, a copy of a poem on the observance of fasts which, except for the incipit recorded by Wanley, had been lost when MS. Otho B XI was burnt in the Cotton fire of 1731. Flower's death prevented him from making the edition he planned, and it fell to Professor Dobbie to publish the *editio princeps* in his *Anglo-Saxon Minor Poems*, 1942. I shall quote his text throughout, take his brief introduction and commentary as a starting-point, and examine afresh some of the emendations on which he invited further discussion.[2]

The poem, which is imperfect at the end, consists of some 230 lines of no high poetical quality. A summary will help the discussion.

In old days Moses, divinely instructed, gave laws to the Israelites, who had God's favour; but in the end they crucified our Lord (1–3).

[1] See his notice in *B.M. Quarterly* viii (1934–5), p. 131; and his lecture 'Laurence Nowell and the Discovery of England in Tudor Times' (1936), *Proc. Brit. Acad.* xxi, pp. 26, 29.

[2] Op. cit., p. xciv.

They kept four fasts, sacrificing a lamb or heifer as a symbol of the dear one (4). But our Lord arose from the tomb and promised us Heaven if we follow his teaching (5). Let us praise him and keep the fasts which Gregory appointed (6): the first in March in the first week of Lent (7); the second in June in the week after Pentecost Sunday (8); the third in September in the week before the Autumn equinox (9); the fourth in the week before Christmas (10). On Wednesday, Friday, and Saturday in each of these weeks the fast is to be kept till the ninth hour except in case of sickness (11). If anybody from the Continent says that you should keep other fasts that Moses appointed for his people, do not assent, but keep those that Pope Gregory from Rome appointed for the English nation (12–13).

Let us also keep the forty days Lenten fast before the Resurrection. Moses fasted forty days before he received God's commands (14–15). So did Elijah, whom an angel fed, before he ascended Mount Horeb and was taken up to Heaven in a fiery chariot (16–19). Lastly, Christ fasted forty days in the wilderness, and was tempted in vain by the Devil. If you follow his example, the Devil's arrows will not harm you (20–22). We command every man to keep the forty days' Lenten fast until noon of each day (23). The priests must sing mass every day and intercede for the people, who must confess their sins (24).

It is very necessary that the priest himself should not sin (25). But if he does, do not let it detract from his good doctrine (26). There are priests who set a bad example. In the morning, immediately after mass, they hurry through the streets seeking the tapster, and persuade him that he can without sin serve oysters and wine before noon, with no more regard for the proper meal-times than a dog or a wolf has. Then they sit and tipple, and say it is permissible to refresh oneself after mass with wine, and to eat oysters and other fish. . . . (27–29).

Flower noted that the poem is in eight-lined stanzas, except that stanza 4 has six and stanza 15 nine lines. In his transcript, which evidently follows the arrangement of the burnt manuscript, Nowell begins each stanza with a new line and a capital, and usually ends it with a special punctuation mark. Stanza numbers are given in the summary, and it will be seen that each is a paragraph dealing with a single topic. This arrangement of alliterative lines, extraordinary in Anglo-Saxon, is evidence of Latin influence and of late composition. Since twenty-six of the twenty-eight completed stanzas are of eight lines, there is a probability that the irregular stanzas 4 and 15 originally had that number. Stanza 4 reads:

We þæt gehyrdon hæleþa mænige
on bocstafum breman and writan,
þæt hie fæstenu feower heoldon
and þonne offredan unmæne neat,
þæt is lamb oþþe styrc, leofum to tacne
þe for worulde wæs womma bedæled.

At the end the expression is bare, and the next stanza begins abruptly:

Ac arisan ongan rices ealdor.

To explain the symbolism of the sacrifice of lamb or heifer, a reference to the Crucifixion is needed.[1] I suggest that two lines with the content 'yet was crucified by the Jews and buried for dead' have been omitted by a kind of homoeoteleuton, because the same thing is said, in a different connexion, at the end of stanza 3. Stanza 15 says that God gave his commands to Moses after his forty days' fast, and told him to teach them to his people, as a token that by fasting we may gain God's grace and the divine doctrines which should instruct every people,

119 gif us þære duguþe hwæt dryhten sylleð.

The editor takes this ninth line to mean 'whether the Lord gives us anything of benefit', but its sense seems to be 'if the Lord gives us any goodness', i.e. 'if there is any goodness in us'. In either case it is so unnecessary that one could hardly imagine an author breaking his stanza scheme to add it. I propose to seclude it as a later addition. Then all twenty-eight complete stanzas would have eight lines.

This regular stanzaic form is not quite unique. In the late-eleventh-century Worcester MS. Junius 121 there is a verse exposition of the Creed which begins with six stanzas of eight, each expounding a clause of the Latin, but breaks away to deal with the crowded last clause phrase by phrase. *Fasting* has two lines in common with this *Creed* that are not found elsewhere in Anglo-Saxon verse:

4 heofna heahcyning, her on life

(= *Creed* 51 with *for* for *on*[2]); and

[1] Cf. Ælfric's exposition, *Catholic Homilies*, ed. Thorpe ii, p. 264 ff.

[2] The flat half-line *her for life* recurs in *Creed* 53, *Fasting* 39, 141, and is current in sermons of the time.

151 and þone uplican   æþel secað

(= *Creed* 37 þone uplican   eðel secan[1]).

Both poems use *unmæne* 'pure', found nowhere else in the poetry, and apply the adjective *wlanc* to the Divinity (*Creed* 48, *Fasting* 54). There are also less distinctive tricks of style such as the use of *mære* 'glorious' as a stock adjective.[2] Taken together with the stanza form, they make it reasonably certain that *Fasting* and *Creed* are by the same author: certainly they belong to the same school. And *Creed* is incorporated in the so-called *Benedictine Office*,[3] of which the prose framework (though not the verse quotations) is generally attributed to Wulfstan, bishop of London,[4] later bishop of Worcester and archbishop of York (1002–23).

If now we look at the content of *Fasting*, the last part, on priests who keep the fasts laxly, gives a lively picture that might be drawn at any period; the middle, on the forty-day fasts of Moses, Elijah, and Jesus, is a commonplace in Lenten sermons;[5] but the times of the four Ember fasts were a matter of contemporary controversy, and probably for that reason they are given the first place: 'Keep the four Ember fasts', our author says, 'at the times appointed by the great Pope Gregory for the English nation. Do not listen to people from the Continent who advocate other dates.'

The controversy in England[6] seems still to await the attention of a liturgiologist able to assemble and interpret the evidence. Failing that, I suppose that an Englishman who crossed the Channel at the beginning of the tenth century would find that in France, or at Rome itself, it was usual to keep the spring and summer Ember fasts at fixed dates, in the first week of March and the

[1] Similarly *Creed* 32: het ða uplicne   eþel secan.

[2] *Fasting* 8 times in 230 lines; *Creed* 3 times in 58.

[3] Edited by E. Feiler *Das Benediktiner-Offizium*, Heidelberg 1901. Other verse pieces in the same collection show the same method of exposition in approximately equal verse paragraphs, but they do not attain regularity.

[4] See especially Miss D. Whitelock, 'A Note on the Career of Wulfstan the Homilist', *English Historical Review* lii (1937), p. 460.

[5] e.g. Ælfric *Catholic Homilies*, ed. Thorpe, i, p. 178.

[6] Dobbie, op. cit., p. xciii, gives references. The most useful collection of English evidence for the late tenth and eleventh centuries is by H. Henel: *Studien zum altenglischen Computus*, Leipzig 1934, p. 60 ff.

second week of June; whereas in England it was usual to make them depend on the date of Easter, so that they fell in the first week of Lent and the week after Pentecost Sunday. The difference of usage was explained in late Anglo-Saxon times by an ordinance attributed to Gregory the Great.[1]

But in the eleventh century several manuscripts give the Continental usage, though they are in a minority.[2] Since their dates exclude post-Conquest influences, the usage is naturally explained as a consequence of the Benedictine Reform in the later tenth century, which depended on the Continent for many of its ideas and practices. The change would be easier to make in a monastic community than in a parish, where laymen were affected; and probably radical reformers favoured the Continental practice, while the more conservative maintained the native tradition. This explanation agrees with the poem, in which the departure from the customary English dates is regarded as a recent innovation from the Continent.

Two English documents from around the end of the tenth century are important. The first, a Latin compilation for the

[1] Printed in Haddan and Stubbs *Councils and Ecclesiastical Documents* iii (1871), p. 52 f. The authenticity of the text has been questioned with good reason. It is probably a practical summary, made before the end of the tenth century, of the scholarly explanation in the eighth-century *Dialogus Ecgberhti*, printed in the same volume, p. 410 ff. Ecgberht infers Gregory's authority from English antiphonaries and missals derived from those brought by Augustine, and claims to have verified the usage in Gregory's copies of these books preserved at Rome. It was a time when Gregory's Registers were being searched (see Boniface to Ecgberht in *Mon. Germ. Hist. Epist.* iii, p. 347); and that Ecgberht should rely on the evidence of service-books indicates that no written instruction from Gregory could be found at Rome or in England.

[2] Henel, op. cit., quotes MS. Laud 482 (Worcester) and the closely related Brussels MS. Bibl. Royale 8558–63; also Vitellius E XVIII (Winchester Cathedral). Important MSS. in which the English practice is mentioned are the Leofric Missal (Glastonbury(?)); Tiberius B V (Christ Church, Canterbury?); Titus D XXVII (Newminster, Winchester); CCCC 422 (Sherborne). The mention of one usage or the other in a literary text belonging to any church is not good evidence for the practice of that church. Otho B XI itself was probably a Winchester copy. Henel notes that Byrhtferth of Ramsey, a pupil of Abbo of Fleury, deals only with the Christmas fast in the text of his *Manual* (ed. Crawford, p. 88), but shows the English dates in the diagram opposite p. 90.

guidance of parish priests which is attributed to Ælfric,[1] says impartially that *Romana auctoritas* supports the one usage, and that the other was prescribed for the English by Pope Gregory. The second is intended to settle the controversy, which would not encourage laymen to observe these exacting fasts. The Laws of Æthelred VI. 23 direct that everybody shall keep the Ember fasts as St. Gregory appointed for the English nation, and the contemporary Latin record has the same rule with the addition 'quamvis aliæ gentes aliter exercuerint'.[2] Again we come round to Archbishop Wulfstan, whose part as inspirer and to some extent drafter of Æthelred's Codes V–X is generally recognized, and whose responsibility for the Latin paraphrase is explicit.[3] The poem on *Fasting* comes from Wulfstan's circle. The censure of lax priests, together with *we bebeodað* 'we command' at line 178, indicates that the writer had authority higher than that of an ordinary monk or mass-priest. Nothing suggests that Wulfstan himself wrote it. Its probable date is covered by the two decades which fall on either side of the year 1000.

Verse written so late is not to be judged by the standards of an earlier period. For instance, in 9ª *þa se leoda fruma* it is not certain that the author wrote *leodfruma* which an earlier poet would prefer. But as he was interested enough in technique to try the stanza form, it is reasonable to suppose that he would avoid half-lines of three syllables: 96ᵇ *þeodlareow*, a compound otherwise unrecorded, was almost certainly *þeoda lareow*, with the same meaning, in the original; 2ª *þurh Moysen* may require the exceptional pronunciation *Moÿsen*; in 117ª *and þa deopan*, the demonstrative may be emphatic enough to carry the stress, but *and þa deoplican* would make a normal half-line.

[1] See B. Fehr *Die Hirtenbriefe Ælfrics*, Hamburg 1914, p. cxxv̄ and footnote. He prints the Latin at p. 240 f. The case of this particular passage is complicated; cf. Fehr's remarks at pp. cii and cx.

[2] Both texts in Liebermann's *Gesetze* i, p. 252 f.

[3] Sermon L in Napier's *Wulfstan*, Berlin 1883, at p. 272, has the sentence: 'and ymbrenfæstena healde man rihte swa swa Sanctus Gregorius Angelcynne sylf hit gedihte.' K. Jost *Wulfstanstudien*, Berne 1950, p. 249 ff., regards this sermon as the work of a compiler who derived the sentence from VI Æthelred 23.

Any failure in the alliteration deserves attention. In

40 deorne dædfruman, and him geara gerim
ælmesdædum ure gefyllan:

the editor has removed *do* after *him*. Clearly the reading should be ***and him dogera gerim*** 'and for his sake fill the number of our days with charitable acts'. *Dogera* (*ge*)*rim* and the compound *dogorrim* are fairly common in verse that is influenced by Biblical models.

168 Higesynnig man, gyf þe susla weard &c.

Here the alliteration appears to fall on the second element of a compound. *Higesynnig* is not recorded elsewhere, and the meaning 'sinful at heart (?)' is unsatisfactory in a compound whose first element does not help the alliteration. Read *Hige*, *synnig man*, &c., 'Consider, sinner, if the Devil dares to tempt you . . .'. The imperative varies 128 *uton . . . rihte gehicgan*, 144 *is to hicganne*.

In one place only the transmitted text has alliteration on the fourth instead of the third stress:

86 þæs þe us boca dom þeodlic demeð.

Here the rare *þeodlic* seems to mean 'national': 'as written authority applying to our nation decrees for us'. To transpose *demeð þeodlic* would separate the adjective violently from its noun *dom*; yet the verse translation of the Lord's Prayer incorporated in the *Benedictine Office* in MS. Junius 121 has:

21 and mandæda, swa we mildum wið ðe
. . . abylgeað,

where *mildum* is unnaturally separated from its pronoun *ðe* to bring the alliteration on to the third stress. It is doubtful whether line 86 is transmitted as the author wrote it. The difficulty is to explain why he introduced *þeodlic* so awkwardly, unless he was translating from Latin.

There remain four exceptional lines:

48 on þære ærestan wucan lengtenes;
58 on þære wucan þe æfter cumeð, &c.;
67 on þære wucan þe ærur byð
emnihtes dæge;
72 on þære wucan þe bið ærur full
dryhtnes gebyrde.

In all these *wucu* 'week' alliterates with vowels. It has been thought that (with the exception of *wuton*, later *uton*[1] 'let us', a kind of interjection in which any phonetic tendency may develop abnormally) Old English initial *w* was stable in words like *wucu*, *wudu* until after the Conquest, when it was affected by Anglo-Norman pronunciation.[2] Pre-Conquest examples like *West Saxon Gospels* Luke xviii. 12 *ucan* for *wucan* in the early-eleventh-century MS. CCCC 140, written at Bath, are very rare. But these verses, composed round about the year 1000, by an author whose opinions exclude the explanation of exceptional French influence, supply the proof that in at least one dialect, perhaps of the South Midlands, initial *w* had become absorbed in *wucan*. The sound-change is concealed by the conventional spelling which spread with the Late West Saxon literary dialect. It appears commonly in the Domesday record of 1086 where the traditional spelling is no longer followed.

In lines 67 and 72 just quoted, Professor Dobbie explains *ærur* as an analogical comparative used as a preposition:[3] 'before the equinox', 'before Christ's birthday'. He does not discuss the awkward *full* in line 72, which can only be construed: 'in that week which, complete, comes before Christ's birthday.' The forced construction suggests literal translation, and the ordinance attributed to Gregory the Great has *in plena hebdomada* here. According to the English usage, the first two Ember weeks followed a Sunday fixed by the date of Easter, whereas Christmas

[1] *Uton* is first recorded in the early-tenth-century Lauderdale MS. of Orosius, probably a Winchester book.

[2] See Sievers–Brunner *Grammatik* (1942), § 172 n.; Girvan *Handboek*, § 199.1; Bülbring *Elementarbuch*, § 464; E. Björkman *Nordische Personennamen in England*, Halle 1910, p. 166 n.; R. E. Zachrisson *English Place-Names and River-Names etc.* (Uppsala Universitets Årsskrift 1926), p. 18 n.; and his essay in *Introduction to the Survey of English Place-Names* (English Place-Name Society i), 1924, p. 113 f.

[3] Grein–Köhler's *Sprachschatz* records this usage only twice, from the verse *Metres* of Boethius xx. 41 *næs æror þe*, and xxix. 26 *ærror sunnan*: in both places the reading is the result of emendation, so that the construction caused difficulty. It varies *ær þonne sunne* in *Metres* xxix. 20, and might be construed as the comparative of the adjective *ær* with a dative of comparison.

might fall on any day of the week: hence 'the complete week' before Christmas was specified. But the same applies to the third Ember week before the autumn equinox, where the ordinance also has *in plena hebdomada*. How is the difference between lines 67^{b} and 72^{b} to be explained? Three possibilities suggest themselves. The author may have been translating from a version of the supposed ordinance which accidentally omitted *plena* for the autumn fast: in fact the word is omitted in MS. CCCC 190.[1] Or *plena* may have been translated at both places, and a copyist or reviser may have dropped the clumsy *full* at the first. Or the author may have been content with the meagre half-line *þe ærur bið* at both places, and a reader may have inserted *full* for the Christmas fast. Perhaps the first is likeliest.

From this point, I deal with some difficult passages in the order of the text.

16 gif hie leohtras heora letan gewyrpan.

The editor, altering MS. *gewyrþan*, renders: 'if they let their sins change for the better.' This would be a strained use of *gewyrpan* 'to recover', and it is better to keep *gewyrþan*, translating: 'if they abandon their sins.' I cannot quote an Old English example of *geweorþan* with the simplex *lætan*, though *lætan* itself, *lætan beon*, *forlætan geweorþan* have the meaning 'abandon', and *leten iwurþen* is frequent in Middle English, usually in the sense 'leave alone'; see *O.E.D.* s.v. *I-worth* 6.

20 ac him [the Jews] se ende wearð earm and þrealic.

Þrealic of the edition is an improvement on manuscript *þreoring*. *Dreorig* gives good sense and is nearer the transcript.

33 ff. After the Resurrection, Christ
ham gesohte,
eard mid englum, and us eallum þone
hyht and gehateð, gyf &c.

The editor takes *hyht* as the contracted form = *hyhteð*, translating 'hopes for it for us and promises it to us'. This meaning is hardly

[1] According to B. Fehr's print in *Die Hirtenbriefe Ælfrics*, p. 241.

satisfactory. Delete *and*, and with *hyht* in the sense 'joy', translate: 'promises all of us that joy if', &c. Cf. 148 ff.

37 f.
Na þær in cumeð atele gefylled,
womme gewesed, ac scal on wyrd sceacan.

The use of *on wyrd* 'to destruction' is unparalleled. *Andreas* 1594[b] *in forwyrd sceacan* suggests the reading *forwyrd* here.

55 ff.
Ofer þa Eastertid oþer fæsten
ys to bremenne Brytena leodum
mid gelicum lofe, †þe gelesen hafað†
on þære wucan. . . .

Professor Dobbie could find no meaning in *þe gelesen hafað*, and I mark it as a crux. Alliteration with *l* is necessary, and the stanza form excludes any considerable lacuna. The editor is probably right in disregarding four letters (? *lefe*) struck out before *lesen* as simply Nowell's correction of a slip in transcription.

65 f. The third Ember fast is

dihte gelicum on þam deoran hofe
to brymenne beorhtum sange.

The commentary suggests that *gelicum* is an adverbial instrumental 'likewise', noting that no other example of the absolute use is recorded. In this stilted verse it is better taken as parallel with *beorhtum*: 'appointed to be celebrated with the like clear song (of praise)' as for the two previous fasts. In the observance of these fasts the author thinks primarily of the services in the church, *on þam deoran hofe*.

73 f.
and we mid deornum scylan
wordum and weorcum wuldres cyninge, . . .
þeodne deman.

Deornum 'secret' is hardly suitable: the word tends to have a bad connotation. Read *deorum* 'good', 'pleasing to (God)'. This is a stock adjective with the author, cf. lines 40, 65, 110, 139, 154.[1]

[1] Miss D. Whitelock in *The Year's Work in English Studies for 1942* xxiii (1944), p. 32 f., correctly restores l. 85 to read: 'þe mot æt oþþe wæt ærur þicgan'; cf. *Wulfstan*, ed. Napier, p. 102/24f. I fear I may have overlooked and duplicated other corrections.

87 ff. Gif þe þonne secgan suþan cymene
bryttan Franca, þæt þu gebann sceole
her on eorþan ænig healdan,
þæs þe Moyses iu mælde to leodum,
na þu þæs andfeng æfre gewyrþe.

The editor notes that the reference to 'Frankish' usage is obscure, and translates the last line 'never value the reception of it', where I prefer to read *andfenga*: 'never be an assenter to it.' Even if *bryttan Franca* (MS. *brytt|franca*) could mean 'lords of the French' it would make no sense in this context. But apart from the doubt whether the genitive *Franca* for *Franc(e)na* would appear so early, the common noun *brytta* always means 'one who gives or disposes of' the thing (never person) expressed by the accompanying genitive, as in 54 *wuldres bryttan.* Read *Bryttan oððe Francan* 'Bretons or French'. The Bretons had an important influence on the English Church in the tenth century, though they were less prominent in the eleventh, when this line may have been corrupted. They began to come in considerable numbers during Athelstan's reign as refugees from the Viking invaders. They brought with them relics and cults which were so eagerly received in South-western England that Bishop speaks of 'a veritable devotional *furore* in Bretonism' in the later tenth century.[1] Their influence was especially strong at Winchester, where Judoc was ranked among the greatest saints, and Machutus, by a confusion of place-names, was adopted as an early bishop of Winchester.[1] So it is natural that our controversialist should join them with the French when he plays on native prejudice against foreigners and their ways.[2] Perhaps Winchester Cathedral, where Æthelwold seems to have made radical reforms following Continental example, had adopted the foreign dates for the Ember fasts. No evidence of this has so far been adduced from the tenth century, but MS. Vitellius E XVIII, which contains an official calendar of Winchester

[1] *The Bosworth Psalter*, 1908, p. 56.

[2] Note his silence about the delicate question of *Romana auctoritas*, which Ælfric (if the passage referred to above, p. 50, is his) quotes on the side of the Continental usage. That our author knew the weight of that argument is fairly clear from his insistence that Gregory's supposed instructions are authority from Rome, lines 45 and 99 ff.

Cathedral, is clear evidence for the Continental practice there some half-century later. The prescription of the English practice in Laws of Æthelred VI, but not in the closely related codes V Æthelred and I Cnut, is an indication that there were powerful interests on either side.[1]

175 gif þu dryhtnes her dædum fylgest.

In the commentary the reading *dryhtne* is suggested, with the rendering: 'if you follow the Lord here with your deeds.' But *fylgan* takes a dative of the thing followed. In 35 f.

gyf we his willaþ
þurh rihtne sefan rædum fyligan,

the Lord's teaching (*rædum*) is to be followed, in 175 his example (*dædum*).

179 þæt manna gehwilc þe for moldan wunað . . .

Read *ofer moldan* 'upon earth', a set phrase.

195 ff. 'Who can make a thrall's peace with his lord, if he has previously angered him greatly, and does not make it good',

ac þa æbyligþe ealdere wrohte,
dæghwamlice dædum niwað?

The editor comments: '*wrohte* for *worhte* "performed" ', and it is not clear how he construes *ealdere*. Translate 'but daily renews by his actions the injury of the old offence (*ealdere wrohte*)'.

202 f. nu þa, folces mann, fyrna ne gyme
þe gehalgod mann her gefremme.

Read *na þu* as at line 91: 'layman, have no regard to the sins that a clergyman commits.'

206 f. drince he him þæt drofe oððe þæt dæghluttre
wæter of wege, þæt is wuldres lare.

The editor has emended boldly. The transcript reads:

drince he him þæt drofe duge hlutter þe
wæter of wege, &c.

Here *lare*, for *lar* which is desirable for metre as well as grammar, is the kind of slip Nowell was likely to make; otherwise the meaning exactly fits the context: 'though he [the priest] should drink

[1] See Note A at p. 278.

dirty (water), let the pure water which is divine doctrine do you good (*duge þe*).' It is hardly possible to translate *of wege* 'from the cup' without giving it undue emphasis. It merely fills out the alliterative phrase *wæter of wege*, cf. 230 *fisc of flode*.

208 ff. Ac ic secgan mæg, sorgum hremig,
hu þa sacerdas sace niwiað,
dæghwamlice dryhten gremiað
and mid æfeste ælcne forlædað
þe him fylian wyle folces manna;
sona hie on mergan mæssan syngað
and forþegide, þurste gebæded,
æfter tæppere teoþ geond stræta.

Æfeste, rendered 'with malice', is an emendation for MS. *æleste*. It is not happy because the author is censuring slack or undisciplined priests, not those who mislead laymen through hate or malice. Although it is not otherwise recorded, MS. *æleste* 'neglect of religious law' fits the context exactly. It assumes a series *ǣ*, *ǣlēas*, *ǣlīest* like *ār*, *ārlēas*, *ārlīest*. The commentary suggests that *forþegide* may be for *forþigede*, weak past participle of an unrecorded *forþicgan* with the meaning 'having overeaten'. But priests are being censured for taking wine and oysters (a delicate and ambiguous food) after mass, so that the grosser offence of overeating before mass could hardly be mentioned so casually. *Hine þegeþ þurst* is recorded from *Leechdoms*;[1] *þurste geþegede* from *Christ III* 1510; so that *forþegide þurste* here means 'consumed with thirst'. For a dative construed with two participles, one before and one after it, of which the second is uninflected, cf. the description of the Cherubim in *Elene* 742 f.:

þa ymbsealde synt mid syxum eac
fiðrum gefrætwad.

216 ff. The lax priest persuades the tapster that he can, without offence, serve oysters and wine before noon,

þæs þe me þingeð
þæt hund and wulf healdað þa ilcan
wisan on worulde and ne wigliað
hwæne hie to mose fon, mæða bedæled.

[1] Ed. Cockayne ii (1865), p. 60/7. *Genesis* 2002 has *ecgum ofþegde* 'destroyed by swords'.

Here *hwæne* is emended from MS. *hwænne*, and the commentary interprets: 'and do not divine (or foresee) whom they may capture for food.' Rather, the point is that beasts observe no mealtimes; cf. Ælfric: 'nytenu ætað swa ær swa hi hit habbað, ac se gesceadwisa man sceal cepan his mæles.'[1] Then MS. *hwænne* 'when' must stand, but *wigliað* cannot. *Wiglian* means 'to practise divination or sorcery', possibly 'to find out by these practices'. But a wolf or dog could hardly be expected to foretell by divination when or what it would eat; and its failure to do so would have no likeness to the conduct of a priest who took wine and oysters before noon on fast-days. *Bewitiað* for *wigliað* gives the required meaning. Apart from the prefix, the misreading is easy, and the simplex is found early in Middle English. Translate: 'it seems to me that dogs and wolves behave in the same way, and take no heed when they eat, lacking all continence.'

224 ff. Hi þonne sittende   sadian aginnað,
sinne semað,   syllað gelome,
cweðað goddlife   gumena gehwilcum
þæt wines dreng   welhwa mote,
siþþan he mæssan hafað,   meþig þicgan,
etan ostran eac   and oþerne
fisc of flode . . .

For *sinne semað*, translated 'pacify enmity' in the commentary, the transcript has *win semað*. Since priests are censured for sitting in the tavern drinking wine after early mass on fast-days, not for making up quarrels (which is their duty), the reading should be *win seniað* 'they bless the wine' before drinking it. This may be no more than vivid description, but probably the author regards the act as irreverent and an exaggeration of the offence. For *cweðað goddlife* I suggest *cweðað þæt Godd life*. The final words could only mean 'and another fish', which is impossible except on the unlikely assumption that another sort of fish was specified in the following lines that are lost. Here the record of the transcript, usually accurate, is at fault. Nowell wrote *oþerre*, and the reading should be *oþerre fiscas*. So the passage runs: 'Then they sit and begin sating themselves. They bless the wine, pour it out again and again.

[1] *Lives of Saints*, ed. Skeat, xvi. 317 f.

They say God gives leave to all men that anyone may drink wine to refresh himself (*meþig*) after he has the sacrament, and may eat oysters too and other fishes . . .'

If these conjectures and explanations are acceptable in the main, they lead to two observations of more general scope. First, the newly discovered text does not favour the opinion that Anglo-Saxon verse has been carefully transmitted. In this short piece, where the transmission has almost certainly been written at all stages, where the burnt manuscript was perhaps not much more than half a century later than the author's original, and that half-century one in which the standard of education was relatively good, there are a number of substantial corruptions over and above those corrected by Professor Dobbie. The exceptional arrangement in stanzas points to an omission of two lines in stanza 4 and the addition of one in stanza 15; there is a crux (57); and the sense is lost at more than one essential place (e.g. 88). It is unlikely that Nowell's transcript is responsible for these. His errors are more probably to be found among the examples of letter-confusion; or in the false grammatical forms of easily recognized words, such as 207 *lare* for *lar* already noticed, and 111 *sylfe dryhten* for *sylfa dryhten*; or in bad spellings like 3 *gelared*[1] for *gelæred*, 195 *þreale* for *þræle*, and 80 *getinge* for *getenge* 'immediately following'.[2] The

[1] Wanley, Catalogue, p. 219, reads *gelæred*. In his quotation of the incipit there are three other minor differences in the first four lines: *Israhela, onlyht, heofona* for Nowell's *Israheala, anlyht* (?), *heofna*, and in every case Wanley's is the spelling one would expect. The transcript has several examples of *i* for *e* which are unlikely in a pre-Conquest MS.: 80 *getinge* (?), 202 *ni*, 205 *rædi*, 214 *forþegide*; *a* is sometimes confused with *e* and *æ*: e.g. 99 *gedemda*, 143 *dyda*, 79 *dag*, 155 *bað*, 174 *ærfeste*; and Nowell's corrections show a tendency to confuse *i* and *y*. In such details the transcript seems to show a mixture of mechanically accurate and careless copying, which makes close consideration of its abnormal forms and spellings unprofitable.

[2] In 79 ff.: On þissum fæstenum   is se feorþa dæg
and sixta samod   seofoþa getinge
to gelæstanne   lifes ealdre,

the editor rightly emends *feoroþa* of the transcript to *seofoþa*. But the suggestion that *getinge* = *getynge* 'eloquent' requires too bold a figure, even if the construction could be paralleled.

proportion of single words omitted,[1] as shown by the metre, is unusually high; but as none of them is essential for the sense, they may be due to an Anglo-Saxon who could follow the sense of alliterative verse better than Nowell could.

The other—that meaning comes first and last in textual criticism—is a commonplace worth repeating. Alliterative verse is not a good medium for precise expression, and Anglo-Saxon vernacular poets did not write their verses, as Virgil did, for an audience trained in literary criticism. Though the effects of Latin education appear in varying degrees, they followed in the main a style suited to improvisation and to the relaxed attention of hall or refectory. Some tolerance is therefore necessary of vagueness or emptiness of meaning, and of set phrases that do not quite hit the mark. Still, in a difficult passage, so many technical conditions of grammar, metre, and textual history have to be considered that, if they are satisfied, one tends to be content with a meaning less apt than the style and context require. The author of *Fasting* was not a good poet, but he was an intelligent and educated man, able to think in an orderly way, and writing for a practical purpose about a subject in which he was interested and well-informed. Any interpretation which makes him say strange or irrelevant things for no apparent purpose is improbable for that reason alone.

[1] In 23 *deadne* is the most likely of the supplements suggested by Professor Dobbie; at 44 read ⟨*her*⟩ *mid Anglum*; at 70 some colourless word like *symle* 'always' is necessary for the alliteration; at 173 supply *werod*.

4

THE BEOWULF MANUSCRIPT[1]

[1916]

A FEW years ago, when turning over the Beowulf MS., I was surprised to observe that certain facts had escaped notice or attention. And they are worth while setting out, if only as an indication of the dangers that beset a historical study in which insufficient attention is paid to manuscript indications, often the clearest indications of time and place.

The manuscript volume Vitellius A xv consists of two separate codices, fortuitously brought together by the binder in the sixteenth or seventeenth century.

The first, ff. 4*a*–93*b* in the present numbering, comes, like the Bede MS. Otho B xi, from the priory of St. Mary's, Southwick, Hants, as appears from the entry on f. 5*b*: 'Hic liber est ecclesie beate marie de Suwika', &c.[2] It is written in two main hands: the first extending to the end of *Augustine's Soliloquies* (f. 59*b*), the second from the beginning of the *Gospel of Nicodemus* to the end of the codex, which is imperfect. Both hands may be assigned roughly to the middle of the twelfth century.[3]

The second codex, ff. 94–209 in the present numbering,[4] is imperfect at beginning and end. It also is written in two hands: the first, extending from f. 94*a* to f. 175*b*, is the first hand of *Beowulf*; the second, extending thence to the end of the codex, is the second hand of *Beowulf*. Taken together they are usually dated *circa* 1000, and with good reason.

From this certain results follow. First, we can no longer say,

[1] From *Modern Language Review* xi (1916), p. 335 ff.

[2] Cockayne's suggested emendation to *Euerwika* (*Shrine*, p. 294), followed by W. H. Hulme *Die Sprache der ae. Bearbeitung der Soliloquien Augustins*, p. 1, is unjustifiable.

[3] Hargrove in his edition of *Augustine's Soliloquies*, with a fine disregard of the facsimile he reproduces, states that his text is in the same hand as *Beowulf*.

[4] [On the variant foliations of the MS., see S. Rypins *Three Old English Prose Texts in MS. Cotton Vitellius A xv*, E.E.T.S. (1924), p. ix ff.]

with the most recent editor of *Beowulf*, 'as to the history of the [Beowulf] manuscript we have no information, till we find it in the collection formed by Sir Robert Cotton'.[1] In the natural place, at the top of the first page of the codex (f. 94*a*), is written the name 'Laurence Nowell' with date 1563; and the credit of preserving *Beowulf* must be given—in part at least—to that indefatigable pioneer in Anglo-Saxon studies.[2] Unfortunately the inscription does not help much more. As far as I know, very few ancient manuscripts, and none of certain provenance, can be traced to Nowell, and so we cannot tell what libraries he drew upon.[3] He was, of course, Dean of Lichfield at the time, and it may be that he obtained the manuscript there or in that neighbourhood. But, failing definite evidence, this must remain a rather remote possibility.[4]

Again, the intolerable confusion in the dating of the prose pieces which precede *Beowulf* in the second codex (ff. 94*a*–98*a* *Christo-*

[1] Chambers, [1914] Introd. p. ix.

[2] He probably did not realize the value of his find. Indeed, although Junius, who had copied *Augustine's Soliloquies* and *Judith* and collated the *Gospel of Nicodemus* from this volume, must have known of the existence of *Beowulf*, there is no evidence that it excited any attention till Wanley set to work upon the MS. in 1700.

[3] [Dr. Flower's researches in 'Laurence Nowell and the Discovery of England in Tudor Times' (1936), *Proc. British Academy* xxi, set a tantalizing problem. Only two MSS. containing Old English texts are known to come from the twelfth-century foundation of St. Mary, Southwick, near Reading. The one, Otho B XI, was transcribed by Nowell in 1562 when it was in the library of Sir William Cecil (Lord Burghley) and Nowell was living in his house as tutor to the young Earl of Oxford. The other, a twelfth-century MS. containing the version of *St. Augustine's Soliloquies* attributed to King Alfred, is bound up with the Beowulf MS. which Nowell acquired in 1563, while he was still living with Cecil in London. The collocation can hardly be due to chance, but there are too many possible explanations. One is that Nowell gave the Beowulf MS. to his patron Cecil when he abandoned his Anglo-Saxon studies in 1566–7, so that it came to Cotton from Cecil's collection together with the two Southwick MSS. But that brings us no nearer to discovering where Nowell got the Beowulf MS. His pluralities, ranging from Chichester to Lichfield and York, gave him many opportunities of acquiring MSS.]

[4] It might be supposed that, in delicate hands, the pictures from f. 98*b* onwards would yield some clue as to provenance. But their nature and style hardly encourage the hope.

phorus fragment, 98*b*–106*b* *Wonders of the East*, 107*a*–31*b* *Letter of Alexander*) comes to an end. The hand of these pieces, which is the first hand of *Beowulf*, is referred to various dates in the eleventh and even the twelfth century.[1] We thus have on the one side complete agreement that the date of the hand in *Beowulf* is '*circa* 1000', or 'late-tenth-century', and on the other the widest discrepancy in the dating of the identical script[2] when it appears in the prose tracts—a phenomenon, to say the least, disquieting.

Literary history must also be brought into line. The appearance of Oriental themes in English literature has been placed at the very end of the Old English period. Wülker thinks these tracts were not translated before the middle of the eleventh century.[3] Brandl speaks of their appearance as 'die fortschrittlichste Erscheinung in der ganzen spätangelsächsischen Prosa'.[4] Stopford Brooke refers to them as 'the last books, save the *Worcester Annals*, which were written in the literary language of Wessex'.[5] But here we have them in a hand which is undoubtedly to be dated *circa* 1000; in a manuscript which is certainly not an autograph, and which seems to represent originals carrying back well into the tenth century. It would appear, then, that the introduction of these Oriental themes belongs to the great period of Continental influence which began with the tenth century,[6] and not to the later period of Norman influence.

One point remains. In the critical examination of early English

[1] M. Förster in *Archiv* cxvii. 367 accepts the later date. [But independently of this article, Professor Förster later published a full and accurate account of the MS.: *Die Beowulf-Handschrift*, Leipzig, 1919.]

[2] Mr. S. I. Rypins, who at my suggestion has undertaken an edition of the prose pieces in the second codex, with a study of the problems they raise, points out to me that Professor Sedgefield in his *Beowulf*, p. xiv, footnote, remarks that 'the first scribe also wrote the MS. immediately preceding the Beowulf MS. in the codex', apparently without noticing the significance of the fact. There can be no real doubt of this identity. The script is very distinctive; and, to mention only one point of detail, the avoidance of the low or long form of *s* is remarkable in a hand which still preserves a good deal of Insular character.

[3] *Grundriss*, p. 505.

[4] Paul's *Grundriss* ii, p. 1132.

[5] *English Literature from the Beginning to the Norman Conquest*, p. 293.

[6] [The study below, p. 65 ff., carries the history farther back.]

texts, the task of distinguishing forms introduced by copyists is usually baffling, and we cannot afford to overlook any source of information. So far, only *Judith*, which is in the second hand,[1] has been used to throw light on the language of the scribes of *Beowulf*. But here, in the first hand, are prose texts of four times the bulk of *Judith*, free to some extent from the circumstances which make poetical texts so confusing in forms, and probably themselves due to more than one author. The detailed comparison of one with another, and of all with *Beowulf*, cannot fail to throw light on the characteristics of the first scribe, and on the explanation of the more obscure dialect forms in *Beowulf*. I need mention only one example. Genitive plurals in *-o*, which are very rare in careful West Saxon texts, occur in the part of *Beowulf* written by the first hand, e.g. l. 70 *yldo*, l. 475 *hynðo*. Surely it is no coincidence that Sievers (*Beitr*. ix. 230) and Klaeber (*Modern Language Notes*, xvi. 17) quote no less than five examples from the *Letter of Alexander* which precedes in the same hand.

[1] Dr. Chambers *Beowulf*, Introd. p. xix, seems uncertain of the identity, but it is not doubtful. The hand is well marked, and has one feature not easily paralleled at this time: the occasional *ȝ* with the bar so swung downwards on the left as to form a loop similar to that of the Continental *g*; see for instance *Beowulf*, l. 2141 *þagyt*, l. 2197 *gecynde* in Zupitza's facsimile. This occurs in *girwan* on the first page of *Judith*. Of course it must not be assumed that the scribe went straight on from *Beowulf* to the *Judith* fragment as we have it.

5

THE COMPILATION OF THE BEOWULF MANUSCRIPT

1. *Introductory*

IN a review of the facsimile edition of the Exeter Book[1] I remarked: 'the Beowulf codex, even allowing for *Judith*, is a collection in verse and prose of marvellous stories.' I hope now to give a reason why its contents were assembled in one book.

The codex (i.e. the second part of MS. Vitellius A xv, copied round about the year 1000) contains (i) *The Passion of St. Christopher*. The leaves containing the early part of this tract were already lost in 1563 when Laurence Nowell wrote his name on the first surviving leaf. (ii) *The Wonders of the East*, with pictures. (iii) *The Letter of Alexander to Aristotle*. (iv) *Beowulf*. The first scribe, who had copied the three previous pieces, ends in line 1939. (v) The end of *Judith*[2] copied by the second hand of *Beowulf*.

How could the *Passion of St. Christopher* be given the first place in a planned collection of this content? He was, of course, a giant, 'twelve fathoms high' the Anglo-Saxon text makes him, improving on the twelve cubits of the Latin original.[3] But the image of him which Chaucer's Yeoman carried on his breast, or Erasmus's

[1] *The Review of English Studies*, x (1934), p. 342; see p. 100 below. I have noticed belatedly that W. W. Lawrence had previously opened this subject in *Beowulf and Epic Tradition*, 1928, p. 14.

[2] *Judith* was in twelve numbered sections, and leaves presumably containing nearly 1,000 lines (sections I–VIII and most of IX) had been lost from the MS. when Junius (d. 1677) transcribed *Judith*. For calculations, see M. Förster *Die Beowulf-Handschrift*, 1919, p. 88; but the indications, especially the crowding and overrunning of the last page of *Beowulf*, are against his suggestion that the end of *Beowulf* itself was lost with these leaves. The last leaf of the codex was loose or torn, and was discarded, perhaps in the course of binding, before the Cotton fire of 1731. The last six verses of *Judith*, after the word *sigorlean*, were preserved by transcribing them at the foot of f. 209*b*, which now ends the codex.

[3] A later age made Christopher 17 foot 8 inches, 5½ inches taller than Colbrand the Giant; see *Reliquiae Antiquae* i (1841), p. 200.

Soldier[1] drew on his tent to keep off danger, was far different from the bizarre conception of the Dark Ages. According to the *Old English Martyrology*[2] 'he had a dog's head, and his locks were extraordinarily long, and his eyes gleamed as bright as the morning star, and his teeth were as sharp as a boar's tusks'. In our fragment[3] King Dagnus calls him *þu wyrresta wilddeor* 'savagest of wild beasts'. The incipit of the same text which Wanley preserves from the burnt eleventh-century MS. Otho B x says: *se wæs healfhundisces mancynnes*.[4] According to a rhythmic *Passio Christofori* which Strecker assigns to Carolingian times:

Hic de Cynocephalorum oriundus genere,
Gente, vultu et loquela ceteris dissimilis,
Vultu pristino retento, loquelam mutaverat.[5]

Christopher, then, was one of the race of dog-headed cannibals, and perhaps for that reason the Cynocephali were, for the early Middle Ages,[6] the most interesting of the Oriental monsters described in *Wonders of the East* and *Alexander's Letter*.[7] It cannot be an accident that the three Anglo-Saxon pieces which certainly mention the *Healfhundingas*[8] are all together in one manuscript; and once it is established that the codex has been planned with some regard to subject-matter, *Beowulf*, the one Old English poem

[1] *Colloquia*, ed. Stallbaum, 1828, p. 20. Erasmus also mentions the superstitious belief in images of 'Polyphemus Christopher' in *The Praise of Folly*, where 'Polyphemus' perhaps means 'giant cannibal'; cp. the further reference in *Colloquia* under *Naufragium*. The superstition has a modern development among motorists.

[2] Ed. G. Herzfeld, E.E.T.S. (1900), p. 66 and note.

[3] Ed. S. Rypins *Three Old English Prose Texts in MS. Cotton Vitellius A XV*, E.E.T.S. (1924), p. 70/5. References to these tracts are given by page and line of Rypins's edition.

[4] See M. Förster, op. cit. p. 77.

[5] *Mon. Germ. Hist. Poetae Aevi Carol.* iv, p. 809.

[6] See the letter of Ratramn of Corbie (*fl.* 850) to Rimbert, *Mon. Germ. Hist. Epist. Karol. Aevi* iv, p. 155, where such curious questions are discussed as whether the Cynocephali were descended from Adam and had souls.

[7] See Rypins's edition, pp. 54 and 33, for the *Healfhundingas*.

[8] Professor Kemp Malone adopts the reading *Healfhundingas* in the difficult line *Widsith* 23; see his edition (1936) p. 69 n. It could be easier defended as a compound of *Hundingas* (*Widsith* 81), like *Dene*: *Healfdene*, than as meaning 'Cynocephali'.

that deals with imagined monsters, may reasonably be associated with the same design. In a brilliant study,[1] Professor Tolkien has defended the monsters as subjects for poetry; and it seems that the preservation of *Beowulf* itself is due to somebody who took a special interest in them.

I shall not attempt to bring *Judith* into the same design. Holofernes was no monster. Nor is it necessary for the argument. Somebody decided that it should be joined to the collection, whether because there was no more convenient place for it, or because Judith was felt to be, like Beowulf, a saviour of her country, at a time when England needed such inspiration in the struggle with the Danish invaders.[2] In any case, it is possible that *Judith* is an accretion to an earlier collection, and one clue leads in that direction. Since Ten Brink presented the evidence from *Beowulf* and *Judith*, it has been generally accepted that *Beowulf* is copied from a manuscript in which *io* often occurred for Late West Saxon *eo* of all origins. *Beowulf*, first hand, has 11 examples of *io* in 87 manuscript pages; *Beowulf*, second hand, 115 in 53 pages; *Judith*, in the second hand, no example in 15 pages. Ten Brink inferred that the second scribe preserved *io* in his copy, while the first usually eliminated it.[3] He did not know that the three prose pieces are in the first hand of *Beowulf*,[4] and that *Wonders* contains a couple of examples of *io*, *Alexander's Letter* has many, *Christopher*

[1] 'Beowulf: the Monsters and the Critics', *Proc. British Academy XXII* (1936).

[2] This was the view of Ælfric about the time when the Beowulf MS. was copied. Referring to his own rhythmic translation of the Book of Judith, he says: 'Iudith . . . hæfð hire agene boc . . . seo ys eac on Englisc on ure wisan gesett eow mannum to bysne þæt ge eowerne eard mid wæpnum bewerian wið onwinnendne here' (Preface to the Old Testament). But his version, as we have it, is addressed to a nun, perhaps an abbess, and Judith is made a pattern of virginity. This is a reminder that one text could be used to teach very different lessons; and it is rash to assume that the poem *Judith* was composed to encourage resistance to the Danes.

[3] Rypins, in the Introduction to his edition of the prose tracts, and in various articles, has produced evidence that the first scribe copied mechanically. Though some of his arguments are inconsequent, this is a valid objection. For a more detailed discussion, see below, p. 92 f.

[4] See above, p. 62 f.

none. This suggests that both *Christopher* and *Judith* were added to a collection characterized by *io* spellings. Too much weight should not be attached to such slight evidence, but it fits another circumstance: additions to an existing collection are easiest made at the beginning and end; and prose and verse would be kept apart if *Christopher* were added at the beginning and *Judith* at the end.

To go deeper into the compilation of the collection requires a close examination of the separate pieces. Unfortunately the three prose pieces have been neglected owing to an old mistake. All through the most active period of Old English studies, *Wonders* and the *Letter* were thought to represent the last stage of Anglo-Saxon literature before the Conquest—twilight fantasies composed as foreign influence and romance crowded in.[1] I propose to examine them with an eye for any evidence bearing on the formation and date of the collection. And two preliminary remarks may help to clear the way. First, it is sometimes necessary to distinguish MS. Vitellius A xv from the collection it preserves: the manuscript may be a copy of an earlier one containing all or some of the pieces. But it would be tedious to labour this distinction when nothing of importance results from it. Secondly, whether or not all five pieces were first assembled in the Vitellius MS., the state of the texts shows that none of them was composed for that codex. They are all copies, and have a previous manuscript history.

II. *The Passion of St. Christopher*

The *Christopher* fragment is in good average Late West Saxon. If it is judged by the standard of Ælfric, a grammarian who took an exceptional interest in vernacular usage, there are irregularities. It has some uncontracted forms in the present indicative, e.g. 70/5 *dyrstlæcest*, 73/3 *nealæceð*. *Sigor* 'victory', occurring once, is usually reckoned poetical and Anglian, but Ælfric has it, and at this date well-known poetical words may be expected in elevated

[1] See e.g. A. Brandl *Geschichte der altenglischen Literatur*, 1908, p. 1132. Authority is so strong in Old English studies that in the latest general textbook I have consulted, G. K. Anderson's *Literature of the Anglo-Saxons*, 1949, p. 379, the *Letter of Alexander* and *Wonders of the East* are still treated as compositions of the mid-eleventh century.

prose. Whether there is any significance in regular *mitty þe* (*mid þy þe*), a translator's phrase for *cum* or *dum*, common in Anglian prose, I cannot say. But these forms might be substituted for *sige*, *mid þæm þe*, &c., in the course of copying.

Two details that may be called scribal are significant. *Christopher* has always (7 times) the spelling *mytty* (*þe*), *mitty*, where *Alexander's Letter*, the only other text in the codex which uses this phrase, has always *mid þy*.[1] *Christopher* has always the spelling *cyningc* (13 times) which occurs nowhere else in the codex. These indicate that *Christopher* came from a distinct manuscript, and that the collection has not been copied often since it was incorporated.

One would not expect the *Passion of St. Christopher* printed in the *Acta Sanctorum* to be the exact text used by the translator, and it certainly differs in some readings. But it is essentially the same story and the same document. Though the Latin is simple, there are a few obvious misunderstandings, e.g. 71/11 where the soldiers are ordered to shoot *ternas sagittas*, and the Old English makes three soldiers shoot arrows. Some scribal errors, also, remain in the text:

68/5 MS. 'he het settan on his heafde þry weras', where *fyrenne helm* = *igneam cassidem* has dropped out after *heafde*, and 'three men' represents the subject of the next sentence.

69/10 'þas tintrego . . . to þinre gecyndnesse and to þinre forwyrde becumað'. To take *þinre gecyndnesse* as genitive, 'of thy race', is awkward syntactically, and the sense is unsuitable; for a saint would not threaten such vicarious punishment. Read *gescyndnesse* 'to thy confusion', with the fair certainty that (*in tua*) *confusione* was in the Latin text used.

70/13 'þæt ic þone god gebidde and minum wiðsace': read *þinne* for *þone*.

71/15 ff. 'ac ne furþon an [sc. stræl] his lichaman ne gehran, ac godes mægen wæs on ðam winde hangigende' renders something like 'sagittae autem divina virtute suspendebantur a vento'. Read: *ac ðurh godes mægen.*

75/4 ' "On naman Cristoforus godes ic þis dem." ' With these words Dagnus applies a plaster made of the martyr's blood to his

[1] Noted by Rypins, op. cit. p. xvi.

blind eyes; and *dem* is best taken here as a miscopying of *dó* 'apply', which is often written with an accent. *Dom* (1 pres. sg.) is possible if the original was Mercian.

These are evidence that the Vitellius copy is not very near to the original translation.

The free handling of the Latin at the end is interesting, whether it is the work of the translator or to some extent due to modifications in the particular Latin text which lay before him. In the original, Christopher prays in a manner familiar in the acts of martyrs: 'in quo loco posuerint corpus meum, non ibi ingrediatur grando, non ira flammae, non fames, non mortalitas; et in civitate illa, et in illis locis, si fuerint ibi malefici, aut daemoniaci, et veniunt et orant ex toto corde, et propter nomen tuum nominant nomen meum in suis orationibus, salvi fiant.' And God grants his petition in the widest terms: 'ubi est corpus tuum et ubi non est.' In the Anglo-Saxon version Christopher asks grace for those who name him in prayer 'where any part of my body lies', referring clearly to relic cults. It makes no mention of hail, and the special benefits for those who have dealt with or been possessed by the Devil: their inclusion in the original suggests that it was composed in a hotter, vine-growing country like Italy. The translation makes Christopher's name a protection against the common evils that touch everybody—poverty, fire (in an age of thatch), all kinds of sickness. And, with a subtle expansion, it follows the Latin in a bold final claim: that Christopher with his last breath prayed for 'a good meed for anybody who wrote his Passion, and eternal rewards for those who read it with tears in their eyes'.[1] Evidently this tract was written to secure the widest popularity for the cult of St. Christopher.

In the later Middle Ages he certainly enjoyed this popularity. But before the tenth century he was well enough known in western Europe. Alcuin names him in a set of verses for the nave of a church.[2] His description from the *Old English Martyrology*, which goes back to the second half of the ninth century, has already been

[1] The Latin in *Acta Sanctorum* is: 'Domine Jesu Christe, praesta bonam mercedem scribentibus et legentibus passionem meam.'

[2] *Mon. Germ. Hist. Poetae Aevi Carol.* i, p. 342.

quoted. But there he is entered at 28 April, whereas the usual day, which is given in the *Acta Sanctorum* text of his 'Passion', is 25 July. And there is no evidence that his cult was exceptionally popular in England till the late tenth and early eleventh centuries. In pre-Conquest calendars the commemoration at 28 April survives only in the very old-fashioned MS. Nero A II, written early in the eleventh century at Nunnaminster, Winchester.[1]

Christopher does not appear in MS. Digby 63, a Northern calendar that reached Southern England about Alfred's time; or in the metrical calendar of martyrs in Athelstan's Psalter, thought to have been composed soon after the year 900;[2] or in the late-tenth-century calendar of Glastonbury in the Leofric Missal;[3] or in Ælfric's *Lives of Saints*, possibly because his life was already available in English. The earliest English notice for 25 July seems to be in the calendar of Salisbury MS. 150 written *circa* 975 for Shaftesbury, a nunnery favoured by ladies of birth.[4] It is regular in the Winchester calendars of the eleventh century; and the calendar of the Bosworth Psalter, prepared early in the same century, shows that the feast had been adopted at Canterbury Cathedral.[5] Other evidence is provided by lists of relics. There were at least two relics of St. Christopher at Newminster, Winchester, and a piece of his skull at Exeter.[6] Finally, in a fire-damaged part of the Nunnaminster prayer-book Galba A XIV, already mentioned, a short prayer to St. Christopher appears among others associated with the favourite devotional cults of the time.[7]

It is a fair inference from this evidence that, perhaps as a

[1] Script and format associate it with the Nunnaminster prayer-book Galba A XIV, and it has a close relation with the litany of the Galba MS. Mr. Neil Ker regards it as probably a piece detached from Galba A XIV (*Medieval Libraries of Great Britain*, 1941, p. 113 n.). For the character and localization of English calendars I follow Edmund Bishop in *The Bosworth Psalter*, 1908.

[2] Bishop, op. cit. p. 51 n.; and *Liturgica Historica*, 1918, p. 141.

[3] Ed. Warren, 1883.

[4] I owe this attribution to the late Edmund Bishop, who did not know when he made it that the later prayer at the end of the MS. shows feminine pronouns.

[5] *Bosworth Psalter*, p. 35.

[6] See M. Förster *Zur Geschichte des Reliquienkultus in Altengland*, Munich 1943, pp. 74, 85, 116, 119.

[7] Bishop *Liturgica Historica*, p. 390.

consequence of relics brought in by King Athelstan, the greatest English collector in this kind, St. Christopher's cult spread rapidly among the devout, especially in select nunneries like Shaftesbury and the Nuns' Minster at Winchester. By the close of the tenth century[1] it had become so popular that it was generally recognized in official calendars. And our tract must have played a considerable part in the success of the movement, of which there are many signs about the time when the Beowulf codex was written. The history of another cult very popular in the late tenth century—that of St. Margaret—is almost identical; and it, too, was propagated by a tract in Latin and English, which promised even more extravagant benefits to devotees.[2]

The Anglo-Saxon version was probably made about or soon after the middle of the tenth century. This date, and the linguistic and orthographical features already noted, exclude the possibility that the whole collection of the Beowulf codex is old as a collection; but they are consistent with the hypothesis that *Christopher* is a late accretion to an older nucleus.

III. *The Wonders of the East*

The Anglo-Saxon version of *The Wonders of the East* is found also in the nearly contemporary MS. Tiberius B v, where each section is preceded by the Latin text, and there are fine illustrations.[3]

[1] In Germany, in the year 983, Walter of Speier produced his verse and prose lives of St. Christopher, to replace one by the nun Hazecha which his bishop had lost *librarii neglegentia*. See Manitius *Geschichte der lateinischen Literatur des Mittelalters* ii (1923), p. 502 ff.

[2] B. Assmann *Angelsächsische Homilien und Heiligenleben*, Kassel 1889, prints the Anglo-Saxon from MS. CCCC 303, and a Latin text from MS. Harley 5327. The Anglo-Saxon text printed by Cockayne, *Narratiunculae*, from MS. Tiberius A III is very different from Assmann's; and the text in the burnt MS. Otho B x differed again, to judge by its incipit and explicit in Wanley's Catalogue.

[3] The Latin text from this MS. is printed in Cockayne's *Narratiunculae*, and by Rypins, op. cit. p. 101 ff. Rypins does not give a collation of its Anglo-Saxon text, which is conveniently printed, together with its Latin, and the Anglo-Saxon text from the Beowulf codex, by F. Knappe *Die Wunder des Ostens*, Berlin 1906. I have used the facsimiles in M. R. James *Marvels of the East*, Roxburghe Club, Oxford 1929.

The text in the Beowulf codex is in fairly good Late West Saxon, with occasional irregularities: uncontracted forms of the 3rd sing. present indicative prevail; there are a few examples of *in* for normal LWS *on*; and the unusual *saragimm* for *searogimm* occurs twice. There are several unique or rare words, but perhaps only 55/14 *gesælan* 'tie up' (where the Tiberius version has *getigan*) and 63/15 *nænig*[1] are more likely to occur in Anglian than in West Saxon prose.

Of scribal forms,[2] note consistent *hy*, *hi* (some 60 instances), whereas *hie* predominates in *Alexander's Letter* and *Beowulf* (first hand), and occurs in about half the examples in *Beowulf* (second hand), *Judith*, and *Christopher*. Beside usual *syndon*, there are three instances of *seondon*, which occurs nowhere else in the codex; and beside usual *swa* there are two examples of the Early West Saxon and dialectal *swæ*,[3] which occurs nowhere else in the codex. But these last appear in the phrase *swæ fon* '(broad) as a winnowing fan', and in both places (57/19, 62/6) the scribe writes *swæfon* as if it were the past tense plural of *swefan* 'to sleep'. Evidently he, and perhaps more than one predecessor, did not follow the meaning. If, as is likely, he copied mechanically, an older or dialectal form *swæ* has been preserved here inadvertently, together with an indication that, in some earlier manuscript, *ŏ* before nasals was more frequent.[4] We must then reckon with the probability that the prevailingly Late West Saxon forms of the Vitellius copy (which I shall call VE to distinguish it from TE, the Tiberius English version) are due to modernization of an older text which had at least a dialectal colouring.

[1] K. Jost *Wulfstanstudien*, Berne 1950, p. 159 ff., has shown that *nænig* is abnormal in the standard West Saxon of Alfred and Ælfric.

[2] In making systematic use of such forms to analyse a composite manuscript written by one hand, I follow a technique suggested to me by my daughter, Celia Sisam: see 'The Scribal Tradition of the Lambeth Homilies', *The Review of English Studies*, N.S. ii (1951), p. 105 ff. Where numbers of examples are given, they are approximate, and intended to indicate the order of frequency.

[3] On the distribution of *swæ*, see Bülbring *Elementarbuch*, § 103 n.

[4] In *Wonders* there are some examples of *ŏ* before nasals in stressed syllables, but *a* predominates. For the distribution of these forms in the other texts see below, p. 91.

The peculiarities that have been noted are enough to show that *Wonders* has a textual history different from that of any other piece in the Beowulf codex; and it alone has illustrations.

THE LATIN TEXT

Materials for the history of the Latin text, which I shall call *Mirabilia* (*Mir.*), are assembled by M. R. James in *Marvels of the East*; but apart from supplying excellent facsimiles, he does not deal with the Anglo-Saxon versions VE and TE.

For the Latin *Mirabilia*, James discovered a second manuscript, Bodley 614 (= B), written in England early in the twelfth century. It is closely related to Tiberius B v (= T), and contains the same series of illustrations.

The primary Latin source is the pretended *Letter of Fermes* (= F) to the Emperor Hadrian, first printed by H. Omont from a ninth-century manuscript,[1] but probably translated into Latin some centuries earlier from a Greek original. To give verisimilitude, imaginary journeys are reckoned precisely in stadia. *Mirabilia* is essentially a selection from F, with a few additional wonders, and some embroideries: thus the distances in stadia are supplemented by equivalents in *leuuae* 'leagues', Gallic *leuga*, which in their uncorrupted form were no doubt derived by simple arithmetic.

Two other texts are related to *Mirabilia*.

One is the pretended *Epistola Premonis* (= P) to the Emperor

[1] *Bibliothèque de l'École des Chartes*, 1913, from the Beauvais MS. now Paris Bibl. Nat. nouv. acq. lat. 1065. This MS. shows some corruptions. Thus a place-name is missing where the late MSS. of *Mir.* § 3 and the English version have *Lentibelsinea* (P *Lentibel*). Omission of a name may also account for the puzzling reading: 'Hic Aegypti partem vicinam vocant quod dicitur maram aquam', where the late MSS. of *Mir.* § 11 have 'quam Aegipti Archoboleta vocant quae est aqua magna', and are supported by the English version.

James prints a late adaptation of F from Gervase of Tilbury. In *Mir.* § 3 he prefers its reading *prandere* to *prendere* of the older Paris MS., quoting a Greek source which says that these birds burn up anybody who eats them. The late MSS. of *Mir.* and the English version support *prendere*. If *prandere* is right, the agreement of *Mir.* with the short letter of Alexander found in the tenth-century Bamberg MS. (ed. F. Pfister *Kleine Texte zum Alexanderroman*, Heidelberg 1910, p. 40) is noteworthy.

Trajan. It was first adduced by E. Faral[1] from the 1829 print of a Strassburg manuscript which was burnt in 1870. This lost manuscript was said to be of the eighth or ninth century, but the dating can hardly be relied on. On the evidence so far available, I take P to be derived from an early state of the text of *Mirabilia*, though a more complex relation is possible.[2]

The second is the *Liber Monstrorum*,[3] known to students of *Beowulf* for its reference to Hygelac, king of the Geats, who was a 'monster' in stature. It contains a number of sections derived from *Mirabilia*, including *Mir.* § 15 on the 'lertices', which F and P omit. Its composition has been tentatively assigned to the eighth century; and A. Thomas,[4] after examining the earliest (Leyden) manuscript, reported to be of the ninth or tenth century, claims that it was compiled in England, partly because of the reference to 'Hyglac' near the beginning, partly because of Insular abbreviations which are found in or misinterpreted in the extant manuscripts.

Precise evidence bearing on the date and provenance of the *Mirabilia* is hard to find. Neither the print of P nor the late manuscripts T and B contain significant abbreviations or spellings. But there is a detail, small in itself, which gains in importance because it fits in with the vaguer indications: near the beginning, the

[1] *Romania* xliii (1914), p. 199 ff. and 353 ff.

[2] For a discussion see James, p. 34 f. He inclines to the other opinion, but perhaps does not allow enough for the demonstrable instability of the text of *Mir.* Briefly: P preserves the epistolary frame, whereas *Mir.* noticeably lacks a beginning and end. P contains nothing of substance from F that is not in the late MSS. (T, B) of *Mir.* or in the English. But P omits matter in *Mir.* that is derived from F, e.g. all the measurements of distance. P ends exactly where *Mir.* ceases to follow F. It has matter corresponding to *Mir.* §§ 14, 18, 19*a*, 21, 23, 29, which are not in F. But it agrees with F in omitting *Mir.* § 15 on the 'lertices', and this must be explained either by coincidence or by later insertion in *Mir.*, if P is directly derived from *Mir.* We have too little evidence for the history of the texts F and P, and for the changes that *Mir.* has undergone in the course of transmission.

[3] Printed by J. Berger de Xivrey *Traditions tératologiques*, Paris 1836; and from a better (Wolfenbüttel) MS., also of the tenth century, by M. Haupt *Opuscula* (1876) ii, p. 221 ff. See also James, *Marvels of the East*, and Manitius *Geschichte der lat. Literatur des Mittelalters* i (1911), p. 114 ff.

[4] *Archivum Latinitatis medii aevi*: Bulletin Du Cange, Paris (1925), p. 232 ff.

Tiberius and Bodley manuscripts read (§ 2): 'usque ad Medorum civitatem cui nomen est Archemedon, quae maxima est ad Babiloniam'. To *ad Babiloniam* both have the interlinear gloss *i. excepto Babilonia*, and the English version reads: *sio is mæst to Babilonia burh.* I have not met with this idiom elsewhere in Latin, and others better equipped have failed to find it. But it occurs in Old English, notably in *Genesis B* 254: *hehstne to him on heofena rice* 'highest next to Himself in heaven'. From the examples given in Bosworth–Toller s.v. *to* I 5e, it appears to be a use of *to*[1] which had a special development with the superlative. To these examples, which include two from Alfred's Orosius and three from Ælfric, may be added a second passage from the *Old English Martyrology*[2] to confirm that the usage is Mercian as well as West Saxon. Wherever a Latin original is available, as for Orosius, the construction is not in the Latin.[3] Unless this idiom can be produced from Late Latin texts free from English influence, the inference is that *Mirabilia* was compiled by an Anglo-Saxon whose simple Latin was influenced by his native idiom.

This agrees with the fact that the only extant Latin manuscripts T and B are English, and the only known vernacular rendering is the Anglo-Saxon. It would account for some corruptions which are best explained from Insular letter-forms,[4] though such confusions

[1] e.g. Ælfric's *Homilies*, ed. Thorpe ii. 522: *he* (Paul) *is geendebyrd to Petre* 'is ranked next to Peter'. In a review of B. J. Timmer's edition of *Genesis B* (*Medium Ævum* xviii (1949), p. 73 f.), Professor Girvan notes on l. 254 that the idiom is Old English, but I have not found examples, other than the two cited by Bosworth–Toller, which support his remark that similar phrases are common in the O.E. version of Orosius. Miss Whitelock drew my attention to a clause in the Chronicle *anno* 876 (which is accidentally omitted in the Parker MS.): B, C, D, E have 'ond him þa gislas sealdon þe on þam here weorþuste wæron to þam cyninge'.

[2] Ed. Herzfeld 128/13: 'he (James) wæs Criste se leofesta þegn to sancte Petre ond Iohanne his breðer.'

[3] Note too the *Letter of Alexander*, near the beginning: 'to minre meder ond geswystrum þu me eart se leofesta freond' = 'secundum matrem meam sororesque meas acceptissime.'

[4] e.g. *Mir.* § 11 *Archoboleta*, where *Liber Monstrorum* has *Anchoboleta* with the confusion of *n* and *r* which is easy in early Insular hands. So in *Mir.* § 10, near the beginning, T and B have the river-name *Gorgoneus* (VE, TE *Wælcyrging*) for F *Gargerus* or *Gargarus*. But a little below T has

might be due to Insular transmission of a Continental text. It also suits the English origin that has been claimed for the *Liber Monstrorum* on other grounds.

There are difficulties in the way of dating the composition of *Liber Monstrorum* later than the first half of the ninth century, and it is unlikely to be older than the eighth, when English trading and missionary relations with the Frisians of the Rhine delta were at a maximum. *Mirabilia*, on which it draws, must have been compiled earlier still—perhaps in the eighth century.[1]

With the materials assembled by James, it is possible to get behind the comparatively late texts in which *Mirabilia* is preserved.

(i) The unrelated fragment of *Jamnes and Mambres*[2] which ends the tract in Tiberius B v (T) is an accretion; as are the further twelve sections of wonders that follow it in Bodley 614 (B).[3]

(ii) In the older part, i.e. §§ 1–37, the order of T and B is wrong: §§ 18–25 should follow §§ 26–33, as they do in P, which keeps the order of F. James suggests that a leaf in a common ancestor of T and B became displaced; but if this ancestor had pictures, wrong folding of a conjugate pair of leaves is likely.[4]

(iii) T and B are closely related in text, as in illustration, but are independently derived from a common ancestor.[5]

Gargulus (P *Gallalis*); and its exclusion from James's print of *Mir.* at this second occurrence is a reminder that his composite text is not strictly based on the evidence.

[1] See Note B at p. 288.

[2] See M. R. James *Journal of Theological Studies* (1905), p. 572. This apocryphal legend was known fairly early in England, for 'the magicians Geamer and Mambres' are mentioned in one of the O.E. expansions of Orosius, ed. Sweet, p. 38/31.

[3] They are from Isidore, except the legends in §§ 42 and 50: the first about two brothers doomed by their parents' curse to fight for ever, except on Sundays; the second containing analogues of the Dancers of Colbeck.

[4] *Liber Monstrorum* selects materials from *Mir.* and separates monsters from beasts. So its order is not decisive, though it seems to derive from a copy in which the original order was preserved.

[5] T is a century older than B; but, e.g. in § 10, B has correctly *accipiunt*, T *aput*; in § 15 B has correctly *auium*, T *ouum*. Despite the great authority of James, who relies on the uniform style of the additional pictures in B, I do not think the twelve added sections found in B were ever in Tiberius B v. Its full-page illustration to *Jamnes and Mambres* seems designed to

(iv) The illustrations and the two copies of the English version, VE and TE, throw some light on the history of the Latin text. The drawings in Bodley 614 may be left out of account, since it has the same series of designs as Tiberius B v. The designs in the Beowulf codex are usually quite different, and bad draughtsmanship gives many of them a ludicrous effect. Unless he found them in his original, a scribe so incompetent in drawing would hardly have ventured on illustrations. We shall find other evidence that they are copies, not originals; so the Vitellius drawings may, after all, represent a remote and debased development of the designs which are executed so brilliantly in the almost contemporary Tiberius manuscript. The following are significant:

(*a*) p. 60/5 f. In VE and TE the Homodubii have *longe sconcan swa fugelas*: T *longis pedibus ut aves*. But both sets of pictures show hooves and something like horses' legs.[1] P reads: *pedes habent ut equus*.

(*b*) p. 61/12 ff. In VE and TE the 'Donestre' are *swa frihteras* 'like soothsayers' from head to navel, and human for the rest. Both sets of pictures show a monster's head and shoulders, the rest human. F lacks the passage; P and T make the upper part of the body human, the rest monstrous. B agrees with the pictures and presumably its Latin reading lay before the designer. *Swa frihteras* of the Anglo-Saxon version represents neither of these variants; it is due to wrong division of the preceding clause, in which *quasi divini* (T *divine*) is given as the explanation of the mysterious name *Donestre*.[2]

(*c*) 67/5 ff. A kindly people present any visitor on his departure with a wife (or woman); VE, TE 'gifað hy him wif ær hy hine onweg læten': T 'cum mulieribus eos remittunt'. Both sets of

mark the end of the copy. It is questionable, too, whether all the matter, particularly the close parallel to the Dancers of Colbeck, was available in England at the beginning of the eleventh century.

[1] Cf. James, op. cit. pp. 28 and 56. His descriptions and notes record discrepancies between the pictures and the Latin text of *Mir.*

[2] *Mir.*: 'genus . . . quod apud nos appellatur *Donestre,* quasi divini', seems to represent a scrap detached and corrupted from F § 32: '(Soraci) qui apud vos *Tritonides* appellantur, quasi divini.'

pictures show a woman being taken away. The true reading is *cum muneribus*[1] (F *remuneratos*), but the corruption is already in P.

(*d*) 62/16 f. At sight of strangers, a people with big ears take up their ears in their hands (VE, TE 'nymað hy hyra earan him on hand'), and run so swiftly that one would think they were flying. T, B read *tollunt sibi aures*. The readings of F, P, and *Liber Monstrorum* show that these people spread out their ears so that they looked like wings. The Vitellius illustration represents this, but in the Tiberius and Bodley manuscripts, long snakelike ears are looped round the supporting hands and arms, in agreement with the mistranslation in the English.

(*e*) 60/15 ff. VE and TE describe two lakes or pools (*seaþas*) of the Sun and Moon, agreeing with the pictures: the wheel-like objects in the Beowulf codex perhaps represent well-heads. T reads *loci*, B *loca*, F *latera*; and only P has *laci* (for *lacus*?).

(*f*) 65/9 ff. Monstrous women have boar's tusks (VE, TE *eoferes tuxas* = F, T, B *dentes aprorum*) . . . camel's feet, and ass's teeth (VE *eoseles teð*). TE has *eofores teð*, answering to T *aprinos*, where *dentes* has fallen out. P has *dentes asinorum* here, agreeing with VE, but it has not *dentes aprorum* above.[2]

(*g*) 57/10 ff. tell of a people who, when they wish to have children, go in ships to India (VE *farað hy on scipum*: TE omits *on scipum*). T, B read *suis manibus transferuntur*; P *immorantur in navibus*, agreeing with VE. The explanation of all these corruptions is supplied by F: 'hii homines in avibus . . . transfigurantur, et apud vos fetus faciunt, quos ciconias appellatis.' As James notes, it is the legend of the stork, and *Ciconia* (VE), corrupted to *Liconia* in T, B, and TE, appears as the scene of the next wonder.

From (*a*), (*b*), (*e*) above it appears that the pictures were designed for a Latin text differing in certain details from T. Both series of pictures agree in these three places. From (*e*), (*f*), (*g*) it appears

[1] James, p. 29.

[2] The corruption in this section goes farther, for all our texts except F describe these hideous women as having beautiful bodies, white as marble. F has 'reliquum corpus pilosum ut structio et camelus', where the last three words mask *struthiocamelus* 'ostrich'. Somehow *pilosum ut structio* has been converted into *speciosus ut marmor*, and *camelus* has been used to describe the feet.

that the text from which VE was translated differed in some of its readings from T. In these three places it agreed with P.

THE TRANSLATION

A translator who at 58/2 faithfully renders T, B: *hi putantur homines fuisse* by *þas beoð men gewende*, without knowing that it represents the earlier *hippopotami appellantur* found in P, may be excused for adding some nonsense of his own. The most notable example is:

(*h*) VE 63/8 ff.: 'þær wæs getymbro⟨d⟩ on Beles dagum and Iobes temple of isernum geworcum and of glæsgegotum; and on þære ilcan stowe is æt sunnan upgange setl Quietus þæs stillestan bisceopes, se nænine oþerne mete ne þig⟨d⟩e buton sæ-ostrum. . . .' This represents T: 'ubi est Belis templum in diebus regis et Iobis æreo et ferreo opere constructum, quod etiam Beliobeles dicitur; et inde est ędis solis ad orientem ubi est sacerdos quietus qui illa oppida maritima observat.' Here *Bel* and *Iob* come from a corruption of *Heliopolis*; *glæsgegotum* 'moulded glass' is due to misreading *uitreo* for *aereo*; and the 'sea-oysters', a semi-fasting diet, are from *oppida* (read as *ostria*) *maritima*.

In the passage just quoted (*h*), TE translates the Latin of T fairly closely; and other examples show the same kind of divergence between VE and TE. Thus:

(*i*) 64/20 VE: Huntresses rear *tigras and leon and loxas* = T 'pro canibus tigres et leopardos nutriunt'. VE makes two nouns of *leopardus*, but TE has correctly: 'fore hundum tigras and leopardos'.

(*k*) 52/19 ff.: Hunters of a dangerous monster *corpora sua inarmant*, i.e. protect themselves with armour. *Inarmant*, a rare word, caused difficulty. P glosses it wrongly *pugnant*. VE, echoing the preceding wonder,[1] treats it as if it were *inurunt*, and makes the monsters burn (*onælað*) pursuers who seize them. In TE the monsters rage against their pursuers: 'gewræðað hy sona grimlice ongen'.

[1] 52/11 f, where hens burn anybody who catches or touches them; see the note at p. 74 above.

What then is the relation between VE and TE? A number of passages help to clarify it:

(*l*) 54/1 VE MS. *geneornesse*: TE *geornfulnysse*. These render T, B *sua industria*, which originally applied to the men who procure pepper, not to the serpents who guard it. MS. *geneornesse* is best taken as for *gecneor*(*d*)*nesse*,[1] and the error was probably in the common source of VE and TE.

(*m*) 56/18 VE: 'seo Nil is ealdor fallicra (TE *fullicra*) ea' = 'Nilus est capud fluviorum'; where the common source had *eallicra* (of all).

(*n*) 57/14 VE: 'þær beoð men acende on ðrys heowes' (TE *þreosellices hiwes*) = 'homines tripertito colore'. Here VE has been troubled by the very rare *þreosel-lice* 'three-fold' preserved in TE, and seems to have hesitated over the alternative *on ðrym heowum*.

In several other places minor corrections of VE can be made from TE. Yet TE has its own errors: e.g. *eastliðende* for VE 66/12 *gæstliþende* = *hospitales*. It sometimes has the common Late West Saxon word where VE has an older or dialectal equivalent: e.g. 55/14 VE *gesælað*: TE *getigað* 'they tether'; or 53/7 VE *eoselas*: TE *assan*, though elsewhere TE has *eosel*—proving it for the original; or 64/3 VE *saragimmas*: TE *swylce meregrota oððe gymmas* = *margaritae*.

This evidence confirms that VE and TE are different states of one text, and shows that they are independently derived from it. Yet TE avoids, or tries to avoid, some of the perversions of VE, whether translator's errors like (*h*), (*i*), (*k*) above, or renderings of variants like (*g*) *on scipum*, which TE omits; or unexplained departures from the Latin like 65/6 *mid heora scin*⟨*lac*⟩*e*:[2] TE omits.

In considering these divergences, we must bear in mind that Latin text, pictures, and translation stand side by side in Tiberius B v, and that was presumably the arrangement of the ancestor which VE and TE represent. In this special case, some revision

[1] Cockayne *Narratiunculae*, p. 77, suggested *cneordnesse*; Knappe and Rypins emend to *geornnesse*, which is possible, but *gecneordnes* is a usual rendering of *industria*.

[2] 'With their magic' apparently renders *cum illis*. Confusion with *illusio* is possible, or it may be an added comment, in the manner of 52/13: 'þæt syndon ungefrægelicu liblac.'

of the translation by the Latin text is probable,[1] and it is the simplest explanation of the 'improved' readings of TE. Similarly, pictures and text may interact, so that the representation in Tiberius B v of men carrying their ears in their hands ((*d*) above) may have been suggested by the mistranslation in the Anglo-Saxon text.

SUMMARY

To sum up. Between the Latin *Letter of Fermes*, which is the main source, and the surviving manuscripts of *Mirabilia*—Tiberius B v of the early eleventh century and Bodley 614 of the early twelfth—there is evidence of the omissions, additions, variations, and extraordinary corruption which are to be expected in the transmission of a popular text through centuries in which Latin learning sometimes fell to a very low level. *Mirabilia* was probably compiled in England in the eighth century.

The pictures were designed for a Latin text differing in substantial readings from T and B. The variants they attest, with others represented in the English of the Beowulf codex (items (*f*) and (*g*) above), show that the *Epistola Premonis* is a valuable witness to an early state of the text. It is not possible to say when the pictures were added; but it was after *cum muneribus* had been corrupted into *cum mulieribus* ((*c*) above), and probably after the corruption of *in avibus* ((*g*) above), since the storks would have been tempting subjects for an illustrator who had the correct text before him.

There is a fair presumption, rather than clear proof, that the illustrations were associated with the Latin text before the English translation was added. This Old English version by an uncritical translator seems to have been added section by section to the illustrated Latin text. There is no certain evidence to show when it was made, but I should assign it to the period beginning with Alfred and ending with Athelstan, when the learning of Mercia,

[1] For this reason I have not relied on several instances where words carelessly omitted in VE are present in TE; or on the omission from VE of sections translated in TE, viz. §§ 5 and 34–37. Of these § 5 has little substance and is corrupt (see James, p. 26). The omission of the final §§ 34–37 may be due to a defective original, since the Beowulf codex is intact at this point.

which was old-fashioned and defective by the standards of the late tenth century, made a valuable contribution by supplying books to the South.

The two surviving manuscripts, both written not far from the year 1000, derive independently from a copy that was already corrupted: see (*l*) and (*m*) above. But apart from errors and omissions, VE is the better witness, because modernization of the language of TE has sometimes been extended to the vocabulary, and its text has been revised in some places by reference to the accompanying Latin. The linguistic forms of VE have also been modernized, so that they are prevailingly West Saxon; but in its details the language points to a transmission different from that of the other texts in the Beowulf codex.

IV. *Alexander's Letter to Aristotle*

The Latin source, from a Greek original, is found in many manuscripts, either independently or associated with the Epitome of Julius Valerius.[1] The earliest manuscripts are of the ninth century; but this Latin version is probably some centuries older. No thorough collation of the published manuscripts with the Old English version has been printed.[2] The more difficult task of establishing the family of manuscripts to which the original of the English version belonged has not, as far as I know, been attempted,[3] and it is unnecessary to my present purpose: for though this

[1] Ed. B. Kübler (Teubner) 1888.

[2] T. O. Cockayne *Narratiunculae*, 1861, p. 51 ff., prints the relevant parts from MS. Nero D VIII and uses also four Royal MSS. in the British Museum. Rypins in the E.E.T.S. edition prints MS. CCC Oxford 82, and gives a number of variants chosen, but not systematically, from other printed sources.

[3] It was probably known early in England. Alcuin sent the more edifying correspondence of Alexander and Dindimus to Charlemagne (*Mon. Germ. Hist. Poetae Aevi Carol.* i, p. 300; cf. L. Traube *Perrona Scottorum* (1900), reprinted in his *Kleine Schriften*, Munich 1920, p. 113). The *Epistola ad Aristotelem* does not seem to be used in *Wonders of the East*; but it is named in *Liber Monstrorum*, which also borrows one of its distinctive phrases, *rapida ferarum genera*. If the argument above, p. 75, is accepted, this is evidence that the *Letter* was known in England in the eighth or early ninth century.

version has been described as close or accurate,[1] it is in fact a free rendering, at times an adaptation, with patches of literalness.

The translator's task was not an easy one. In *Wonders*, though there are many strange names, the Latin itself is simple. The *Epistola* has more elaborate constructions and some pretensions to 'high style'. At 25/6 'ad Nothi venti spiracula tendi iussi' is rendered: 'Het . . . þa fyrd faran forð þy wege þe we ær ongunnen hæfdon', which at 12/3 translates 'inceptum iter agere institui'. At 35/17, to appease the anger of the gods, shown by a rain of fire, Alexander orders his men 'scissas vestes opponere ignibus'; and though *scissas vestes* is a Biblical phrase, and the context helps, the English runs: 'then I ordered my men to tear up old clothes, and hold them against the fire, and shield themselves therewith'.

Besides, any one manuscript has a full share of corruptions, though they are less extraordinary than in *Mirabilia*. When in difficulty, our translator often omits the phrase or passage that puzzles him. There is an obvious lack of continuity at p. 47/1, because a reading like *clibatura*, corrupted from *gleba turis*[2] 'lump of frankincense', led him to omit a sentence. The crocodile is omitted at 21/15, where there is a difficult description in the Latin; and again at 31/3, when a monster appears with two heads, one of a lioness, the other of a crocodile, he cuts out the crocodile's head altogether. It is true that in this last passage he has to make the best of a manuscript which read *lunae*, a recorded corruption, for *leaenae*.[3]

Still, after making all allowances for a difficult or corrupted original, and for corruption of the English itself,[4] there is evidence

[1] R. Wülker *Grundriss zur Geschichte der ags. Litteratur*, 1885, p. 505, calls it 'eine recht getreue Übersetzung'. Stopford Brooke goes farther when, referring also to *Wonders*, he says 'both are accurate translations, and done in excellent English' (*English Literature . . . to the Norman Conquest*, 1898, p. 293).

[2] Kübler's reading.

[3] 'Duo capita habens, alterum lunae simile . . . cocodrilli alterum simillimum' is rendered 'hæfde þæt deor seonowealt heafod swelce mona, ond þæt deor hatte *quasi caput luna*': 'the beast had a head quite round like the moon, and the beast is called 'quasi caput luna.'

[4] For example, 2/15: 'Hio is cennende þa fulcuþan ond wecga oran ond wunderlice wyhta' is probably the fault of a copyist who has dropped *wildeora ond wæstma* after *fulcuþan*. The Latin has: 'terra . . . parens

enough that the translator was shaky in Latin: At 20/20 serpents are described as having *pectora erecta*, which becomes: 'their breasts were turned upwards, and they moved along on their backs.' At 23/12 noxious creatures attacked the army from above (*e caelo pestes venere*). Although the context makes the meaning clear, he takes these to be pestilential vapours in the air, and is interested enough to repeat the rendering *wolberende lyft*, adding that many died *for heora þæm wolberendan stence*. At 34/18, the wind dropped before snow (*flatus Euri deciderat*), but he translates 'then the winds began to increase again, and the weather became stormy'.

Insufficiency in Latin may show itself at any time. In the twelfth century, at Canterbury Cathedral, and in the superbly executed Eadwine Psalter, 'similis factus sum pellicano in solitudine' (Ps. ci. 7) is glossed: 'gelic geworden ic eom felle hundes on licnesse': 'I am become like to the skin of a dog in likeness.' But such weakness in the translator of a difficult text like the *Epistola* becomes less likely as the tenth century advances.

A certain uncouthness in the translation also points to an early date; and it is strange that literary historians have grouped this awkward style with the light-running prose of *Apollonius of Tyre*. The Latin word-order is sometimes followed against English idiom (e.g. 14/20 ff.). The connective *þæt* is used where it is unnecessary to the construction (this occurs also in *Wonders*). There are clumsy combinations with the demonstrative, e.g. 11/9 ff. 'he sylfa þursti wæs *se min þegn . . . þone minne þegn . . . þæs mines þegnes*'. The style is distinguished from that of *Wonders* (VE) by tedious doubling of expressions, a practice common in early English translations, but here carried to excess: e.g. 3/5 'Nu ic hwæþre *gehyhte ond gelyfe* þæt þu þas þing ongete swa þu me ne talige owiht *gelþan ond secgan* be þære micelnisse ures *gewinnes ond compes*; forðon ic oft *wiscte ond wolde* . . . .'[1] Sometimes he drops a

publica ferarum et fructuum, metallorum atque animalium'. Several corrections are suggested by H. Bradley and K. Sisam *M.L.R.* xiv (1919), p. 202 ff.

[1] This trick of style makes it possible to emend with some confidence the closing passage: 'ond . . . ecelice min gemynd stonde ond [h]leonige (*h* burnt away) oðrum eorðcyningum to bysne.' *Hleonige*, which means 'bend down', 'lie down', cannot be coupled with *stonde*. Read *hleouige* from

string of words round about the meaning: At 30/18: 'palus erat sicca et canna abundans' is rendered 'the land was all dried up and fen and canes and reedy swamps'. At 27/20: 'cum essem gregarius ex Macedonico miles exercitu' he misunderstands *gregarius* 'common' as 'herd-keeper' and translates: 'forþon þe ic wære his þegnes mon ond his ceapes heorde ond wære his feohbigenga.' His difficulty in this place lay partly in *miles*, which he understood as a man of rank, a 'thane'. He had no equivalent for 'ordinary soldier',[1] and so at 21/11 he translates 'triginta servis et viginti militibus (amissis)' by: 'þrittig monna þære fyrde ond minra agenra þegna twentig'.

There are other interesting adjustments. The ideal leader of the Greeks and Romans thinks first of his army, but our English translator felt that the general should come first. When water failed in the desert (14/1), Alexander was concerned 'first about my own necessity and that of my army', where the Latin has 'primo de statu exercitus magis quam de proprio meo sollicitus sum periculo'. And at 12/8 he camps 'because of the intolerable thirst that afflicted myself and also all my army and (transport) animals', but the Latin has nothing equivalent to 'myself'.

Perhaps the best way of conveying the translator's manner is to give a literal rendering of an incident that took his fancy, with the Latin in a footnote[2] for comparison:

'Then he [Porrus] wanted to know about me and my thanes. When he enquired and asked from those going in and out of my camp, I was

hlifian 'to tower up', which is found with short as well as long *i* in the stem. In *Wonders* in the same hand *leone* appears six times for *leoue* 'league'; and by a queer chance the one example of *u* for medial *f* in the codex is *hliuade* 'towered up' *Beow.* 1799. Again, at 29/6 where Porrus becomes Alexander's *gefera ond gefylcea*, the disputed *gefylcea* should be taken as nom. sg. *gefylca* 'comrade (in arms)', in accordance with the Aldhelm gloss *commanipulares: i. socii vel conscios: gefylce*; see Napier *Old English Glosses*, p. 24/859 and note.

[1] Attempts to meet this deficiency in Old English by borrowing from Latin—*militisc monn* in *Gregory's Dialogues*, *milite* plural in the first Vercelli Homily—were unsuccessful, for the later copies substitute *þegn(as)*.

[2] Cupidusque me nosse, milites meos subinde commeantes interrogabat ubi ego essem vel quid agerem. Qui cum incerta responderent, ipse, auditis eius interrogationibus (omnia enim mihi regi magno Macedonum

told that he wanted to know about me and my army. Then I took off my royal garments, and clothed myself in undistinguished dress and mean garments, as if I were a common man and had need of food and wine. When I was in Porrus's camp, in the condition I have already described, at once he heard that I was there and he was told that somebody had come from Alexander's camp. Then he ordered me to be brought to him at once. When I was brought to him, he inquired and asked me what King Alexander did, and what kind of a man he was, and of what age. Then I fooled him with my answers and said that he was very old, and so old that he could not keep himself warm anywhere but by the fire and the burning coals. Then at once he was very glad and rejoicing at these answers and words of mine, because I told him he was so old; and then too he said: "How indeed can he, such an old man, succeed against me in any battle, for I myself am young and active?" When he questioned me closer about his doings, I said that I did not know much about his doings, and seldom saw him, the King, because I was (I pretended) man to one of his thanes, and herdsman of his beasts, and keeper of his livestock. When he heard these words he gave me a letter or epistle, and commanded me to deliver it to King Alexander, and also promised me a reward if I would deliver it to him; and I promised him that I would do as he commanded. After I had gone thence, and was come again to my camp, both before I read the letter and also afterwards [that] I was mightily shaken with laughter. These things I tell you, my master, and Olimphiad my mother, and my sisters, in order that you should hear and know of the arrogant temerity of the barbarian King. Then I had spied out the King's camp and his strongholds into which he with his army had betaken himself.'

Here we see how freely he translates when his interest is engaged; for instance, he adds spying out the enemy's positions as

referebantur), sumpto habitu militari positoque meo cultu, perveni in castra vinum et carnes quidem empturus. Casu Porus sciscitans me interrogavit quid faceret Alexander aut cuius esset aetatis. Quem eludens mendacio temporis 'tanquam homo senior' inquam 'dux noster in tabernaculo se accenso igni calefícat.' Tum ille gaudio alacer, quasi cum decrepito sene esset prelium commissurus cum esset ipse iuvenis, elatus tumore, 'Quid ergo' inquit, 'non respicit aetatem suam?' Respondi uno id proposito ignorare me quid faceret Alexander cum essem gregarius ex Macedonico miles exercitu. Tradidit mihi minis plenam epistolam quam si regi Alexandro darem pollicitus est praemium; cui iuratus dixi futurum ut in manus eius hae litterae pervenirent. Reversusque protinus in castra, et antequam legerem et postquam legi epistolam in magno risu sum dissolutus; cuius tibi et matri meae sororibusque meis superbam ut barbari inclitam temeritatem mireris exemplar misi.

a motive for Alexander's visit.[1] And his interest is mainly in the campaign and the general. This explains why, with more marvels still to come in his original—serpents, griffins, great fishes, river sirens—he stops the translation short as soon as the oracles of the sun and moon have foretold Alexander's death: the real interest ends there. It explains too the absence of all moralizing. The gods Libri and Hercules, heathen oracles and sacrifices, are accepted without explanation or apology. The spirit of the translation, like its style, accords well with the period of King Alfred's wars.

LINGUISTIC

There remains the language of the *Letter*, and I take the opportunity of making some comparisons with the other texts in the Beowulf manuscript. 'VPs' refers to the late-ninth-century Mercian gloss to the Vespasian Psalter; 'R[1]' to the late-tenth-century Mercian gloss to the Rushworth gospel of Matthew.[2]

(i) Two isolated forms, 8/6 *foeran* 'to go', and 34/13 *gehliuran* 'warmer', have no parallels in the rest of the codex. In West Saxon *oe* forms are rare by the end of the ninth century, but they survive much later in Anglian. *Gehliuran* is more un-West-Saxon in its spelling than in its form, since in Early West Saxon *gehliwran*

[1] William of Malmesbury *Gesta Regum* (ed. Stubbs) i, p. 126, has a story of King Alfred visiting the Danish camp in disguise to spy out their plans, and a similar story of the Danish leader Anlaf visiting Athelstan's camp before Brunanburh, i, p. 143.

[2] There is a useful factual dissertation on the phonology: *Lautlehre der angelsächsischen Version der 'Epistola Alexandri ad Aristotelem'*, by A. Braun, Leipzig 1911, who thinks the Anglian forms are due to a scribe.

Many forms which are not standard West Saxon are consistent with Anglian origin, though they are not strong evidence by themselves because they could easily arise in the course of transmission: for example, regular uncontracted *-eþ* in the 3rd pers. sg. pres. indic. (the 2nd pers. is less regular); *eo* without umlaut in *unheorlic* 34/6 and possibly 16/1; *e* as the umlaut of *ea* in *bergan* 'taste', *ferd* 'army', *gerwan* 'prepare'; *ē* as the umlaut of *ēa* in *ned, geceged, bedegled, geherde*; *e* after palatals in *agef-, onget-, gelpan, sceldan*; the umlaut in *-beorende, siogorum*; the rare *ea* for *eo* in *hread* 'reed' and in 22/3 *laforas* for *eaforas* 'boars', cf. *Beowulf* 2152. Such forms are often described as 'Saxon patois'; but they may be due, for example, to composition in a mixed dialect, or to copying of a non-West-Saxon composition by West Saxon scribes, or to copying of a West Saxon composition by non-West-Saxon scribes.

might be found beside typical **gehliewran*; but again *iu* survives comparatively late in Anglian.

(ii) The vocabulary is interesting—certain words,[1] taken together, point to an Anglian original: e.g. *eþian* 'to breathe' and its noun *eþung*; *nænig*; *nymþe* 'unless'; *aræfnan* 'to endure' with *unarefnedlic*; rare *(h)rif* 'fierce' thrice in the set phrase *(h)rifra wildeora*; *þecelle* 'torch' twice. Frequent *semninga* 'at once' is common in Mercian, occasionally found in Late West Saxon, unrecorded in Northumbrian prose. Words otherwise recorded by Bosworth–Toller from Wærferth's version of Gregory's *Dialogues* or the Old English Bede, both texts with Mercian features, are *gehyld* 'safe', *gelis* 'studium', *widgalnes* 'wide extent'. Words notable because they are otherwise recorded only from verse are: *byrnwiga* 'warrior clad in mail'; *unheorlic* 'violent'; *treowgeþofta* 'faithful comrade'; and *hronfisc*, which in the *Letter* 33/7 is applied to river and lake fishes.[2] The verb *mæran* in the exceptional phrase *ut mæran* (beside *ut cyþan*) 'to make public' is also confined to verse, though *gemæran* is found in Gregory's *Dialogues* and the Old English Bede. Finally, there is the remarkable word *ealfara* for *alfara* 'beast of burden', a borrowing from the Arabic-speaking invaders of Spain[3] which seems to have reached England through Frankish channels in the ninth century.

(iii) A mark of Anglian transmission is the frequent use of the preposition *in* with the meaning 'in', where West Saxon has *on*. The *Letter* has *in* 'in' almost as often as *on* 'in'. *Christopher* has only *on*. *Wonders* has a few examples of *in*. *On* predominates by far in *Beowulf* and to a less extent in *Judith*.

[1] These, except *nænig*, for which see K. Jost *Wulfstanstudien*, p. 159 ff., are selected from R. Jordan *Eigentümlichkeiten des anglischen Wortschatzes*, Heidelberg 1906. Other words in the *Letter* which Jordan regards as Anglian are *hleoþrian* 'resound' with *oferhleoþrian*; *gewinn* in the sense 'toil' with *gewinful*. I exclude words like *gefeon* 'rejoice', *frignan* 'ask', which are recorded from Early West Saxon and Anglian texts, but are abnormal in Late West Saxon. There is not enough evidence to assign reasonably exact geographical boundaries to any of the words that are called Anglian; see below, p. 128.

[2] Possibly as the result of corruption in the Latin or English, since there is no equivalent of the adjective *crudos* (pisces), and the point is that these fishes were eaten raw, cf. *Wonders* 55/3.

[3] R. Jordan *Säugetiernamen*, Heidelberg 1903, p. 126.

(iv) There are some thirty examples of the accusative form *mec* 'me', including about a dozen where a corrector has erased final *c*; and seven examples of *usic* 'us', in three of which *-ic* has been erased.[1] These forms are not found in standard West Saxon prose. *Christopher* has only *me*; examples of the accusative are lacking in *Wonders* and *Judith*. *Beowulf* has sixteen examples of *mec*, four of *usic*, but all are correctly used for the accusative, whereas the *Letter* extends *mec* to the dative.[2]

(v) For the preterite of *cuman*, the *Letter* has regular *cwom(on)* both in the simplex and compounds. *Christopher* and *Judith* have *com(on)*; *Wonders* no example; *Beowulf* has both forms in almost equal numbers.

In the simplex VPs. has regular *cw-*, which is usual in R[1]. In Early West Saxon the Parker Chronicle has usually *cu* = *cw* up to the annal for 877; thereafter *com-* is usual; and entries made at Winchester in the early tenth century have only *com-*. *Pastoral Care* and *Orosius* usually have forms without *w*. See p. 101 below.

(vi) The *Letter* has more examples of Early West Saxon *ie* than the much longer *Beowulf*: *nieten* (6 times), *uniepe*; *giet*; *þrie*; *hiera*; *wæfersien*; *gesiehst*; *ongietan*; *wætersciepe*. So, if it was of Mercian origin, it was subject to West Saxon influence not later than the first half of the tenth century.

(vii) The pronoun *hie*, nom. acc. pl. and acc. sg. fem., is normal in the *Letter*: according to Braun it occurs 137 times against *hi* thrice. *Wonders* has no *hie*; in *Christopher* and *Judith hie* and the

[1] In the Exeter Book *Soul and Body* and *Descent into Hell*, *mec*, *þec*, *usic* have been corrected to *me*, *þe*, *us*; and as these poems are both on popular sermon themes, probably the same man corrected both. Such erasures, applied only to parts of a codex (for *mec*, *þec*, *usic* are common throughout the Exeter Book), are a reminder that, when dealing with literary transmission, we have to reckon sometimes with the irregular intervention of contemporary editors and not only with authors and scribes.

[2] e.g. 39/1 'hwæþer hie mec soð sægdon'. In the Exeter Book Riddles 5, 5 and 66, 10, all modern editors alter MS. *mec* to the usual dative *me*. This would be justified in a normalized text, but not in one which aims at preserving all forms that are historically defensible. The examples in *Alexander's Letter*, in *Salomon and Saturn* B 18, and in VPs. xxx, 5, are enough to show that linguistic confusion of the forms was not confined to late Northumbrian texts like the *Durham Ritual*.

alternatives *hi*, &c., are about equally divided. So it is in *Beowulf*, second hand; but in *Beowulf*, first hand, *hie* predominates by about 5:1.

In VPs. *hie* is regular; it is common, beside *hiæ*, in R^1. In Early West Saxon *hi* is common beside *hie*; and during the later tenth century *hy*, *hi*(*g*) replace *hie* in normal West Saxon, e.g. Ælfric. See below, p. 102; and Sievers–Brunner *Altenglische Grammatik* (1942), § 130.3.

(viii) Before nasals, e.g. in *comp*, *noma*, *hond*, *ongon*, short *o* predominates in stressed syllables.[1] *Christopher* has *a* (*mon* once). *Wonders* has several instances of *o*, with signs that it had been more frequent. In *Beowulf*, first hand, *a* has a considerable majority; in the second hand *o* is the commoner.[2] In *Judith* the forms are almost equally divided.

In VPs. *o* is regular; in R^1 it is usual. In early West Saxon *o* is the commoner, but there is considerable fluctuation.[3] From Athelstan's reign onwards *a* prevails in West Saxon contemporary charters, but, for example, Bishop Oswald's Worcester charter of 984 has *o*. Late West Saxon (Ælfric) has regularly *a*.

(ix) (*a*) Characteristic for the South-West Mercian of VPs. is *e* for *ǣ*, whereas in the North-East Mercian of R^1 *æ* predominates. In the *Letter* *e* for *æ* is rare; but it occurs in both examples of *þecelle* 'torch', and in five out of the six examples of the verb-stem *-ræfn-*, which are reckoned Anglian words.

(*b*) In the *Letter*, West Germanic *ā*, West Saxon *ǣ*, appears regularly as *æ*, where VPs. has regular Anglian *e*, but R^1 a strong minority of *æ* forms. Middle English evidence and place-names like *Stratton* show that *æ* was common in a considerable area of the East Midlands.[4]

(*c*) Characteristic also for the Mercian of VPs., as contrasted

[1] For lists, see Braun, op. cit. p. 8 f.

[2] See Klaeber's edition, Introd. vii, § 24 n. 7.

[3] The evidence is set out by Cosijn *Altwestsächsische Grammatik* i, p. 13 ff. For suggested explanations, see Sievers–Brunner *Altenglische Grammatik*, § 79, Anm. 1.

[4] For a summary and references see R. Jordan *Handbuch der mittelenglischen Grammatik*, § 49.

with R[1], is *ea* for normal *ă* in words like *featu* pl., West Saxon *fatu*. There is no trace of this in the *Letter*.

These negative indications suggest that the *Letter* is East rather than West Mercian.

(x) The characteristic marks of Kentish, *e* for *y* and confusion of *æ* with *e*, do not appear in the *Letter*, in *Wonders*, or in *Christopher*.

(xi) The way is now clear to examine the spellings with *io*, where normal Late West Saxon has *eo*. The historical development has been traced by Sievers.[1] Briefly: original *eo*<*eu* and *io*<*iu* are still kept apart in Northumbrian of the late tenth century. In Kentish they are confused from the early-ninth-century charters[2] onwards, and *io* for *eo* is characteristic of Kentish at the end of the tenth century. In Mercia *eo* has begun to replace *io* by the late ninth century (VPs.), and there are irregularities; but a minority of historical *io* forms survive in the late tenth century (R[1]). In the archetype of our earliest manuscripts of Alfred's *Pastoral Care*, *io* and *eo* can still be fairly well distinguished. Early in the tenth century *eo* prevails in West Saxon, and by the late tenth century (Ælfric) *eo* is regular for original *io* and *eo*. So in a manuscript in which Late West Saxon predominates, only *io* forms need special explanation.

In the *Letter io* is relatively frequent, though it tends to appear in patches—some 66 examples in 50 pages of the manuscript. (*Christopher* has none in 9 pages; *Wonders* 2 in 17; *Beowulf*, first hand, 11 in 87; *Beowulf*, second hand, 115 in 53; *Judith* fragment none in 15 pages). Most of the examples in the *Letter* are survivals of historical *io*.[3] Only two words show *io* for older *eu*: *diora* g. pl. at 32/6 stands against 27 examples of *deor*, *-deor* 'beast', and such an exception is in keeping with the usage of VPs. and the Early West Saxon manuscripts. But there are 15 instances of

[1] *Zum angelsächsischen Vocalismus*, Leipzig 1900, p. 26 ff., continuing Paul und Braune's *Beiträge* xviii (1894), p. 411 ff.

[2] Sievers relies on *triow* 'tree' in the uncial charter of Œthelred dated 692–3; but the copy is much later; see p. 3 n. above.

[3] viz. *sio* (6 times), *hio*, *hiora* (19 times), *þrio*, *hiow* (4 times), *edniowunga*, *dioglum*, *londliod*, *onsion* (twice), *þiostre*, *getiod*; *siond*, *sioððan* (9 times), *siogorum*, *tiolodon* (twice).

trio(w)-, all in the account of the trees of the sun and the moon, against 19 forms with *eo*. Scribes sometimes repeat an exceptional spelling in one particular word; but it is curious that this word belongs to the same phonetic group as *þeow* 'slave', which has an exceptional number of *io* spellings in VPs.[1] Taken with the other evidence, the survivals of *io* are consistent with Mercian origin.

In *Wonders*, which has been almost completely normalized, the two examples *hio*, *sio* contain historical *io*, and may be regarded as survivals. In *Beowulf*, first hand, none of the eleven examples[2] of *io* contains old *eu*: they too must be survivals from a dialect in which *io* was not substituted for old *eu*. In *Beowulf*, second hand, *io* is much more common even than in the *Letter*, and here *io* is freely substituted for old *eu*, e.g. in *biorg*, *biorn*, *hioro-*, *Hiorot*, *Iofor*, *siomian*; *biodan*, *ciosan*, *hiofende*, *hiold*, *bior*, *diop*, *drior-*, *iode*, *sioc*, *þiod*; as well as *-ðio(w)*. Such forms, which one would expect in the South-East, begin to appear on the first page written by the second hand. There is no obvious explanation of the complete absence of *io* spellings from the *Judith* fragment copied by the same hand.[3] It is conceivable that this scribe standardized his practice after he had copied *Beowulf* and before he copied the final sections of *Judith*; or that in a previous copy of *Beowulf* a new scribe came on at about the same place; but these are long chances. The first scribe cannot have eliminated *io* spellings from his part of *Beowulf*, for even if the evidence that he usually copied mechanically is set aside, he admits *io* spellings freely in the *Letter*, and he could hardly distinguish the few examples of historical *io* which remain in his part of *Beowulf*.

V. *Conclusions*

It is now possible to consider the compilation of the Beowulf codex with better information. We began with the supposition that the first and last pieces, *Christopher* and *Judith* (which themselves

[1] Sievers' *Zum ags. Vocalismus*, p. 38 f. In *Beowulf*, second hand, the word which most often has *io* for old *eu* is *-ðio(w)* 7 times against *-ðeo(w)* 10 times.

[2] viz. *frioðu-*, *giogoð* and *iogoðe*, *hio* (thrice), *hiora*, *niowan*, *scionon*, *gewiofu*, *wundorsiona*.

[3] For further discussion see below, p. 104 ff.

show no signs of having had a manuscript transmission in common), differ in transmission from the remaining three, *Wonders*, the *Letter*, and *Beowulf*. This fits all the evidence.

But although these last three texts are fairly old, no evidence has appeared to support the hypothesis that they, or any two of them, make an old nucleus for the collection. *Wonders* is not only distinguished by its illustrations: it has been almost completely turned into normal Late West Saxon. It contains no example of *hie*, few of *in* 'in', relatively few of *ŏ* before nasals. Presumably, then, it came into the collection at some time between the middle of the tenth century and the copying of the extant manuscript, which is usually dated 'about the year 1000'.

The *Letter* and *Beowulf* may possibly have been together for a generation or two. Anybody who accepts the emendation *hleouige* (above, p. 85 n. 1) will note in it and *Beowulf* 1799 *hliuade* a hint that these two texts had been previously copied by one scribe; and not very long previously, since *u* for *f* is rare before the late tenth century. Again, genitive plurals in *o* seem to be confined to the *Letter*[1] and *Beowulf* (first hand). But the much better preservation in the *Letter* of *hie*, *in*, and *ŏ* before nasals, its regular *cwom*(*on*) forms, its more frequent *ie* forms, and different treatment of *io*, are against a manuscript association with *Beowulf* going as far back as the early tenth century.

It is possible that all five pieces were first assembled in the Beowulf codex; possible, alternatively, that *Christopher* and *Judith* were added to a slightly earlier collection; but fairly certain that there was no such collection until the second half of the tenth century.

To go farther involves speculation. *Wonders*, the *Letter*, and *Beowulf*, which are contiguous, preserve in different degrees forms which point to an Anglian, or more specifically a Mercian dialect. Obviously the separate manuscripts were together at the place where they were assembled into a collection. And most likely it was some place in Mercia where West Saxon influences were strong in the later tenth century. This last condition does not help very much, because West Saxon as a literary language had spread

[1] See p. 64, above.

to places like Worcester and York by the time the Beowulf manuscript was written. Still, it favours South Mercia.

To avoid misunderstanding, the vagueness of our knowledge of dialect geography must be appreciated. Mercia—the Midland kingdom—was not divided from the West Saxon kingdom by a deterrent physical boundary, or even by a political line that remained fixed for centuries. In the late eighth century Mercian political influence was strong in Kent and in Wessex. In Alfred's reign Mercian literary influence was strong. In the tenth century Wessex dominated Mercia. These conditions are against well-defined dialectal boundaries. Then, again, our late-tenth- and early-eleventh-century texts come from monasteries, and the local character of monasteries was disturbed by the Benedictine Reform. Men moved about: Ælfric, for instance, worked at Winchester, Cerne, Eynsham, and seems to have been far enough north to see the twilight nights of summer.[1] Manuscripts moved freely too. And so, inevitably, texts and styles of writing or illustration were not for long confined to one place. With so much movement, very little can be known of the geographical limits within which any word, inflexion, sound, or syntactical peculiarity was current in the late tenth century; and no system of linguistic calculation can refer a text or manuscript safely to its home. With this large reservation, I suggest that London itself is the kind of place in which the collection might have been formed, for there Mercian and West Saxon met, and there the South-Eastern *io* forms of *Beowulf*, second hand, would also be possible. Strangely enough, no book surviving from pre-Conquest times has been assigned to the principal city, though it must have used and produced many books, and at least one manuscript, Otho B II, derives from the copy of the *Pastoral Care* that Alfred sent to Heahstan, bishop of London.

A few more inferences may reasonably be drawn from the manuscript. The two hands indicate that it was the undertaking of

[1] See *De Temporibus*, ed. H. Henel, E.E.T.S. (1942) vi. 18, with the editor's comments at pp. xlv and 94 f. But Ælfric's remark, which a summer journey would account for, hardly justifies the suggestion that he was born in the North.

a community, not of an individual who made a copy for his own use. Their ill-matched styles, the poor capitals, the childish draughtsmanship of the illustrations to *Wonders*, and the modest format are evidence that the book was not produced as a present for some great man, whether an ecclesiastic or a lay patron. The late tenth and early eleventh centuries were a golden age of English book-production, and this manuscript does not compare in elegance with the nearly contemporary Exeter and Vercelli books, or the Junius 'Cædmon', or Tiberius B v. It is the plain everyday work of a good period, well suited for reading in a monastic library or cloister. And if a cataloguer of those days had to describe it briefly, he might well have called it 'Liber de diversis monstris, anglice'.

6

THE EXETER BOOK

I[1]

. . . The experience of the editors has enabled them to select those subjects and methods of presentation which are most serviceable to users of the facsimile, and to omit vague and controversial matter that might detract from the value of a permanent standard of reference. But perhaps I may be allowed here to suggest briefly some of the subjects for speculation that remain.

For instance, shall we ever know more about the way in which this miscellany was compiled? The earlier part contains longer religious poems, and the later part shorter poems, religious and secular; but in both the order of contents is generally haphazard.[2] Thus, in the first part, the two poems signed by Cynewulf are divided by non-Cynewulfian matter; and in the second the Riddles appear as two large groups and a separated pair, one of which is a variant text of a riddle that appears some twenty-eight pages earlier. It seems that the collection was put together by tacking on new groups or items as codices or single pieces came to hand. And it is unlikely that the compilation was first made in the Exeter Book, whose stately, even style indicates that it was transcribed continuously from a collection already made.

Because the copy may be several times removed from the original miscellany, not much light on the method of compilation can be expected from the study of the scribe as a copyist (even the authority of Mr. Flower will not persuade me that more than one scribe was employed). Yet a detailed study would be valuable. It might be inferred that such a well-trained hand would transcribe mechanically, bringing to English the habit of literal reproduction that was required in Latin. In fact his one consecutive scrap of

[1] Section I is from a review in *The Review of English Studies* x (1934), p. 339 ff., of *The Exeter Book of Old English Poetry*, with Introductory Chapters by R. W. Chambers, Max Förster, and Robin Flower, 1933.

[2] See Note C at p. 291.

Latin (f. 129*b*) is barbarous, probably because he had no thought of correcting a corrupt original. There are many signs of mechanical copying, such as *swist*, which is no word, written three times for common *swift* (f. 104*b* corrected, f. 105*a*, f. 128*b*). In the only place where the Exeter Book can be compared with a much older copy, the Leiden Riddle, it comes fairly well out of the test, though it has lost the last two lines, or rather, has in their stead a commonplace riddle-ending. But the desirability of transposing dialectal or obsolete forms interfered with the literal transcription of Old English poetry, and transposition itself tends to become mechanical. Thus in *Christ*, l. 875, and again l. 899, the facsimile shows *onsyne beorg* for 'on Mt. Sion', because some copyist mistook *onsione* in his original for a case of the common word meaning 'face' (dialectal *onsion*) and substituted the equivalent *onsiene*, later *onsyne*. Similarly *hyra dreorge* for *heorudreorge* in *Juliana* 482 arises from the substitution of regular *hyra* (gen. pl. of *he*) for what a copyist took to be its variant *heora*. How far and when the scribe of the Exeter Book normalized as he copied it is hard to say. A distinctive feature that runs through the whole miscellany, such as the usual retention of *ie* in words like *giet*, *giefan*, may possibly be due to the manuscript copied. The erroneous *helwerena* for *helwarena* (*Christ* 731; *Juliana* 322 corrected, 437 corrected, 544) might be regarded as a peculiarity of the Cynewulf poems were it not paralleled by *burgwerena* (*Widsith* 90 corrected) and *Hætwerum* (*Widsith* 33). We are left to guess whether the sudden appearance three times on f. 113*a* of the rare *fer-*, *fer* = *for-*, *for* represents an exceptional lapse into the scribe's forms or an exceptional outcrop from some earlier manuscript.

But it is certain that after the Exeter Book left the scriptorium, little was done by later readers to remove even crude errors from the text. One might be tempted to seek in the history of the mānuscript some special explanation for the rarity of late corrections, were not the case of the Vercelli and Beowulf codices the same. No doubt some readers of English poetry could not write, and others had not pen in hand. But when the few feeble glosses to the main hand of the Junius manuscript are taken into account, the likeliest explanation is that not many in the eleventh century understood the harder poetry well enough to read it critically. The few later corrections in the poetical manuscripts are usually concerned with variant forms, less often with patent errors. To the recording of textual variations (which were certainly numerous), the explanation of hard places, and the detection or removal of deeper-seated corruptions, they contribute practically nothing.

That a full understanding of the older poetry should become rarer as the eleventh century progressed is natural enough. But something more is necessary to account for the clustering of our four great poetical manuscripts towards the end of the tenth century; for all may well be the products of one generation (970–1000), which has thus an importance for the preservation of Old English poetry comparable with that of the age of Charlemagne for Latin. The circumstances of that generation were, in fact, peculiarly favourable. A widespread revival in the Church had brought into being many active scriptoria. Not only the family of Æthelweard but noble families generally supported the monasteries as patrons or inmates, and having little Latin, they would welcome books in English. Above all, national spirit ran strong after a century of consolidation under great kings like Alfred, Athelstan, and Edgar, and a great minister Dunstan, who is distinguished as churchman and statesman for his Englishry. It could not be the same in the later days of Æthelred, or when the Danish kings ruled, or under Edward the Confessor. In the leading churches, too, with a necessary exception for sermons, there seems to have been a hardening against English as a literary medium—partly, perhaps, because there was less need for compromise as reform became established, partly because the best Continental models did not admit the vernacular to a place beside Latin. The fine books of the eleventh century are nearly all Latin; and it can scarcely be an accident that our one late specimen of an Old English poetical codex (the *Waldere* fragments) makes such a poor showing beside the four earlier books. In format it has none of the magnificence which safeguarded the Exeter, Vercelli, and Junius manuscripts; and its careless, uncouth style is what one would expect from some backward eddy, while theirs belong to the full stream.

One further point in the relation of the four codices is worth notice. Professor Chambers reminds us that the smallness of their overlap is some measure of the quantity of Old English poetry that was available when they were written: only about 200 lines are duplicated. The prospect of lost riches to be derived from this figure would be almost incredible if we had to do with four poetical miscellanies. But, in fact, the Vercelli Book is a collection in prose and verse of homiletic matter earlier than Ælfric; the Beowulf codex, even allowing for *Judith*, is a collection in verse and prose of marvellous stories, with a strong secular bent; the Junius manuscript, as originally written, is a book of Old Testament history in verse. There is no great likelihood that these three would overlap; and in an age when the circulation of books was active, it is probable that more or less standard collections, designed to limit repetition, would find favour. Only the Exeter Book (so far as its scope can be discerned without knowledge of the collections it was designed to supplement) is a poetical miscellany, open to any English verse that was written by the middle of the tenth century.

II

I return to the linguistic forms of the compilation, in order to explore some by-paths.

Examination of the pieces copied by the first *Beowulf* scribe[1] revealed no linguistic peculiarity running through them all, so that it could be attributed to the scribe, or (what is indistinguishable in practice) to an earlier copyist of the collection whose forms have been preserved in the extant manuscript. In the main hand of the 'Cædmon' manuscript Junius 11, it is again hard to find any distinctive feature that appears throughout.[2] For most of the verse

[1] Above, p. 93 ff.

[2] The spelling *y* for *e* in unstressed *-en, -el, -er* as in: *mægyn Gen. A* 52; *æfyn Gen. B* 313; *engyl Gen. B* 262, 293, and the description of the picture on p. 3; *eðyl- Gen. A* 224, 962, 1492, 2225, 2708; *swefyl Gen. A* 2417, binds together *Genesis A* and *B*; but one example *fæderyn-* in *Exodus* 560 is hardly enough to cover *Exodus* and *Daniel*. Again *somed* 'together' is the common spelling of *Genesis A* and *B* (13 times), where *Exodus* and *Daniel* have only *somod, samod* (5 times), but *somod* also occurs in *Gen. B* 242, *samod* in *Gen. A* 1701, so that mere chance cannot be excluded.

and prose of the Vercelli Book there is a sprinkling of forms showing confusion of etymological *geo-*, *gea-* with *eo-*, *ea-*, apparently a South-Eastern characteristic.[1]

But in the Exeter Book several unusual features appear throughout the miscellany. I select some for which a background has already been provided in the examination of the Beowulf codex, and add a brief comparison with the Junius and Vercelli manuscripts.

(i) The past tense forms *cwom*, *cwomon*, etc., are found without exception, both in the simplex and the compounds of *cuman*. In the Vercelli Book *cwom(on)* and *com(on)* are used indifferently in the verse, and *cw-* forms appear in some of the prose, notably Sermons XVII and XVIII. For the Junius 'Cædmon' see below, p. 103.

(ii) Short *o* in stressed syllables before nasals is usual in words like *noma*, *bona*, *long*, *conn*, *born* pa.t.sg. The spelling with *a* is exceptional, and appears beside *o* chiefly in common words like *mann*, *hand*, *scamu*, *wanian*, *ongan*. The province of *o* seems to have been extended in the course of transmission: for *mon* = *mān* 'evil' in *Precepts* 82, *Maxims* I, 195, *Rhyming Poem* 62; and *monþeawum* in *Juliana* 410 (where Thorpe's correction is certain), are the result of mechanical substitution by a scribe who took *man* in his copy as *homo*, and wrote it, as usual, *mon*.

Although stressed *a* before nasals was normal in the known dialects of Southern England (except the South-West Midlands) in the later tenth century, the three other poetical codices have *o* beside *a*. For the Beowulf manuscript see p. 91 above. The 'Cædmon' manuscript is in this respect patchy and irregular, but *a* is the commoner, and *o* is rare in past tenses like *cann*, *band*. In the Vercelli verse *o*, rare in the prose, tends to be confined to a limited number of words, in which it is accompanied by labials, e.g. *from* adj., *clomm*, *geblonden*, *blon* pa.t.sg., *wonn* adj., *swon*; but irregularity extends to rhyming phrases like *Andreas* 9 *rond* 7 *hand*.

[1] Examples are: f. 44*a* (*Andreas* 1122) *eogoðe*; f. 51*a* (*Andreas* 1627) *eador*; f. 60*a* *eallan* 'gall'; ff. 60*b*, 61*b*, 62*b*, 64*a*, 84*b*, 85*a*, 94*a*, 112*a*, 116*a* *geearw-* (for *gegearw-*); ff. 56*a*, 59*a*, 66*a*, 124*a* (*Elene* 322) *eorne*; f. 103*a* (*Soul and Body* 116) *eaglas* 'jaws'; f. 125*a* (*Elene* 399), 135*b* *earė*, *earo*; f. 61*b* *geardungstowe*; f. 80*a* *gearnian*; f. 101*b* (*Soul and Body* 24) *fulgeodest* (for *fuleodest*); f. 112*a* *geardige*, f. 134*a* *geardodan*; f. 134*b* *geadiga*.

(iii *a*) In the late-tenth-century Vercelli, 'Cædmon', and Beowulf manuscripts, and in the roughly contemporary *Blickling Homilies*, *ie* is common in the pronoun *hie*. In the Exeter Book the usual forms are *hy*, *hi*, and *hie* is rare. The difference is not due to relative date, since palaeographically the Exeter Book has claims to be reckoned rather earlier than the rest; and *hi* is already common in the two manuscripts of the *Pastoral Care* that were written in Alfred's time. In this respect the Exeter Book, like Ælfric's work, represents an area in which *hie* was a monosyllable at the end of the ninth century; and the usage of the other poetical manuscripts is influenced by dialects in which it remained disyllabic throughout the tenth century. The verbal forms *sie*(*n*) are usually associated with *hie* in manuscript spelling; but in the Exeter Book they are relatively commoner: here the disyllabic pronunciation was favoured by the analogy of other optatives; and the early manuscripts of the *Pastoral Care* also prefer *sie*(*n*).

(iii *b*) Characteristic Early West Saxon *ie* is more frequent in the Exeter Book than in the other three poetical codices. But the majority of the examples are in the initial combination *gie*-, e.g.: *giedd*, *gief*-, *giefl*, *gield*-, *giell*-, *widgiell*, *gielp*-, *giestron*, *-giet*-, *giest*, *gierwan* (*gierede*), *gierela*; *gīem*-, *gīet* adv., *gīen*. These forms appear throughout the miscellany. Apart from this special feature, the *ie* spellings are a thin scattering of forms current in Early West Saxon.[1] MS. *þreamedlum* in *Guthlac A* 696 and *þreamedlic* in *Juliana* 128 (for *þreaniedl*-) indicate that the scribe found *ie* spellings in his pattern manuscript. The emendation seems to be necessary, though curiously enough MS. *þreamedl*- occurs also in *Salomon and Saturn* 241 and 428.

Thus certain linguistic features have been imposed or allowed to survive throughout all the miscellaneous contents of the Exeter Book, so that we can speak, in a limited sense, of the language of the collection. It seems unlikely that the latest scribe is responsible. His highly schooled, monumental hand, the frequent confusion of similar letters mentioned above (p. 98), and slips like *Azarias*

[1] They include such irregular spellings as *Phoenix* 461 *gielt* for *gylt*; with *Maxims* I, 111 *ieteð*, Riddle 12, 6 *triedeð*, *Phoenix* 199 and *Order of the World* 64 *biereð*.

148 *sacerdos saðfæst* for *sacerdas soðfæst*, all point to a mechanical copyist. Yet if these characteristics are due to a previous scribe or scribes, they might possibly be found together, towards the middle of the tenth century, in the South-Western district where the Exeter Book itself was copied. Not much is known about dialect distinctions within Southern England at that time.

If now we look for forms or spellings that distinguish one part of the collection from another, the contrast with the Beowulf codex is equally sharp, while the Vercelli and 'Cædmon' manuscripts are intermediate, though nearer to the Exeter Book.

In the main hand of the Junius 'Cædmon' there are four poems certainly by different authors: *Genesis A*, the interpolation *Genesis B* translated from Old Saxon, *Exodus*, and *Daniel*. *Genesis A* and *B* have only past tense *com*(*on*) in the simplex and compounds of *cuman*, whereas the older or dialectal *cwom*(*on*) is preserved 7 times against 5 *com*(*on*) in *Exodus*, 10 times against 6 *com*(*on*) in *Daniel*. This suggests (though it is insufficient to prove) that *Exodus* and *Daniel* have not for long had the same transmission as *Genesis A* and *B*. But I have found nothing to support the view,[1] based on hypothetical reconstructions of the early gatherings, that *Genesis B* was first interpolated in the extant manuscript.

In the Vercelli Book, all in one hand, *Andreas* has a sprinkling of *io* for normal Late West Saxon *eo*: *sio* twice, *bioð*, *gesion*, *dioful* twice, *niowinga*, *niowan*, *frioðo*, *giofum*, *sionwe*; and *Fates of the Apostles* has *edgiong*. In these *io* is explained by the etymology; and

[1] e.g. Gollancz in his introduction to the facsimile (1927), p. liii; B. J. Timmer *The Later Genesis*, 1948, p. 15. The beginning of the interpolation is lost from the MS.; but where it ends, *Genesis A* follows in the same line of writing (MS. p. 40/8) without a space or even a capital to mark the change of source. The occurrence of *niotan* three times in *Genesis B* for normal *neotan* may be regarded as a reflection of Old Saxon *niotan*, since in all *Genesis A* the only close parallel is 182 *liodende* 'growing'. But on Dr. Timmer's view that the scribe of the 'Cædmon' MS. copied the original translation from Old Saxon, and that this translation was made by an Old Saxon in the reign of Alfred, the general adjustment to the usage of *Genesis A* is hardly credible. Sievers, using arguments from 'Schallanalyse' which I cannot follow, concludes that the translator of *Genesis B* produced the whole work *Genesis A* and *B* by a process of compilation and revision (*Britannica*, Leipzig 1929, p. 57 ff.).

if it is right to accept the emendation 1647 *se ar* for MS. *sio ar*, the *io* forms in *Andreas* cannot all be attributed to its author. Sermons follow, and Förster has noted[1] that sermons VII–XI, counting from the beginning of the manuscript, are numbered by the scribe II–VI, which is their order if the count is begun after *Andreas* and *Fates*.[2] These numbers may be vestiges of a separate collection or of an earlier state of the compilation. However that may be, the sermons (up to XIV) that immediately follow *Andreas* and *Fates* have, besides frequent *sio*, *hio*, *bion*, *diofol*, a considerable number of examples of *io* for etymological *eo*: e.g. *hiofon*, *biorht*, *wiorc*, *iorðe*, *giorne*, *wiorþan*, *wiorðan*, *sioc*, *lioht*, *hiofað*. But in the prose life of Guthlac, at the very end of the manuscript, there are no *io* forms at all. Here the difference of usage seems to distinguish three sources of the compilation.

A similar difference of usage is noticeable at the very beginning of the Exeter Book. Whereas *Christ II* (*The Ascension*), which has Cynewulf's signature, shows no *io* spellings, *Christ I* (*The Advent*) has a sprinkling throughout: *sio* (twice), *hio*, *sioh*, *giofu*, *lioþucægan* with etymological *io*; *niedþiowa* with etymological *eo*; and *iowa* 'show', *nioda* 'wishes', where either *eo* or *io* might be explained. This difference between two consecutive pieces may indicate a difference of source, and so strengthen the arguments against Cynewulf's authorship of *Christ I*.

But such negative evidence as the absence of *io* from a poem of no great length is inconclusive. No convincing explanation has been given for the case of *Judith* (above, p. 93). In the main hand of the 'Cædmon' manuscript, *io* forms fade out long before the end of *Genesis*.[3] In the Vercelli Book most of the pieces have

[1] Introduction to the Facsimile (Rome 1913), p. 56 f.

[2] There is a case for regarding Vercelli Homily VI as number I in this sub-series; but it may be a substitute. Obviously it is not by the same author as VII which follows it or V which precedes *Andreas*.

[3] After *Genesis B* the examples are 1103 *scio* from *sceon* v.; 1439 *hlioðo*, 2091 *nior*. The last is interesting because MS. *oð leni|or*, with *en* formed as a ligature, shows that the scribe did not understand it. He or a predecessor seems to have misread *eðle* (or *oeðle*) *nior*, 'nearer to his homeland' as the preposition *oð* followed by a place-name; and the context encouraged Junius and other early editors in the same interpretation. *Nior*, if correct, should be Kentish (Sievers–Brunner, § 128, 3), and may

some *io* forms, but they cluster or thin out in a way that is hard to explain: for instance, *Dream of the Rood* and the three following sermons would make a well-defined stretch of some twenty-four manuscript pages without *io*, were it not for *bion* 'bees' on f. 107*b*. In the Exeter Book, examples of *io*, mostly in the pronouns *hio*, *sio*, appear sparsely and unevenly.[1] There are a few in *Christ III*, in *Guthlac A* and *B*, in *Phoenix*, and in *Juliana*. Thereafter, long gaps are broken by rare *io* forms, until a patch of *hio*, *sio* (14 examples) appears in Riddles 31–39.

It would not be safe to build on such evidence, and it seems that *io* forms are often unsatisfactory as an indicator. One difficulty is that they are so widespread: their absence is a peculiarity of standard Late West Saxon; and even *io* for etymological *eo* is found, in greater or less degree, in Early West Saxon and Mercian as well as in Kentish. So in any older text there may be traces of different treatments of the sounds concerned; and similar treatments may appear in different parts of a collection as the result of coincidence: it is remarkable that examples of etymological *io*, unmixed with *io* for *eo*, survive in *Beowulf* (first hand), *Andreas*, most of the Exeter Book, and *Salamon and Saturn*.

Two other interrelated difficulties affect all investigations of this kind. One is the irregularity of scribes, who cannot all be expected to treat their copy in the same way at beginning and end of

be a form from an earlier MS. which has survived because it was not recognized as an English word. But such a corrupt place is not good evidence for an OE. *oðel*, beside normal *eðel* which occurs many times in *Genesis A*.

[1] Apart from *hio*, *sio*, the examples I have noted are: *Christ III* 1653 *gioguð*; *Guthlac A* 175 *biorg* (the only clear example of *io* for *eo* after *Christ I*); *Guthlac B* 912 *spiowdon*; *Phoenix* 299 *nioþoweard*, 355 *giong*, 581 *edgiong*; *Juliana* 215 *tiohhast*, 476 *spiowedan*; *Maxims* I 145 *unwiotodne*; *Soul and Body* 75 *tiolode*; Riddles 61, 6 *nioþan*; 73, 18 *swiora*; 87, 8 *niol*. I exclude MS. *wiolane* in the obscure line *Widsith* 78:

MS. wiolane ond wilna   ond wala rices,

where most modern editors read *wiolena* = *weolena*, *welena* 'riches'. The phrase *wilna ond welena* (*weolena*) occurs in Alfred's *Pastoral Care* 387/7 and 391/18; but the spelling *wiol-* is not in keeping with the usage of the Exeter Book. It may be due to anticipation of *wilna*, or the words may be corrupted from proper names.

a long work, or even at beginning and end of the day's task. The other is the complexity of manuscript transmission, which in an age of active copying, like Alfred's or the later tenth century, is certain to go beyond our powers of detection. An example of the complications that can arise at the first launching of a new work is given by Alfred's translation of Gregory's *Pastoralis*;[1] and the later transmission offers many more possibilities.

How then is the difference between the Beowulf collection and the Exeter miscellany to be accounted for? In the former, every text is distinguished from the rest by the presence or absence or relative frequency of certain forms; and no really distinctive form runs through the collection. In the latter, several forms are characteristic of the whole miscellany, and it is hard to be sure of any that distinguishes one text or group from another. The explanation is that the Beowulf collection has, in the main, been mechanically copied from the time it was formed, while the Exeter collection has at some time been copied by one or more scribes who freely substituted forms to which they were accustomed for those in the copy before them.

These two ways of transcribing may coexist at any time; but some conditions favour one or the other. The second half of the tenth century was the period of the Benedictine Reform. Its sources were Continental, and that assured a primary place to Latin. The best pupils of the new monastic schools, such as Ælfric and Byrhtferth, expressed themselves easily in sober, practical Latin prose, and Wulfstan the Cantor wrote a considerable amount of Latin verse; the extent of the reform appears when their works are compared with the tortured prose of Æthelweard or the verse of Frithegoda's *Life of Wilfrid*, written a generation or two earlier. New Latin psalters, service-books, and reading-books were adopted, so that Continental texts had to be copied on a grand scale. How deeply scribal practice was affected is shown by a notable break with the past: during the second half of the tenth century the Continental style of handwriting became firmly established as proper for Latin; the native hand, which had served all purposes for three centuries, was relegated to vernacular texts, for which

[1] See p. 140 ff. below.

there could be no Continental pattern-books; and even there it was radically modified towards the Caroline minuscule. A new hand, different abbreviations, more classical Continental spelling, new texts intended to be read aloud in church or refectory to keen and educated listeners—all these made the standards of copying more exacting; and the scribes, who were often poorly equipped in Latin, found it quickest and safest to aim at following the pattern-copy in all details. From this time until the twelfth century, mechanical copying often preserves minutiae from the pattern, and they may provide valuable evidence on the history of texts. As an example, the Salisbury MS. 150, written about 975, is one of the earliest extant Gallican psalters produced in England as a service-book. The native script is still used, but the abbreviations in the text follow a Continental original. The same scribe copied the Latin headings to the psalms, which come from an English source, and they are clearly distinguished by an Insular system of abbreviations: there is no mixing of the two streams. This is a Latin parallel to the distinctions preserved in the Beowulf codex, and we have seen that the whole history of that volume, as a collection, probably falls within the second half of the tenth century.

The revival under Alfred was less thoroughgoing and different in character. Though he had Continental helpers, he depended chiefly on native resources. More copying of Latin books was necessary, and, as in the later period, it is reflected in the handwriting; but the massive, regular English hand of which so many examples survive from Athelstan's time to the end of the tenth century owes its character to a new draught on the native majuscule or 'quarter uncial', which was used for fine books in the eighth and ninth centuries and for headings far into the tenth: when the scribe of the Exeter Book copied the Latin half-lines in *Phoenix* 667 ff., he used letter-forms distinctive of this older script.[1]

[1] As E. A. Lowe remarks (*Codices Latini Antiquiores* ii (1935), Introd. p. xi), the 'shibboleth' of this script is α, with which *s*, *N*, *R*, and *d* are often associated. The Exeter Book scribe usually reserves α for Latin, for Biblical names like *adam*, eu*an*, or for small capitals. In the Vercelli Book and the Junius 'Cædmon' a debased *α* appears occasionally as a mere variant of minuscule *a*.

Alfred aimed at the spread of a working knowledge of Latin rather than at the revival of Latin studies (the one considerable Latin composition of the years 875–925 is the work of the Welshman Asser). His great achievement was the development of English as a means of national education, and the provision in English of a selection of books 'most necessary for all men to know'. In his time, and in the following generation, vernacular texts were more than a subsidiary part of a scribe's work. Now, in copying the vernacular, exact reproduction of the pattern was unnecessary. When a Mercian text like the Vespasian Psalter gloss had to be transcribed for use at Winchester in MS. Junius 27 (written about the year 925), adaptation was desirable, and adaptation was easy for a scribe writing his own language. These conditions encouraged the habit of free copying. The signs of it that appear in the Exeter Book are to be expected if the whole miscellany was assembled in the time of Alfred, or his successors Edward and Athelstan, all of whom appreciated Old English poetry.[1]

[1] See below, p. 137.

7

MARGINALIA IN THE VERCELLI BOOK

REFERRING to the ninth century, the late Robin Flower remarked that 'Irish scribes—and only Irish scribes at that time—had a habit of setting down in the margins and on blank spaces of their manuscripts personal memoranda, invocations of saints, little fragments of verse, and all the flotsam and jetsam of idle fancy';[1] and among his examples he translates from a copy of Cassiodorus on the Psalms: 'Pleasant is the glint of the sun to-day upon these margins, because it flickers so.' If Anglo-Saxon scribes caught these gleams, they did not record them. Their marginalia as a rule are severely practical. Occasionally they leave traces of a wandering mind, but they are inarticulate. In the Vercelli Book a dog trots gaily and irrelevantly across the foot of a page of *Andreas* (f. 49*b*); written unobtrusively at the end of f. 41*b* of the same poem is a half-erased *eadgiþ*, but only a romancer could make anything of this Edith. Anybody who scans the margins of the facsimile edition[2] must be content with very little things.

I begin with xƀ at the extreme top of folios 119*a*, 121*a*, 123*a*, 126*a*, which is due to the scribe. It is a prayer at the beginning of the sitting, probably *X*(*riste*) *b*(*enedic*), though the expansion has not been recorded; but it is also, I think, an inconspicuous pen-trial to make sure that pen and ink will go smoothly: it is very like the secular ꝑƀ = *probatio* (*pennae*). This symbol xƀ carries us back to the earliest Christian times in these islands. It is characteristic of Irish scribes.[3] Warren noted examples from the Lambeth MacDurnan Gospels which King Athelstan gave to Christ Church, Canterbury, and from the Scottish Book of Deer.[4] But if xƀ was an

[1] *The Irish Tradition*, 1947, p. 36.

[2] *Il Codice Vercellese*, Rome 1913, with Max Förster's admirable introduction.

[3] W. M. Lindsay *Early Irish Minuscule Script*, 1910, p. 47 and note.

[4] *Academy*, 23 Mar. 1889, p. 205, following up a note by Neubauer, 16 March, p. 186, who refers to the 'Cædmon' MS., Vercelli Book, and MS. Barlow 35.

Irish invention, which English scribes adopted, it had Italian analogues or antecedents; for Lowe has noted that $\overline{\text{XF}}$ occurs as a beginning prayer in sixth-century South Italian books long before $\overline{\text{XPE}}$ FAVE appears in the Northumbrian Codex Amiatinus (*circa* 700) or the Irish St. Gall Priscian (*circa* 850).[1]

In English manuscripts xƀ is commonest round about the end of the tenth century. Napier[2] assembled instances from Bodleian MS. Digby 63 (late ninth century), the Caius College MS. 144 (late ninth century), the Junius 'Cædmon' (*circa* 1000), and from Barlow 35 (*circa* 1000). To these may be added Durham Ritual (tenth century) pp. 22, 94, 139;[3] Bosworth Psalter (B.M. Addit. 37517, late tenth century) f. 55*a*, and Royal 15 A xvi (early eleventh century) ff. 75*b*, 77*b*, 78*b*, 80*b*: it is curious that in this last manuscript, as in the Vercelli Book, the symbol appears in a fairly regular series at one part of the book only. The list could no doubt be lengthened, but these are enough to show that the practice was widespread, and that, although Christ Church and St. Augustine's books predominate in the list above, the mark is not, as James suggested,[4] specially connected with Canterbury.

At the foot of f. 63*b*, *writ þus* is written inconspicuously in a hand rather later than that of the text. It appears to be a pen-trial made by somebody who was copying the text. *Writ ðus* occurs as a later addition on f. 1*a* of the Worcester MS. Junius 121 (end of the eleventh century). In MS. Hatton 20, which King Alfred sent to Worcester,[5] an expansion of it is added at the top of f. 53*b* in a rough hand of perhaps the early twelfth century: *Willimot, writ þus oððe bet.* Here it can no longer be an admonition to copy the

[1] *Codices Latini Antiquiores* ii (1935), p. xv.

[2] *Academy*, loc. cit.

[3] Ed. Surtees Soc. (1927), p. xlvii.

[4] *Ancient Libraries of Canterbury and Dover*, 1903, p. xxv.

[5] See below, p. 142. Cockayne, who had explored many Anglo-Saxon MSS., quotes the marginalia from Hatton 20 and Harley 55 at *Leechdoms* ii, p. xxii in connexion with the colophon of the late-tenth-century MS. Royal 12 D xvii:

Bald habet hun*c* librum quem Cild conscribere iussit.

But his inference that later scribes had degenerated into 'tipsy drudges' is freakish. In the colophon the nicknames *Bald* and *Cild* are used alone for metrical convenience, and *Cild* indicates that the scribe was young.

style of handwriting, because the text-hand of Hatton 20, which is akin to the contemporary first hand of the Parker Chronicle, went out of fashion early in the tenth century; just as the hand of the Vercelli Book, with its Insular combinations of *e* with a following *m*, *n*, *r*, low *s*, *t*, *g*, sometimes *c*, *a*, *o*, went out of fashion early in the eleventh century.[1] It is a tag from the writing-schools, and Willimot, whose name reflects the new French fashion, was doing a copying exercise at Worcester.

In the Middle Ages free use of the whip was the mark of a good schoolmaster, and at the top of f. 55*a* of Hatton 20, Willimot gives another variant, with an attempt at rhyme:

Writ þus oððe bet oððe þine hyde forlet,

'Write thus or better, or lose your skin.' In a twelfth-century addition to yet another Worcester book, Harley 55, f. 4*b*, the pupil Ælfric names his schoolmaster:

Writ þus oððe bet; ride aweg; Ælfmær Patta fox, þu wilt swingan Ælfric cild:

'Write thus or better; ride away. Ælfmær Patta "the Fox", thou wilt thrash the boy Ælfric.' He would hardly have been so bold if Ælfmær Patta's sharp eyes looked beyond the exercises to the manuscripts from which they were copied.

I have assumed that Willimot and Ælfric 'cild' were doing exercises at Worcester, not multiplying books. Delisle has assembled Continental evidence that quite young boys sometimes did this work;[2] but their ignorance and irresponsibility were dangerous to

[1] In the usual Insular script, *e* standing alone is almost evenly divided by the horizontal bar. In continuous writing, this bar often joined a following letter on the upper line, and the upper part of *e* was formed above the line as in Roman cursive and derived scripts. Caroline minuscule attained a more compact form by making the bar of *e* not horizontal, but inclined upwards towards the line, where it joined a following letter, so that the part of *e* above the bar was a small arc within the line. In eleventh-century English Insular script the Caroline practice was adopted, and the combinations with high *e* or *æ* rapidly disappeared. They survive occasionally, e.g. in an original grant by Thurstan, dated 1049 (*Facsimiles of Ancient Charters in the British Museum* iv, pl. 33), and were imitated in some forged charters.

[2] *Le Cabinet des Manuscrits* i, p. 315. For a modern instance see Thoresby's *Diary* for 8 July 1712, quoted by D. C. Douglas *English*

the texts they copied, so that Charlemagne forbade their employment on books important for the church services:

Pueros vestros non sinite eos vel legendo vel scribendo corrumpere. Et si opus est evangelium, psalterium et missale scribere, perfectae aetatis homines scribant cum omni diligentia.[1]

This good rule seems to have been followed in Anglo-Saxon times. In the eighth century we hear of Bede on his death-bed dictating his translation of St. John's Gospel to his pupil Wilberht;[2] and after the terrible winter of 763–4 Abbot Cuthbert of Wearmouth excuses himself for sending Lul only Bede's Lives of St. Cuthbert, because, though he and his pupils (*cum meis pueris*) had done their best, the excessive cold had numbed their fingers.[3] But *pueri* was often used to include all those who were training to become priests or monks. The context suggests that Wilberht was one of Bede's senior pupils; Cuthbert's *pueri* were youths selected for their aptitude in calligraphy rather than children; and when Alcuin proposes to send *aliquos ex pueris nostris* from Tours to copy texts at York and bring them back to France,[4] he evidently has in mind young men of considerable training and discretion. The only extensive early English example of irresponsible copying I have noticed is in the Eadwine Psalter, from the first half of the twelfth century. There the English interlinear version of the Roman text[5] is copied in several hands which probably belong to younger members of the scriptorium at Canterbury Cathedral; but they made such nonsense that a corrector erased most of the glosses up to the end of Psalm 77, and replaced them with a good version of the gloss found in the Regius Psalter.[6]

Scholars, 1939, p. 87: '[Elizabeth Elstob] showed me a delicate copy of the Textus Roffensis, wrote by a poor boy she keeps, most of it before he was quite ten years of age. . . . I saw the boy who has imitated the Saxon and other antique hands to a wonder.'

[1] Capitular of 789, ch. lxxi.

[2] Letter of Cuthbert to Cuthwine, ed. E. v. K. Dobbie *The Manuscripts of Cædmon's Hymn and Bede's Death Song*, New York 1937, p. 118 ff.

[3] *Mon. Germ. Hist. Epist. Karol. Aevi* i, p. 406.

[4] Op. cit. ii, p. 177.

[5] Ed. F. Harsley, E.E.T.S. 1889.

[6] MS. Royal 2 B v, ed. F. Roeder, Halle 1904.

Besides *writ þus*, Förster[1] has noticed a few words, letters, and numbers in the Vercelli Book which seemed to him to be not by the original scribe. To distinguish and date such tiny scraps with certainty is hardly possible. The scribe himself may add or correct at another time, with another pen or different ink, or he may be cramped for space when writing between the lines, or he may fall short of the regularity of his set hand. Hence there is room for differences of opinion, and I should assign the longest item in Förster's list, *mægenþrymme* interlined in *Elene* 735 (f. 128*a*), to the text hand. But, taken together, *writ þus*, *sclean*[2] added above the line on f. 99*a*, and the minuscule scribbles *st*, *est*, *æ* on the last fly-leaf,[3] indicate that the book remained in English use in the eleventh century, so that it was not specially written to be sent abroad. None of these is good evidence that it was still in English hands after the Conquest.

One later addition remains. On the lower part of f. 24*b*, the first blank space in the manuscript, is the excerpt from Psalm xxvi. 9:

> R̅ Adiutor meus esto domine ne derelinquas me deus
> salutaris meus V̅

written in a small Caroline minuscule, with delicately formed neums above. This Förster assigns to the thirteenth century.[4] In his careful study of the provenance of the codex, he established two alternatives: either it came to Italy between the years 1000 and 1175, when Englishmen might still read Anglo-Saxon, or it came as a curiosity in the sixteenth century.[5] But if this psalm-verse was added in England in the thirteenth century, the first alternative is excluded; and if it was added in Italy in the thirteenth century, the second is excluded. So it is an entry of some importance.

At the outset we are faced with difficulties. Who in Italy in the

[1] Introd. to Facsimile, p. 15.

[2] There is no other example of *scl-* for *sl-* in the MS. On these forms see K. Sisam, Herrig's *Archiv* cxxxi (1913), p. 305 ff.; and add an outcrop of *stl-* forms, *stlea, stlog, stlaga,* &c., in the eleventh-century MS. Tiberius B v, f. 74.

[3] The capitals CUM PERVENISSE on this fly-leaf are too artificial to be helpful.

[4] Facsimile, Introd. pp. 16, 52.

[5] Op. cit. pp. 33, 39, 40.

thirteenth century would have an Anglo-Saxon book open before him, and think it a good place to record a scrap of chant that interested him? In England the book might be looked at in the early thirteenth century in some place like Worcester, where old men still pored over Anglo-Saxon texts. But we have seen that there are no late entries in the Vercelli Book such as those that are characteristic of Worcester.[1] And who in England in the thirteenth century, or even the twelfth, wrote a hand like this? If it is English, with the reservations necessary because the scrap is so small and the writing compressed to carry the neums, I should place it in the eleventh century, and in the first rather than the second half of that century.

Here, perhaps, I may be allowed to become anecdotal. When I was an undergraduate, and until his death in 1917, I had the privilege of knowing and corresponding with Edmund Bishop, the greatest of English liturgical scholars. He was then in retirement at Barnstaple or Downside, and I used to send him scraps that might interest him from manuscripts, except those in the British Museum which he knew familiarly by the process of working through the medieval collections from the first shelf-mark to the last. It was a point of method with him to have these oddments without comment. 'Let us each work from his own angle', he would say, 'and if our results converge or agree, we shall be encouraged to think that we may be on the right track.' So I sent him the Latin of this psalm-verse from Oxford simply as from the margin of an Anglo-Saxon MS.

His reply gives an example of his flair and minute attention to little things. He was rather surprised that I should find this in an English manuscript (he had inferred that it was in Oxford), for he would have guessed Northern Italy! He gave his reasons. He could find the omission of *neque despicias me* after *derelinquas me* only in an eleventh-century Milan manuscript printed in M. Magistretti's *Manuale Ambrosianum*, p. 451.[2] There too the psalm-

[1] For a list of Worcester MSS. with glosses by a tremulous hand see N. R. Ker *Medieval Libraries of Great Britain*, 1941, p. 117, n. 3.

[2] Milan 1905. The standard Psalter text, Old Latin, Roman, and Gallican, is: 'Adiutor meus esto. ne derelinquas me neque despicias me Deus

verse is not divided into

V(ersicle): Adiutor meus esto Domine ne derelinquas me
R(esponse): neque despicias me Deus salutaris meus,

as in the Roman Breviary; but the whole forms the *capitellum*[1] at Terce on ordinary days. Until these peculiarities can be matched from early English use, they are good evidence that the entry was made in Northern Italy.

The next step was to get expert opinion on the neums. After a minute examination, the late Dr. H. M. Bannister, editor of *Monimenti Vaticani di paleografia musicale latina*, and the late Dr. G. H. Palmer, an expert in early plainsong, agreed that the notation belonged to the eleventh century, and were inclined to think that it was English: the national differentiation of neums had hardly begun so early. They could not identify the melody in English or foreign books. In the available English examples, this psalm-verse had the same Latin text and the same division into versicle and response as the Roman Breviary.[2]

It was still necessary to have an opinion on the script from someone thoroughly at home among medieval North Italian hands, and Cardinal Mercati, who then presided at the Vatican Library, readily gave his help. After consulting colleagues, he thought the script was of the eleventh century, and that the first half of the twelfth was the extreme later limit. He thought it could be North Italian, but at this date, and on so small a specimen, it was impossible to distinguish North Italian Caroline minuscule with any confidence.

In sum, there is reasonable certainty that this entry was made in the eleventh century, and in Northern Italy. Whether an Englishman or an Italian made it is uncertain on the evidence of script and

salutaris meus.' There is an old and widespread variant *es tu* for *esto*; and the insertion of *Domine*, or *Deus* (e.g. Eadwine Psalter), is not uncommon in psalters, perhaps by influence of the *capitellum*, which usually has either *Domine* or *Deus*. But the Milan MS. quoted has not this addition.

[1] On the nature and history of these *capitella*, see E. Bishop *Liturgica Historica*, 1918, p. 127 f.

[2] Dr. Palmer compared the earliest available text with neums from Exeter (Leofric Collectar), Worcester, Peterborough, Gisburne, and York, as well as the common Sarum form. These include both monastic use (Septuagesima Sunday at Lauds) and secular (same day at Terce).

neums; but an Englishman is more likely to have had this book in use.

Then one alternative—that the manuscript reached Italy after the Renaissance—can be dismissed. So, too, can the agency of Cardinal Guala, which despite its inherent improbability has cumbered all discussion of the subject for more than a century: he was active in England and Vercelli in the first quarter of the thirteenth century. Nor, though he comes within the indicated period, is Bishop Ulf a likely carrier of the book.[1] He was a Norman priest of the Confessor's household, whose promotion to the see of Dorchester caused a scandal. In 1050 he was examined by a papal synod at Vercelli and found incompetent to do the duties of a bishop; but lavish bribery enabled him to hold his see until he was driven out of England in 1052.[2] Such a man was not likely to be interested in an old-fashioned collection of English sermons and religious verse, or to detect and record a variation in the music of the services at Vercelli. Mr. Herben thinks he took the book to serve as a bribe, but that overrates the simplicity of Ulf and the Italian officials: it had no use or money-value in Italy.

Ulf's visit to Vercelli would need closer consideration if the number of eminent men from England who travelled that way had been few. In fact, the way through the Alps was the usual route from England to Rome, and for those who took the Great St. Bernard Pass Vercelli was on the road: it was the forty-second halt on Archbishop Sigeric's return journey from Rome in 990–1, or roughly half-way.[3] Archbishops of Canterbury usually went to Rome for their *pallia* from Athelstan's reign, archbishops of York from the reign of Cnut; and several of them must have stopped at Vercelli, going or coming.[4] Bishops or abbots would often take the

[1] His claims have been restated by S. J. Herben *Speculum* x (1935), p. 91 ff. [2] *Chronicle*: E under 1047 and 1052; D under 1050.

[3] Stubbs *Memorials of St. Dunstan*, Rolls Series, 1874, p. 394.

[4] W. Levison *England and the Continent in the Eighth Century*, p. 241 ff., has shown that a letter of protest against the exactions of the papal court on these occasions, and the fatigues of the journey, belongs to the beginning of the eleventh century, not to the year 805. Miss D. Bethurum *Philologica: Malone Anniversary Studies*, 1949, p. 97 ff., has brought evidence to show that the compiler was Wulfstan, among whose collections it is preserved.

same way when business or devotion called them to Rome. There were royal missions such as that of Bishops Herman and Ealdred in 1050, which included the author Goscelin. King Cnut himself travelled through the passes of the Alps, accompanied by Bishop Lyfing of Crediton, in 1027 and has left a letter recording his protests against the exorbitant tolls levied there on English travellers, 'tam mercatores quam alii orandi causa viatores'.[1] Other great laymen who went on pilgrimage must be reckoned with, because a scholarly priest might make one of their party, as the future Archbishop Oda went to Rome when a young man with his patron Æthelhelm.[2] The stream of ordinary pilgrims across the Great St. Bernard hardly enters into the question, for they would not easily borrow manuscripts from a church, or carry anything so bulky as the Vercelli Book across the Alps. But there were so many possible carriers in the first half of the eleventh century that there is no justification for choosing one or another.

There is something unattractive about an argument which leaves bare ground where before there was a rich crop of interesting hypotheses;[3] so I shall attempt a purely conjectural reconstruction.

At some time in the first half of the eleventh century an eminent Englishman decided to make the journey to Rome. To and fro, it was a journey of months, with many hours of rest or waiting on

[1] Liebermann *Gesetze* i, p. 276; iii, p. 191.

[2] See the early-eleventh-century *Life of St. Oswald*, ed. Raine, *Historians of the Church of York* i (1879), p. 399 ff. In the same work, p. 409, Oda appears in a vision to warn his successor Ælfsige, who later died of frostbite in the Alps, that he would cross the sea and climb the mountains but never be enthroned as Archbishop at Canterbury: 'mare transfretabis, montes ascendere valebis, sed nequaquam in apostolica sede sedebis.'

[3] I pass over a suggestion which Förster made in order to explore all possibilities: that the book reached Vercelli by way of some Continental centre like Fulda or Würzburg (Introd. to the Facsimile, p. 34 ff.). This only removes the problem to another place. The close connexion which brought Latin books from England to Fulda and Würzburg belongs to the eighth century, and there is no record of a late-tenth-century book in Anglo-Saxon reaching either place. Nor is there a parallel for the further transfer of such a book to Vercelli. The transfer of the tenth-century sacramentary, Vercelli MS. CLXXXI, from Fulda or Würzburg to Vercelli, at a period when German influence was strong in the Lombard Church, is wholly different in kind.

the weather, which good reading for himself and his company would help to pass. As its head or patron, he was able to borrow from the library of a monastic church, and the choice fell on the Vercelli Book. It is essentially a reading-book: there is nothing in it that would support a claim at Rome, or help in a controversy on liturgy or doctrine; and whoever chose it had old-fashioned tastes, for it is an out-of-the-way collection. It includes nothing by the new popular sermon-writers Ælfric and Wulfstan; and in a period from which many collections survive, it is the only manuscript for about half its sermons. Crossing by the Great St. Bernard, the party halted at Vercelli. At the cathedral service there, the leader (if he was an ecclesiastic) or an attendant priest skilled in music, heard the *capitellum* 'Adiutor meus esto' sung with a text, division, and melody strikingly different from the English use, and noted it, or perhaps asked an Italian to write it, in a convenient place—the first blank space in the English sermon-book. At this stage it was intended to bring the manuscript home again; but some chance intervened. Possibly one of the party stayed behind sick at Vercelli, and the book was left to comfort him. Possibly on the outward journey it was left for safe keeping in the cathedral, to be picked up on the return, which some change of plan, such as a diversion via Mont Cenis, prevented. Possibly when the loads were made up to recross the Alps, something had to be sacrificed, a new treasure was preferred to the old book, and conscience was salved by leaving it to the cathedral. Such commonplace reasons, which no chronicle or document is likely to record, would account for its remaining with the books of Vercelli Cathedral.

8

DIALECT ORIGINS OF THE EARLIER OLD ENGLISH VERSE

DO the linguistic tests now available enable us to determine the dialect in which any longer piece of the earlier Old English poetry was composed? There seems to be no recent general treatment of this question, though it is customary for editors to say something about the original dialect of the particular poems they present. When reviewing a modern edition of exceptional interest,[1] I indicated some reasons for doubting the view that practically all the early poetry is demonstrably of Anglian origin:

> The method of approaching this problem which has become almost traditional is by no means securely based. It assumes that dialect colouring traceable to the original form of an Old English poem is evidence of the poet's natural dialect, though consideration of dialect conventions in Greek literature must raise doubts. From the fact that some early poems were composed in the Anglian dialect, it reaches the conclusion that no extant early poem was composed in the South, though practically all the surviving verse was preserved there. Yet, without early Southern texts, there is no sure distinction between words, forms and constructions unknown to Southern poets in early times, and those, once general, that survived in Anglian only.

A development of this summary criticism may help to distinguish fact from opinion, and may encourage others to produce more convincing arguments.

The stock to which the poet belonged and the locality in which he composed may be left out of account: we are concerned only with the dialect he used. But at once a difficulty arises. A dialect is recognized by a combination of features in its sounds, vocabulary, accidence, or syntax. Within Anglo-Saxon England there were not many forbidding physical barriers, political boundaries seldom remained fixed, and the surviving texts that can be dated and

[1] *The Poetical Dialogues of Solomon and Saturn*, ed. R. J. Menner, New York 1941, reviewed in *Medium Ævum* xiii (1944), p. 31 f.

localized with reasonable certainty are so few that we do not know the geographical limits within which any dialectal feature was current at a given time. A philologist, asked what were the characteristics of West Saxon about the year 800, and in what districts they prevailed, would have very little direct evidence on which to base an answer. So 'West Saxon', 'Mercian', 'Anglian' in this connexion are vague terms.

If, in the attempt to be more precise, one of the principal dialects is closely defined as the language of a particular text or author, it ceases to be comparable with others more vaguely defined. Some not very critical studies of Anglian elements in Ælfric's vocabulary have raised doubts about the purity of his West Saxon; and to avoid these doubts there has been a tendency to rely chiefly on the prose works for which Alfred's authorship is generally accepted as the standard of pure West Saxon vocabulary. But if a poem has to be attributed to one or the other, 'West Saxon' in such a narrow sense is at a disadvantage compared with 'Anglian' in the vague sense, because differences from standard West Saxon will be relatively clear and certain.

A new difficulty appears when the definition of dialects by texts is carried through—if, for instance, 'West Saxon' is defined as the language of Alfred and Ælfric, and 'Mercian' as the language of the Vespasian Psalter and Royal Glosses, which correspond roughly in dates. In its regular characteristics the dialect of Alfred's prose was probably that of the districts around Winchester the capital and Wilton a principal residence of the kings of his line. The regularity and widespread literary use of Ælfric's dialect is easiest explained if it was the language of Æthelwold's school—again at Winchester.[1] Similarly both the Vespasian Psalter and Royal Glosses[2] seem to represent the dialect of the district around Worcester. So large parts of the South and Midlands are not covered by these specimens of the late ninth and tenth centuries. For the period to which the earlier poetry is commonly assigned

[1] See below, p. 153.

[2] For non-linguistic evidence that MS. Royal 2 A xx was a Worcester book, see I. Atkins and N. R. Ker *Catalogus Librorum MSS. Bibliothecae Wigorniensis*, 1944, pp. 18, 67.

—the seventh, eighth, and early ninth centuries[1]—hardly any consecutive prose survives.

Nor is it safe to treat the few surviving specimens of local dialects as true samples for larger areas and earlier centuries. The work of historians and archaeologists does not suggest that the Anglo-Saxon invaders settled and remained in big homogeneous blocks, segregated according to their Continental homes, so that original differences of dialect would persist and new features develop uniformly. There are many indications of irregular conquest and subsequent advances or recessions as one Anglo-Saxon leader or group came into conflict with others. In the later period, when evidence is fuller, one century is enough to produce considerable differences between the standard West Saxon of Alfred and of Ælfric. We find Mercian influence at Canterbury, where the Mercian gloss seems to have been copied into the Vespasian Psalter; and West Saxon influence at Worcester, where the Royal Glosses, in the texts used and the script as well as the language, are an old-fashioned survival; contemporary Worcester charters leave no doubt that West Saxon had become the official language at Worcester by the end of the tenth century. In earlier times, when evidence is scarce, conditions were certainly simpler in one respect only—that dialect differences were less well marked—and this makes it harder to determine the original dialect of early poems.

So much preamble may help to explain why the question of origin is difficult, and why it is often reduced to the crude alternatives: Anglian or West Saxon? If the issue could be so simplified, there is a fair chance of getting a right or at least a defensible answer even if the methods used are faulty. But it is to the quality of the arguments, rather than to particular results, that I wish to call attention.

It is important to distinguish words and forms that could arise in the course of transmission from century to century, or from dialect to dialect, from those that are structural in the verse, i.e. necessary to the metre. Most of the poetry is preserved in single

[1] The eighth century is favoured by most critics, and the ninth tends to be a blank. By 'earlier poetry' I mean poetry generally thought to be of the period specified above.

manuscripts of the late tenth or early eleventh century, and in a language that is predominantly West Saxon in forms, though it differs in many details from the standard Late West Saxon of Ælfric's prose. Then any reliance on words or forms that are not confirmed by the metre will tilt the balance against West Saxon origin. For all such forms that are regular in West Saxon are naturally accounted for by the transmission. Yet those that are irregular are often treated as evidence that Anglian originals have been incompletely transposed into West Saxon. This assumes that the history of the earlier poetry is simply one of composition in Anglian with a one-way transmission ending in the Late West Saxon manuscripts: which is really the thing to be proved.

It is true that any Anglian poem that survives in a late Anglo-Saxon manuscript has passed into West Saxon. Yet whenever a few facts are known, they do not suggest that transmission was simple. The *Dream of the Rood* appears first in extracts on the eighth-century Ruthwell Cross in Dumfriesshire. A complete text, West-Saxonized and probably expanded from the original poem, is preserved in the late-tenth-century manuscript at Vercelli. There are echoes in the couplet inscribed on an Anglo-Saxon reliquary of the eleventh century now at Brussels.[1] The history that links these three survivals must be one of movement and change that stretches the imagination. And there are no historical reasons why poems composed in the South should not pass to the North and Midlands, assume an Anglian dress or colouring there, and return to the South. The Northumbrian version of the Mailcoat Riddle is found in a ninth-century manuscript at Leyden, together with Latin riddles by Aldhelm, who wrote its Latin original. This would be good evidence that Latin texts composed in the South came into Northumbrian hands in early times, even if Aldhelm's dedicatory letter to the Northumbrian King Aldfrith ('Acircius') were not extant.[2] Had Aldhelm himself made the English translation it might travel the same way; and there is nothing in the

[1] First printed by H. Logeman *L'Inscription anglo-saxonne du Reliquaire de la Vraie Croix*, &c., Brussels 1891.

[2] *Aldhelmi Opera* (*Mon. Germ. Hist.*), ed. R. Ehwald, Berlin 1919, p. 61.

Northumbrian version to prove that it was not transposed from West Saxon. The Mailcoat Riddle, wherever it was translated, is an example of literary or learned communication. But in an age when recited verse was one of the few means of popular instruction and amusement, and when travelling entertainers carried verse to all classes of society, the chances are not great that poems, whether secular or religious, would remain localized for long periods or would move uniformly southwards. Obviously oral transmission at any point in the chain would eliminate non-structural forms of the original, unless the reciter spoke the local dialect in which it was composed.

It is desirable then to confine attention to words and forms that are confirmed by the metre. The doubt will remain whether a poem preserved in one late manuscript has been interpolated or partly recomposed in a dialect different from that of the original; or whether the original itself contained things imitated from other dialects. But an inquiry that begins by accepting as original what is structural in the verse will not be overburdened with evidence.

The most important structural test that has been proposed concerns forms of the present indicative, which are so common that they are pretty certain to occur in any longer poem. It was formulated by Sievers in a classic study:[1] poems that have only uncontracted forms of the 2nd and 3rd person singular present indicative such as *bindest*, *bindeð*, are of Anglian origin, and poems that show some short forms such as *binst*, *bint*, are Saxon, or Kentish. In fact, the Anglian prose texts from the late ninth and the tenth century have uncontracted forms; the standard West Saxon of Alfred at the end of the ninth century normally has the short forms, which are regular in Ælfric a century later; the poems thought to be early have long forms with insignificant exceptions; and several poems from the South that are known to be later, e.g. Alfred's verse epilogue to the *Pastoral Care*, the verse *Metres* of Boethius, *Menology*, and *Seasons of Fasting*, have some short forms.

Yet there are wide gaps in the argument. Evidence is wanting that the short forms were characteristic of West Saxon in earlier times, say in the eighth century. Even in Alfred's day it is not

[1] Paul und Braune's *Beiträge* x (1885), p. 464 ff.

clear that they were used all over the South—in Devon, for instance, or Surrey or Middlesex. Æthelwulf's charter of 847, which Sweet classes as Saxon,[1] has only long forms; so have the Surrey charter (871–89), and the Kentish charters of Oswulf (805–10) and Abba (833–39). These are perhaps the best witnesses for the South before Alfred's reign, and though the number of examples is small, their consensus carries weight. Many Southern prose texts also show a significant number of long forms.[2] Then again, the long forms may have been a feature of the old poetic diction, and the appearance of short forms in some late pieces may be part of the breakdown in the traditional verse technique of which there is other evidence. Sievers, who seems never to have regarded the test he proposed as decisive,[3] in his latest work is said to have preferred the view that the uncontracted forms belong properly to slow, dignified speech. This has been questioned.[4] But there is clear evidence that these forms were associated in the South with the language of verse. In the verse *Metres* of Boethius there are more long than short forms, and those who doubt Alfred's authorship[5] usually agree that this paraphrase comes from the South, and is based on a prose version containing only short forms. The evidence of Alfred's verse epilogue to the *Pastoral Care* in the contemporary manuscript Hatton 20 (H) is more precise. Here, as Sievers noted, the short form 469/7 *werð* is required by the metre: the prose text has contracted *wierð*, *wirð*, *wyrð* in some sixty-six

[1] *Oldest English Texts*, p. 433 f. The other three are at pp. 451, 443, 447. An instance of *limpð* occurs in Æthelberht's charter dated 858, p. 438/25.

[2] J. Hedberg *The Syncope of the Old English Present Endings*, Lund 1945, aims at collecting all the examples from printed texts, but does not undertake the critical study of each text that is needed to show the significance of this great body of materials.

[3] In the article cited, p. 473 and note, he attributed *Exodus* to Kent though it has only uncontracted forms: 282 (bis), 540 (restored), 543, 544, 555.

[4] A number of long forms in Ine's Laws (MS. CCCC 173, *circa* 925, from Winchester) may be archaisms. Alfred's formal *Ælfred kyning hateð gretan* has often been noted, and a good late example is Dunstan's letter of 980–8: *þis gewrit sendeþ se arcebisceop* (Napier and Stevenson *Crawford Charters*, p. 18).

[5] On this question see Note D at p. 293.

places and only once 255/5 *weorðeð* (H and C).[1] But the epilogue contains two other examples, 469/4 and 469/6 *tofloweð*, both required by the metre. In the whole prose text H and C (where it is available) have only short forms, four of *toflewð*, three of the parallel *grewð*. So although Alfred admitted the short forms, normal in his prose, when they were metrically convenient, he associated the long forms with verse and did not use them to vary the rhythms of prose.

All the evidence is consistent with the view that the uncontracted endings were general Old English in early centuries, and were regarded as appropriate to verse, at least till the end of the tenth century, by writers for whom the short forms were normal in prose. It is possible that the short forms, which most philologists[2] explain as by-forms derived from the inverted *bindis þu*, *bindið he*, had become generalized by the late ninth century in the spoken language of the districts around Winchester; that the rapid development of prose under Alfred established them as the standard literary prose forms in the South; and that they were extended to verse by prose-writers like Alfred and other late composers of prosaic verse.[3] But it is unnecessary for the present purpose to

[1] Cosijn *Altwestsächsische Grammatik* ii, p. 149. Long forms usually have the unmutated vowel, restored by analogy.

[2] Since A. Walde *Die germanischen Auslautgesetze*, Halle 1900, p. 125 n.

[3] The occurrence of short forms beside the long as a test of Southern origin does not concern the earlier poetry, because all poems containing a significant number of short forms are known to be of Alfred's time or later. Generally there are grounds other than linguistic for associating them with the South, though Jordan *Eigentümlichkeiten*, p. 67 n., inclines to Imelmann's view that the *Menology* is of Anglian origin. The particular case is unconvincing, but it brings to mind a possibility that deserves attention. In the tenth and eleventh centuries West Saxon had a position as the literary and official language of England which no dialect had previously attained (see above, p. 94 f.). A good deal of work has been done on borrowing in this period from Anglian into West Saxon, which is to be expected. But borrowing by Anglians from West Saxon, which was almost inevitable, has not been much considered; and it is important, at least theoretically, when the distribution of words in Middle English is used as evidence for Old English, or when the preference in Modern English for West Saxon words, rather than the Anglian prose alternatives, has to be explained (see Jordan, op. cit. p. 108 ff.). It should be considered before the presence of West Saxon words or forms in the structure of late verse is treated as decisive against Anglian authorship.

establish this last hypothesis. The considerations that have been mentioned are enough to show that the consistent use of long forms in a poem presumed to be early, say before 850, is not good evidence of Anglian origin. No other test from inflexion or phonology is so widely applicable or so much respected.

On the usefulness of vocabulary for determining the dialectal origin of early verse there is some difference of opinion. Jordan, whose *Eigentümlichkeiten des anglischen Wortschatzes* is distinguished by its strict method, uses the poetry only when it supports the evidence from prose.[1] On the other hand, the late Professor Menner, who faced the difficulties with characteristic fair-mindedness, concluded that vocabulary supplies 'striking testimony to the provenience of a [poetical] text'.[2] The chief difficulty lies in the artificial, often archaic vocabulary of Anglo-Saxon alliterative poems, whatever may be the period or dialect which produced them. The technique and style of the verse kept the poet hunting for synonyms or variant expressions, and encouraged the persistence of set phrases. Hence many poetic words are not found in prose at all, and many compounds are hardly conceivable except in poetic diction. If then some words of an early poem occur in the prose of one dialect only, it cannot safely be argued that the poem was composed in that dialect. For words that were once general Old English may survive into the comparatively late prose period in one local dialect after they have become obsolete in others. Or again, a local dialect may adopt for use in elevated prose words that belonged only to the poetic dialect in earlier centuries. Two examples will make the problem more concrete:—

Mēce 'sword' is notable foı its phonology. From the cognates Gothic *mēki*, Old Norse *mǽkir*, Old Saxon *māki*, it should be standard West Saxon *mǣce*, but in Southern manuscripts of the later tenth and the eleventh centuries it is regularly spelt *mēce*, which is the form to be expected in Kent and a large part of the Anglian area. It appears mostly in poems in which there is a good deal of fighting, for instance *Beowulf*, *Waldere*, *Exodus*, but not in

[1] See his Introduction, p. 3.

[2] 'The Vocabulary of the Old English Poems on Judgment Day', *P.M.L.A.* lxii (1947), p. 588.

Genesis, the Riddles, or the signed poems of Cynewulf. It is not always required by the alliteration; it makes the second half of poetic compounds like *beadumece*; and it occurs in a fair variety of half-lines, with one stock phrase *meces ecgum* (cf. *Heliand* 2807, 4877), and one recurring pattern *bradne* (*scirne*, *scearpne*) *mece*. There is no indication that, like the adjective *weird* in modern English, it spread from one famous passage. Most West Saxon scribes of the later period seem to have known the word,[1] but only in the non-West-Saxon form; that is to say, as a borrowing from a dialect other than standard West Saxon. This has been treated as evidence that the poetic vocabulary, and consequently the earlier poetry, was Anglian.

But there are complications. *Mece* is used in several late poems connected with the South: in the *Metres* of Boethius, *Brunanburh*, *Maldon*, and last in Layamon's *Brut*. Again, the Anglian prose evidence for it is slight. It renders *mucro* once in the Corpus Glossary (*circa* 800), a composite word-list which has Mercian elements. It renders *machaera* in the influential Vespasian Psalter (lvi. 5), whence it passes unchanged into the West-Saxonized copies Junius 27 (Winchester *circa* 925) and Cambridge University Ff. I. 23 (before 1050); and from the Junius tradition it was transferred by a corrector to another Winchester Psalter, Vitellius E XVIII, about the middle of the eleventh century. But *mece* also occurs several times in eleventh-century glosses to Aldhelm;[2] and once in the early-twelfth-century Eadwine Psalter xvi. 13 *frameam* = (*sword*) vel *meche*.[3] Even if it is coincidence that the Corpus Glossary, the Vespasian Psalter, the Eadwine Psalter were all Canterbury books, and that the Aldhelm glosses bear the marks of a Kentish ancestry,[4] we have here an illustration of the impor-

[1] The Winchester scribe who copied *Brunanburh* into the Parker Chronicle has *mecum* 24, but *mæcan gemanan* 40, a bungling of the difficult phrase *mec(e)a gemanan* B, C; D reads *mecga* in this phrase but *mecum* 24.

[2] See Napier *Old English Glosses*, 1900. *Mece* renders *machaera*, *framea*, *romphea*, once in the phrase *mid awendenlicum mece* (Digby gloss 1151).

[3] There is no means of telling whether this particular rendering is a recent addition to the complex gloss, which in parts may go back to the ninth-century period of Mercian influence at Canterbury. The spelling is late, and a thorough contemporary corrector allowed the word to stand here.

[4] For the relations of the extant MSS. see Napier, op. cit. p. xxiv f.

tance of Canterbury in the transmission of certain texts. There is one more vagary in the record of this word: *mecefisc* is used to render *mugil(is)* 'mullet' in Ælfric's *Grammar* and its appended list of the names of well-known fishes.[1] Yet this book may be taken to represent what was taught in Æthelwold's school at Winchester, the stronghold of West Saxon; and the mullet, which is more common in the South, is not likely to have a name borrowed from the North or Midlands.

In sum: *Mece* is an old word in Germanic poetry which survives very late in Southern England. All the prose examples belong to the artificial and often unpredictable language of glosses to hard words. West Saxons seem to have known it in the tenth and eleventh centuries, and even used it in the name of a fish; but they wrote it regularly in the exceptional, presumably borrowed form *mece*, which is Kentish as well as Anglian. The occurrence of *mece* is not evidence for the Anglian origin of particular poems; and it should be noted that evidence of this rare kind could never be used to establish West Saxon origin: if any word were borrowed into the general vocabulary of Old English poetry in a specifically West Saxon form, there would be no way of detecting it in the late manuscripts.

The second specimen word is *leoran* 'to go', hence 'die', with its compounds *be-*, *forð-*, *ge-*, *ofer-*, *þurh-leoran*, and derivatives like *geleor(ed)nes*. Jordan, who assembles prose examples,[2] calls it the most important distinguishing mark of the Anglian vocabulary. The occurrences of very distinctive words are generally too few to give a just idea of the boundaries within which they were current, and there is no reason to think that the natural use of many words stopped short at political boundaries. But the evidence for *leoran* is full. It is common in the Northumbrian Gospels (Lindisfarne,

[1] Ed. J. Zupitza, Berlin 1880, pp. 39/1, 308/5. One MS. J(ulius A II) has the spelling *mæce*, but though it was copied rather before than after 1050 it has irregular spellings elsewhere, e.g. 155/10 *mælce* for the verb *melce*: so it is not good evidence for the true West Saxon form. For the compound Bosworth–Toller compares *garfish*, which is not really apt: the grey mullet could be likened to a sword; the garfish has a *gar* on its snout.

[2] Op. cit. p. 44 ff.

Rushworth), and *Durham Ritual*; in the Mercian Rushworth Matthew and the Vespasian Psalter; common, too, in the early prose texts that preserve Mercian features—*Martyrology*, Old English Bede, *Gregory's Dialogues*; and it survives in the Blickling and Vercelli Homilies. On the other hand, it is replaced by *feran*, *wendan*, &c., in some West Saxon copies of the *Martyrology*, Bede, and *Dialogues*, and in others it is confused with *leornian* 'to learn' often enough to show that some scribes of the tenth or early eleventh century did not understand it.[1] There is no example in Alfred. The apparent instances in Ælfric distinguish pieces that are not by him.[2] A few in the West Saxon Gospels (Matt. i) probably derive from a gloss. A better-attested Anglian and non-West-Saxon word could hardly be expected.

Yet this outstanding Anglian word, whose meanings 'go (away)', 'die', made it usable whatever the subject-matter might be, is rare in verse. In poems that can be reckoned fairly early it occurs twice in *Andreas*: *lungre leorde* (*leordan*), once in *Guthlac A* 726 *oferleordun*; otherwise twice in a *Prayer* in the Exeter Book and once in the late Southern *Menology* 208 *geleorde*: this last is the only place where it is not held by alliteration.[3] The inference to be drawn is not that *Beowulf*, *Genesis*, the signed poems of Cynewulf, and the rest are non-Anglian, but that vocabulary is a tricky guide to the original dialect of verse.

The late Professor Menner suggested a method which seemed to him to meet objections. Referring to the review quoted at the beginning of this paper, he wrote:

> According to Sisam, *Solomon and Saturn* II, for instance, if of Early West Saxon composition, might possibly have preserved Common Old English words or meanings, used in early but lost Saxon poetry, which have died out in West Saxon, but not in Anglian prose. That is, *gēna* 'yet', 241; (*eormen*)*strynd* '(mighty) race', 322; *þecele* 'torch', 410;

[1] For Bede see Miller's edition (E.E.T.S. 1890), p. xlix f. In MS. Otho C I of the *Dialogues*, ed. Hecht (Leipzig 1900), the confusion appears, e.g. at 136/5, 138/29.

[2] *Lives of Saints*, ed. Skeat ii (1900), xxiii B. 752, 761, 804; xxxiii. 285. On xxiii see Jordan, p. 45 n.; on xxxiii see below, p. 185, n. 1.

[3] *Geleorene* rhyming with *forweorone* in *Ruin* 7 is taken to represent a related strong verb: Sievers Grammar § 384, n. 3.

gewesan 'converse', 'debate', 172—recorded in Anglian but not in West Saxon prose—might have been part of a common poetic vocabulary cultivated in the South as well as in Anglia in early times. This contingency seems highly unlikely in itself. But, if it were true, we should then certainly expect that some words which became restricted to West Saxon prose (as opposed to Anglian) would be found in the poem, just as we have in admittedly Anglian poems, words which became restricted to Anglian prose (as opposed to West Saxon). Such words, with one doubtful exception, *clūd* 'rock' 185, we do not find.[1]

Since he used 'West Saxon' in the strict sense, excluding texts that are not pure, 'Anglian prose' should be similarly defined. Then several words in *Salomon and Saturn II* that are (I believe) lacking in Anglian prose are found in Alfred's West Saxon prose, e.g. *gielpen* 'boastful', *leoftæl* 'well-liked', *getigan* 'to tie', *weorðgeorn* 'desiring honour'; indeed, Bosworth–Toller records *gielpen* only from the poem and from four places in Alfred's *Pastoral Care*. These words are not put forward as evidence that the poem is a West Saxon composition. They can be disposed of by good arguments. But arguments as good can be turned against the words used to show its Anglian origin. To take one as a sample:—From the parallel passages cited above, p. 31 ff., and the Old Saxon lines corresponding to the end of *Genesis B*, it appears that the alliterating sounds are fairly stable; they are usually preserved even though the wording is altered in transmission. Of the four words mentioned by Professor Menner, only the very rare *gewesan* (*ymb*) lit. 'be together', is held by the alliteration; and the evidence is insufficient to show that it is Anglian.[2] The other three are not

[1] 'The Vocabulary of the Old English Poems on Judgment Day', *P.M.L.A.* lxii (1947), p. 585 f.

[2] On *gewesan* see Jordan, p. 56. The details are worth examining as an example of the kindness shown to Anglian claims. The verb *gewesan* is recorded in English only at *Salomon and Saturn* 172, where the collocation with *geflitan* indicates the meaning 'to dispute' (not necessarily 'to quarrel'). This is the text whose provenance is to be determined:—

(*a*) In the Late Northumbrian gloss to the *Durham Ritual* an unexplained *giwosa* thrice glosses *conversatio*; but grammar, meaning, and the occurrence of simple *wosa* twice to render the same word, make the relation with *gewesan* 'to dispute' uncertain; the parallel with *to-wesnis* translating *di-vortium* is worth noting, and all these compounds of *wesan* may be translator's compounds.

structural in the verse, and so might be substituted if a poem composed in standard West Saxon were adapted to Anglian use, and if none of them belonged to the traditional language of poetry.

In the present state of the investigation, vocabulary remains unsatisfactory or inconclusive as evidence of the original dialect of poems presumed to be early; and too many favourable hypotheses are used to produce the result that all the earlier poetry is Anglian. No doubt some of it is, if only because more than half the country and perhaps more than half of the population were under Anglian rule for most of the early period. Still, it is safer to work with no prepossession against West Saxon or Kentish origin. Where there is enough decisive evidence, a prepossession is soon corrected.

(*b*) In Miller's edition of the OE. Bede 274/5 *gewesnis ond unsibb* translates *dissensio*, and *gewesnis* is not otherwise recorded. The argument from this seems to be: 'The O.E. Bede, though attributed to Alfred in early times, bears marks of Mercian origin; so *gewesnis* implies that *gewesan* "to dispute" was used in Anglian, *and it was not used in West Saxon*.' The unsupported tail of this argument is its effective part. But was *gewesnis* used by the translator? The relationship of the MSS. of the OE. Bede needs more study in detail, but broadly: T (a good MS.) and B (sophisticated, but not derived from T) form one branch of the tradition against C, O (not derived from C), and Ca (essentially derived from O). At 274/5 *gewesnis* is the reading of T only: B, C (in Nowell's transcript B.M. Addit. 43703), O, and Ca have spellings of *towesnis* which in the sense *dissensio* 'quarrel' is a natural development from unrecorded *to-wesan* 'to be divided'. But *dissensio* is translated again at 300/3 where T, C, O, Ca read, effectively, *towesnis ond unsibb*: T has *towestnis* altered from *towæstnis*, and B, which often smooths out difficulties, omits the word, so that it was probably disguised in the common source of T, B. From this evidence, the natural inference is that the translator rendered *dissensio* by *towesnis ond unsibb* in both places, and that *gewesnis* in T is a variation introduced at some place indeterminable: purely graphic confusion of *to-*: *ge-* is possible. In that case, so far from *gewesan* 'to dispute' being an Anglian peculiarity, evidence is needed that it was used in Anglian.

There are no late OE. examples of *towesnis*, which seems to have gone out of use early in the tenth century; but its distribution does not suggest that it was limited to any one dialect. Besides the examples from the OE. Bede, Bosworth–Toller records four in the sense 'quarrel' from Alfred's *Pastoral Care*, the standard of Early West Saxon. Among glosses to Bede, thought to be Kentish, it renders *divortium* (Sweet *O.E.T.* 181/41); and among glosses from the West Country (?) MS. Harley 3376 which have a dialectal element, it renders *dissolutio* (Wright–Wülker *Vocabularies* i. 224/11). All these uses develop naturally from **to-wesan*.

But where, as in this case, much depends on the selection and interpretation of tangled or fragmentary evidence, a bias at the outset is likely to influence the result. The example of the series of investigations which gave Cynewulf most of the early poetry is comparatively recent.

It may be said that what I have called a prepossession is a reasonable presumption; that the background of history makes decisive for Anglian linguistic symptoms which are inconclusive when taken by themselves. A short survey of non-linguistic considerations may therefore be useful.

From the beginning of the study of Anglo-Saxon poetry, Northumbria has always been favoured. Her early eminence in Latin learning and the arts, the advantage of Bede's historical record, above all the story of Cædmon, gave Northumbria the first claim to the early poetry. On a simplified view, catastrophic Danish invasions made the ninth century a blank in literary production. As the attributions to Cædmon broke down under closer examination, the vagueness of these considerations became generally admitted. Critics still feel the fascination of Bede's Northumbria as a setting for poetry, but the pieces for which there is specific evidence are very few, though they are historically precious. Two short poems that were certainly composed in Northumbria are preserved by quotation in Latin texts: Cædmon's *Hymn* and the verses Bede made on his death-bed. The inscriptions on the Franks Casket are probably of Northumbrian origin.[1] The inscriptions on the Ruthwell Cross make it reasonable to claim the *Dream of the Rood* for Northumbria: not the whole text that appears centuries

[1] See Napier in *An English Miscellany presented to Dr. Furnivall*, 1901, p. 379 ff., who shows that the forms are Anglian and regards the loss of inflexional *-n* in *sefu(n)* as decisive for Northumbrian. This test is properly used where we have the original. As a curiosity, I note Sweet's remark on the Hatton MS. of the *Pastoral Care* in the Introduction to his edition, p. xxxii: 'Dropping of final—generally inflectional—*n* is very frequent in H. The *n* is frequently added above the line, but often the correction is neglected, especially towards the end of the MS. It is the *n* of the infinitive, weak adj. inflection and subjunctive that most frequently suffers this apocope.' Yet the author was Alfred, the MS. was sent out from Winchester (see p. 142 below), and the handwriting tells against Northumbrian tendencies in the scribe.

later in the Vercelli Book, but the best of it, which is the best of Anglo-Saxon religious poetry. Of these pieces, which have been preserved by exceptional chances, only the *Dream of the Rood* survives in the West Saxon collections; and it is to be expected that Northumbrian poetry would suffer most losses in transmission, owing to the misfortunes that came on the Northern kingdom and the consequent weakening of contact with the South in the ninth and tenth centuries.

When the Mercian dialect was recognized[1] and studied, the difficulty of distinguishing West-Saxonized copies of Northumbrian from similar copies of Mercian poems became evident. The term 'Anglian' was conveniently used to cover both dialects, and though Northumbrian origins were favoured, Mercian was often admitted as a second string. But the historical claims of the Mercian kingdom are better than secondary. Even after Sir Frank Stenton's *Anglo-Saxon England*, their importance for literary history needs to be emphasized. Mercia was a formidable power in the critical period 650–850, coming into prominence under Penda and reaching its zenith under Offa, who seems to have had all the attributes of a great ruler except a contemporary historian. When he died in 796 he had attained an authority unequalled by any other English king before Athelstan. Outside his Midland kingdom he had the overlordship of Kent and Wessex and a powerful influence in Northumbria. He dealt firmly with Charlemagne; the Pope treated him with deference; his new archbishopric of Lichfield challenged Canterbury's leadership of the English Church; Alcuin praised his encouragement of learning.[2] The production of verse was favoured throughout the period of Mercian predominance because prose was not yet a serious competitor in vernacular literature.[3]

[1] In 1875 J. A. H. Murray suggested that the gloss to the Rushworth Gospel of Matthew was Mercian. By 1889, when Zupitza published the Royal Glosses, the characteristics of the dialect were established.

[2] *Mon. Germ. Hist. Epist. Karol. Aevi* ii, p. 107.

[3] A rich Mercian religious prose before Alfred is sometimes assumed without good evidence; cf. Menner, art. cit., p. 585. The poverty of the Mercian 'Register' which is incorporated into some texts of the *Chronicle* is notable. From Alfred's Prose Preface to his *Pastoral Care*, it appears that he knew no English versions of the classics of Church literature earlier than those he made or promoted. No doubt prose was used for

For transmission Mercia had the advantage over Northumbria of a central position, close political relations with Kent and Wessex, and—what was particularly important for written transmission—an area in the South and West Midlands which escaped the Danish attacks and linked Alfred's revival of education to the earlier English tradition.

No extant verse is proved to be Mercian by external evidence. But we are dealing with presumptions, and the two long poems on Guthlac, the hermit of Crowland in the Lincolnshire fens, are presumptively Mercian, probably from East Mercia like Felix's Latin *Life* (*circa* 740) on which they depend. Such compositions are signs of an active cult, and there is no evidence that Guthlac was popular outside Mercia before the late ninth century.[1] These poems, especially *Guthlac B*, are remarkably like the signed poems of Cynewulf in language and style. It may be inferred either that the Anglian dialect[2] of Cynewulf was Mercian, which fits the available data very well; or that in his time Northumbrian poetry and the poetry of Guthlac's country, cut off by the Humber and the fens, were uniform: in which case little is to be hoped for from stylistic and linguistic studies.

Mercian claims extend to secular poetry. Interest in a royal house can be as significant as interest in a local saint; and the episode of Offa's Continental namesake and ancestor, with a fragment of the Mercian royal genealogy, is loosely inserted in *Beowulf* in a way that is hard to account for unless it was a compliment to his great Mercian namesake. Those who believe that *Beowulf* is the work of one man, in the sense that one man made all its verses,

sermons and other necessary purposes; but the extant Mercian glossaries, and interlinear versions of psalters and Matthew's Gospel, are rather tools for education than prose literature.

[1] Guthlac, who died in 714, is not mentioned in Bede; in the York Poetical Calendar *circa* 800; in the Northern calendar of the late ninth century in MS. Digby 63; or in the metrical calendar of Athelstan's Psalter composed at Winchester *circa* 900. The language of the Anglo-Saxon prose version of Felix's *Life* shows signs of Mercian origin (Jordan, p. 11). In a classic article, *Anglia* x (1888), p. 131 ff., Napier proved that the prose life of the Lichfield saint Chad is also Mercian.

[2] For the rhyming passage in *Elene* as evidence of Anglian dialect, see above, p. 2.

should see in this episode an indication that the poem was composed in Mercia in the late eighth century. But it is a safer inference that Mercia had a share in the transmission of *Beowulf* and the moulding of it into its extant form.[1] Signs of Mercian transmission at a fairly late period have been noted in an earlier chapter.[2]

For the dialect of the Kentish kingdom there is very little evidence—some early charters, the *Glosses* from the end of the tenth century, a colouring in many texts that are predominantly West Saxon. Perhaps for that reason orthodox modern criticism allows Kent no part in the making of extant Anglo-Saxon verse: the so-called *Kentish Hymn* and *Kentish Psalm* are preserved with the *Kentish Glosses* in the St. Augustine's MS. Vespasian D VI, and may owe their dialectal colouring to that chance. Yet, historically, Kent should not be barren ground. In the seventh and eighth centuries the Kentish kingdom had a considerable though diminishing importance, and it maintained some coherence through the ninth century. Its population was perhaps not greatly less than that of Northumbria. It was the main gateway to the Continent from which Northumbria drew so much inspiration. In so far as learning favoured the writing of religious verse, Kent with the primacy of the English Church was always favourably placed. In so far as an unbroken tradition from the earliest centuries to the latest favoured the preservation of what was written, no Anglo-Saxon centre compared with Canterbury.

Even if religious verse is discounted as a secondary growth, Kent has a specific claim to consideration. Hengest was the ancestor of the Kentish kings, and in Bede's time Horsa's tomb was shown in Kent, so that the story of Hengest and Horsa, mentioned in

[1] Cf. Miss Whitelock's discussion, *The Audience of Beowulf*, 1951, p. 57 ff. Similar considerations apply to the less striking but still excrescent account of the Continental Offa in *Widsith* 37 ff. Sir Cyril Fox 'The Boundary Line of Cymru' (*Proc. Brit. Acad.* 1940), p. 21, has suggested that when Offa built Offa's Dyke against the Welsh he had in mind his namesake's fame as a marker of lasting boundaries. This is not fanciful. *Beowulf* contains plenty of evidence that heroic poetry was much occupied with examples to follow or avoid. The confused *Vitae Duorum Offarum*, written in the twelfth century at St. Albans in old Mercian territory, is evidence that parallels were drawn between the two Offas.

[2] See above, esp. p. 94 f.

Bede, Nennius, the Anglo-Saxon Chronicle, and the very late list of popular legends which Imelmann discovered,[1] has its natural origin there. No verse fragment of it survives; but some good authorities identify this royal ancestor with Hengest of the Finn story. Whether they are historically the same hardly matters, because there is no reason to think that poets of later centuries could distinguish two legendary heroes of that name. In the *Finnsburh Fragment* Hengest is in the background, but a special interest in him is clear in the expression:

And *Hengest sylf* hwearf him on laste.

Sympathy with his dilemma and gentleness towards his treaty-breaking are features of the Finn episode in *Beowulf*. There is a presumption that these stories, though not necessarily the extant forms of them, were told to his successors at the Kentish court, and were favoured (if secular stories found favour at all) in the many South-Eastern religious foundations that were associated with the families of the early kings of Kent.[2]

There remains the Saxon kingdom, with its stablest territories in the western and middle South. It too had influential rulers in early centuries: Ælle and Ceawlin are in Bede's list of overlords; Cædwalla and Ine were no petty kings. From the beginning of the ninth century the West Saxon kingdom was usually the strongest. It had learned men too—Aldhelm of Malmesbury, Bede's correspondent Daniel of Winchester, and Boniface, a Devon man, the greatest of Anglo-Saxon missionaries. After all, Aldhelm, not a Northumbrian, was the first Englishman to practise classical metres, and he is credibly reported to have been Alfred's favourite poet in the vernacular.[3] The correspondence of Boniface's circle, which is remarkable for the literary interests it reveals, preserves

[1] In MS. Vespasian D IV, f. 139*b*; see *Deutsche Literaturzeitung* xxx (1909), p. 999.

[2] See the first part of the text edited by Liebermann as *Die Heiligen Englands*, Hannover 1889, which is a unique record of the early ramifications of the royal family.

[3] By William of Malmesbury *Gesta Pontificum*, ed. Hamilton, p. 336: 'nativae quoque linguae non negligebat carmina; adeo ut, teste libro Elfredi, de quo superius dixi, nulla umquam aetate par ei fuerit quisquam.' The book referred to is Alfred's lost *Handbook*.

the earliest recorded couplet of secular verse.[1] Aldhelm, Boniface, and Tatwine, a Mercian from the Worcester district who became archbishop of Canterbury, are the three chief English writers of Latin verse riddles, so that it would be strange if all the English riddles are Anglian. Still, *Ruin* is the only surviving poem presumed to be early which has a specific claim to be West Saxon, if, as is most probable, it describes the ruins of Bath; and even here an Anglian poet visiting Somerset might be invoked.[2]

But there is a compelling reason why West Saxon claims to a share in the production of early verse should not be discounted as unlikely. For at least four generations their royal house showed a remarkable interest in English poetry, and gave it an honourable place in education. Alfred's mother Osburh, who came of Jutish, not of Anglian stock, offered a book of English poems to whichever of her sons could read it first.[3] As a boy, before he could read, Alfred listened day and night to English poetry.[3] Later he delighted to read English poems and learn them by heart.[4] His children, the future King Edward and Ælfthryth, were taught the psalms, English books, and above all English poetry;[5] and no doubt the schooling of promising young men[4] was similar. Edward's son Athelstan followed in the same tradition. *Nemo literatius rempublicam administravit* says William of Malmesbury. English and Latin panegyrics survive to show his interest in verse.[6]

At a critical period, the example of the royal house was an

[1] The *Saxonicum verbum* beginning *Oft daedlata*, ed. with bibliography in Dobbie *The Anglo-Saxon Minor Poems*, 1942, p. 57. The name of the monk who quoted it is still a puzzle: see W. Levison *England and the Continent in the Eighth Century*, p. 130 n.

[2] Miss C. A. Hotchner's *Wessex and Old English Poetry, with special consideration of* The Ruin, New York 1939, deserves mention. Miss Hotchner, a champion of Wessex, assembles many interesting facts and opinions bearing on dialect in the early poetry, but the arguments are uneven in quality.

[3] Asser, ch. 22–23.

[4] Op. cit., ch. 76.

[5] Op. cit., ch. 75.

[6] On the verses beginning *Carta dirige gressus* see W. H. Stevenson *E.H.R.* (1911), p. 482 ff. When Dunstan's detractors tried to deprive him of Athelstan's favour by reporting him *avitae gentilitatis vanissima didicisse carmina* (*Memorials of St. Dunstan*, p. 11), they meant heathen charms and incantations, not ancient poetry.

important factor, perhaps the decisive factor, in securing that so much early verse was handed on to the late tenth century. Alfred's praise of Aldhelm as the best English poet is evidence that some old West Saxon verse was known at the West Saxon court. According to William of Malmesbury, Alfred also explained in his *Handbook* that a *carmen triviale quod adhuc cantitatur* (perhaps a riddle) was composed by Aldhelm in order to attract people to his serious teaching.[1] It is of course possible that by some chance all West Saxon poetry was lost in the following century of West Saxon predominance; but that would be one more doubtful hypothesis necessary to maintain the Anglian origin of the older verse.

This survey does not support a presumption that the extant earlier poetry is Northumbrian or Anglian. Rather it suggests that while verse was the medium of vernacular literature, it was produced in all the Anglo-Saxon kingdoms. As we go farther back in time, the grammarian's conception of poetry, classified according to the local dialects spoken by its makers, becomes less useful and creates many difficulties. More attention should be given to the probability that there was a body of verse, anonymous and independent of local interest, which was the common stock for the entertainment or instruction of the English peoples. A poem, wherever composed, might win its way into the common stock. The native metre, based primarily on the alliteration of stressed syllables, carried well because in this essential the usage of seventh-century Northumbria and tenth-century Wessex was the same; but any local dialect forms that affected the verse-structure were a handicap to circulation. A poet might prefer to take his models from the common stock rather than from the less-known work of his own district. In this way poems could be produced that do not belong to any local dialect, but to a general Old English poetic dialect, artificial, archaic, and perhaps mixed in its vocabulary, conservative in inflexions that affect the verse-structure, and indifferent to non-structural irregularities, which were perhaps tolerated as part of the colouring of the language of verse.

[1] *Historia Pontificum*, ed. Hamilton, p. 336. From the same source William learnt how Aldhelm was related to the royal family, op. cit. p. 333.

Once produced, the prospects of any one poem surviving are very much a matter of chance. On the whole, the opportunities of transmission were most favourable for the survival of Southern poems into the late collections, and least favourable to Northumbrian. Because the requisites for making books were always limited, and were mostly at the disposal of the Church, religious verse had the advantage in transmission over secular stories. Most of them would not be written down at all if sound churchmen like Alcuin and Ælfric had their way; and the chances are small that any of them would be made into fine books, which have the best prospect of survival to modern times.

9

THE PUBLICATION OF ALFRED'S *PASTORAL CARE*

THE evidence on the publication of Alfred's version of Gregory's *Pastoralis* is exceptionally good; and the details are important because two manuscripts of his time are the prime sources for the study of Early West Saxon. These are Hatton 20, Sweet's[1] H, in the Bodleian, and Tiberius B XI, Sweet's C, which, apart from some charred fragments, is preserved in a transcript made by Junius when the manuscript had already been mutilated at the end. Both were prepared by the King's orders, yet they differ in many details of forms or spellings and in some readings of substance: thus in the famous Prose Preface H reads: 'ðone naman anne we lufodon ðætte we Cristne wæren, ond swiðe feawe ða ðeawas', where C has *hæfdon* for *lufodon*; and in ch. viii H reads: 'for hiera gitsunge hie doð him to leafe ðone cwide ðe Sanctus Paulus cwæð . . .' where C has *lade* 'excuse' for *leafe*. In the first of these H's reading *lufodon* may be a mechanical repetition of the preceding *lufodon*, which survived because it made passable sense. The second is clear evidence of intelligent revision before copies were sent to the bishops.

Nothing in Asser's *Life* suggests that Alfred wrote with his own hand. After hearing explanations from Plegmund, Asser, Grimbold, or John the Old Saxon,[2] he would presumably dictate his version piecemeal, at the times he could spare, to one or more scholarly amanuenses, who would give his words the written form they thought best. Here the first complication arises. It has been noticed that at the end of the book (after ch. 50) psalm numbers are usually given when the psalms are quoted, as if a different clerk

[1] Sweet prints both in his edition, E.E.T.S. 1871. K. Jost *Anglia* xxxvii (1913), p. 63 ff., has shown that Junius's transcript of C cannot be relied on in some details.

[2] Prose Preface, p. 6.

were responsible for that part.[1] Sweet, referring particularly to *e* for *ie*<*ea*, remarks that the end of the Hatton MS. is on the whole more archaic than the earlier part,[2] and *ē* for *ǣ* becomes frequent in the part where the psalms are numbered. At about the same place, *sua* as alternative to *swa* ceases to appear,[3] and *ðæra* as alternative to *ðara* becomes common. Such differences may be due to the first manuscript and not to the scribes of the Hatton manuscript.[4]

When the translation was complete, the problem of dissemination arose. If the original would serve for the King's own use—and we know from Asser § 88 that he was content to read in manuscripts that had no calligraphic elegance—perhaps a dozen more copies would be needed: up to ten for his bishops, if Dorchester and Hereford were included; a few more for favoured non-cathedral foundations like Shaftesbury, where his daughter was abbess, or for helpers like Grimbold and John. In the early days of his revival of letters it is unlikely that Alfred would have around him, or at any one place, enough trained scribes to deal promptly with this and other literary or administrative copying. So several copies of the text were made at his literary headquarters (probably Winchester) by scribes of whose linguistic background nothing is known. At this stage differences between copies could arise, and modification of the original forms and spellings is likely.

Some of these copies of the text were sent to other scriptoria for copying, in order to distribute and speed up the work. According to the Verse Preface, where the book itself speaks:

> 'King Alfred turned every word of me into English, and sent me to his copyists, south and north, instructing them to produce more of the same from the pattern-copy, so that he might send them to his bishops. . . .'

In alliterative verse 'send south and north' means 'send in all directions'; and possibly help was sought in such strong centres as

[1] S. Potter 'The Old English Pastoral Care' *Trans. Phil. Soc.* for 1947, p. 119 f.

[2] Introduction to his edition, p. xxx.

[3] Cosijn *Altwestsächsische Grammatik* i, p. 81.

[4] The problem of distinguishing hands other than the main hand in the text of Hatton 20 is still unsettled. After consulting Mr. Neil Ker, I am satisfied that what is said above will not be seriously affected by any demonstrable change of scribe in that MS.

Worcester under Wærferth and Canterbury under Plegmund. In this third group of copies there were further opportunities for confusion of forms and for colouring from dialects. They would be returned to headquarters with the pattern copies.

It is unlikely that all the copies made at headquarters were sent out as patterns. At least one would be useful for reference and for making others. Tiberius B XI seems to have been produced at headquarters and retained there. It was not prepared for sending out, because a blank is left at the beginning of the Prose Preface for the name and title of the person addressed. It was at headquarters while other copies were being distributed, for at the beginning of the Prose Preface it contained the note:

+ Plegmunde arcebiscepe is agifen his boc 7 Swiðulfe biscepe 7 Werferðe biscepe.[1]

'Archbishop Plegmund has been given his copy, and Bishop Swithulf [of Rochester], and Bishop Wærferth [of Worcester, who received the Hatton copy].'

More decisive palaeographical evidence will be noticed later.

When enough copies of the text were assembled at headquarters, the prose and verse prefaces, containing the King's personal message, were added there. As the Prose Preface was transcribed, the name and style of the person for whom the copy was intended were included at the beginning, e.g. in the Hatton manuscript: 'Ælfred kyning hateð gretan Wærferð biscep . . .'; and to avoid any confusion after this had been done, the destination was boldly marked on the first page:

+ ĐEOS BOC SCEAL TO WIOGORA CEASTRE

'This copy is to go to Worcester.'[2]

The evidence for this procedure is clear. The prefaces in the Hatton manuscript are on two added leaves conjoined; they are not

[1] Wanley, Catalogue, p. 217. The special status of Plegmund and Wærferth indicates that these were the first three copies sent out. Possibly Swithulf was senior to Wærferth, but his priority may have been due simply to the convenience of sending to Canterbury and Rochester together.

[2] It is uncertain whether the copies were bound before they were sent out; and it is not clear that the texts were checked at headquarters. Certainly Hatton 20 was not corrected by Tiberius B XI.

part of the gathering with which the contents and the text begin; and they are in hands[1] which do not appear in the contents and text. Again, Wanley tells us that in the headquarters copy Tiberius B XI the prefaces were in a hand different from that of the text,[2] so they were pretty certainly on added leaves.

The question of the hands is interesting. Wanley, who examined the Tiberius manuscript before it was burnt, and made facsimiles, both from it and from Hatton 20, which required careful study of the letter-forms, says that the Hatton prefaces are in a script very like (*proxime accedunt ad*) the text-hand of Tiberius B XI.[3] Mr. Neil Ker thinks that they are identical, relying not so much on direct comparison with the charred and shrunken fragments as on the identity between the hand of the Hatton Prose Preface and the Kassel Leaf of the *Pastoral Care*,[4] and on the probability that this Kassel fragment is one of the lost leaves from the end of Tiberius B XI. After examining the photographs of the Kassel Leaf which he kindly lent me, I accept his view. Even if we have to do with two scribes of identical training, it is reasonably certain that the text of Tiberius B XI was copied at headquarters, where the scribe or his 'twin' added the Prose Preface to Hatton 20.

But as the prefaces were also added to Tiberius B XI in a hand different from that of its main text, it is a fair inference that they were not both ready at headquarters when the text was first handed over for multiplication; in other words, that Alfred finished them while copies of the text were being prepared. The thrifty use of time is natural to a great administrator; and certainly he gave much time and reflection to the Prose Preface.[5] He may have worked on it with a special amanuensis, so that the Prose

[1] The hand of the Verse Preface has distinguishing characteristics. The Tiberius scribe, who wrote in the Prose Preface, was apparently a person of some importance whose time had to be used sparingly.

[2] Catalogue, p. 217: 'utraque præfatio, sicut in Cod. Werferthiano ab aliena manu scripta, Codici præmittitur.' Enough of the charred MS. remains to confirm this difference of hand.

[3] Catalogue, p. 71. For his facsimiles see Hickes's *Thesaurus, Gram. Anglo-Saxonica*, &c., pp. 3 and 78.

[4] The Kassel Leaf contains Sweet p. 385/20 *beæftan* to 387/7 *sumum*. It is printed by H. M. Flasdieck *Anglia* lxii (1938), p. 208 ff.

[5] See F. Klaeber *Anglia* xlvii (1923), p. 53 ff.

Preface would show forms and spellings differing from those of the main text.

In fact Cosijn noticed that the Tiberius Prose Preface contains forms that do not occur in the main text, and explained them by a change of scribe.[1] But if such forms were mainly due to the latest scribes, the Hatton Prose Preface should agree with the Tiberius text, since the same hand copied both. Generally they do not agree: thus, the Hatton Prose Preface has regularly (7 times) *liorn-* 'learn', which appears only 3 times in the Tiberius main text against 28 *leorn-*, and it has regular *giond* (6 times) which appears only once in the Tiberius main text. Again, when Sievers investigated *io* forms by noting the places where Tiberius and Hatton agree (so that they probably represent a common source), he found that relatively frequent *io* for etymological *eu*, as in *hioldon*, *ðioda*, *bebiode*, distinguished the common source of the Prose Preface from the common source of the main text.[2] The discrepancies are accounted for if the Prose Preface was dictated to an amanuensis who was not used, or not much used, for the main text.

I have noticed nothing distinctive in the language of the short Verse Preface, which follows the Prose Preface in the manuscripts. It is matched by a verse epilogue, and may have been intended originally as the only preface to appear in the book. Before the Prose Preface, Tiberius B XI (which is most likely to preserve traces of the first draft) and the Cambridge University manuscript have the heading, "Ðis is seo forespræc hu S(ancte) Gregorius ðas boc gedihte þe man Pastoralem nemnað'; 'This is the preface (telling) how St. Gregory composed this book which is called *Pastoralis*.' The heading does not answer at all to the Prose Preface, which has no mention of Gregory and merely names the *Pastoralis*. But it would serve as heading for the Verse Preface, which begins: 'This work Augustine brought from the South across the salt sea to (us) island-dwellers, as God's champion, the pope of Rome, had previously written it. The learned Gregory, in the wisdom of his heart, had considered many good doctrines, the treasure of his mind. So he who was the best of Romans, wisest of men, highest

[1] *Altwestsächsische Grammatik*, Pref. p. vi.

[2] *Zum angelsächsischen Vocalismus*, p. 42.

renowned for glorious deeds, won the greatest number of mankind for the Lord of heaven.'[1] It seems then that the Prose Preface was inserted, in Tiberius B XI or an earlier draft, between the Verse Preface and its heading. The alternative is that the heading belongs to Gregory's own preface and has been separated from it by successive insertions of the long table of contents and Alfred's Verse and Prose Prefaces. On either explanation it looks as if the inclusion in the book itself of Alfred's famous letter to his bishops was an afterthought, made possible by the interval necessary to produce enough copies of the text.

Thus the first issue of an Anglo-Saxon book, and even the original copy as it came from the author, may exhibit different usages of form or spelling in different parts. I cannot follow the investigation into the later manuscripts of the *Pastoral Care*, nor are they likely to throw much clear light on the forms and spellings of the earliest copies. Their importance lies in the substantial variants they may contain. MS. Otho B II, now fire-damaged, seems to have been a tenth-century descendant of the copy Alfred sent to Bishop Heahstan of London, whose name is in the Preface. Cambridge University Library MS. Ii.2.4, said to be of the mid-eleventh century, has the name of Bishop Wulfsige (of Sherborne) in the Preface. So both these are prima facie independent authorities for the text. Trinity College, Cambridge MS. 717 (R. 5. 22), copied rather later in the eleventh century, probably came from Salisbury.[2] It has no preface, and its affiliations are unsettled, though certainly it has been modernized in places. MS. CCCC 12, *circa* 1000, has no name in the Preface. It comes from Worcester, yet it is not copied from the original Worcester MS. Hatton 20.

[1] The translation of these clumsy verses is not free from doubt. *Ærendgewrit*, chosen to alliterate with *Agustinus*, means 'a writing carried by a messenger', here the 'work in Latin'. It is likely enough that Augustine brought a copy with him in 597, for Gregory gave his *Pastoralis*, written in 591, to other leaders of the Church; see Manitius *Geschichte der lat. Literatur des Mittelalters* i (1911), p. 104. For *ær fore*, in *swæ hit ær fore adihtode*, cf. Alfred's prose usage *ær beforan*, Orosius 12/30, &c.

[2] Wanley, Catalogue, p. 168, argues acutely that Bishop Jewell's letter to Archbishop Parker, expressing inability to identify the author or the work, cannot refer to Cambridge University MS. Ii.2.4 (in which it is now inserted), but would suit Trinity MS. 717, which lacks the preliminary matter.

Miss M. Ångström[1] has claimed that it derives from Tiberius B xi (C). Though 62/22 *geswenced* C and Corpus 12: *gescinded* Hatton and the rest,[2] is the only reading she cites that is clear evidence for the relation, it is supported by 52/8 *lade*: *leafe* already mentioned, where the manuscripts divide in the same way. In the Prose Preface Corpus 12 agrees with C in two good readings: 2/10 'þa ðeowutdomas þe hie Gode don sceoldon', where H and the Cambridge University manuscript omit *don*, and 4/7 *hæfdon*, where H and the Cambridge University manuscript read *lufodon*. Collation of the whole text of Corpus 12 is needed to establish that it is simply derived from C, of course with errors and unauthoritative variations of its own. If, as seems likely, the relationship is the same throughout, Corpus 12 has special authority for the latter part of the text, which was missing from C when Junius transcribed it before it was burnt. For the part that Junius transcribed, Corpus 12 should serve as a check: thus at 114/3 Junius has *tælwierðe* 'blameworthy', H correctly *stælwierðe* 'serviceable'; and at 158/19 Junius has *on hiera scyldrum* 'on their shoulders', H correctly *on hiera scyldum* 'in their sins': in both places Corpus 12 agrees with H, indicating that C also agreed and that Junius slipped in transcribing it.

Though most of the literary prose texts survive in more than one manuscript, for practical reasons (the difficulty of the task, the advantage of quick publication, an excessive preoccupation with phonology) the conception of a critical text, formed by weighing the authority and merit of the variants, is a refinement that has seldom touched Anglo-Saxon studies.[3] But if a future editor should aim at getting as near as possible to the wording Alfred sent to be multiplied, he would do well to prefer the charred fragments of Tiberius B xi, the Kassel Leaf, Junius's transcript, and Corpus 12,

[1] *Studies in Old English Manuscripts*, &c., Uppsala 1937, p. 37 f.

[2] Professor Simeon Potter has kindly supplied me with the readings of the Cambridge MSS. in the samples quoted. The Prose Preface is printed from the Corpus and Cambridge University MSS. by F. P. Magoun Jr. *Mediaeval Studies* xi (1949), p. 113 ff.

[3] For Alfred's *Boethius*, cf. p. 294 n. below; for the OE. Bede, p. 130 n. above; for *Gregory's Dialogues*, p. 229 n. below; for Ælfric's *Catholic Homilies*, p. 165 ff. below.

which between them present a state of the text earlier than that in the Hatton manuscript and the other three. In this connexion one more reading deserves close consideration. At 198/22 C and Corpus 12 have: 'Gif him ðonne weas gebyrige oððe ungewealdes' 'If then he happens by mischance or unintentionally . . .': H and the rest read *wealdes* 'intentionally' for *weas*. Though it cannot be decisive where the paraphrase is free, the Latin original (si quando vero contra eos vel in minimis lingua labitur) favours *weas*, and so does the English context, since its trend is that to speak against one's lord in any circumstances is a grave matter. But apart from the exceptional status of Tiberius B XI, the rare word *weas* 'by chance' has the better claim to be original. Outside this passage it occurs many times, usually with *gebyrian*, in Alfred's prose paraphrase of *De Consolatione*, from which it passes twice into the verse Metres.[1] Otherwise it is recorded only once, from the Bede Glosses of Alfred's time, which are thought to be Kentish.[2] It seems to have been used in a limited circle, possibly under Kentish influences, and to have died out soon after Alfred's day. *Wealdes* in the Hatton tradition, which is suggested both by the form of *weas* and by the following *ungewealdes*, is naturally explained as a contemporary substitution made by somebody who either did not understand *weas* or thought it would be unintelligible to readers.

[1] On the authorship of the verse Metres see note D at p. 293 below.
[2] Sweet *Oldest English Texts* 181/54.

10

MSS. BODLEY 340 AND 342: ÆLFRIC'S *CATHOLIC HOMILIES*[1]

ONE can seldom look at an Anglo-Saxon manuscript without thinking gratefully of Humfrey Wanley.[2] His portrait hangs in the Manuscript Room of the British Museum by virtue of his work as Harley's librarian; but Bodley was his training-ground, and he might have been Bodley's librarian in succession to Hyde had he not failed, for all his learning, to take a degree. During his term as assistant in Bodley, he completed the index to Bernard's Catalogues, and laid the foundation of his own Catalogue, which opens with an unusually full description of our MSS. Bodley 340 and 342.

I should rank Wanley's Catalogue among the half-dozen satisfying books on Anglo-Saxon, and after two centuries and a quarter its usefulness is not lessened. Plan and execution are alike good; every accessible manuscript containing Old English words is described in detail; his search for material went far beyond the obvious sources; his eye was quick to light on the things that matter; and he combined with the natural aptitudes of a great palaeographer a sureness of method which has made it possible to reconstruct his reasoning from his short conclusions.[3] So when the revival of

[1] [From *The Review of English Studies* vii (1931), p. 7 ff.; viii (1932), p. 51 ff.; ix (1933), p. 1 ff.]

[2] [On Wanley, see p. 259 ff. below, to which a few footnotes have been transferred. I apologize for some overlapping.]

[3] The text of Asser's *Life of Alfred* depends on a single MS., once part of Otho A XII, which was entirely destroyed in the Cotton fire of 1731. The early descriptions of this MS. are vague and conflicting. Thomas James in 1600 says it is in at least two hands, of which that which is 'much the latest' still contains many Saxon letters. In 1639 Ussher, whose authority is deservedly high, says it is in Saxon characters of Asser's time, or not much later. Wise, in his edition of 1722, speaks of several hands, one of which he calls *recentior*; gives a bad specimen of the first hand which contains no Anglo-Saxon letter forms; and quotes Wanley's opinion that this first hand is to be dated 'about A.D. 1000 or 1001'. In his *Asser*, p. xlv, the late W. H. Stevenson, who knew and appreciated Wanley's

Anglo-Saxon studies came in the nineteenth century, scholars found the bulk of the manuscript materials collected, described, dated, and indexed by an expert. With Wanley's Catalogue as a guide, they could go straight to the particular materials they required, or send a copyist or photographer. This facility led to the rapid and efficient printing of the texts, and enabled scholars from abroad, who could not have found time to sift the mass of material scattered through the English collections, to share and even lead in the work of editing.

Yet efficiency has its drawbacks. It was not altogether desirable that workers should be relieved from foraging among manuscripts as Wanley himself had done; or that the technique and range of Old English studies should be so much influenced by the difficulties of foreign scholars whose time available for studying manuscripts in England is short, and whose curiosity about matters not directly in hand is necessarily limited. The leading scholars have set the best example,[1] and in principle the manuscripts have always been

methods, conjectured that he gave this precise date after comparison of the script with a Cotton charter of the year 1001 (Augustus II 22). Wanley's brief answer to Wise's questions, which is extant in a letter to Charlett (2 June 1721) in Ballard MS. 13, confirms this acute conjecture, and clears up all the difficulties:

'As to Mr. Wise's other quæres, he may please to know that his Cottonian Asser is not written by one hand, but by several, and much about the same time, according to the custom of writing books of old. The beginning is of the best and stanchest hand, and seems to have been written about A.D. 1000, in the English hand of that time, and not all in Saxon letters as misrepresented by Archbishop Parker, who printed from this very book; yet proper names (according to custom then very common) are written with Saxon letters when required, as with ð, þ, ƿ, etc. My authority for adjusting the age of that exemplar is an original charter of King Æþelred, dated A.D. 1001, which as to the hand, agreeth very well with the first part of the Asser, OTHO. A.12. I do not remember any MS. in Oxford exactly of that hand, yet I fancy some notion may be had of it, if Mr. Wise pleases to look upon those Canons in Bibl. Bodl. marked SUPRA. M.4. ART. 138.'

This last MS. is now called Bodley 865, and a reduced specimen of the hand may be seen in Napier's *Chrodegang* (E.E.T.S.) opposite p. 112, though only the last line is in the Latin script which Wanley had in mind.

[1] In recent years Professor Max Förster has given us admirable detailed descriptions of several complex MSS., such as the Vercelli Book (Introduction to the facsimile edition, Rome 1913); the Beowulf MS. (*Berichte*

regarded as the *fontes vivi*: still, in practice there has been a tendency to use them with economy, or to prefer more convenient sources. And now that the flow of new materials and ideas is drying up, there is something to be said for the pre-systematic way of turning over one manuscript after another, with no set purpose except to follow up anything of interest that may arise. At least, that must be my excuse for a rambling comment on a few selected points in these two manuscripts.

I

There is no need to describe the two volumes in detail, because their contents are listed fully in Wanley's Catalogue, pp. 1 ff.; and a description has appeared in a recent volume of the Bodleian Summary Catalogue.[1] It should be noted that:

MS. Bodley 340 = Wanley's N.E. F.4.10 = Summary Catalogue 2404;
MS. Bodley 342 = Wanley's N.E. F.4.11 = Summary Catalogue 2405.

Together they make a single homiliary, built up for the most part from Ælfric's *Catholic Homilies*; they are written in the same main hand; and they were kept together through careless centuries until 1761,[2] when they suffered a change of name and were separated by the unrelated MS. Bodley 341.

The Anglo-Saxon text falls into three parts:

(*a*) The main hand which runs through the original parts of both volumes (MS. 340, f. iv and ff. 1–169*a*, *Explicit Hic Liber*; MS. 342, ff. 1–202*b* top, *Explicit Hic Liber*) is a fine square English hand

über die Verhandlungen der Sächs. Acad. der Wissenschaften, vol. lxxi. 4); MS. Vespasian D XIV in *Englische Studien*, vol. liv; and MS. Tiberius A III in Herrig's *Archiv für das Studium der Neueren Sprachen*, vol. cxx.

[1] Vol. ii, p. 351 f. From Wanley's time it has been customary to describe MS. Bodley 342 first, because it begins with the rubric *Incipit Liber catholicorum sermonum anglice in anno primo*. In fact MS. Bodley 340 is the first, and MS. Bodley 342 the second volume of an annual cycle; but roòm was found for the first of Ælfric's two accounts of the Creation by placing it out of series at the beginning of the second volume (MS. 342). Its rubric has been carried over from the original issue of the *Catholic Homilies*, where it is the first sermon of the first volume. The true order is confirmed by comparison with MS. CCCC 198 (see below, § II).

[2] I owe this date to the kindness of Dr. Craster.

which, if normal conditions are assumed, would fall in the first quarter of the eleventh century.[1] The initials at the beginning of each volume, and one that has escaped colour-washing at f. 57*a* of MS. 342, show the laced designs, and animal heads with flat lower jaws and serrated crests, that are typical of the native style round about the year 1000.

(*b*) In MS. Bodley 342, folio 202 is followed by added leaves ff. 203–18, which I shall call the Supplement.[2] Of these, ff. 203–6*a* mid. are written with blacker ink in a good flowing script that need not be much later than the original hand.

Then at f. 206*b* top a new sermon begins in a weaker hand which would normally be dated about 1050. This hand runs to the end (f. 218*a* foot) of the Supplement, of which the last leaf is cut away down the middle from top to bottom.

(*c*) On 202*b*, immediately after the original *Explicit*, a large rough hand,[3] which is not easy to date, but may be placed round about the year 1100, has filled the blank space with the following:

Se halga papa Gregorius asende (hider on eard) þisne eadigan biscop Paulinum, þe we todæg weorðiað, Godes word to bodianne; and he swa dide unforhtlice swa lange, oð he gehwyrfde Eadwine, Norðhembra cyng, to cristendome, and ealne his þeodscipe; and þærr wearð ærcebiscop on Euerwic; and þær wunede þa hwile þe se cyng Eadwine leofode, and Norðhembram (*sic*) þæs cristendomes gyman woldon, þe se ærcebiscop Sanctus Paulinus heom bodade forðy þe se cyng Eadwine hæfde (Æþelburge) to cwene, Æþelbrihtes dohtor cynges. Þa gelamp hit þæt se cyng Eadwine wærð ofslegen, and se cristendom mid Norðhembrum acolade swiðor þanne hi beþorfton; and he geseah ða se halga

[1] An idea of it may be obtained from two reduced specimens which are used as illustrations in S. H. Gem's *An Anglo-Saxon Abbot*, 1912.

[2] The contents of this Supplement, which begins in the middle of a sermon as if some previous leaves were missing, are from Ælfric's *Catholic Homilies*, viz.:

f. 203*a* First Sunday in Lent (ed. Thorpe ii. 106, l. 15 ff.).
f. 204*b* Septuagesima Sunday (ed. Thorpe ii. 72).
f. 206*b* St. Andrew (ed. Thorpe i. 576).
f. 211*b* St. Andrew's Passion (ed. Thorpe i. 586).

Whether from carelessness or because the two volumes were temporarily separated, the person who added the first two items failed to notice that both are already in MS. Bodley 340 (f. 106*b*; f. 87*a*).

[3] It appears again on the margin of f. 139; and more than once in MS. Bodley 340.

ærcebiscop þæt he nare nota þær nytt beon ne mihte. Gewende þa *hider to Cent* he and seo cwen, Eadwines laf cynges; and he wearð þa mid myce(l)re arwyrnesse undorfangen fram þam cynge Eadbolde, Æþelbrihtes suna cynges. *Þa wæs þes stede biscopleas, and he ða Sanctus Paulinus be þæs cynges bene undorfeng þisne biscopstol, and her ?þa? þurhwunode oð his liues ende: wearð þa her bebyrged, 7 her gyt aligð and nis nan . . . .*[1]

The historical information about Paulinus has no special interest, and is derived from Bede.[2] But the Anglo-Saxon tract on the *Resting Places of the Saints* tells us: 'Đonne resteð Sanctus Paulinus on Rofeceastre';[3] and the italicized words in the passage above are clear evidence that the manuscript was at Rochester when they were written. This is confirmed by two early catalogues. At the end of *Textus Roffensis* is a catalogue[4] which has been printed in *Archæologia Cantiana*, vol. vi, and which mentions (p. 127) *Sermonalia anglica in duobus voluminibus*. The second catalogue of Rochester, made in the year 1202 by Alexander 'huius ecclesiæ quondam cantor', is in Royal MS. 5 B XII, and has been printed in *Archæologia Cantiana*, vol. iii: item 112 at p. 57 of the print is *Omeliaria anglica II*. We may be sure that both these entries refer to our manuscripts.[5] Until Sir Walter Cope (*d.* 1614) presented them to Bodley, I have not noticed any other record of the manuscripts.

Now a pre-Conquest manuscript from Rochester is a rare thing. It would be still more interesting if the whole manuscript were

[1] The writing is sometimes faint, and difficulty is increased by a deceptive later freshening of the ink, so that *Gregorius* has been altered to *Gregoryus*; for *þeodscipe* the surface reading is *beodscipe*; for *leofode* the freshened ink seems to give *leofdoe*; and I have guessed that *bæþorfton* represents an original *beþorfton*. Words and letters in round brackets are written above the line; and of these *Æþelburge* is certainly in another hand. At the bottom the text has been shorn away by the binder.

[2] *Historia Ecclesiastica*, Bk. II, especially c. xx. His day is 10 Oct.

[3] Edited by F. Liebermann *Die Heiligen Englands*, Hannover 1889, p. 15; cf. p. 1. A French version of this tract is printed in Gaimar's *Lestorie des Engles* (Rolls Series) i, p. xxxix.

[4] Not included in Hearne's edition of 1720; but Wanley, in the description of *Textus Roffensis* at p. 276 of his Catalogue, excerpts this and another Anglo-Saxon item.

[5] A table of contents for MS. 342, written in an early-thirteenth-century hand, is headed *Sermones anglici. A.*

demonstrably written at Rochester; but we must be content with the presumption that it was. All the evidence is consistent with that reasonable presumption, though there is none which excludes the possibility that the original part was written at some other centre, such as Canterbury, and transferred very early to Rochester. Indeed, there are two indications which might seem to favour this latter alternative, though both are illusory. First, Ælfric's sermon on St. Andrew, the patron saint of Rochester, appears in the later Supplement, not in the original homiliary. This is evidence that the selection of sermons was not made for Rochester, but tells in no way against the copying at Rochester of a recognized course of sermons such as this appears to be. Secondly, whereas the portions which were certainly or probably written at Rochester (the Supplement, especially ff. 206*b*–18; the account of Paulinus; and scattered glosses, e.g. *senfullum* for *syn-* in MS. 340 f. 37*a*, *grere* for *gryre* f. 38*a*) show well-marked Kentish features, the original homiliary is in fairly normal West Saxon. But apart from the consideration that Ælfric wrote his sermons in West Saxon, the early eleventh century was the period in which West Saxon was recognized all over England as the official and literary language. The York surveys of about 1030 supply a good instance in local documents from the North.[1] The prayers to St. Dunstan and St. Ælfheah in MS. Arundel 155 give an equally striking example from Kent, for though they were certainly copied at Christ Church, Canterbury, into an official service-book, and were presumably composed and Englished at Canterbury, yet they are normal West Saxon. Dialect does break through, the more frequently as the eleventh century advances; but good West Saxon may be written anywhere in its first half.

For textual purposes it will be convenient to give these two manuscripts the siglum R(ochester).

II

Ælfric issued his *Catholic Homilies* in two volumes, each of which provided a course of sermons for the principal occasions of the

[1] Edited W. H. Stevenson *English Historical Review*, January 1912, p. 15 ff.

Church year; and this is the arrangement which appears in the printed text.[1] But he expressly authorized a rearrangement which would make a single annual cycle out of the two volumes.[2] MSS. Bodley 340 and 342, which were written in Ælfric's lifetime, are perhaps the earliest example of such an alternative grouping; and as there are several Anglo-Saxon books that draw upon the *Catholic Homilies*, it is of some interest to see whether any of them is closely related to our manuscripts.

The order of contents is the best guide, though the risk of coincidence is considerable where the arrangement is that of the Church year. But our manuscripts are not simply a reshuffling of Ælfric's two volumes; several of his sermons are omitted, and the sermons for certain days (among them the greatest such as Christmas and Easter) are drawn from other sources. Thus, in Bodley 340, Wanley's items 20–27 (ff. 108*a*–52*a*) are an alien group. The same eight items in the same order appear in CCCC MS. 198 (Wanley's S.8), which is also mainly drawn from the *Catholic Homilies*; while no other manuscript contains more than three of them. This clue is proved right by a detailed comparison:

(*a*) Items 1–19 of Bodley 340 correspond with items 1–19 of CCCC 198 in Wanley's description,[3] except that item 8 of Bodley 340 beginning *Men ða leofostan, us manað* (which is not Ælfric's, but is found in the older Vercelli collection) is replaced in CCCC 198 by Ælfric's sermon for the same occasion beginning *Johannes se godspellere cwæð* (Thorpe, ii. 54).

(*b*) Items 20–27 of Bodley 340 are covered by items 20–23 and 26–29 in CCCC 198. In the latter manuscript items 24 (= Thorpe, ii. 110) and 25 (= Thorpe, ii. 224) are extra sermons for the Second and Fifth Sundays in Lent, which have each one sermon only in Bodley 340. They are in the same hand as the sermons noted

[1] Edited B. Thorpe, 2 vols., 1844–6.

[2] Latin Preface to vol. i, ed. Thorpe, p. 2: 'Duos libros in ista translatione facimus, persuadentes ut legatur unus per annum in ecclesia Dei, et alter anno sequenti, ut non fiat tedium auscultantibus; tamen damus licentiam, si alicui melius placet, ad unum librum ambos ordinare.'

[3] I have used Wanley's numbering of the items (Catalogue, p. 125 ff.), because it is simpler for comparison than that of M. R. James's Descriptive Catalogue of the CCCC MSS., p. 475.

under (*d*) below;[1] they occupy a self-contained quire of 10 leaves (against the normal 8); and are evidently an addition to the book, for they were not included in the original table of contents.

(*c*) Items 28–34 of Bodley 340 = items 30–36 of CCCC 198. Here Bodley 340 ends. Here ends, too, the original list of contents for CCCC 198, which, like that of Bodley 340, contains 31 heads.

(*d*) Items 1–9 of Bodley 342 are different from items 37–42 of CCCC 198, though all are by Ælfric. But this section of CCCC 198 is marked by three peculiarities: it is written in a different hand from the rest with 23 lines to the page against a normal 26 lines; it ends abruptly in the middle of a sentence; and it breaks the regular sequence of the Church year. It may be concluded that it is an intrusion upon the original volume, and that it takes the place of items 1–9 of Bodley 342, which preserve the order of the Church year.[2]

(*e*) Items 10–14 of Bodley 342 correspond with items 43–46[3] of CCCC 198. Item 15 (Thorpe, i. 338) is not in the Corpus MS. Items 16–21 of Bodley 342 are items 47–52 of CCCC 198.

Here the Corpus manuscript loses its orderly character and the correspondences cease; but up to f. 291*b* it is a copy, with displacements and modifications, of the series found in Bodley MSS. 340 and 342; and as it is known from glosses written in a characteristic shaky hand that CCCC MS. 198 was at Worcester in the twelfth century,[4] it appears that this particular selection of homilies had some circulation. For the purposes of textual work on Ælfric's

[1] [Mr. Neil Ker has re-examined the MS., and enabled me to correct a misstatement at this point in the original article. Its removal simplifies the argument.]

[2] Except Item 1, for which see note 1 on p. 150.

[3] By a slip Wanley assigns the same number XLV to two consecutive sermons.

[4] It must not be assumed that this book, which belongs to the early eleventh century, was actually written at Worcester, for on f. 321*a*, written over an erasure, is an inscription beginning *þis his þæt boc þæt ic Ulf* . . . which is unfortunately undecipherable in its essential part, even with the help of ultra-violet rays. There are certain signs of Kentish dialect in the MS. which indicate either that it was written in the South-East, or, as is perhaps more likely, that it has a South-Eastern book (not our Bodley MSS.) in its pedigree.

Catholic Homilies, these two manuscripts R and W(orcester) represent a branch which had separated off in Ælfric's own time; and a few sample collations show that, though they are closely related, the texts of the sermons in the two manuscripts do not stand in the simple relation of original and copy.

III

There appears to be a short way of determining the type of text to which these manuscripts (R, W) belong. Since 1855, when Dietrich published the first part of his classic study of Ælfric, the authorities[1] are agreed that in Thorpe's print of Ælfric's Second Series, the six sermons which follow the passage headed *Excusatio Dictantis* are not part of the original work but are a later supplement, added by Ælfric in a 'second edition'. All these six are found in the first hand of MS. Bodley 342; whence it would follow that the selection was made from Ælfric's second edition.[2] The odd thing is that when this test can be applied to a collection of sermons, it always gives the same result, leading us back to Ælfric's second edition; and to find the explanation we must go over the ground afresh.

Light is thrown on the date and composition of the *Catholic Homilies* by the following prefaces and notes, all written by Ælfric, and all printed in Thorpe's edition:

Series I: (*a*) Latin letter to Sigeric, Archbishop of Canterbury; (*b*) English Preface; (*c*) Latin note on the needlessness of a table of contents.[3]

Series II: (*d*) Second Latin Letter to Sigeric; (*e*) Second English

[1] Dietrich in *Zeitschrift für historische Theologie*, 1855, p. 507 ff.; Miss C. L. White *Ælfric*, 1898, p. 102 ff. (mainly translation of Dietrich); ten Brink *History of English Literature*, transl. Kennedy, i. 105 n.; R. P. Wülker *Grundriss zur Geschichte der angelsächsischen Litteratur*, 1885, p. 460; W. Hunt in *Dictionary of National Biography* and in *History of the English Church* i. 374; A. Brandl *Geschichte der altenglischen Literatur*, 1908, pp. 163, 165; *Cambridge History of English Literature* i. 116 ff.

[2] Dietrich draws the conclusion, p. 513, and is followed by Miss White, p. 106 ff.

[3] No closing words for this volume have been preserved, though it is likely that there was something of the kind in the first separate publication.

Preface; (*f*) *Ammonitio* or warning against drunkenness, in Latin;[1] (*g*) *Excusatio Dictantis* or Author's Apology, in English (Thorpe, ii. 520); (*h*) Final Prayer (Thorpe, ii. 594).

That Sigeric became Archbishop in 990 (probably at the beginning of the year) rather than in 989 as Dietrich supposed, is now generally agreed. The day of his death was 28 October, or thereabouts.[2] The year of his death, like so many points in the troubled chronology of his times, cannot be established beyond the reach of doubt; and yet it is critical for our purposes. In the Parker manuscript of the Chronicle it is entered by a contemporary hand under the year 994, whereas the late Canterbury MS. Domitian A VIII has it at 995.[3] But these two witnesses are easily reconciled: in both of them a single entry reports the death of Sigeric and the election of his successor, which took place on Easter Day (21 April) of the next year;[4] so that the whole entry might well be transferred to the later year. Thus far the case for 994 seems to be clear, and that date is accepted by Stubbs,[5] Freeman, Liebermann, and the *Dictionary of National Biography*. But then they are compelled to

[1] This is a postscript to (*d*)—Ælfric takes leave of Sigeric at the end of it—and it has been understood as a rebuke to Sigeric himself (see Plummer *A.-S. Chronicle* ii. 173). But Ælfric would hardly expose the Archbishop, whose imprimatur he was seeking, to such public criticism. He quotes the Lord's rebuke to Aaron (*Leviticus* x. 9), not because the Archbishop stands in Aaron's place, but because Aaron typifies the whole priesthood; and drunkenness was then a besetting sin of English priests. The *Ammonitio* was presumably written in Latin so that it should reach the priests rather than their congregations. Its abrupt intrusion seems to be due to some incident which forced the subject upon Ælfric's attention.

[2] The early-twelfth-century fragment of a Christ Church obituary in MS. Nero C IX has his obit at II Kal. Nov.; but the name *Sirichus* has been erased at V Kal. Nov. above, where his obit was coupled with that of Archbishop Æthelnoth. The Christ Church obituary of about a century later in the same MS. has Sigeric and Æthelnoth at V Kal. Nov., but no entry at II Kal. Nov.

[3] Florence of Worcester agrees. Other MSS. of the Chronicle have it at 995, but they represent a single source.

[4] After 'Ælfric Wiltunscire biscop wearð gecoren' MS. Domitian A VIII has the addition 'on Easterdæi on Ambresbyri fram Ægelrede cinge and fram eallan his witan'.

[5] *Registrum Sacrum Anglicanum*, p. 30.

reject the testimony of a good charter, Harley 43 Ċ 7, which bears the date 995 and has Sigeric among the witnesses. Relying on this charter, Dietrich, and more recently Plummer,[1] prefer 995 as the year of Sigeric's death; but it will be seen that they must reject either the autumn date for his death, or the Easter date for the election of his successor, or another good charter dated 995 which his successor witnesses as 'archbishop elect'.[2] Neither of them notices the evidence of the Leofric Missal, where *Depositio Sigerici Archiepiscopi* is entered by a contemporary hand opposite the year 994 in the Paschal tables; and this should be allowed to settle the issue.[3] Hence Ælfric completed both series of the *Catholic Homilies* between 990 and the end of October 994.

In the Second Latin Letter to Sigeric which introduces the Second Series, Ælfric says: '. . . et licet multis iniuriis infestium piratarum concutiebamur postquam præfatum libellum [i.e. the First Series] tuæ Sanctitati transmisimus, tamen nolentes repperiri falsidici promisores, dolente animo hoc opus perfecimus.' Dietrich, interpreting this as a reference to the fierce raids of Olaf and Swein in 994, concludes that the Second Series was completed after that invasion and before Sigeric's death (which he places in 995); and this has been accepted as one of the few fixed points in the chronology of Ælfric's life and works. Yet it is impossible if Sigeric died in October 994.[4] For the Chronicle tells us that the invaders attacked London on the Nativity of St. Mary (8 September), and went on to harry the south and west of England in the later autumn. So even if we suppose that Ælfric wrote his preface in October, the last month of Sigeric's life, he would be writing,

[1] *Anglo-Saxon Chronicle* ii, p. 178.

[2] No. 692 in Kemble's *Codex Diplomaticus*. See also the Rochester charter, No. 688.

[3] I take Harley 43 C 7 to be a nearly contemporary copy rather than an original charter, and a slip in the date DCCCCXCV is probable. Two other charters from a late source (Kemble's 689 and 690) are also connected with Æscwig of Dorchester, have the same witnesses, and are dated 995; but they are obviously untrustworthy. One gives Sigeric's successor the title of archbishop, though Sigeric himself is in the list of witnesses, and both are dated in the seventh year of the indiction, which should be 994.

[4] Miss White *Ælfric*, pp. 52–55, accepts this date, but follows Dietrich's chronological scheme, without noticing the inconsistency.

whether at Cerne or at Winchester, in the very thick of the troubles; he could not speak of them as past, and as happening 'after I sent you my First Series'.

I have little doubt that Ælfric refers to the earlier heavy attacks of 991. These are chiefly remembered for the Battle of Maldon in the east; but that they touched the south-western counties closely appears from the treaty of peace which is preserved among Æthelred's laws; it was made after negotiations by Archbishop Sigeric, Alderman Æthelweard of Devonshire (our Ælfric's patron), and Alderman Ælfric of Hampshire, who persuaded the King to buy peace for their provinces.[1]

It follows that the First Series was completed after Sigeric's election in 990, and before the autumn raids of 991.[2] As a refinement, it may be argued that Ælfric would not fail to refer to Sigeric's election if he were writing to him immediately after it, and that the time while the Archbishop was abroad seeking his *pallium* is also excluded. If an ingenious calculation by Stubbs is accepted, he was at Rome in July 990,[3] and would not be home till the early winter; so that the first half of 991 is the likeliest date for the completion of the First Series.

This coincides roughly with the result (990–1)[4] that Dietrich obtains by mere spacing out from his fixed date for the Second Series (994–5). But the words of the Second Latin Letter, 'per codicellum quem *nuper* tuæ auctoritati direximus . . . *festinavimus*

[1] F. Liebermann *Gesetze der Angelsachsen* i, p. 220. It is significant that Sigeric was not the representative of the Church when peace was negotiated with the invaders of 994; on that occasion, according to the Chronicle, Ælfheah Bishop of Winchester acted with Alderman Æthelweard. This is accounted for if Sigeric died in October 994; but it would require explanation if he were alive and at work after the peace.

[2] That Maldon was fought on 11 Aug. is known from Byrhtnoth's obit in MS. Titus D XXVII (R. T. Hampson *Medii Ævi Calendarium* i, p. vi). [Professor Dickins *Leeds Studies in English* vi, 1937, p. 17, records an obit from the Ely MS. Trin. Coll. Camb. O.2.1, late twelfth century, giving the date 10 Aug.]

[3] *Memorials of St. Dunstan* (Rolls Series), p. 391 n.

[4] Dietrich and those who follow him do not see how unlikely it is that Ælfric, writing in 994–5 of invasions which began in September 994 and were just ended, would describe them as happening 'after I sent you my First Series in 990–1'—for that is the effect of their datings.

hunc sequentem librum', coupled with the statement in the First Letter to Sigeric that the second volume is already in hand ('alterum vero librum modo dictando habemus in manibus'), indicate a shorter interval between the two volumes, perhaps no more than a year; and the issue of both may be assigned to the years 991–2. So much for the chronology.[1]

In the First Latin Letter, Ælfric says: 'quadraginta sententias in isto libro posuimus'; in the Second: 'Igitur in anteriore opere ordinavimus XL sermones, in isto vero non minor numerus sententiarum invenitur'; and in the Second English Preface: 'In each book there are forty sermons, excluding the preface.'[2] The Latin note (*f*), which Thorpe prints as the end of the First English Preface, confirms the number of forty sermons for the First Series, but

[1] [The following note was added in *R.E.S.* viii (1932), p. 67 f.] For the completion of the First Series I have proposed the date 990–1 and for the Second 992. It has since occurred to me that Ælfric would arrange his sermons according to the calendar of the year in which he assembled them for publication, or, more probably, the year in which they would first be used by others. In that case something might be inferred from the relative order of fixed and mobile feasts. Attention may be confined to the years 989–95, as the extreme limits which have anywhere been suggested for the archbishopric of Sigeric, to whom both Series are dedicated. In the First Series the only condition suggested by the order of contents is that Mid-Lent Sunday should not be later than the Annunciation (25 March), a condition which was fulfilled in 989, 991, 992, and 994. The Second Series has more fixed points. The Second Sunday in Lent should not be later than 12 March (St. Gregory), which excludes 990 and 995. Mid-Lent Sunday should follow St. Benedict (21 March): this excludes the other years except 993. But in the second half of the year the order of the Sundays after Pentecost gives a different result: The Ninth Sunday should not be later than 25 July (St. James—Thorpe's date is wrong); and the Twelfth Sunday should not be later than 15 August (the Assumption of the Virgin). These conditions are satisfied in 989, 992, and 994. But as the Sixteenth Sunday is not later than the Nativity of the Virgin (8 Sept.), 994 is excluded. And 989, which was included at all by excess of scruple, is out of the question for the completion of the Second Series. Thus the first half-year agrees with the calendar of 993, and the second half of the year agrees with the calendar of 992, which is what one would expect if Ælfric issued the book about Midsummer 992. Then the only calendar that need be considered for the First Series is that of 991, which would suit publication at the turn of 990–91. This line of argument confirms the dates proposed on quite different grounds.

[2] In the English Preface to his next book, the Grammar, he again speaks of the two books as containing eighty sermons.

adds a complication: 'Quid necesse est in hoc codice (i.e. the First Volume) capitula ordinare, cum prediximus quod XL sententias in se contineat? excepto quod Æþelwerdus dux vellet habere XL quattuor in suo libro.' When this is read in connexion with a sentence in the Second English Preface: 'Before each sermon we have set the title in Latin, but anybody who likes may dress a table of contents after the preface',[1] it appears that Ælfric, having come to the end of the preface, which the table of contents would naturally follow, makes a note for his copyists that in Volume I such a table of contents is unnecessary; for if it is known that there are forty sermons and that they are arranged in the order of the Church year (with which all users of the collection would be familiar), there is no need for a table of contents to prove the completeness of any copy or the order of its parts. But then, to avoid a possible error, he reminds the scribes that his patron Æthelweard wants forty-four sermons in his personal copy. Chance has thus preserved a note intended not for the reader, as the prefaces are, but for the workers in a scriptorium.

In Thorpe's edition, the First Volume contains 40 sermons. But the Second Volume, on Thorpe's count, contains 45 sermons, of which 39 precede and 6 follow the Author's Apology. Dietrich, by counting as two a composite sermon which Thorpe counts as one (Thorpe's item xii for choice), brings the number of sermons before the Author's Apology up to 40; and assumes that the Second Series originally ended here. He takes the six following sermons to be a supplement added by Ælfric in a later issue. He thinks that the first four of them are the four extra sermons which Æthelweard desired for his own copy, and is confirmed in this view when he detects evidences of later composition in the fifth sermon *In Natale Sanctarum Virginum*.[2] This explanation has been generally accepted.[3]

[1] Thorpe mistranslates, and is followed by Miss White, p. 105. Ælfric's prefaces show a keen interest in the details of the scribes' work; and we shall see that there was more reason for a table of contents in the Second Series.

[2] Op. cit., p. 508.

[3] W. Hunt makes the supplement 5 sermons, apparently by taking one from the 6 and adding it to the 39; but his account of the matter in *History of the English Church*, vol. i, 374 ff. is far from clear.

But great and deserved as Dietrich's authority is, his solution is not so satisfactory that it should pass without question.

(1) There is nothing in the Author's Apology to suggest that the six sermons which follow it are a later supplement to the original issue of the Second Series; and these six sermons are followed by a normal *Explicit Liber Secundus*, &c.

(2) The Apology itself cannot be very much later than the original issue of the Second Series. In it Ælfric explains that he omits the story of St. Thomas of India (21 December), because it has long since been translated into English verse, and because St. Augustine questions the incident of the cupbearer who boxed the Apostle's ear.[1] This explanation must have been written before the *Lives of Saints*, in which Ælfric includes St. Thomas (but without the story of the cupbearer's hand) at the special request of his patron Æthelweard—i.e. before 998, in which year Æthelweard is presumed to have died.

(3) When he supposes that the fifth sermon—*In Natale Sanctarum Virginum*—is later than the four which precede it, and indeed later than the year 1000, Dietrich disregards two points: First, it is expressly mentioned with the rest in the Author's Apology which, as we have just seen, cannot be late: 'We dare not make *this book* much longer, lest it pass beyond bounds and induce weariness in readers by its bulk. We will, however, set out *in this book* a few more sermons of general application on apostles and martyrs, confessors and *holy virgins*.' Secondly, the division of saints into four classes, Apostles, Martyrs, Confessors, Virgins, is standard form; it is the essential framework of a litany of saints; and a writer who had provided for the first three classes could hardly fail to go on to the fourth. So far, then, from the fifth sermon being separable from the previous four, it is indissociably linked with them by its subject, and, as we shall see, by its purpose.

(4) The suggestion that the first four sermons are the four specially prepared for Æthelweard's copy is not convincing. For Æthelweard's copy containing forty-four sermons was of the First Series, not the Second. If Ælfric wanted to use these extra sermons,

[1] For the legend, see M. R. James *The Apocryphal New Testament*, Oxford 1924, p. 367.

he would naturally make them a supplement to the First Series, or absorb them into the body of the Second Series; to make them a supplement to the Second Series was not the obvious way of publishing them. Besides, it is unlikely that Æthelweard, who presumably wanted four sermons for special feasts,[1] would ask for any of these six.

(5) Up to the Author's Apology, Ælfric follows the course of the Church year in his Second Series, assigning sermons in order of date to particular saints, such as St. Benedict on 21 March, or to festivals such as Palm Sunday; until he boggles over St. Thomas whose day (21 December) is the last great general feast before Christmas.[2] But the six sermons that follow the Apology—*In Natale Unius Apostoli*; *In Natale Plurimorum Apostolorum*; *In Natale Martyrum*; *In Natale Confessorum*; *In Natale Sanctarum Virginum*; *In Dedicatione Ecclesiæ*—do not in themselves belong to particular days of the year. They are written to suit the commemoration of any apostle or group of apostles, any martyr, confessor, virgin, or dedication, and cannot be given a place in the yearly round of a church until its preacher says, for example: 'I want a sermon for the feast of St. Grimbold. He is a confessor, so I shall take Ælfric's *In Natale Confessorum*, put St. Grimbold's name in the blanks left, and preach it to celebrate his day, July 8th.' The need for such a class of sermons is plain. In Ælfric's time there was great diversity of practice. The feast-days recognized by all the English churches were the backbone of every calendar; but any church might have its special celebrations, depending on its relations with other churches, or local interest, or the possession of relics. Even if Ælfric knew of all these special feasts, which is unlikely, it was impossible to provide for them specifically in a reasonable compass; and yet

[1] His other demands on Ælfric are precise enough; he asks for a translation of Genesis as far as Isaac (Preface to Genesis), or for the Book of Joshua (Letter to Sigweard); or the Life of St. Thomas of India (*Lives of Saints* ii. 400). And Ælfric's reminder to the scribes would hardly be necessary if he intended them to add the four sermons on extra leaves at the end of Æthelweard's copy (which would call for no special forethought). It rather implies that these sermons were to be distributed through the special copy in order of feast-days; and this could not be done unless they were sermons for specific occasions.

[2] Ælfric begins the year with Christmas in both series.

he wanted to supply the English clergy with a foundational book which would cover the principal occasions for preaching. The six sermons that follow the Apology cover the gaps in his selection of occasions; they may be an afterthought, but they may just as well be a part of the original design; and their place at the end of the Second Series is naturally explained because it was impossible to arrange them among the sermons for particular days.

In sum, Dietrich's explanation, which is the basis of the accepted view that these six sermons are a later supplement, is open to several objections, and has the single merit that it solves the numerical difficulty.

Yet it is a wrong solution. In the Second English Preface Ælfric says that he includes the lives and passions of those saints 'whom the English honour with feast-days'. An earlier tenth-century document, the verse *Menology*, professes to give the 'feast-days that the King of the Saxons orders to be kept by all',[1] and comparison with it shows that Ælfric held closely to his plan. He even felt it necessary to apologize for omitting the feasts of St. Thomas and the Birth of St. Mary (Thorpe, ii. 466), because they are in the number of great general feasts of the English Church.[2] Then what title to inclusion have 'the Saints Alexander, Eventius, and Theodulus' who are celebrated in Thorpe's Sermon xx of the Second Series? Only this—that theirs is the secondary feast for 3 May. The Invention of the Cross (Thorpe II, xix) is the great feast of that day, and it alone is mentioned in the verse *Menology*. The subjects are distinct, but Ælfric would naturally reckon these two items as one, because they serve for only one day in the Church year.[3] Similarly, Thorpe's II, xv and xvi, are both for Easter Day; and his II, xxii and xxiii (to which xxiv is a mere pendant), are both for

[1] Edited Grein-Wülker, vol. ii, p. 293.

[2] Only Matthias (24 Feb.) passes unnoticed, though contemporary calendars leave no doubt of the importance of his feast. The sermon *In Natale Unius Apostoli* would serve for the occasion, and the confusion of his legend with that of Matthew probably accounts for Ælfric's silence. Cf. Thorpe ii, p. 520.

[3] The scribes well understood this, for they are found together in six MSS. but never apart. In the contents of Bodley MS. 340 and CCCC MS. 198, written by the original hands, *Inventio Sanctæ Crucis* covers both items.

Tuesday in the Rogation Days. II, xxvii is also a pendant. Thus Thorpe's 39 sermons before the Apology cover only 34 feast-days, and when the 6 sermons after the Apology are added we get the exact number 40 that Ælfric promised.[1] The number 40 for the First Series is also calculated by days, not by items.[2]

So these six sermons, like the Author's Apology, belong to the original issue of the Second Series, and, with the supposed supplement, the evidence for the 'second edition' disappears.

This conclusion does not imply that Ælfric produced only one edition of the *Catholic Homilies*, but rather that we know almost nothing of his work on the text of the classic example of Anglo-Saxon prose. Although Dietrich raised it three-quarters of a century ago, and many minute studies of Ælfric's work have appeared since then, I cannot find any published evidence of curiosity about the problem. For Wanley the *Catholic Homilies* were represented by a number of manuscripts, whereas for modern scholars they are represented by Thorpe's printed text.

IV

In the previous section I digressed so far on the text of Ælfric's *Catholic Homilies* that I must go a little farther, premising that the problem is one for an editor with full collations, and that the materials I can bring to it are no more than enough to make a beginning.

CAMBRIDGE UNIVERSITY LIBRARY MS. GG.3.28

Wanley's full description (Catalogue, p. 153) directed Thorpe to this codex as the best single source of the *Catholic Homilies*. No

[1] It is often stated that Ælfric's *Lives of Saints* (for which he chose saints whom 'monks among themselves honour in their offices' as distinct from those 'whom the English people honour with feast-days') also contains forty sermons. This is no more than a conjecture based on the analogy of the two earlier volumes; it is not supported by any statement from the author; and the attempts of Dietrich, pp. 517–18 (1855) and of MacLean (*Anglia* vi, p. 441) to make the contents of MS. Cotton Julius E VII conform to the number are unsatisfactory.

[2] It follows that the four extra pieces in Æthelweard's copy of the First Series are to be sought—if they are extant—among Ælfric's sermons for days other than the forty days for which the First Series provides.

other manuscript contains the Latin and English prefaces, or has the text of both the volumes that these prefaces describe. We have seen, too, that in a Latin note on the special copy for Æthelweard and on the needlessness of a table of contents, it preserves Ælfric's direction to the scribes who prepared the early copies of his First Series.

Thorpe[1] prints the bulk of the contents in their order, which is: (*a*) *Catholic Homilies*, First Series; (*b*) the Second Series, with the author's closing prayer (Thorpe ii. 594); (*c*) Ælfric's *De Temporibus Anni* (ff. 255*a*–61*b*, not printed by Thorpe), with a heading which may be rendered: '*Hereafter* follows a little piece on the Times of the Year, *which is not accounted a sermon*, but is rather to be read by anybody whom it pleases.' It begins 'I purpose *also*, if I may venture to do so, to collect briefly some information from the book that Bede made . . .';[2] (*d*) translations of the Paternoster, Creeds, and some short prayers (Thorpe, ii. 596–600); (*e*) A Lenten sermon *De Penitentia* (Thorpe, ii. 602–8), proved to be Ælfric's by the reference (p. 604) to his previous sermons on the Paternoster (I, xix) and the Creed (I, xx); (*f*) a few lines on abstinence in Lent (Thorpe, ii. 608) which are closely connected with the preceding sermon; (*g*) Ælfric's *Epistola de Canonibus* (not in Thorpe's edition), a pastoral letter prepared for the third Bishop Wulfsige of Sherborne. It is imperfect at the end (f. 266*b*), for the last two leaves have been lost.[3]

There is precise evidence that all these works are Ælfric's, except for the Creeds and Prayers, which may safely be assigned to

[1] *The Homilies of the Anglo-Saxon Church*, ed. B. Thorpe, Ælfric Society, 2 vols. 1844–6. Some leaves have been lost, and Thorpe fills the gaps from MS. Royal 7 C XII for the First Series and from our Bodley MSS. for the Second. He does not mention that the last leaf of the First Series is missing, with the words following *gemænelican* (p. 618 of the print near the foot) and presumably a colophon. In his Preface (p. vii, note) he explains that long passages translated from the Gospels have been abridged. His paragraphing has generally no MS. authority. His text is reasonably accurate in matters affecting the sense, but minor words are sometimes carelessly treated. An editor would do well to begin by collating it on the MS.

[2] Printed from this MS. by K. W. Bouterwek *Screadunga*, 1858, p. 23 ff., and with full collations by O. Cockayne *Leechdoms* iii. 231 ff.

[3] The latest edition is by B. Fehr, *Die Hirtenbriefe Ælfrics* (Bibliothek der angelsächsischen Prosa, ix), Hamburg 1914, p. 1 ff.

him on grounds of style and of aptitude to the purpose of the whole collection. That purpose was to supply ordinary priests, in clear English, with the religious instruction necessary for their congregations, together with some related writings for the guidance of the priests themselves—the *De Temporibus* to deepen their knowledge of matters which are frequently touched upon in the *Homilies*, the Pastoral Letter to show them their duties. Unity of aim, and the exclusion of works by other authors,[1] mark the contents of MS. Gg.3.28 as a compilation made under Ælfric's own direction.

But probably none of the items (*c*)–(*g*) went out with the *Catholic Homilies* as they were submitted to Archbishop Sigeric: all follow the prayer with which Ælfric closed the work; the prefaces to the *Homilies*, which are almost pedantically minute, give no hint of them; and the first piece, *De Temporibus*, is copied separately, beside matter relating to Sigeric, in the contemporary miscellany MS. Tiberius B v,[2] which would be natural enough if it were issued as a separate tract, but not so likely if it were known to be a part of the book of *Catholic Homilies*. Now there is evidence elsewhere[3]

[1] Ælfric took pains to segregate his own writings. In the prayer at the end of the *Catholic Homilies*, he begs other translators or expounders of the Gospels to keep their work apart from his own. Again, at the end of the Preface to the *Lives of Saints*, he asks that his work should be copied without interpolations. There is thus a presumption that MSS. prepared under his direction do not include the works of others; and conversely that collections in which his works are mingled with alien matter have not his authority.

[2] This is supported by indications that Ælfric retouched the version in Tiberius B v at beginning and end for the separate issue. In MS. Gg.3.28 it begins 'Ic wolde eac, gyf ic dorste, *gadrian* . . . of ðære bec þe Beda . . . gesette and gegaderode . . . .' Tiberius B v has *pluccian* 'excerpt' (cf. Thorpe i, p. 212, foot), which seems to be an improvement made because *gegaderode* followed so closely. Cf. p. 172 n. 5 below. [For objections to this view, see Professor H. Henel's edition of *De Temporibus*, E.E.T.S. (1942) p. xvi f. I cannot believe that a scribe, or anybody except Ælfric himself, would trouble about the fine point of style involved in the substitution of *pluccian* for *gadrian*. Certainly *De Temporibus* was intended to supplement and to be closely associated with the *Catholic Homilies*; but if the second volume of the *Catholic Homilies* was sent to Archbishop Sigeric and others before *De Temporibus* was written as a supplement to it, Ælfric would send out *De Temporibus* separately, and no recipient would fail to connect it with the *Homilies*.]

[3] See below, p. 176 (*d*).

that when Ælfric was moved by one of his correspondents to write a new short piece, he kept a copy by having it entered at the end of a suitable codex. The *De Temporibus*, as its preamble shows, he placed at the end of a copy of the *Catholic Homilies*. Probably the items (*d*)–(*g*) were added to the same 'official' volume in their chronological order by his directions.

There is no reason to think that MS. Gg.3.28 is itself that authoritative copy. It is not a codex built up quire by quire, or item by item, as matter became available, but is written from beginning to end in one main hand,[1] on a uniform plan, and with a strict economy of vellum. A new item usually follows on in the same quire, the same page, and sometimes even in the same line. Only the Second Series begins a new right-hand page, but apparently it is the second leaf of a quire, so that the book was not designed to be bound in two volumes. It is, then, a copy, direct or indirect, of a collection built up under Ælfric's instructions; and is thus very near the fountain-head.

Where it was written is not known. The signature of Leonard Pilkington[2] and a pressmark at the top of the first page indicate that it came to Cambridge from Durham. The main hand, which

[1] There is no change of hand at the beginning of the Second Series. A rounder, more upright hand, with distinct letter forms, appears in short passages here and there, e.g. ff. 225*a*, 226*b*, 240*b*–1*b*. I take this to be the hand of the miniator; cf. the minuscule headings of *De Temporibus* at f. 261*b*. The initial capitals throughout the book are simple, and yet unusual enough to deserve attention; the broader strokes are outlined in brown-black ink and filled with a zigzag pattern in bright red.

[2] See *D.N.B.* The mark is reproduced in New Palæographical Society, pl. 147, 4*a*. [Professor Henel in his edition, p. xxviii n., objects that this pressmark is assigned to Norwich in *New Pal. Soc.* I, pl. 147. Pressmarks are not always distinctive because the same system was used in more than one library, and the attribution to Norwich is corrected in the indexes to the work. Professor Henel adduces valuable new evidence for the history of the MS.: it was one of twenty given to Cambridge in 1574 by Bishop Pilkington of Durham, Leonard's brother. That Bishop Pilkington was a theologian, not an antiquary, is really no objection to his ownership of the MS., or to Durham provenance. It was their theological implications that first drew attention to Ælfric's works; and, as Professor Henel notes, Pilkington was one of the bishops who testified to the accuracy of the texts in *A Testimonie of Antiquitie*, 1566–7, where Ælfric's Easter Homily and Letter for Wulfsige were first printed.]

is strongly influenced in duct by the Caroline minuscule, would normally be assigned to the last years of the tenth or the first years of the eleventh century. Any closer dating must depend on the contents themselves, and particularly on the last item, the Pastoral Letter for Bishop Wulfsige, which, apart from its order in the codex, is pretty certainly the latest in date of composition. The extreme limits of Wulfsige's bishopric are 992–1002. Since Dietrich wrote, this letter has usually been assigned to 998, or later, because in that year Wulfsige established monks at Sherborne in place of canons. But there is no necessary connexion between the letter and this reform. The unusual asperity of Ælfric's preface would best be accounted for if he still felt freshly the contrast between Æthelwold's school at Winchester and the backward districts round Cerne; and if he feared that Wulfsige, who belonged to the more patient reforming school of Dunstan, might not press on fast enough. The tone throughout seems better suited to the bishop's early days[1] than to the later years in which he enjoyed the reputation of a saint—a reputation which at that time almost implies success as a reformer. I see no reason for placing the composition

[1] B. Fehr (op. cit. p. liii) shows that the Pastoral Letters for Wulfstan belong to the beginning of Wulfstan's archiepiscopate, not to the end as Dietrich argued. But Fehr (p. xxxviii) thinks that the Letter for Wulfsige is later than the year 1000 because it contains no reference to the approaching end of the world in that year. The argument from silence is dangerous. But a positive statement that the end was near would have no value for close dating in England, as the following facts will show: (i) The most moving warning of imminent doom is Wulfstan's *Sermo ad Anglos* written in 1014. (ii) The reference to the end of the world which Fehr quotes from the Preface to the First Series was transferred unchanged in MS. CCCC 188 to be a permanent part of the first Advent sermon; and this MS. represents a collection that was in Ælfric's own hands after 1005 (see p. 177, below). (iii) Before 1000 Ælfric discusses the end of the world in *Catholic Homilies* i, p. 608 ff. 'If the end were a thousand years off', he says, 'that would not be long.' The whole discussion would be idle if he believed, in defiance of the famous Gospel text, that the time could be fixed by the calendar, which he does not mention. (iv) His teaching is explicit in the sermon 'for Holy Virgins', which, as I showed in the previous section (p. 162 ff.), was included in the original issue of the Second Series about 992. 'No one except God alone can know when the end will come' (Thorpe ii, pp. 568, 574). This was, I think, the teaching of the English Church in the years immediately before 1000.

of the Pastoral Letter after 993; the compilation copied in MS. Gg.3.28 was probably closed about that date; and the codex itself need not be very much later.

To a date so early there is one serious objection. The English Preface to the First Series, found only in this manuscript, runs:

I, Ælfric, monk and masspriest (though in strength unequal to these orders), was sent in King Æthelred's day by Bishop Ælfheah, Æthelwold's successor,[1] to a monastery called Cernel, at the request of thane Æthelmær. . . . Then I conceived the plan, I believe by God's grace, of writing this book, &c.

Ælfric became abbot of Eynsham in 1005, and after that date would no longer call himself 'monk and masspriest'. Ælfheah succeeded Æthelwold in 984, became archbishop of Canterbury in 1005, and was martyred in 1012. Æthelmær, the son of 'Æthelweard dux', founded the Benedictine house at Cernel in 987 and Eynsham Abbey in 1005. So far all the indications are consistent with the first issue of the First Series in 990–1. But though the interpretation has been questioned on general grounds,[2] 'in King Æthelred's day' has not unnaturally been taken to imply that the King was dead, and he died in 1016. Accordingly the *Cambridge History of English Literature* says 'the whole preface was composed probably after 1016'; while Thorpe, Dietrich, Miss White, the *Dictionary of National Biography*, and Brandl assume retouching by the author after 1016. But there is a parallel in Ælfric's *Lives of the Saints*:[3]

A very learned monk came north across the Channel from St. Benedict's [Fleury] *in King Æthelred's day* to Archbishop Dunstan [*d.* 988], three years before he died; and his name was Abbo. When they were talking together, Dunstan told the story of St. Edmund, as Edmund's swordbearer had told it to King Athelstan when Dunstan was a young man and the sword-bearer was very old. The monk wrote all the story in a book, and when the book came into my hands a few years later, I turned it into English, as it stands hereafter. Within two years [987] this monk Abbo returned home to his monastery, and soon afterwards [988] was appointed abbot there.

[1] To Ælfric, an alumnus of Winchester Cathedral, this would be the familiar description of Ælfheah; it was necessary to distinguish him from the earlier Winchester bishop and saint Ælfheah, who died in 951.

[2] Notably by Cockayne *Leechdoms* iii (1866), p. xviii, and B. Fehr, op. cit. p. xxxviii.

[3] Ed. Skeat, E.E.T.S. ii, p. 314.

The *Lives of Saints* may be dated between 993 and 998.[1] From the passage just cited it is clear that the Life of St. Edmund is not a later addition; and the introductory words are of a piece with the text, for they summarize Abbo's dedicatory letter to Dunstan. Evidently Ælfric used the phrase '*in King Æthelred's day*' during the King's reign as a formal indication of date; and this is confirmed when we find *regnante Æthelredo rege Anglorum* in Ælfric's Latin life of Æthelwold, written in 1005–6.[2]

ROYAL MS. 7 C XII

This is the copy of the First Series to which Thorpe turned when leaves were missing from MS. Gg.3.28. The contents, which are

[1] The later limit is set by the dedication to Æthelweard, who seems to have died in 998. The earlier limit has been fixed at 996 by Dietrich and later writers, on the ground that Æthelwold is referred to as a saint, and he was translated in that year. But it would be difficult to stretch the 'few years later' of the careful preface to St. Edmund as far as 996, so that this Life at least is earlier. Besides, the prefaces to the *Lives* indicate a close relation with the *Catholic Homilies*, for which I have proposed the date 990–2; and Ælfric makes it clear that his *Grammar* is the only major work that comes between the *Homilies* and this 'quartum librum'. Then are the references to Æthelwold decisive? He is twice referred to in the *Lives* as 'now working miracles' (i, pp. 264–6 and 470). If it be conceded that both passages are original (in the first *halga* may well have been substituted for the regular alliterating adjective *arwurða*, just as *sancte* is interpolated at i, p. 442), still Ælfric himself says in his Life of Æthelwold 'ad eius mausoleum miracula fieri audivimus, *et antequam ossa eius elevarentur e tumulo*, sed et postea' (ed. J. Stevenson ii. 265). The translation in 996 no doubt marked a great step in the spread of Æthelwold's cult, but it was not necessary for the existence of that cult at Winchester, any more than a formal act was necessary to make Dunstan a saint soon after his death. I incline to place the *Lives* early in the period 993–8. This crowds his principal English works into a few years. But he was uneasy about the policy of Englishing, and from the outset we find him closing the ways against more: *Catholic Homilies* ii. 594: 'I declare now that henceforth I will never translate Gospel or exposition of the Gospel'; Preface to *Genesis*: 'I declare now that I dare not and I will not translate any book [of the Bible] after this book'; Preface to *Lives of Saints*: 'Decrevi modo quiescere post quartum librum a tali studio, ne superfluus judicer.'

[2] Ed. J. Stevenson, *Chronicon Monasterii de Abingdon* (Rolls Series), 1858, ii, p. 265. The date is fixed by Ælfric's statement in the preface that it was written twenty years after Æthelwold's death (1 August 984), and by the dedication to Kenulf, who became bishop of Winchester in 1005–6 and died soon after his election.

listed by Wanley (Catalogue, p. 174 ff.), correspond generally with those of Part I of Thorpe's manuscript, except that the prefaces are lacking. The Royal manuscript belonged to Cardinal Wolsey, but its earlier history is unknown.[1] It is written in two main hands;[2] the first, which is the more archaic, covering ff. 4–25*a* and 46–90; the second covering ff. 25*b*–45 and 91–218*a Explicit hic liber*.[3] Taken together, they indicate a date near the end of the tenth century.

There are an unusual number of contemporary additions and corrections, some interlined, some in the margins, and two on slips attached to ff. 165*a* and 169*b*.[4] They result in a text which is substantially that of MS. Gg.3.28, and some undoubtedly repair careless errors or omissions. But closer examination does not suggest that the copyists were abnormally careless. The omissions are often not due to homoeoteleuton, which is the usual explanation in a manuscript like CCCC 188; and when, for instance, *drihtnes* is corrected to *godes* (Thorpe i, p. 600, l. 2), *sindon* to *beon* (p. 602, l. 12), *getiþode* to *forgeaf* (p. 604, l. 4), or the words *þe man deadra manna lic mid behwyrfð* are struck out after *sealfe* (p. 220, l. 31),[5] we have to do not with a scribe but with a fastidious reviser. The manu-

[1] There are a number of twelfth-century glosses in English which do not show the characteristics to be expected in a book from the South-East. On f. 124*b* is a late-eleventh-century note indicating that the quires were then misbound, though they are now in order: 'séc hér æfter ofer þaræ feorðan cýna,' where *cine* 'quire', which Bosworth–Toller Supplement gives only as masculine with short vowel, is feminine and has the vowel marked long. M. Förster, 'Keltisches Wortgut im Englischen', in *Festschrift für F. Liebermann*, 1921, p. 142, shows that *cine* is a borrowing from Irish *cin* 'quire', from Latin *quina* 'five each', so that it was properly a quire of five sheets folded to make ten leaves. The figurative meaning 'deep subject' deduced for this word from a passage of Byrhtferth (ed. S. J. Crawford, p. 182) should be replaced by the simple meaning 'quire'.

[2] A third hand writes the first five lines of f. 197*b*.

[3] An erasure follows.

[4] A third slip, which presumably contained the words *Se engel . . . of middangearde* (i, p. 222, ll. 8–13) has been lost between ff. 77 and 78. It repaired an omission due to homoeoteleuton.

[5] Because words to the same effect occur above in the translation of the Gospel for the day, which Thorpe omits. There is a good deal of evidence to show that Ælfric carefully avoided repetitions which had no stylistic purpose.

script may have been made from very bad copy, such as an author's draft; or it may have been itself the basis for a revision; or it may have been collated with an improved authoritative text; or it may partake of all these characters. The early correcting hands in themselves present a problem. Most of the alterations may be assigned to the scribes, of whom the second is the more active; but a few seem to exhibit other contemporary hands, which are yet near enough to the second to raise embarrassing doubts. Fortunately I can leave these problems for a more detailed study,[1] and limit attention to two corrections which Wanley noticed.

On f. 64*a*, in the sermon for Mid-Lent Sunday, after *eallum cristenum folce* (Thorpe i, p. 186, l. 18) a surrounding line secludes a passage of twenty-six lines, beginning *Gif hwa smeað* and ending *smeagunge*, of which, as far as I know, there is no trace in any other manuscript. In the margin, mutilated by the binder, is the following note in a contemporary hand: 'ðeos racu [stent] | fullicor on ð[ære] | oðre bec. and w[e hy] | forbudon on [þys-]|sere þylæs þe h[it æ-]|þryt þince gif [heo] | on ægðre bec b[eo].' 'This explanation appears more fully in the second volume, and we forbade it in this, lest it should seem tedious if it appeared in both volumes.' An

[1] Mr. J. C. Pope of Yale has very courteously communicated to me his survey of the MSS. that contain homilies by Ælfric. He has independently noted the importance of the Royal MS., and proposes to print the additional passages and sermons in MS. CCCC 188, with other unpublished homilies which may reasonably be attributed to Ælfric. It is to be hoped he will undertake the task of collating the important MSS. and re-editing the *Catholic Homilies*. [I take the opportunity of calling attention to Professor Pope's opinion, communicated to the Old English section of the M.L.A. at the end of 1931, that the marginal note mentioned above and a few less important entries in the Royal MS. are in Ælfric's handwriting. Professor Pope had generously told me of this, and, expecting an early article from him, I did not explore questions of the relations between author and scribes which the MS. raises. These entries are almost certainly in Ælfric's hand, which is distinct from that of the scribes engaged on the MS. The alternative is to suppose that somebody else selected from another copy and entered into the Royal MS. just these few notes which by their content or comparative insignificance suggest the intervention of the author himself. There is no need to dwell on the importance of having a specimen of Ælfric's hand, and a long MS. prepared under his own supervision at a time when he was engaged in thorough revision. It is possible that the same hand may turn up in another MS.]

expansion of the cancelled passage is in fact found in the Second Series (Thorpe ii, p. 198 ff.). Clearly the author of the marginal note is Ælfric himself. When he had finished the First Series and came to compose or revise the sermon for the same day in the Second, he decided to use this matter there, and accordingly cancelled it in the First Volume. The decision may have been made after the First Series was issued, in which case he might circulate his correction; or it may have been made when the First Series was in book form, in the Royal manuscript at least, but not yet issued; or it may have been noted in Ælfric's draft—we must attach some meaning to the past tense *forbudon*—and neglected by the copyists. In any event Royal MS. 7 C XII, which alone has the passage and note, has strong claims to be considered the earliest extant state of the First Series—certainly earlier than MS. Gg.3.28, which has no trace of the excised passage.

The second notable correction is in the Sermon on St. Andrew, which is made up of two parts, *In Natale* and *Passio*. The Royal manuscript has the text as Thorpe prints it from MS. Gg.3.28; but after the closing Amen, the following words in the text-hand[1] are crossed out:

'Hit wære gelimplic, gif þises dæges scortnys us geþafian wolde, þæt we eow þæs halgan apostoles Andrees þrowunge gerehton. Ac we wyllað on oðrum sæle, gif we gesundfulle beoð, eow gelæstan, gif we hwæt lytles hwonlicor gefyldon. Uton nu eadmodlice, &c.' (f. 211*a*). 'It would be fitting, if the shortness of the day would permit, to tell you of the holy apostle Andrew's passion. But, if we have health, we will make it good another time, if we have fallen short in any detail, &c.'

I may not have interpreted the last few words correctly, but the significance of the passage is clear enough. The leaders of the Benedictine reform in England knew how important it was that able young monks should be sent from great monastic schools like Winchester into the strongholds of the unreformed clergy, where they could prove their worth in ministering to laymen. Ælfric was called to Cerne not simply as a monk but as a masspriest. In the Preface to his First Series, where he speaks of Cerne, he styles him-

[1] i.e. the hand of the second scribe, who is thus proved to be a mechanical worker.

self 'monk *and masspriest*' instead of, as elsewhere, 'monk' and later 'abbot'. As a masspriest it would be his duty to preach to an ordinary congregation;[1] and we should think of the *Catholic Homilies* not as literary exercises, but as, in the main, a two years' course of sermons actually preached by Ælfric, and later revised and made available for other priests. This cancelled note belongs to a special occasion —a dark day at the end of November when he could not find time to prepare and deliver an account of St. Andrew's Passion. But he was conscientious about giving full measure. He apologizes for the shortness of some of the sermons in the Second Series,[2] and we shall find him expanding the shortest of the First Series. He duly completed the Passion with a regular ending, and marked the leaves with some such direction as 'After In Natale Sancti Andree', with perhaps an insertion mark at the proper place in the original text. The scribe followed the direction; but, failing to notice that the original closing words must be omitted, he copied them mechanically after the inserted passage, so that they appear after the revised close. If this happened for the first time in the Royal manuscript, it is the nearest thing to Ælfric's draft. If other copies were made before the error was discovered—and the slavish way in which Anglo-Saxon scribes reproduce gross errors is remarkable—it is still the only extant witness to this early state of the text. As such, it deserves minute study, with close attention to the Latin sources.

CORPUS CHRISTI COLLEGE, CAMBRIDGE, MS. 188

Details of the contents of this manuscript—the only other of the First Series that survives—are given in Wanley's Catalogue, p. 123 ff., and also in M. R. James's Catalogue of the Corpus MSS. It is written in two hands that would normally be dated round about the year 1025; and there is no mark of ownership before it came into Archbishop Parker's possession.

Dietrich showed conclusively that it contains a later stage of the text than MS. Gg.3.28, though his view was troubled by a radical

[1] 'On Sundays and feast-days the masspriest must explain the meaning of the Gospel to the people in English' (Pastoral Letter for Wulfsige, ed. Fehr, p. 14; cf. Letter for Wulfstan, ibid. p. 130).

[2] Latin Preface 'quamvis aliquæ illarum brevitate angustentur'.

misunderstanding of the latter manuscript. The chief features of the Corpus manuscript are these:

(*a*) It begins, not with the opening sermon of the First Series called *De Initio Creaturæ*, but with Ælfric's treatment of the same subject commonly known as the *Hexameron.*[1] This was probably preferred because it is fuller. We know from its opening words 'On sumum oðrum spelle we sædon hwilon ær' that it is later than *De Initio Creaturæ*, and it was presumably written after the *Catholic Homilies* had been issued.

(*b*) In the Second Series of the *Catholic Homilies* Ælfric excused himself from writing a sermon for the Nativity of the Virgin on the grounds of difficulty in matter and doctrine (Thorpe ii, p. 466). Here the day (8 September) is supplied with a short historical account of the birth of the Virgin, and a long discourse on virginity.[2] No doubt his friends overcame his doubts by arguing that a feast-day of the first importance could not in practice be left without an expository sermon; and that it was better to steer a discreet way through the difficulties than leave them to unlearned preachers.

(*c*) At the appropriate places there are two other sermons which are not found in Thorpe or the Royal manuscript: one for the Third Sunday in Lent, which has been printed by George Stephens from Cotton MS. Faustina A IX;[3] the other for the Sunday after Pentecost, which is as yet unprinted. On grounds of language and style, quite apart from their occurrence in this manuscript, they may safely be attributed to Ælfric.

(*d*) The last sermon in the codex, *In Natale unius Confessoris*,[4] is introduced by a note which led Wanley to think that this manuscript belonged to Ælfric himself: 'Hunc sermonem nuper rogatu

[1] Edited by S. J. Crawford (Bibliothek der ags. Prosa x, Hamburg 1921) from a good but late MS., with full variants.

[2] Printed by B. Assmann, Bibliothek der ags. Prosa iii, Kassel 1889, p. 24 ff.

[3] *Tvende Oldengelske Digte*, Copenhagen 1853, p. 81.

[4] Printed by B. Assmann, op. cit. p. 49. One general sermon for such an occasion had already been provided in the Second Series. But the reform movement had multiplied the popular commemorations of confessors, both by its own saints—Dunstan, Æthelwold, Oswald, Wulfsige—and by the inevitable spread of relic cults such as that of St. Judoc; so that there was a need for an alternative to avoid repetition.

uenerandi episcopi Athelwoldi, scilicet Iunioris, anglice transtulimus, quem huius libelli calci inscribi fecimus ne nobis desit, cum ipse habeat.' The younger Æthelwold was bishop of Winchester from 1006 to 1012, or possibly 1014; and the composition of the sermon falls between these dates. As Ælfric had become abbot of Eynsham in 1005, it is a fair inference that CCCC MS. 188 is an Eynsham book prepared under his eye, or a close copy of such a book. Presumably he would draft his sermon on wax tablets, make a fair copy to send to Bishop Æthelwold, and order a scribe to transcribe this into a codex for safe keeping before it was dispatched. The Corpus manuscript shows no abnormality at the beginning of the new sermon. It is in the same hand (the second scribe's) as the preceding pieces; the heading is in the ordinary style; the quiring is normal; and at the end of the sermon, on the foot of the last page of the manuscript, another, *De Die Judicii*, has been begun in the usual style, and erased. It is possible that, just when Ælfric had finished his task, a copy of his revised First Series was nearing completion, so that, without delaying the dispatch of the new piece to Æthelwold, he could order it to be transcribed in regular style and in its natural place at the end of the series of homilies for specific days. But when all the circumstances are considered, there is a balance of probability that the Corpus manuscript is a copy, direct or indirect, from a book in which Ælfric kept a record of his alterations and additions.

(*e*) Some of the sermons have been retouched. I need mention only two which Wanley noticed as longer than in other copies. In the sermon for the Second Sunday after Easter, the passage 'Be ðisum awrat se witega Ezechiel . . . he bysnað' (Thorpe i, p. 242, ll. 7–24) is omitted; the original text runs on to *life* (p. 244, l. 6); and the matter of the excised passage is then expanded in some 300 manuscript lines. Style and language show that the addition was made by Ælfric,[1] who thus brought this exceptionally short sermon up to normal length.

[1] For instance, the verb *gynan* 'to drive' is recorded once in the compound *wiðgynan* 'to repel (a doubt)' from Ælfric's *Lives of Saints* (ed. Skeat i, p. 520), and once as simplex: 'oð þæt hi man *gynde* ongean eft to Judan' in the same work (ii, p. 108). In the addition the same alliterative

The sermon for the First Sunday in Advent is also very short in Thorpe's text. In the Corpus manuscript, instead of the last line printed by Thorpe (i, p. 606), there is a long passage from the English Preface to the First Series, beginning *Men behofiað godre lare, and swiðost*, ending *For swylcum bebodum*,[1] and followed by new closing words. With so many evidences of his revising hand in the manuscript, we can be fairly sure that this change is also due to Ælfric. It means that, so far from modifying his prefaces after Æthelred's death in 1016, he had discarded them before 1014, and used their permanent material elsewhere. Extensive revisions and additions had made this course inevitable. It was no longer possible, even if it were useful now that the *Catholic Homilies* had become firmly established, to claim Sigeric's authority for the whole contents; and it was no longer true to say that the volume contaïned forty sermons. This is one reason for the absence of the prefaces from all extant manuscripts except MS. Gg.3.28: Ælfric himself suppressed them.

We have now surveyed the three extant copies of the First Series. Each bears special marks of Ælfric's supervision, and each presents a different stage in the development of the text. The order of the stages corresponds with the probable age of the manuscripts: first Royal MS 7 C XII; second MS. Gg.3.28, which Thorpe printed; third CCCC MS. 188; and the latest of the three may possibly have been copied in Ælfric's lifetime if he died about the year 1020. These are the foundations on which an editor must build; since there is no other copy of the Second Series to compare with MS. Gg.3.28, and the many manuscripts in which different arrangements or selections of the *Catholic Homilies* appear can only be appraised by reference to these three. Yet three is a tiny fraction of the copies that existed in Ælfric's lifetime; for this was a standard work which every church of any importance would require, and his time was the golden age of Anglo-Saxon book-production. It would be too much to expect that blind chance, saving three copies

phrase occurs: 'ðu wylt losian on leahtrum and æthleapan þæm hyrde, ac he ðe wyle *gynan* ongean to ðære eowde' (MS. p. 186).

[1] Thorpe, p. 2, l. 17 to p. 6, l. 34.

from the mass, should also save one of each important state. Nor can it be maintained that these three were preserved with special veneration by reason of their close connexion with Ælfric: the copies he sent to Æthelweard and to Sigeric, the originals of the sermon he sent to Æthelwold, and of the letters for Wulfsige and Wulfstan, are all lost—whether they went to Canterbury or Winchester, Sherborne or Worcester. The facts are best explained if we suppose that Ælfric was constantly retouching the collection or adding to it at the suggestion of friends; and that at any given time he would have a copy by him which embodied these alterations. If someone applied to him for the *Catholic Homilies*, he would either lend this authoritative book as a pattern or, more probably, arrange that a copy of it should be made in his own scriptorium. If the new copy went to an important centre, it might there become the model for others; but still the mechanical habits of Anglo-Saxon scribes and his own repeated urgings to write 'according to the pattern'[1] would tend to preserve the notes he made on the pattern books. In this way many successive states of the text might be issued, of which we happen to have three. They should not be called first, second, and third editions, since these terms would suggest that the series is complete in three sharply defined stages.

V

It is now possible to frame more precisely the question from which this excursus began: to which of the three states is the text in MSS. Bodley 340 and 342 (= R) nearest allied? Evidently not to the latest, for it has none of the improvements in MS. CCCC 188. As between Royal MS. 7 C XII (= A) and MS. Gg.3.28, its affinities seem to be with the former. Thus (1) after *handa* (Thorpe, i, p. 10, l. 1) R and A have the words 'and ealle eorðan he belycð on his handa', which are not in Gg.; (2) for *wuldre* (p. 46, l. 21) R has wrongly *wuldor*, A *wuldre* altered from *wuldor*; (3) for *onfoh* (p. 48, l. 4) R, A have *underfoh*; (4) before *fæder* (p. 52, l. 29) R, A have *heofonlica*; (5) R, A have not the Latin at p. 300, l. 20; (6) for *forhtiað* (p. 304, l. 2) R reads *bifiað*, A *biuiað* corrected to *forhtiað*;

[1] Thorpe i, p. 8 and ii, p. 2; Preface to *Latin Grammar*, repeated in the Preface to *Genesis*; *Lives of Saints* i, p. 6.

(7) R, A have not Ælfric's Latin note, p. 304, ll. 9–15;[1] (8) for 'ðurh his ænne ancennedan sunu' (p. 500, l. 24) R, A read 'ðurh his ancennedan bearne' (*bearn* R); (9) before *Paulus* (p. 520, l. 13) R, A have the words 'Salomon cwæð "Rihtwises mannes sawul is wisdomes setl"', which are not in Gg.

It is necessary to distinguish variants of probable authority, such as items (6) and (8), from the idiosyncrasies and errors of MS. Gg.3.28. Thus item (1) is an obvious instance of homoeoteleuton in Gg.,[2] and so is item (9). In items (3) and (4) MS. CCCC 188, the latest of the three stages, agrees with R, A. Such readings dissociate R from Gg., but are not evidence of a close relation between R and A.

The best evidence of this relation is their agreement in a free use of the dative after prepositions, where Gg. has the accusative: e.g. Thorpe i, p. 10, l. 26, *ongean god ælmihtine*: R, A *ongean gode ælmihtigum*; ibid. l. 27, *wið þæt werod*: R, A *wið ðam werode*; ibid. l. 29, *ofer hi ealle*: R, A *ofer him eallum*; p. 50, l. 22, *for his cwelleras*: R, A *for his cwellerum*; p. 132, l. 13, *embe godes beboda*: R, A both originally read *ymbe godes bebodum*; p. 296, l. 22, *oð þisne dægðerlican dæg*: R, A *oð þisum dægðerlicum dæge*; p. 354, l. 1, *þurh oðre halige geearnunga*: R, A *þurh oðrum haligum geearnungum*; p. 402, l. 18, *on ða oðre apostolas*: R, A *on ðam oðrum apostolum*.

It will simplify a complex problem if attention is confined to the common preposition *þurh*, which is found only with the accusative in Old English poetry, in the Vespasian Psalter (Mercian), in the Kentish Psalm and Hymn, and in Alfred's West Saxon. So, whereas most of the other prepositions ordinarily take dative or accusative according to the meaning, every dative with *þurh* is abnormal; and a local explanation of the abnormality is excluded, as might have been expected from the evidence already given that R is a South-

[1] Most, if not all, the Latin gospel texts are squeezed into the Royal MS. by contemporary hands. Latin notes that certainly derive from Ælfric himself are more significant for textual history; but it is hard to decide whether they were omitted in A and R, or were added by the author after the first copies had been issued.

[2] The words appear in MS. Vitellius C v, which generally presents a late form of the text.

Eastern book, probably with a South-Eastern tradition behind it, while A shows no trace of South-Eastern ownership,[1] and is intimately connected with Ælfric's South-Western original. The construction with the dative is evidently late, and might spring up anywhere from the common instrumental use of *þurh*, and the analogy of other prepositions with the dative which it overlaps.[2]

In the Royal manuscript the dative is used frequently after *þurh*, though not to the exclusion of the accusative; and there is no consistent principle of choice. But a closer examination of the manuscript shows that the province of the dative was originally wider than now appears. There are a number of erasures and alterations which convert it into the accusative: e.g. *þurh his wisdom* (Thorpe, i, p. 10, l. 6): so A, altered from *wisdome*; *þurh deofles swicdom* (p. 20, l. 3): so A, altered from *swicdome*; *þurh manna mandæda* (ibid. l. 24): so A, altered from *mandædum*; *þurh his bearn* (p. 102, l. 14): so A, altered from *bearne*; *þurh ða twegen dælas* (p. 130, l. 20): so A, altered from *þurh ðam twam dælum*. Again there is no obvious reason why the dative should be sometimes corrected and sometimes left, though the corrector seems to have been more active near the beginning of the manuscript.[3]

A comparison of the first few sermons in the Royal manuscript with the corresponding pieces in R (MS. 340) gives the following results: (i) Where the dative has been altered to the accusative in the Royal manuscript, R has often the uncorrected dative; e.g. in all except the first of the instances quoted above. This fact, which corresponds with the evidence of items (2) and (6) cited at p. 179, above, is important for the analysis of the corrections in the Royal manuscript, some of which clearly do not belong to the first issue of the text. (ii) Wherever the dative occurs in R, it stood originally in A.[4] In fact, in the early sermons the choice of cases, haphazard

[1] See above, p. 172, n. 1.

[2] The MSS. sometimes show variants like *for eallum ðam tacnum* (Th. i 108, l. 22), where R has *þurh*; *for ðam heofenlican leohte* (Th. ii 548, l. 1); R *þurh þæt heofenlice leoht*.

[3] There are similar corrections with other prepositions. The questions of syntax involved deserve a dissertation.

[4] The converse does not hold through R, which is not homogeneous in this respect. Thus *De Initio Creaturæ*, the first sermon in the Royal MS.,

as it seems, is identical in R and A. For instance, R, A have *þurh þæt tacn* (Thorpe, p. 58, l. 14); *þurh tacen* (p. 62, l. 12); *þurh tacne* (p. 106, l. 4), where the *e* has been erased in the Royal manuscript. The agreements are such as to exclude coincidence, and there can be no doubt that R is closely related to the earliest extant state of the text in the Royal manuscript, as against the later states in MSS. Gg.3.28 and CCCC 188.

Turning now to MS. Gg.3.28, I find no instance of the dative after *þurh* in the First Series: the accusative is invariable. For the Second Series, of which Gg. is the only complete copy, the same contrast of regular accusative in Gg. against frequent dative in the corresponding sermons of R might be expected. But it is not so. From the Preface (Thorpe ii, p. 2, l. 18) onwards, the Second Series offers many examples of the dative after *þurh* in Gg.,[1] not evenly distributed as they were in the Royal manuscript of the First Series, but sometimes isolated, sometimes in patches, as at p. 304 ff., where there are six instances in five pages. Not only are similar phrases found in one place with the dative and in another with the accusative,[2] but the two are several times combined in hybrid constructions of the type *ðurh ða treowu* (acc.) *and ðam streawe* (dat.) *and ðam ceafe* (dat.).[3] Evidently the two Series contained in MS.

is also the first in MS. 342, and here there is close agreement in the use of the dative. But at the other end of the volume, in the sermon for the First Sunday in Advent, the Royal MS. has several instances of *þurh* with the dative where MS. 342 has the accusative throughout. The difference is probably due to uneven correction of the dative to the accusative in the copies from which R derives.

[1] The other prepositions affected seem to be treated similarly in Gg. Thus R. Gottweiss *Anglia* xxviii, p. 380 ff., lists the examples of *ymbe* with the dative in Thorpe's print, and of twelve instances only one is in the First Series.

[2] *ðurh þæt fyr afeormode* (ii, p. 590, l. 14), but *ðurh ðam fyre fornumene* (ibid. l. 27).

[3] Ed. Thorpe ii, p. 590, l. 13. Such hybrid constructions are mostly due to partial correction. The process may be seen, for instance, where (Thorpe i, p. 354, top) A has *ðurh martyrdome oððe ðurh oðrum haligum geearnungum*: R substitutes *martyrdom* for the first dative, making a hybrid; Gg. has the accusative in both members. Again (at i, p. 408, top) A originally read *ðurh godcundum tacnum ne ðurh liflicre lare*, but a corrector has altered *liflicre* to the accusative; R reproduces the hybrid thus formed; Gg. has the accusative in both places. It is worth noting that Gg. and R

Gg.3.28 derive from separate manuscripts of the First Series and the Second Series which had not the same textual history. Our previous conclusion that MS. Gg. is but a copy is confirmed. And the scribe who made it must have been unusually mechanical, for he not only followed his originals exactly in their divergent treatment of the cases after *þurh*, but (as Thorpe first pointed out, supposing it to be evidence for a change of hand) he usually spells *middangeard* in the First Series and *middaneard* in the Second.[1]

To sum up: the earliest state of the First Series in the Royal manuscript frequently has the dative after *þurh*, and R shows that a text containing these forms was issued. The First Series in Gg. has no such forms; nor has the later stage shown in MS. CCCC 188.[2] All these manuscripts are closely associated with the author. In the Second Series the dative appears in Gg. and the corresponding parts of R.[3] Clearly, on this evidence, Ælfric is responsible for the

sometimes agree in preserving the hybrid; e.g. *ðurh drycræft oððe ðurh runstafum* (ii, p. 358, l. 11); or *þurh freonda fultum* (acc.) *and ælmesdædum* (dat.) *and swiðost þurh halige* (acc.) *mæssan* (ii, p. 352, l. 25). And there are instances in the original form of A: e.g. *ðurh ðisne geleafan and ðurh godum geearnungum* (i, p. 294, l. 8). It is possible, then, that some of them may be due to Ælfric himself, especially where the accusative is an abstract noun and the dative more concrete.

[1] [There are exceptions in both volumes. Curious is the appearance of *middangeard* thrice in *De Temporibus* ch. v, perhaps as the result of special correction in that chapter, since elsewhere in the tract MS. Gg. has *middaneard*. The form *middaneard* must have been a neologism when Ælfric began writing, though it became common in the early eleventh century and is often substituted for *middangeard*, e.g. in MSS. C and H of *Gregory's Dialogues*, in MS. B of Alfred's *Boethius*, and in MSS. W and Bd of Cædmon's Hymn (ed. Dobbie). That the substitution of *eard* for *geard* was primarily phonetic appears from the parallel late *wineard* for *wingeard*.]

[2] As far as I have checked it. Lack of full collations, particularly for the Cambridge MSS., must be my excuse for neglecting some refinements of method and conclusion. Mr. E. S. Murrell has kindly rechecked for me some critical places in Gg.

[3] An examination of all the corresponding passages leaves no doubt that the datives after *þurh* in Gg. and in R derive from a common source, which is pretty certainly Ælfric's MS. of the Second Series. For instance, R agrees in all the examples on p. 376 of Thorpe's print. But, as might be expected, Gg. sometimes preserves the dative where R has the accusative: e.g. *ðurh his mandædum*: R *mandæda* (p. 310, l. 5); and conversely Gg. has

abnormal use of the dative in both the First and Second Series as originally issued; and he regularized his usage with prepositions after the Second Series had been published, revising at least the First Series minutely to bring it into line.[1]

It is even possible to specify a likely date for the reform. The Second Series was followed by the *Latin Grammar*,[2] in which Ælfric gave a considerable space to prepositions and the cases they govern.[3] The task of explaining Latin usage and translating the examples would bring home to him the anomalies of his own practice in English, and the advantages of regularity.

In that case, one would expect anomalous datives to disappear from his later works. I give a superficial account of the facts, still using *þurh* for simplicity: In the *De Temporibus*, which is closest in time to the Second Series, the dative still appears both in Gg. and the separate issue contained in MS. Tiberius B v.[4] The minor pieces in Gg. which Thorpe prints have only the accusative. So has the Letter for Wulfsige with which Gg. ends. In the *Latin Grammar* the accusative is regular. The compilation of the *Lives of Saints*

examples of the accusative where R preserves the dative, e.g. *ðurh leahtras*: R *leahtrum* (p. 338, l. 16). Thus R sometimes has readings nearer the original text of the Second Series than Gg. In one place (ii, p. 526, l. 14, after *sylfwilles*) R has words: *and wæstm brohton þurh godum weorcum. Hi ferdon sylfwilles* that are lost by homoeoteleuton in Gg. But as they are found also in MS. Junius 23, this is merely an error of Gg. It is curious that these words should contain an isolated example of *þurh*+dative, for elsewhere in this sermon MS. 342 agrees with Gg. in having only the accusative.

[1] That Ælfric also corrected the Second Series in this detail is likely but not demonstrable. Late MSS. are poor witnesses on such a point. The best evidence is MS. Vitellius C v, dating from about 1025, which contains a few sermons from the Second Series. Usually it has the accusative after *ðurh*, e.g. in Sermon XXVI, especially p. 376, where R and Gg. have several datives. But even this MS. preserves a few instances of the dative, as in the hybrid *þurh ða ealdan æ and ðæra witegena cwydum* (ii, p. 398, l. 13).

[2] [I do not mean 'followed immediately'. The small tract *De Temporibus* almost certainly intervenes, and so may other minor pieces. See Note E at p. 298, below.]

[3] Ed. J. Zupitza, p. 268, beginning, 'Case is the one feature of this part of speech'.

[4] See Bouterwek's *Screadunga*, p. 24, ll. 19 f., where both MSS. have *þurh acennedum cildum . . . þurh forðfaren(d)um.*

followed closely, though single Lives were probably written earlier:[1] in the two volumes of Skeat's edition instances of the dative after *þurh* are very rare.[2] In the Pastoral Letters for Wulfstan there is one example of the dative in a corrupt passage,[3] but a good manuscript has the accusative. The later sermons that have been mentioned already—*Hexameron*, *De Virginitate*, *In Natale Unius Confessoris*—have only the accusative. I may have missed a few examples, but the contrast between the *Catholic Homilies* and *De Temporibus* on the one hand and the later works on the other is confirmatory evidence of Ælfric's change of practice.

That he should be found overhauling the details of his English syntax may come as a surprise to those who think of the tenth century as an uncouth age. But he took an artist's pleasure in all the little things that make for good writing. His handling of the prepositions reveals at once the care that lies behind his finished prose, and the Latin standards by which he moulded it.

VI

LATER ADDITIONS

Many phases of Old English studies might be illustrated from the two Bodley manuscripts, for the old language and favourite sermons died hard. The last medieval reader who marked these volumes could do little more than add Latin glosses to familiar Gospel texts. Then from the early thirteenth to the sixteenth century they were preserved by the blessed inertia of ecclesiastical libraries, until the revival of antiquarian studies, and their application to religious controversy, again brought readers to the old

1 Besides St. Mary of Egypt, which is obviously interpolated, I reject on internal evidence Sermon XXXIII, St. Euphrasia, as not by Ælfric. Both are misplaced in the annual cycle. Sermon XXIII, The Seven Sleepers, is remarkable for a number of rhymes of the type *Mycel is me unbliss minra dyrlinga miss* (ed. Skeat, i, p. 504).

2 I, p. 30, l. 96, *ðurh . . . mycelre eadmodnesse*; p. 530, l. 686, *þurh þinre leasan tale*. But at ii, p. 128, l. 39 *-um* in *þurh Oswoldes geearnungum* is a later correction; and *þære* is perhaps gen. pl. in *þurh þære deofla grimetunge* (p. 294, l. 1206).

3 Ed. B. Fehr, p. 80, § 25: *þurh þas myngunge* (acc.) *and manegum oþrum wordum* (dat.).

sermon-books. But I shall limit attention to two kinds of later additions.

The first is a group of accents, associated with marks of word-division and punctuation. Some are in ink, some in a coarse brown pencil which occasionally leaves no more than a scratch; and both kinds often suffer later erasure. The accents in ink vary in appearance as though they belonged to different strata.[1] Those in pencil are easier to describe briefly, because they seem to come from one hand. As they occur in the sermons added to MS. 342 by later scribes, they are presumably not earlier than 1050. The form of certain marginal notes in similar pencil, taken in conjunction with places where the pencil is crossed by later corrections, suggests that they were made round about the end of the eleventh century.

Some sermons and passages are densely marked, others lightly, others not at all; and an examination of these last in favourable places[2] reveals the marker's practical purpose. The unmarked passages, which are often secluded by a pencil line in the margin, are evidently the 'cuts' made by a person who was preparing the sermon for delivery. The marks, then, were intended to guide him in reading aloud, and are thus free from many of the doubts that embarrass the study of accents in Old English manuscripts. But the consistency of a grammarian is not to be expected in markings made with such a purpose, and conclusions can be more safely drawn from their presence than from their absence.

(i) The commonest accent is the acute, which is sometimes doubled in a way that suggests careless or hasty marking rather than a considered distinction. It is applied to the vowels of stressed syllables: (*a*) most frequently to a vowel

[1] All the usages noted below for the pencil occur also in the ink markings. Many of these may come from the same hand as the pencil, if it be allowed that the use of a pen would result in forms different from those produced by a hard point.

[2] e.g. MS. 340, ff. 30–32. In other places the process is not so clear, either because the cuts were decided upon after some markings had been made, or because the text was worked over for more than one occasion. The nature of the revision is of interest, for we know all too little of the habits of English preachers at this time. The sermon for 'the Second Sunday after Epiphany and for general occasions' (Thorpe ii, p. 54) has had unusually heavy correction.

certainly or probably long: e.g. *fótum*, *hǽlan*, *éac*, *wórd*, *ýldinge*; (*b*) commonly to a short vowel in a heavy syllable: e.g. *stíncende*, *cwéartern*, *búrgum*; (*c*) commonly to a short vowel in a stressed prefix: e.g. *únasecgendlice*; (*d*) occasionally to a short vowel in a stressed open syllable: e.g. *wúnunge* (MS. 340, f. 10*a*); *sámod* (f. 20*b*).

(ii) (*a*) Stressed short vowels in closed syllables are often indicated by a curl above, which is a variant of the short sign:[1] e.g. *Gòd* (so distinguished from *gód* 'good'), *gòdspelle*, *gòdcundnysse*, *gecỳd*, *lìm*, *anìm*, *càn*(*n*), *màn*(*n*) and *mànnum*, *forhwàn*, *ongàn*, *mùntum*, *getrỳmman*, *gæ̀mnie*, *fùlne*, *pàlm*, *cwèlmbærum*, *þwỳr*, *onbrỳrd*, *gefỳrn*, *awùrpon*, *geànbidode*, *wànspédigum*. A short sign was first noticed in Old English by Napier, who cited the eleventh-century MSS. Cleopatra B XIII and Tiberius A III.[2] It occurs also in MS. CCCC 190,[3] and a systematic search would add to the list.

(*b*) Sometimes an angular sign like the circumflex is used with the same purpose, e.g. in *hûlcum*, *ândgyt*, *genâm*, *stêmn*, *þrŷm*, *gôdcundan*, *gesêt*, *fŷr* (compar. of *feorr*), *þûs*. Occasionally it spans the space between the word to which it belongs and the next; and in *manncynn* (MS. 340, f. 30*a*), where it should appear over both syllables, it is doubled over the first. This angular sign has not been noticed elsewhere, and is the more curious because the circumflex is traditionally a mark of vowel-length. But in the original script (late tenth century) of Salisbury Cathedral MS. 150 it is used both in words like *timêbo* and in words like *dûx*, *nîx*, where the vowel is short but the syllable is long because it is closed by two consonants. This may be the starting-point of the usage here.

[1] In other OE. MSS. the short sign is like a *c* written above the vowel: this modification in the position of the brevis ᵕ avoids confusion with the marks of abbreviation usual in Latin MSS. of the time. In the Bodley MSS. the short sign is a curl open on the left-hand side: this variant of the brevis would be inconvenient in Latin, where a similar mark indicates the contraction *-us*; but it serves well enough in the vernacular.

[2] *The Academy*, Oct. 1889, p. 221.

[3] See B. Fehr *Die Hirtenbriefe Ælfrics*, 1914, p. xviii, and for examples, pp. 9, 15, 25.

(iii) In other manuscripts in which a short sign has been noted, the curl is applied indifferently to short vowels in open and closed syllables. Here the former are distinguished by a new mark—a very long macron which is usually extended over the following consonant and vowel:[1] e.g. in *godes*, *bodum*, *brudon*, *gelaðode*, *wracu*, *strecan*, *cuma*, *nama*, *wanian*, *toslopen*, *beran*, *warum* (dat. pl. 'wares'), *hryre*, *hwate*, *þrotan*, *plegan*, *ege*, *onsigon*, *geflogen*, *clawum*, *cneowu*.

Now grammatical devices in English of this period generally reflect the revived teaching of Latin, since Latin, not English, was studied grammatically. And it is at least curious to find that, quite apart from their importance in metre, the Latin short vowels in open syllables had been recently the subject of controversy. Ælfric in the Preface to his *Grammar* speaks of the many who pronounce *pater*, *malus*, &c., in prose after what he calls the 'Welsh manner' (*Brittonice*), i.e. with a short vowel, and defends the lengthened pronunciation, which had become established in late Vulgar Latin, by arguing that to address the Heavenly Father with a short vowel in *Pater* is to subject God to the rules of grammar. Evidently the school of Æthelwold was on its defence in this matter, and fell back on an old dispensing argument for want of grammatical authority. Such a dispute might lead to the practice of distinguishing the short vowels of open syllables in Latin, whence it might be transferred to English.[2]

But however that may be, here, a century before the *Ormulum*, is the distinction between short vowels in open and in closed syllables which lies at the root of the long controversy about Orm's system of spelling. Orm doubles a consonant after a short vowel, *except* when the vowel is in an open syllable: thus *mann*: gen. *manness*; *Godd*: gen. *Gŏdess*; *namm* 'he took': but *năme* 'name'. According to one view, he doubled the consonant to show that the

[1] Once (MS. 342, f. 120*b*) *gegrîpan* (pa.t.subj.pl.) has been corrected to *gegripan*.

[2] If this use of the long macron had its origin in the teaching of Latin, it may have been suggested by the metrical equation: two shorts = one long.

preceding vowel was short. According to a view which seems to be more favoured by recent writers,[1] his primary purpose was to show that the consonant was long; and the exceptional treatment of *năme*, &c., is in the forefront of their evidence.

The arguments from phonology are fine-drawn, because in English a short stressed vowel is usually associated with a long following consonant in the same syllable. But the tradition behind Orm has not, I believe, been discussed. Our Bodley manuscripts, almost as regularly as far as the markings go, have the same distinction of short vowels in open and closed syllables: *mȧn(n)*: *mȧnnes*; *Gȯd*: *Go̅d̅es*; *nam* (pa.t.sg. of *nĭman*): *nam̅a̅*.[2] Yet I have detected no signs of interest in consonant-length. If that were in question, the marker would not help himself by such markings as *þæt hi wæ̅r̅e wǽron*

[1] There are three main views—I mention only their earliest or principal exponents:

(i) That Orm wished to mark the quantity of vowels (A. J. Ellis *On Early English Pronunciation*, 1869, pp. 55, 486; H. Sweet *History of English Sounds*, 1874, p. 48 (508); second edition 1888, §§ 616–17; L. Morsbach *Mittelenglische Grammatik*, 1896, p. 31 ff.).

(ii) That he wished to mark the quantity of consonants (M. Trautmann *Anglia* vii (1884), Anz. pp. 94 ff. and 208 ff.; *Anglia* xviii (1896), p. 371 ff.).

(iii) That observation of the varying length of consonants first led Orm to adopt his system, though in the result it came to indicate the quantity of vowels (E. Björkman *Anglia* xxxvii (1913), p. 351 ff., who gives a useful history of earlier work; K. Luick *Historische Grammatik*, 1914, p. 87 f.; R. Jordan *Handbuch der mittelenglischen Grammatik*, 1925, p. 37).

The symmetrical evolution of opinion—two opposed views followed by a compromise—is noticeable. There are elements of chance in the fortunes of theories, and it is worth remarking that when Sweet first published his view in 1874, he left the single consonant in words like *năme* as 'a formidable difficulty' unsolved. In his second edition of 1888 he gave a competent explanation. But in the meantime the active and influential school of Trautmann had become committed to consonant-quantity as the solution. It is a question whether this doctrine would have gained so strong a hold if Sweet had been able to state the case in 1874 as he did in 1888.

[2] There is a difference in the treatment of short diphthongs or virtual diphthongs. The marker of the Bodley MSS. has *cla̅w̅u̅m*, *cneo̅w̅u*, so grouping these words with others in which a short vowel stands in an open syllable. Orm writes *clawwess*, *cnewwess*, and divides at the line-end *claw-wess*, &c., exactly as if he were dealing with a short vowel in a closed syllable.

'that they should be wary' (MS. 340, f. 61*a*), because in both words the medial consonant is the initial sound of the second syllable.[1] Indeed, it is hard to see how an Englishman reading his own language aloud could attach practical importance to marking the niceties of consonant-length; or why his mind should be directed to it at all as a matter of theory or tradition. Then, and long afterwards, Latin grammar was the only linguistic discipline; and Latin grammar meant the more practical parts of a few standard textbooks. If unpractical elements appear, it is because they have the authority of Donatus, Priscian, or Isidore. And though these grammarians deal with the length of vowels and syllables, and were eagerly read and developed because the subjects were necessary for the writing of Latin verse, they and their medieval successors seem to be indifferent to the length of consonants.[2] They were either unconscious of subtle variations (as most of us still are unless our interest has been awakened by modern phonetic theory), or else they thought discussion of them unprofitable.

Orm, too, must have been steeped in the current teaching of Latin. His sermons are translated from old-fashioned sources; he gives his title a flavour of modesty and latinity by clapping *-ulum* on to his own name;[3] he abandons native metres for a Latin type without rhyme or alliteration. So he might be expected to look at English from the standpoint of Latin grammar, and from that standpoint the study and markings of consonant-length would be an original exercise in phonetics. It is not very likely that an author who is otherwise pedantically attached to tradition should strike

[1] It might be thought that the mark indicates an abnormal absence of syllable-division, such as is found in similar forms in modern German: that instead of *nă-ma*, &c., the pronunciation was *năma*. But the practice of scribes and the later lengthening of short vowels in open syllables confirm the normal division *nă-ma*.

[2] What is in question is not the patent difference between a single consonant as in *many* and a true double consonant as in *pen-nib*. Orm is supposed to have observed and recorded such differences of length as that between *d* in *God* and *d* in *goad*, *t* in *pit* and *t* in *feet*.

[3] According to H. Bradley *Collected Papers*, 1928, p. 219, *Ormulum* was 'probably an imitation of *Speculum*, a common medieval name for books of devotion or religious edification'. But though it is known earlier, *Speculum* as a title seems to have become popular after Orm's day.

out this new line, without any explanation, in a work which he expected to have some currency.

Let us then see what difficulties stand in the way of assuming that he kept to the path of tradition with an eye on the habits of writers and readers of his own time, and that he was particularly interested in the quantity of vowels and syllables.

(i) To distinguish long vowels the Latin grammarians recommended the macron; but except in formal scansion it had been made impracticable in Christian times by the spread of the similar mark of abbreviation—a spread which was suddenly accelerated in the twelfth century. The acute accent was also used in special cases;[1] but it had so many values in Old English writings that its failure as a distinctive mark of length was inevitable; and still another complication was added in the twelfth century when, from forms like *abíít*, it began to spread to *i* in all positions. The doubling of the long vowel was not usual or elegant in Latin orthography; it was not very common in late Old English; and it had become associated with a disyllabic pronunciation in words like *abíít*. Thus there was no clear and familiar way of marking the long vowels, and Orm generally leaves them unmarked.

(ii) The short mark of the grammarians was not a convenient way of distinguishing the very numerous short vowels in closed syllables, e.g. *Gŏd*, *măn*(*n*): it was rare in Latin and English texts; it was easily confused with abbreviation-marks; and by tradition it belonged equally to the short vowels in open syllables. But in Latin a doubled consonant usually follows a short vowel, and in late Old English every doubled consonant followed a short vowel and closed the syllable. This association of short vowel and doubled consonant in the minds of Englishmen is early, for Byrhtferth, writing in 1011, gives as an example of barbarism *þu sót*, where one should say *þu sott*.[2] Here, ready to Orm's hand, was an unmistakable method of indicating the short vowels in closed syllables, which are the great majority in English.

[1] e.g. to distinguish *pópulus* 'poplar' from *populus* 'people'.

[2] Ed. S. J. Crawford, E.E.T.S. 1929, p. 96.

It is the most regular feature of his spelling, and the only one he mentions in his Preface.

(iii) There remain the short vowels in open syllables, such as *năme*, OE. *năma* 'name'. Orm, like the marker of our Bodley manuscripts, may have aimed at distinguishing them from the short vowels in closed syllables. But even if he had no such purpose, he could not double the consonant in this case without getting into difficulties: for *namme* would inevitably suggest the pronunciation *nam-me*, with a true double consonant; and such words as *sŭne* 'son', *bĕde* 'prayer', would assume the forms of *sunne* 'sun' and *bedde* (dative) 'bed'.[1] To his contemporaries the double consonant between vowels had a significance which it has lost in modern English; and sensitiveness on such a point would be increased by the training in division of syllables which was then usual:[2] Orm himself would have to consider how he would divide *namme* at the end of a line of his manuscript, and would find *namm/e*, *na/mme*, and *nam/me* all intolerable. Yet if he left the short vowels in open syllables unmarked, they might be confused with the long vowels; and the difference was sometimes of practical importance in the *Ormulum*, because a word of the type *năme* could not fill the last foot in the verse. I should not care to assert that he explored and was oppressed by all these difficulties. A phonetician bent on marking the quantity of these vowels would find an easy solution in the use of a special diacritic such as that found in the Bodley manuscripts. In fact Orm writes words of this kind with a single consonant, sometimes adding a short sign, e.g. *năme*, and sometimes not. As a system designed to mark the length of vowels his spelling breaks down.

Must we then conclude that it was a system designed to mark the length of consonants? I think not: for there is the possibility,

[1] The point was first made by Sweet, *History of English Sounds*, 2nd ed. 1888, §§ 616–17. I differ from this classic account only in the explanation of Orm's purpose.

[2] Scribes sometimes wrote in syllables, e.g. Cotton MS. Vespasian D xx (tenth century), f. 18*a*, 'am bu las ti pe di bus u bi li ci tum non fu it.'

even the likelihood, that Orm's interests were not those of a phonetician at all, and that the end he had in view required neither consistency nor completeness of notation. A phonetic system should represent every sound precisely and uniformly, taking nothing for granted except the reader's willingness and ability to interpret the system. But a working orthography for a special purpose may be produced on a different principle. Its deviser may well consider who will read it, and how, and for what purpose; what knowledge and habits these readers may be assumed to have, and what difficulties they may be expected to feel. Its success will depend on the discreet selection of points at which special help is given, whereas a phonetic notation succeeds by the even fullness of its record.

Clearly, in a working orthography designed for English readers there was no need to distinguish all short vowels in open syllables from long vowels. Uncertainty was likely only when they occurred in words of similar form, and more particularly in contexts that were not plain at the first glance. Orm meets this special case very often by marking the short vowel with the short sign, or the long vowel with the acute, or by using both: thus *bigrĭþenn* pa.t.pl.: *bigriþenn* infin.; *wrĭtenn* p.p.: *wrítenn* infin.; *hătenn* 'to hate': *hátenn* 'called'; *hĕre* 'of them': *hére* 'here'; *hĕte* 'hate': *hæte* 'heat; *lăte* 'late': *láte* 'appearance'; *răþe* 'quickly': *ráþenn* 'advise'; *rŏtenn* 'rot': *róte* 'root'; *to tăkenn* 'to take': *to tákenn* 'as a token'; *wăke-menn* 'watchmen': *wáke* 'weak'; *wĕre* 'man': *wære* 'were'; *wĭte* 'wise man': *wíte* 'punishment'. Regularity cannot be claimed for these markings, but there is enough to indicate a practical purpose other than the scientific representation of sounds.

Nor is this practical purpose hard to find. It can scarcely be coincidence that Orm's book and the older Bodley manuscripts are both complete[1] courses of sermons for the common people; that Orm was a canon of the Augustinian order, which undertook the care of lay congregations; and that his age saw the revival of popular preaching at widely distant points in Europe. In his Preface he says repeatedly that he explained the Gospel in English because he

[1] The extant MS. in Orm's own hand (MS. Junius 1 in the Bodleian) is only the first part of the larger scheme indicated by his Preface and table of contents.

wished that all English folk should hear it, believe it, and follow it in deed, and so win salvation for their souls. This was possible only if his book were read to them by preachers, and the orthographical devices are—as in the Bodley manuscripts—intended to help preachers reading aloud to their congregations.

One can imagine the discussions Orm had with his brother Walter, a fellow canon, who encouraged him to write the *Ormulum*. The signs of change about them were alarming to good churchmen. A ferment of new ideas, many of them worldly in tendency, had unsettled the rank and file of laymen. Might they not still be saved by sound instruction in the Gospel, such as Bede gave in Latin? Sermons in English were needed to reach the people; yet there was no foundational course in English now that Ælfric's language, despite patching and modernizing, was out of date. To supply the want would be a great work for religion. Verse should be the medium, because the people preferred rhythmic forms and remembered them better. But the apathy and ignorance of congregations were partly due to the way preachers mumbled and blundered in reading the sermon; and no wonder, when the spelling of the English texts available had become a medley of archaisms, tricks borrowed from French, and careless eccentricities. Something ought to be done to help preachers to read the Gospel truths to their congregations as they were trained to read Latin—'distincte et aperte atque verbatim sed et syllabatim ac sensatim'.[1]

This I take to be the subordinate but not insignificant part of orthography in Orm's ill-fated design for saving the souls of Englishmen.[2] If so, we may put aside many of the phonological subtleties that have been suggested to account for details in his spelling: even if they crossed his mind, they would be neither

[1] The jargon is Ælfric Bata's in *Early Scholastic Colloquies*, ed. W. H. Stevenson, 1929, p. 68.

[2] This practical motive played a large part in the medieval development of calligraphy and orthography, which took place mainly in books intended for the use of clerics. So Alcuin, one of the great initiators and guiders of reform, enjoins accuracy:

Ne vel falsa legat, taceat vel forte repente
Ante pios fratres lector in ecclesia.
(*Mon. Germ. Hist. Poetae Latini Aevi Carol.*, i, p. 320.)

intelligible nor useful to preachers in the act of reading aloud. To attain his object he was bound to take familiar usage as a basis, and to improve it by devices which were transparent and not puzzling.[1] So he points his text very carefully, and specially marks the division of words, which is often troublesome at first glance to readers of manuscripts. He introduces a rule like the doubling of consonants after short vowels in closed syllables which puts no strain on the memory or intelligence of readers. Generally he avoids freakish and misleading spellings; and, as we have seen, he tries to help in special difficulties.[2] It is natural that the reasons why he chose to help in one place and not in another should often escape us, and that his enthusiasm for an ingenious device should lead him to use it more often than was strictly necessary. There are elements of caprice and carelessness in his work which defy rational explanation. But even in these lapses from scientific perfection he has a kinship with men of his own time and training, among whom it is hard to find a place for Orm the rigorous phonetician.

VII

The scribbles on the blank leaves of old manuscripts are always worth notice, because the broken scraps that were running in the minds of scribes or readers floated to the surface when a new pen had to be tried.

[1] Even where he distinguishes the sounds in *egge* 'edge' and *eggenn* 'to egg on' by using a different form of *g* (Napier *Academy*, 15 March 1890), his practical sense appears. The distinction of sounds, which was then what it is now, requires no nice observation; the finer distinction of the symbols will help readers who notice it, but those who do not notice it will at least have the customary spelling of the time, since both the symbols are unmistakably 'g'.

[2] Some peculiarities of Orm's orthography may be intended to counteract habits which a preacher would derive from his training in the reading of Latin. Thus it is a safe rule that all Latin vowels before a final *t* are short: *at*, *et*, *-it*, *tot*, *ut*, *caput*, &c. Orm's emphatic double and treble accents are almost confined to syllables containing long vowels followed by *t* in the same syllable: *wra̋t*, *gæ̋t*, *ʒe̋t*, *fe̋tless* 'vessel', *sı̋t* 'pain', *főt*, *űt*. The two or three exceptions ending in *d* might be explained in the same way, but are better accounted for by special circumstances. M. Deutschbein collects the materials in Herrig's *Archiv für das Studium der neueren Sprachen*, vol. cxxvi, p. 49 ff., and vol. cxxvii, p. 308 ff., and attempts to find a phonological exlpanation.

The last fly-leaf of MS. Bodley 342 has been cut in half from top to bottom, so that little is left intelligible, except the copy-book verse 'Dicite Pyherides non omnia possumus omnes', often repeated, and the line-ends of a *quid inde?* poem in five lines, which show variants from the longer version printed in Wright and Halliwell's *Reliquiæ Antiquæ*, i, p. 57.

The last fly-leaf of MS. Bodley 340 is headed by the alphabet followed by *In principio* and many half-erased scribbles. One scribe, regardless of grammar, writes *Probatio penne incaustum.* Another begins *Anno millesimo sexageno quoque seno*, placing musical notes over *sexageno*, and then stops short. Another, with a neat pointed hand of the second half of the eleventh century, tumbles out a more curious rag-bag. He begins with formal pen-trials: *Probatio penne si bona sit*; *Probatio incauxti si bonum sit*. Next comes a prayer to the popular Saint Nicholas: 'O beate pater Nicolæ, pium dominum Iesum pro impietatibus nostris deposce!' Then

Scribere qui cupiunt sensum Deus augeat illis!

Next he remembers some leonine hexameters whose mangled text proves that he did not understand them:

Cordarum modulos pangamus nobile melos,
singula dulcisonum quo s(int)[1] discrimina vocum
callemus resono leviter dinoscere plectro,
et (sic) dissimiles melius formare tenores,[2]
accentusque gravis ne s(it)[3] moderando suavis
aptemus citara[4] fides feriendo canora,
nunc leviore modo clangentes nuncque suppremo. Alleluia.

Then *Quid expectamus nunc?* with a wholly unexpected sequel:

Abent omnes volucres nidos inceptos nisi ego et tu[5]

and below it

Hebban olla vogala nestas hagunnan hinase hi | anda thu.

[1] Letters in brackets are not legible in the MS. For help in emending the text I am indebted to Mr. Stephen Gaselee, Mr. F. J. E. Raby, and Dom André Wilmart.

[2] tenora *MS.*

[3] sit] *MS.* ? fit.

[4] ceteras *MS.*

[5] He begins *Abent omnes* again below, but goes no farther.

This is by far the earliest scrap of Netherlandish that has been recorded in England, and I doubt if it can be matched anywhere.[1] It recalls a whole series of literary contacts with the Low Countries: Dunstan in exile and in power again; Womær, abbot of Ghent, retiring to die at Newminster, Winchester, in 981;[2] the unlucky clerk of Liége, *omnium fæx Christicolarum*, whom Archbishop Æthelgar employed to work with the Newminster copy of Aldhelm's *De Virginitate*;[3] nearer our date, Athelard of Liége and Utrecht, who was appointed by Harold to instruct the canons in his favourite abbey of Waltham;[4] and, lastly, the *Flandrenses* who came in the train of the Conqueror. The Latin sentence looks like a fragment from one of the colloquies which were used to teach Latin, and there may well have been a Fleming among the monks of Rochester.

Readers who have been so patient as to follow the rambling course of these articles may wish to be reminded that they were written to commend the irregular study of Old English manuscripts. Many manuscripts would offer less variety of interest than the example chosen. But MSS. Bodley 340 and 342 are not fresh ground: they have been expertly described since Wanley first made them known in 1705; they are easily accessible, and they have been used by competent modern philologists. If they still offer good gleaning, it is because the attention of the scholars who used them was concentrated on other things.

A persistent restriction of curiosity is not altogether surprising. When a new subject is advancing, as Old English studies did after 1870, with everything to be done and none too many workers, more rapid progress can be made if wandering eyes are disciplined: so we put blinkers on young horses. When the subject becomes established academically, teaching tends to follow the lines that have

[1] Dr. M. Schönfeld, to whom I communicated the scrap, examines its interest for Netherlandish philology in *Tijdschrift voor Nederlandsche Taal- en Letterkunde* lii (1933).

[2] Anglo-Saxon Chronicle, MS. C under that year.

[3] *Memorials of St. Dunstan* (Rolls Series), ed. W. Stubbs, p. 388.

[4] *The Foundation of Waltham Abbey*, ed. W. Stubbs, Oxford, 1861, p. 15.

been worked successfully; they become implicit in systematic training, and are fortified by a professional technique. But with limited materials, the law of diminishing returns presses inexorably. The advances which are the real life of a study become smaller, fewer, and more hardly won. Some will then say that the subject is worked out. It is more cheerful to believe that certain veins, once rich, are no longer yielding enough, and to look for others to supplement them. The manuscripts, at least, have still plenty to offer.

11

AN OLD ENGLISH TRANSLATION OF A LETTER FROM WYNFRITH TO EADBURGA (A.D. 716–17) IN COTTON MS. OTHO C I[1]

IN the *Modern Language Review* for April 1922, p. 166, Professor Toller quotes three words excerpted by Cockayne from an Old English tract named *Wynfrith*, and refers to Wanley's Catalogue (1705), p. 212, where the opening and closing sentences are quoted from the Cotton MS. Otho C I.

This manuscript suffered in the fire of 1731, especially at the beginning, which was most exposed because the book stood first on its shelf. The bulk of the text is fairly well preserved, although towards the end the leaves are increasingly shrivelled, split, or holed. All that survive are skilfully mounted on cardboard frames, and bound up in two volumes.

The first volume of 110 folios contains a copy of the West-Saxon Gospels, written in one bold, rough hand which may be dated about the middle of the eleventh century. At the end of the Gospel of St. John the scribe gives his name: *Wulfwi*[2] *me wrát* (f. 110*a*). The

[1] From *Modern Language Review* xviii (1923), p. 253 ff.

[2] The identification of this *Wulfwi* with *Wulfwinus*, the scribe of the Paris Psalter (Bibl. Nat. MS. Lat. 8824), by Bruce (*Publ. Mod. Lang. Assoc. of America* ix. 47–50), Plummer (*Life and Times of Alfred the Great*, p. 150), Bright (*Gospel of St. John*, Boston 1904, p. xix n.), and, on their authority, by Wildhagen (*Festschrift für Lorenz Morsbach*, Halle 1913, p. 471) shows how the survival of errors is favoured by indirect methods. *Wulfwi* can hardly be miswritten for *Wulfwī* = *Wulfwine*, as Wildhagen suggests, because the contraction mark in OE. represents *-ne* only in words like *þoñ* = *þonne*: it is not added directly to a vowel. And although the latinized forms of *Wulfwi*(*g*) and *Wulfwine* occasionally cross in late texts, the names are usually well distinguished; and both are so common that there is no prima facie case for connecting two MSS. because one is signed *Wulfwi* and one *Wulfwinus*. Bright finds corroboration of the identity in the likeness of the scribal errors in both texts, but he quotes no examples, and they are not obvious. The real test, which none of these

folios containing the text up to Matthew xxvii. 6 were lost when Wanley saw the book; and since then fire has completely destroyed another 25 leaves, as far as Mark vii. 22, and reduced those that immediately follow to charred fragments.[1] This volume is free from glosses or other extraneous matter, save for an Old English rendering of a letter from Pope Sergius to St. Aldhelm, which is added at the end of St. Luke's Gospel (ff. 68*a*, l. 5 to 69*b* foot) in a smaller and smoother hand, nearly contemporary with Wulfwi's.[2] As the letter gives privileges to Malmesbury, it has been inferred that this copy of the Gospels belonged to Malmesbury Abbey in the eleventh century.

The second volume appears to be a single manuscript of distinct origin, which was fortuitously bound up with the Gospel manuscript in Cotton's time. Scattered through it are many Latin and a few English glosses by hands of the end of the twelfth or the beginning of the thirteenth century; and as the method of glossing

writers appears to have made, is a comparison of the hands, and it would be hard to find two more unlike in the first half of the eleventh century: that of Wulfwi is large and rough, with the tops of the high letters deeply cloven; that of the Paris Psalter is earlier in style, and is as smooth and regular as can be found in the records of Old English penmanship. The direct test should be decisive; but even against this emergency Plummer (loc. cit.) has prepared a life-line for the hypothesis by reviving the suggestion that the colophon of the Paris Psalter may be a copy—that Wulfwinus may be the scribe not of the book itself but of its archetype. This suggestion was advanced by Thorpe (*Libri Psalmorum*, &c., Oxford 1835, p. vi n.), who was misled into thinking that the Paris MS. was a copy made by a French monk; and fortunately it can be disposed of. For a contemporary hand has added above *Wulfwinus* in different ink his distinguishing name —*cognomento Cada*. I have little doubt that Wulfwine himself wrote these words—*cognomento* in his Latin, *Cada* in his English script; but in any event, here is clear evidence that Wulfwine was a known person when the entry was made in the Paris MS.; and the ascription of such a book as the Psalter to a known and obscure copyist who did not actually write it is a piece of motiveless falsification that should not be assumed. The identification fails, and with it must go any support it affords to the Malmesbury provenance of both books.

[1] See the description in *The Holy Gospels in Anglo-Saxon*, &c., ed. Skeat (Cambridge 1871–87), Preface to *Mark*, p. viii ff.

[2] Printed by Birch *Cartularium Saxonicum*, No. 106 (vol. i, p. 154 ff.), and by Hamilton *Willelmi Malmesbiriensis de Gestis Pontificum* (Rolls Series 1870), p. 370 ff. footnote.

agrees in some minute points with that found in manuscripts which certainly come from Worcester,[1] it may be taken that the whole of our second volume belonged to Worcester about the year 1200. It consists of 155 mounted leaves, containing as principal text (ff. 1–137*a*) Wærferth's Old English version of Gregory's *Dialogues*,[2] which for some reason was left incomplete.

I. The First and Second Books (ff. 1–61*b*) are written in a hand that preserves many features of the old national script, and may be dated—if normal conditions be assumed—in the first quarter of the eleventh century. They are preceded in the same hand by a metrical preface which is preserved only in this manuscript, and contains the puzzling lines:

Me awritan het   Wulfstan bisceop,
Þeow ond þearfa   þæs þe alne þrym a⟨h⟩of . . .
Bideþ þe se bisceop,   se þe ðas boc begeat
Þe þu on þinum handum nu   hafast ond sceawast,
Þæt þu him to þeossum halgum   helpe bidde
Þe heora gemynd her on   gemearcude siendon;
Ond þæt him God ællmihtig   forgyue þa gyltas
Þe he geworhte, . . .
Ond eac resðe mid him   se ðe ah ealles rices geweald;
Ond eac swa his beahgifan,   þe him ðas bysene forgeaf,
Þæt is se selesða   since brytta,
Ælfryd mid Englum,   ealra cyninga
Þara þe he sið oððe ær   [fore] secgan hyrde,
Oððe he hiorðcyninga[3] ær   ænigne gefrugne.

Since Krebs[4] first printed the passage in 1880, the association of the names of Bishop Wulfstan and King Alfred has been much debated, with the result that later critics are at one with Keller[5] in the con-

[1] I have not relied on identification of the Worcester gloss-hands, because the point deserves a lengthy and difficult palaeographical study.

[2] See Hecht's edition, *Bibliothek der ags. Prosa*, vol. v, especially Pt. I (Leipzig 1900), p. vii f.

[3] = *iorð-, eorð-cyninga.*

[4] *Anglia* iii, p. 70 ff. He used Cockayne's transcript.

[5] *Die literarischen Bestrebungen von Worcester in ags. Zeit*, Strassburg 1900, p. 6 ff.; and also Holthausen *Archiv* cv (1900), p. 367 f.; Cook *Mod. Lang. Notes* xvii (1902), col. 14 ff.; Hecht in his edition, Pt. II (1907), p. 36, &c.; Brandl *Geschichte der altenglischen Literatur* (Strassburg 1908), p. 1063 f.

clusion that the preface is by the translator, Bishop Wærferth; that *bysen* means the King's 'command' or 'commission' to translate the *Dialogues*; and that the copyist of MS. Otho C I has substituted for *Wærferð* of the original preface the name of *Wulfstan*, which was more famous at Worcester in the eleventh century. Yet the manuscript itself discloses a much more interesting scrap of literary history. In *Wulfstan*, the last three letters *-tan* stand on an erasure, and are, I should think, not earlier than the time of the second Wulfstan, who was bishop of Worcester from 1062 till his death in 1095.[1] It is pretty clear that the name of *Wulfsige* stood here originally, and any doubt is removed by the trace of the erasing tool below the line, where the tail of *ʒ* would fall.[2] The preface then is by a Bishop Wulfsige; and who can doubt that this was King Alfred's friend Wulfsige, bishop of Sherborne?[3] To him Alfred sent a copy of his translation of Gregory's *Pastoralis*, which was the archetype of MS. Ii. II. 4 (1737) in the Cambridge University Library;[4] and evidently the King distributed copies of *Gregory's Dialogues* among his bishops in the same way. On the model (*bysen*)[5] of this gift-book, Wulfsige ordered another copy to be made, and wrote for the occasion the rhythmical preface, which is the only

[1] The substitution was probably made during the bishopric of Wulfstan II, for the prayer would be more appropriate in his lifetime. Keller (p. 66) apparently assumes that the first scribe of MS. Otho C I wrote during his bishopric, which is untenable. Hecht (Pt. II, p. 27) and Cook accept Keller's view; but it is hard to see how they square it with the date 1025–50 which they assign to the MS. Cook's further suggestion that the scribe was Wulfgeat (loc. cit., col. 18) is far astray.

[2] See the discussion at p. 225 ff., below.

[3] The dates of his consecration and death are unknown; cf. Asser's *Life of King Alfred*, ed. W. H. Stevenson (Oxford 1904), p. lxvi. In fact his memory is preserved chiefly by doubtful or spurious charters, and by the inscriptions in books.

[4] See Wanley's Catalogue, pp. 153, 168; he concludes that the Trinity MS. R.5.22 (717) was the one sent by Bishop Jewell to Parker from the Salisbury Library, where one would expect to find Sherborne books. The same history is claimed for the University Library copy.

[5] Wülker's objection to this interpretation (*Grundriss zur Geschichte der ags. Litteratur*, p. 439, n. 2) is invalid; cf. Ælfric's Preface to the second series of his *Catholic Homilies*: 'Nu bidde ic . . . gif hwa ðas boc awritan wylle, þæt he hi geornlice gerihte be ðære bysne', &c. (ed. Thorpe ii, p. 2); and particularly the metrical preface to *Pastoral Care*, ll. 12–16.

surviving piece of his composition. Perhaps because their own good texts had been lost or depraved, the Worcester community subsequently obtained a transcript of the copy that had been made by Wulfsige's instructions, and with it his preface reached Worcester. Later still, some reader to whom the name of Wulfsige was meaningless substituted the great Worcester name of Wulfstan in our manuscript. To broach all the questions of textual history that arise would lead me too far from my present purpose. But here at least is the reason why the rhythmical preface is absent from MS. CCCC 322 of the *Dialogues*, which belongs to a tradition independent of Wulfsige's copy. And the Mercian forms of Books I and II of MS. Otho C I may be traced to Wærferth's original with more certainty now that it is established that this manuscript does not represent the continuous tradition of Worcester or any other Mercian centre.[1]

II. With the Third Book (f. 62*a*) begins a hand formed in the tradition of the Carolingian minuscule, and distinctly later in appearance than the first. It is not uncommon to find two hands of the same date differing in the stage of script-development attained: but in this instance I am not satisfied that the second hand is strictly contemporary with the first. The ruling is for 30 lines as compared with 27 lines of the first part; the colouring of sentence-initials is not carried into Books III and IV; and it may well be that the original manuscript was divided for practical use into two halves each containing two books (a division which would be easy because Book II ends with a quire); and that the second scribe was employed a generation or two later than the first to supply Books III and IV, which had become defective or had gone astray in the meantime.[2] Leaving the *Dialogues* incomplete at the end of l. 10 on f. 137*a*, this scribe goes on to fill ff. 137*b* to 139*b*, l. 4 with two Lives translated from the *Vitae Patrum*,[3] Bk. v.

[1] For a possible doubt see p. 229 n., l. 13, below.

[2] The first scribe clearly did not intend that the copy should end with Book II, for on f. 61*b* he writes: *ond æfter þisse ongynneð seo þridde* [sc. *boc*], &c. There is some confirmation for the division into sets of two books in the other Worcester MS. of the *Dialogues*, now Bodleian MS. Hatton 76 (*circa* 1075), which contains only the first two books of the late revision of Wærferth's text.

[3] Migne *Patrologia Latina*, vol. lxxiii. The Old English renderings are

III. On f. 139*b*, l. 5, *Malchus*, which has the same source (Bk. I), begins in a new hand, weaker at times, and later in appearance than the preceding, yet perhaps not very much later in fact. This hand runs to f. 148*b* and so includes the text called *Wynfrith* (ff. 143*b*, l. 7 to 146*a*, l. 21). Folios 146*a*, l. 22 to 148*b* are very much damaged, and contain a sermon on the text 'Domine, libera animam meam a labiis iniquis et a lingua dolosa',[1] which I shall call *Evil Tongues*. It has not been printed, and there seems to be no other copy.

IV. Then follows a group of seven leaves, before and after which there were lacunae already in Wanley's time. The first page (149*a*) is very much blackened, and at a glance appears to contain twelfth-century writing; but closer examination shows that many letters had been unskilfully freshened up before the fire of 1731,[2] and probably the text was originally in the same clear hand of the second half of the eleventh century that appears on the verso of f. 149 and on the following leaves to the end. It is not probable that these leaves were originally written to form part of the volume. They are ruled for 32 lines as against 30 lines of the two preceding hands; the name of each sermon is entered in capitals as a running title at the head of the pages it occupies—an unusual feature; and though the Worcester style of glossing is continued, a twelfth-century reader, whose hand appears nowhere else in the volume, has made several corrections in this part. Folios 153 and 154 have been transposed by the binder, and in detailing the component pieces I shall therefore use f. 153* = the present f. 154 and f. 154* = the present f. 153:

Ff. 149*a*–151*b*, l. 27 contain a sermon *De Creatore et Creatura*,

printed, with *Malchus*, by B. Assmann *Bibliothek der ags. Prosa*, vol. iii (Kassel 1889), p. 195 ff. *Malchus* was first edited by Cockayne *The Shrine*, London 1864–70, p. 35 ff.; and Cockayne's notes of words from the following tract, which came into Professor Toller's possession, were presumably made when he was preparing his text. He also transcribed the *Dialogues* in 1863.

[1] Ps. cxix. 2.

[2] The letter *ȝ* is usually changed to *g*. At the foot of this page a hand of saec. xii–xiii has entered a list of books which is now imperfect owing to crumbling of the burnt margins: '*Liber dialogorum Gre⟨gori⟩ . . . Vitas Patrum*. Item *Beda de gestis Anglorum* anglice. Item *Vita* . . . . Item *Synonima Ysydori*. Item *Beda* . . . *De consola⟨tione⟩* . . .' (i.e. Boethius).

imperfect at the beginning. Very little of the first page (149*a*) is legible. From the top of f. 149*b* the text is made up chiefly of passages from Ælfric's *Hexameron*,[1] viz. ll. 73–80+; 85*b*–95+; 103–6; 306–19+; 324*a*, 325–6*a*+; 344–55+; 360–75+; 376–404; 413–542 (end). The addition of the sign + indicates that the passage is followed by a few lines of matter not in the *Hexameron*, or by a junction in which matter suggested by the *Hexameron* is differently expressed. If now we turn back to the difficult page 149*a*, we shall find no legible word from the *Hexameron*, though the subject is clearly the nature of the Creator. Apparently, then, the second part of the sermon (*de Creatura*) was formed by excerpting the framework passages of the *Hexameron*; and the first part (*de Creatore*) was newly composed, or drawn from some other source which I have not identified. The existence of this manuscript for nearly half of the text seems to have escaped the notice of editors and critics of the *Hexameron*.

Folios 151*b*, l. 29 to 153**b*, l. 14 contain a sermon *De sex etatibus huius seculi*; as far as I know it is the only copy extant, and is unprinted.

Folios 153**b*, l. 16 to 155*b* contain the sermon *De populo Israhel* (*quando volueris*), wanting the end:[2] but the whole text occurs at f. 101*b* ff. of Bodleian MS. Hatton 115 (*olim* Junius 23), a contemporary Worcester manuscript. It also appears to be unprinted.

From Wanley's report of the closing words it is plain that *Wynfrith* is a misnomer for the piece beginning on f. 143*b*, which is a version of the extant Latin letter written by Boniface (Wynfrith) to Eadburga about the year 717. For the historian of Old English literature this version has interest as an early vernacular example of a vision of the other world;[3] and it would be more important still

[1] The line-numbers quoted are those in S. J. Crawford's edition: *Bibliothek der ags. Prosa*, Hamburg 1921.

[2] The last words on f. 155*b and þær æt⟨eowde⟩* correspond to f. 105*b*, l. 18 of MS. Hatton 115. The two texts are closely related, but the Cotton MS. sometimes has the better reading, e.g. *mid anrædum mode*, where the Hatton MS. (f. 102*a*, l. 22) has *mid rǽdum mode*; and *to his geferum*, where the Hatton MS. (f. 105*a*, l. 12) has *gerefum*.

[3] From the reference to Ceolred in the Latin text (§ 15), the vision itself must be dated just before that king's death in 716. The slightly earlier vision of Drihthelm comes into Old English in the translation of Bede's History

if it could be claimed as witness to a late appreciation of the familiar letters of eighth-century Englishmen, or as a tribute to the memory of the greatest of English missionaries. But there is little doubt that the letter was translated and preserved chiefly for the sake of its theme. Perhaps because his great work was done abroad, and no influential religious house at home was interested in the glory of his name by reason of local associations or the possession of relics, Boniface was not ranked among the chief saints of England in the tenth and eleventh centuries: his feast on 5 June is never of the highest grade; he is commemorated neither in the *Old English Martyrology* nor in the verse *Menology*; no other letter of his circle is extant in an Old English rendering; and little would be known of his Latin correspondence had we to depend on the surviving copies from English scriptoria.[1]

So by curtailing the beginning and the end, the translator has removed the personal touches and the exact notes of time and place that are proper to the letter form. He omits even the paragraph on Ceolred (†716), whether because it had no longer a living interest, or because it was felt that there was some indelicacy in recalling the misdeeds of that scandalous king of the Mercian line.[2] He con-

(Bk. V, c. xii), and in Ælfric's sermon (ed. Thorpe ii. 348). The vision of Fursey is also the subject of a sermon by Ælfric (ed. Thorpe ii. 332).

[1] The translation gives slight indications that the lost MS. from which it was made was independent of the four Continental MSS. used by the *Monumenta* editors to establish the text of this letter. At § 10, l. 8 *usque ad medium* is M. Tangl's emendation for *usque ad genua medium* (*-a*) of the MSS.; and the OE. *oð ðone middel* reflects an uncorrupted text. At l. 13 only one of the three best Latin MSS. has the accepted reading *castigatione* (variants *correctione, cogitatione*), which the OE. *clænsunge* fortifies. In § 16, l. 8, *Begga* of the Latin MSS. seems to be unexampled among Anglo-Saxon men's names, but the OE. *Bogia* = *Boia* is well established. From the errors made by the late glossators, e.g. *videndo* for l. 47 *héapiende* (confused with *hawiende*); *muscas* for l. 99 *fleogan* v.; and *persecutus es* for l. 66 *eahtodest* (confused with *ehtan*), it may be inferred that about the year 1200 these diligent readers did not know where to find a Latin text of Boniface's letter in the rich library of Worcester. [On the English evidence for the text of Boniface's letters see W. Levison *England and the Continent in the Eighth Century*, 1946, p. 280 ff.]

[2] That such visions could be turned into instruments of scandal is shown by a slightly later English example in *Mon. Germ. Hist. Epist.* vol. iii, p. 404–5. It seems to have been suggested by Boniface's letter.

centrates attention on the vision, and the name of Wynfrith is hardly more important for his purpose than the name of Bogia, which is also preserved by a casual reference. For the rest the rendering is close: the omission of the last of the Vices after l. 70 *unnytnys* (itself a strange rendering of *iter otiosum*), and of the first of the Virtues at the middle of l. 86, must be accidental; and the only noteworthy addition—the bracketed words at l. 66—is of the nature of a gloss. Barbarisms are not infrequent, e.g. l. 17 *under ánre gesihðe* = *sub uno aspectu*; constructions of the Latin are often confused, as at ll. 9–13; 49–52; 71–74; 92–94; the words *et diversorum . . . commorantium* at the beginning of § 13 have been wrongly joined to the end of § 12; and there are several verbal faults: for instance at l. 16 *lichaman gesihðe* seems to arise from construing *carnis* with *conspectum* instead of *velamine*; l. 36 *þære beorhtan gesihðe an engel* = *splendidae visionis angelus* could hardly have been written if the translator saw that *splendidae visionis* = *splendidus aspectu*; l. 116 *sweg* = *fraglantia* (i.e. *fragrantia*) is due to a rather common confusion with *fragor*; l. 127 *fotes deopnesse* may follow from misreading of *pene* as *pede*; and at l. 129 *helan* translates *ascellas* 'armpits'.

That the extant copy is not the translator's original is clear from the scribal errors mentioned in the footnotes; and consequently the linguistic forms cannot be relied on to prove the place of composition. There are well-marked deviations from standard Late West Saxon: *tealode* 82, with *u*-umlaut, for normal *talode*, and *nioðeran* 97, 107, 110 are strictly Anglian. So are p.p. *gesegen* 12, 44, 146 and pa.t.subj. 3 sg. *gesege* 134, 186 beside *geseage* 97, 179, though such forms of (*ge*)*sēon* seem to occur in the South in very late Old English. The same remark applies to Anglian (or Kentish) *nedbade* (normal *nȳd-*) 7; *ungehersumnes* 63 beside normal *ungehyrsum* 63; *stemende* (normal *stȳm-*) 80; *lég* (normal *līg*) 27, 32, 38, 99, 112; *cegan* 53, 80, 91; and *awerged* 43, 155 beside normal *awyr*(*i*)*gd-* 45. Next comes a group of forms that are usually associated with South-Eastern dialects: (*a*) common *io* for *ĕo* as in the pronouns *hiom* 111, &c., *sio* 79, &c.; with *siocum* 89; *friode* 189; *feorpiode* 199; *hīofigende* 101, 108; *triowe* 'tree' 126; *ungetriowan* 193; *diofol* 177; and (*be*)*fiollan* 103, 127; *niorxnawang* 119; *biorht-* 129, 135.

(*b*) occasional *ia* for *ēa*, *éa* in *hiaf* 159, *hiardran* 209. (*c*) rare *io* for *ĕa* in *gesioh* (pa.t.sg.) 180.

It is often assumed that the provenance of an eleventh-century copy can be determined from its linguistic forms; and since in our second volume we have specimens of the work of four scribes, of whom the first three at least were pretty certainly engaged in one place (probably Worcester) and on a single book, it is worth following these abnormalities through the volume:

Hand I (ff. 1–61*b* = *Dialogues*, Bks. I and II) has common *gesēge*, *gesegen*; common *nēd*, &c. for normal *nīed*, *nȳd*, &c.; frequent *io* for *eo*.

Hand II (ff. 62*a*–137*a* = *Dialogues* Bk. III–) has common *gesēge* (*-sēage*), &c.; common *nēd*, &c.; but not *io* for *eo*. When, however, the same scribe comes to copy the first two Lives (ff. 137*b*–9*b*) he writes regularly *gesēge* (*-sēage*); no *nēd*, &c.; no *io* for *eo*; and these two Lives have usually *æ* for mutated *ĕ* before a covered nasal (e.g. *lotwræncas*), though the number of such forms in the *Dialogues* is inconsiderable.

Hand III (ff. 139*b*–48*b* = *Malchus*, *Wynfrith's Letter*, *Evil Tongues*) is in language fairly uniform; for instance *Malchus* has frequent *io* for *eo*; occasional *ia* for *ēa* in *hiafde*,[1] and probably once *io* for *ĕa* in *niorwedon*;[2] but no significant use of *æ* for *ĕ*+covered nasal.[3]

Hand IV (ff. 149*a*–55*b* = *Hexameron*, &c.) has none of the abnormalities of *Wynfrith's Letter*.

It seems that the applied theory of eleventh-century English dialects is much simpler than the reality: there is no necessary uniformity of language in the copies produced by a single scriptorium; and in the manuscript before us, the forms *gesēge* (*-sēage*),[4]

[1] For *Evil Tongues* cf. f. 147*b* . . . *gif us abelgað ure efenhiafden*.

[2] Presumably for *nearwedon* rather than for early *nierwedon*: cf. *niorog-lice* as variant to *nearulice* in *Dialogues* (ed. Hecht), p. 29, l. 21.

[3] *Mænnen*, l. 189, is the only example in *Wynfrith's Letter*.

[4] The forms *gesēage*, *-sēagon* are perhaps to be explained as mere spellings for *gesēge*, *-sēgon*, reflecting the reduction of historical *-ēag-* to *-ēg-*. It is true the late glossator by superscription converts *gesege* f. 140*a* into *iseȝe*, and *geseage* f. 139*a* into *iseawe* = *isawe*; but this is not good evidence that the vowel in *geseage* differed from that in *gesege*.

gesegen are the only abnormalities that run through the three hands, and so may fairly be used as evidence for the provenance of the manuscript. Even here there is a difficulty: for since our volume was at Worcester about the year 1200, and almost certainly at Worcester a century earlier, in Bishop Wulfstan's day,[1] there is good reason for believing that it was produced at Worcester; and yet its characteristic forms *gesēge*, *gesegen* are by no means typical of the many Worcester books that have come down from the second half of the eleventh century. I shall not attempt to unravel these perplexities, which might be fewer if we knew more about the literary language of Worcester in the time of Oswald († 992). But it is possible to reach some conclusions on the history of the texts. It may be inferred that forms like *nēd* in the *Dialogues* from Bk. III onward are not due to the latest scribe, since they are absent from the two Lives in his handwriting; that in previous textual history these two Lives are dissociated from the *Dialogues*, and that their characteristic *æ* for *ĕ*+covered nasal is also not due to the latest scribe. Again, while at first sight *Malchus* (*M*) must be associated closely with the two Lives that immediately precede it, because they have the same source, on its linguistic forms it must be grouped with *Wynfrith's Letter* (*W*) and *Evil Tongues* (*E.T.*): either, then, these characteristic forms are due to the latest scribe, or the three pieces have an earlier history in common distinct from that of the other Lives from the *Vitae Patrum*.

The vocabulary supports the second alternative. Jordan[2] has listed a number of words that are rarely found in Late West Saxon texts, and though it would not be safe to rely on any single example, in texts so short the cumulative weight of the following is considerable:—Pure Late West Saxon has *clipian* 'cry out' where early texts, or late texts with an Anglian colouring, have *cēgan* (*cīgan*):

[1] It is tempting but hardly safe to identify MSS. Otho C I and Hatton 76 with the '*II Englissce Dialogus*' mentioned in the brief catalogue at f. 101*b* of the Worcester book CCCC MS. 367 (late 11th century): see James *Sources of Archbishop Parker's Collection of MSS.*, p. 62, and Hecht's edition, Pt. II, p. 29.

[2] *Eigentümlichkeiten des anglischen Wortschatzes*, Heidelberg 1906. See also Klaeber 'Zur altenglischen Beda-übersetzung' *Anglia* xxv and xxviii; Hecht, op. cit., Pt. II, p. 134 ff.

the two Lives have only *cleopian*; *M*, *W* have only *cēgan* (*cīgan*), and so has *E.T.*, e.g. f. 146*a* 'þonne ic cige ane siðe, þonne gehyreð he me æfter þære gecigednesse'. *Semninga* 'suddenly' in pure Late West Saxon is replaced by *færinga*, &c., but it occurs in *W* 8, 10, 177 f.; *M* 218. Of *midnes* = Lat. *medium*, Toller has only four examples, all from *M*; but there are two more in *W* 56, 174. Another word uncommon in pure West Saxon texts is (*ge*)*fir*(*e*)*nian*: there are three examples in *W* 60, 62, 175, and it occurs more than once in *E.T.*, e.g. in a passage on f. 146*b* that gives three examples of *yfelsian*, another Anglian symptom: 'and þæt is þonne swiðe micel yfel þæt se man onsace Drihtne hælendum Criste, and hine yfelsige, and his halgum téonan do . . . Hwæt bið mare synn þonne man yfelsige his Drihten? Forþan sé yfelsað his Drihten se þe his gesceafte tæleð oððe his gesceafte wyrgeð, þeah hine hwa abelige; and þurh þyllicu þing gefirenað seo tunge oft.' The word *godwrecnis* 'crime' pretty certainly lies behind *godwyrcnis* at l. 49; the recorded literary examples are from the translation of Bede's History, a text with well-marked Anglian features, and the substantive *godwreca*, which is also uncommon, occurs in *M* 389 'gangað ut, ge godwrecan'. It is a fair inference that the three texts—*Malchus*, *Wynfrith's Letter*, and *Evil Tongues*—were composed in territory once Mercian; and when the opening words—*M*: *Sagað her on þissum bocum*; *W*: *Her sagað on þissum bocum*—are added to the list of similarities, it seems likely that the translator of *Malchus* was also the translator of *Wynfrith's Letter*. The vocabulary does not warrant the conclusion that *Evil Tongues*, which is probably based on Latin materials, is also the work of this translator, but it is possible; and the possibility is strengthened if the exceptional phonological forms that the sermon shares with *M* and *W* go back to the translator's draft. If common authorship could be established, we should have a useful clue to the date of the translations; for the sermon contains many references to the monastic life: e.g. f. 146*b* 'And forþan ne tælen þa munucas[1] æfre, ne ne cweðan "We wæron

[1] Note *þa munucas* here, and yet the preacher identifies himself with the monks in the next passage. If the original wording has been correctly preserved, it would indicate that the preacher of the English sermon was placed in charge of monks, as bishop or abbot.

nu þráge on mynstre and we on þam fæce micclum ne gefírnodan"; forþan hig liogað gif hig tælað, forþan hiora tunga gefirenað dæghwamlice'; or f. 147*b* '. . . and gif we hit gewrecan ne magon, þ⟨o⟩nne biotiað we to him: "Hwæt, we syndon munucas ge-cweden," þeh we þone munuchad rihte ne ⟨he⟩aldon. We us sceolon gebiddan to Drihtne, gif we þone munuchad rihte healden willa⟨ð, on⟩ ǽrne morgen and on underne, and on midne dæg, and on þa nontid, and on æfenne, and æt ⟨n⟩iht, and æt honan sange', &c. Such a sermon is not likely to have been composed in English, or translated for English use, before the Benedictine Reform in the latter part of the tenth century.

Wynfrith's Letter contains other matter of lexicographical interest. There are two examples of the unrecorded verb *oðlengan* (*to*) = *pertinere* (*ad*) ll. 53, 74. One clear instance of the simplex *blǣstan* = '*anhelare*', '*erumpere*' (of fire) occurs at l. 31; another at l. 98, which is better not taken as a compound with *up*; and a third at l. 27 favouring the compound *forþblǣstan*, which is probably to be assumed for Toller's first example of *blǣstan* (*Suppl.* p. 96). *Feorþīod* = '*longinqua regio*', l. 199, and *sceaððignes* = '*laesio*', l. 38, are also new. *Lihtian*, l. 48, in the literal sense 'to reduce the weight of' is not elsewhere recorded for Old English; nor does Toller give examples of *ormǣtlic* adj., ll. 159, 182, though the adverb is not uncommon. The sense of *nȳdbād* in *þurh nēdbāde* at l. 7 is not easy to determine; while *pund* = *pondus*, l. 47, and *geswēge* = *consonantes*, l. 74 (cf. l. 21), owe their unusual meanings to bad translation. Other words of interest because they are comparatively rare are: *ārēceleāsian* 72; *domne* 1; *forstynted* 35, 142; *gegītsian* 58; *gemánes* (from *gemāh*) 62; *gylplīce* 59; *héapian* 47, 82; *lorh* 181; *picen* adj. 130; *unārǣfnedlīce* adv. 33; and the contexts are now available for *bewrigennys* 11, 14, *drūþung* 64, *cwealmlic* 160, which Toller has already quoted from Cockayne's notes. Perhaps none of these is so interesting as a sentence from *Evil Tongues* that the fire has spared, f. 147*a*: 'Ac he ymbgæð hus and sægð oþrum men oþres synne, and cwið "Ic eom fyrenfull 7 þés man is fyrenfull." "Ac hwæt belangað þæs þonne to eow?" cwæð se Godes lareow.' The verb *belong* is not recorded in the Oxford Dictionary till the fourteenth century, and here it has exactly the sense (*quid interest?*) that one would expect in an Old English example.

The print of the Latin original, which I am able to reproduce from the *Monumenta Germaniae Historica*[1] by the courtesy of the directing authority, will provide what more is necessary to explain the text. Considerable passages or phrases which are not represented in the translation are italicized. In the Old English, contractions are expanded without notice; and to avoid descriptive footnotes, any letter of which an identifiable trace remains is treated as if it were preserved intact. Letters of which no identifiable traces remain are printed in italics within brackets ⟨⟩. Where the Latin source, the style, or the context give sufficient indications of the reading of the manuscript in its perfect state, I have tried to fill gaps due to crumbling. It is not easy; for the vellum is so much distorted in the worst places that the number of missing letters can be determined only by the crude method of averaging several whole lines; but the attempt may serve a useful purpose so long as it is clear that italicized words within brackets have no better authority than mere conjecture.

f. 143*b* § 1. Her sagað on þissum bocum þæt domne Wynfrið sende þis gewrit ærost to þissum leodum, bi sumum preoste se wæs þrage forðfered and gehwyrfde þa eft to his lichaman. He sæde þæt he bicome to þisse þeode, and þæt he spæce wið ðone preost, 'and he me þa rehte þa ⟨*wundorlica*⟩n gesihðe þa þe he geseah þa he wæs buton lichaman, and þis he me rehte eall his agene worde.

1. *Rogabas me, soror carissima, ut admirandas visiones* de illo redivivo, qui *nuper in monasterio Milburge abbatissae* mortuus est et revixit, *quae ei ostensae sunt,* scribendo intimare et transmittere curarem, *quemadmodum istas veneranda abbatissa Hildelida referenti didici. Modo siquidem gratias omnipotenti Deo refero, quia in hoc, dilectionis tuae voluntatem eo plenius liquidiusque, Deo patrocinium praestante, implere valeo, quia* ipse cum supra dicto fratre *redivivo*—dum nuper de transmarinis partibus ad istas pervenit regiones—locutus sum; et ille mihi stupendas visiones, quas extra corpus suum raptus in spiritu vidit, proprio exposuit sermone.

---

3 he bicome] *so Wanley: now only the last two strokes of* m *and the final* e *remain.*

5 wundorlican] *Lat. stupendas; cf.* wundorlicre = *stupendae*, l. 135.

[1] *Epistolae*, vol. iii, p. 252 ff.; see also *Epistolae Selectae*, vol. i, ed. M. Tangl, Berlin 1916. There is a modern English rendering in E. Kylie's *English Correspondence of St. Boniface* (King's Classics), London 1911, p. 78 ff.

§ 2. 'He cwæð þæt him geeode þurh nedbade þæt his lichama wære seoc geworden, and he wæs semninga þy gaste benǽmed. And him þuhte þæt hit wære on þære onlicnysse þe him man þa eagan weccende mid þicce hrægle forbrugde; and þa semninga wæs seo bewrigennys onweg anumen, and þa wæs him ætywed on gesihðe ealle þa þing þe him næfre ǽr gesegen næron ne onwrigen; and him wæs æghwæt swiðe uncuð þæs þe he geseah. And þa æt nyxtan wæs eall seo swearte bewrigennis aworpen fram his eagum: þa þuhte him þæt eall þes middaneard wære gesamnod biforan his lichaman gesihðe; and he sceawode eall folc, and ealle eorðan dælas and sǽstreamas, under ánre gesihðe. And him þuhte þæt þa englas wæron swilce hig byrnende wæron, þa þe hine læddon ut of þam lichaman, and he ne mihte nænig þinga locian on hig for þære micclan beorhtnesse þe hig mid ymbseted wæron; and hig sungon swiðe wynsumum stefnum and swiðe geswégum, and hig cwædon "*Domine, ne in ira tua arguas me, neque in furore tuo corripias me*": þæt is: "Drihten, ne þrea þu us in þinum yrre, ne þu us ne steor in þinre hatheortnysse."

§ 3. 'And he sæde þæt hig hine abrudon up in þone lyft; and he þa geseah fyr beornan ymb ealles þyses middaneardes ymbhwyrfte, and se lég wæs forðblæstende mid swiðe únmætre micelnysse, and he wæs swiðe egeslic upastigende; "and næs eall þes middaneard, þa ic hine sceawode, buton swilc he wære on anes †cleowen†

2. Dicebat quippe, se per violentis egritudinis dolorem corporis gravidine subito exutum fuisse. Et simillimum esse collatione, veluti si videntis et vigilantis hominis oculi densissimo tegmine velentur; et subito auferatur velamen, et tunc perspicua sint omnia, quae antea non visa et velata et ignota fuerunt. Sic sibi, abiecto terrenae velamine carnis, ante conspectum universum collectum fuisse mundum, ut cunctàs terrarum partes et populos et maria sub uno aspectu contueretur. Et tam magnae claritatis et splendoris angelos eum egressum de corpore suscepisse, ut nullatenus pro nimio splendore in eos aspicere potuisset. Qui iucundis et consonis vocibus canebant: 'Domine, ne in ira tua arguas me, neque in furore tuo corripias me.'

3. 'Et sublevabant me—dixit—in aera sursum. Et in circuitu totius mundi ignem ardentem videbam et flammam inmensae magnitudinis anhelantem et terribiliter ad superiora ascendentem, non aliter pene quam ut sub uno globo totius mundi machinam conplectentem, nisi eam

---

22 *Psalm* xxxvii. 2. 29 cleowen] *read* cleowenes.

onlicnysse, and eall his weorc; and ic geseah þæt þæt fyr wolde blæstan ofer ealne middaneard, gif se engel ne sette Cristes rode tacen ongéan þam fy⟨*re: and*⟩ þonne gestilde hit, and se lég swiðf. 144*a* rode on | micclum dæle. And ic wæs swiðe unaræfnedlice geþræ̈sted on minum eagum for þiss⟨*es*⟩ micclan brynes ege; and me wæs ealra swiðost seo gesihð †forstynded† for þara scinendra gasta beorhtnesse; and þa æthrán þære beorhtan gesihðe an engel minum heafde, and ic wearð þurh þæt gescyld and gesund gehealden fram þara léga sceaððignesse."

§ 4. 'And he sæde, on þære tide þe he wæs of his lich⟨*a*⟩man, þæt þyder wære gesamnod of lichamum swa micel menego forðferedra sawla swa he ne wende þæt ealles mennisces cynnes nære swylc unrim menego swilce þæt wæs. And he sæde eac þæt þær wære micel meniu ǽt awergedra gasta, †and† eac þam beorhtum englum þe þær gesegene wæron: hig hæfdon micel geflit wið ða awyrigdan gastas bi ⟨*þam soðf*⟩æstan sawlum þe þær wæron útgongende of lichaman: and þa deoflu wæ⟨*ron wregende þa s*⟩awle, and hig wæron héapiende hiora synna pund on hio; þa ⟨*englas wæron*⟩ ládiende and lihtigende hiora synna.

sanctus angelus inpresso signo sanctae crucis Christi conpesceret. Quando enim in obviam minacis flammae signum crucis Christi expresserat, tunc flamma magna ex parte decrescens resedit. Et istius flammae terribili ardore intollerabiliter torquebar, oculis maxime ardentibus et splendore fulgentium spirituum vehementissime reverberatis; donec splendidae visionis angelus manus suae inpositione caput meum quasi protegens tangebat et me a lesione flammarum tutum reddidit.'

4. Praeterea referebat: illo in temporis spatio, quo extra corpus fuit, tam magnam animarum migrantium de corpore multitudinem illuc, ubi ipse fuit, convenisse, quam totius humani generis in terris non fuisse antea existimaret. Innumerabilem quoque malignorum spirituum turbam nec non et clarissimum chorum supernorum angelorum adfuisse narravit. Et maximam inter se miserrimos spiritus et sanctos angelos de animabus egredientibus de corpore disputationem habuisse, daemones accussando et peccatorum pondus gravando, angelos vero relevando et excussando.

---

33 unaræfnedlice] *second* n *added above line.*

35 forstynded] *read* forstynted*; cf. l. 142.*

43 and] *delete* (*?*).

45 soðfæstan] *only the* e *part of* æ *survives. Nothing equivalent in the Latin.*

47 on hio] o *uncertain: but the letter is not* g; *for* hio *cf. ll. 56, 112.*

§ 5. 'And se man sæde þæt he sylf gehyrde ealle his †godwyrcnisse† and his agene synna—þa þe he of his giogoðe gefremede, oððe þæt he on receleaste gefremode, þæt he nolde his synna ándettan, and þæt he on ofergitolness gefremode, oððe þæt he eallunga nyste þæt hit to synna oðlengde: and ælc þara synna cégde his agenre stefne wið hine, and hio hine †hig† ardlice þreadon; and anra gehwilc þara synna þe he of his iugoðe gefremede, on †ænigum† hade þær wæs forðgeboren on hiora midnesse; and hio wæron þus sprecende:—Sum cwæð: "Ic eom þin gitsung þe þu unalyfedlice gegitsodest wið Godes bebodu." Sum cwæð: "Ic eom idel gilp þe þu mid mannum gylplice ahofe." Sum cwæð: "Ic eom leasung in þære þu gefírenadest þær þu wære lígende." Sum cwæð: "Ic eom unnyt word þe þu idelice gespræce." Sum cwæð: "Ic eom gesihð þurh þa þu gefirenadest." Sum cwæð: "Ic eom gemánes and ungehersumnes, þær þu ealdum gastlicum mannum ungehyrsum wære." Sum cwæð: "Ic eom drupung and sleacnis þe þu wære receleas in haligra gewrita geornesse." Sum cwæð: "Ic eom swiciende geþoht and unnyt †gamen† (þe þu oðra manna lif eahtodest and þin agen lif forlete), and ic þe ofer gemet on cyrican and buton cirican gebisgode." Sum cwæð: "Ic eom slapolnis mid þam þu wære

5. Et se ipsum audisse, omnia flagitiorum suorum propria peccamina —quae fecit a iuventute sua et ad confitendum aut neglexit aut oblivioni tradidit vel ad peccatum pertinere omnino nesciebat—ipsius propria voce contra illum clamitasse et eum dirissime accussasse et specialiter unumquodque vitium quasi ex sua persona in medium se obtulisse dicendo quoddam: 'Ego sum cupiditas tua, qua inlicita frequentissime et contraria praeceptis Dei concupisti'; quoddam vero: 'Ego sum vana gloria, qua te apud homines iactanter exaltasti'; aliud: 'Ego sum mendacium, in quo mentiendo peccasti'; aliud: 'Ego sum otiosum verbum, quod inaniter locutus fuisti'; aliud: 'Ego visus, quo videndo inlicita peccasti'; aliud: 'Ego contumacia et inoboedientia, qua senioribus spiritalibus inoboediens fuisti'; aliud: 'Ego torpor et desidia in sanctorum studiorum neglectu'; aliud: 'Ego vaga cogitatio et inutilis cura, qua te supra modum sive in ecclesia sive extra ecclesiam occupabas'; aliud: 'Ego somnolentia, qua

---

49 godwyrcnisse] *conceivable as a barbarous rendering of* '*beneficia*': *but in fact there is nothing in the Latin to suggest it. Read* godwrecnisse, *a word which occurs in the OE. Bede and in glosses: cf.* godwræc *adj.* '*impious*'.

54 hig] *delete* (?).

55–56 ænigum] *read* æg(e)num: *Latin* 'quasi ex sua persona'.

66 gamen] *read* gymen *or* gemen: *Latin* 'cura'.

geþricced, þæt þu late arise Gode to ándettenne." Sum cwæð: "Ic eom unnytnys"—and hig him on sædon manega þing þissum gelic. And ealle þa þe he on his lifes dagum lifigende gefremod⟨*e*⟩, þe he
f. 144 *b* areceleasode to ándettenne, | and manige synna þær cirmdon swiðe egeslice wið hine þa þe he næfre ne wende þæt hio to synnum oðlengdon; and þa awyrigdan gastas wæron geswege eallum þam synnum; and hig wæron hine swiðe heardlice wregende, and hig wæron secgende ealle þa stowe and ealle þa tide þe hig þa mándæde on gedydon. And he þær geseah eac sumne þara manna þe he ær gewund⟨*od*⟩e þa hwile þe he lifigende wæs;—and se man lifde þagyt—, and to gewitnesse his yfela he wæs þider gelǽded; and sio wund wæs open, and þæt blod wæs stemende, and he wæs cegende his agenre stefne and he⟨*fi*⟩estu edwit cweðende, and he s⟨*tælde*⟩ þæs blodes gyte swiðe wælhreowlice, and he tealode and héapode micel m⟨*eniu synna on hine*⟩; and þa ealdan feond trymedon and sædon þæt he wære hira gew⟨*ealdes and hira hlytes*⟩.

oppressus tarde ad confitendum Deo surrexisti'; aliud: 'Ego iter otiosum'; *aliud: 'Ego sum neglegentia et incuria, qua detentus erga studium divinae lectionis incuriosus fuisti'*; et cetera his similia. Omnia, quae in diebus vitae suae in carne conversatus peregit et confiteri neglexit, multa quoque, quae ad peccatum pertinere omnino ignorabat, contra eum cuncta terribiliter vociferabant. Similiter et maligni spiritus in omnibus consonantes vitiis accussando et duriter testificando et loca et tempora nefandorum actuum memorantes eadem, quae peccata dixerunt, conclamantes probabant. Vidit quoque ibi hominem quendam, cui iam in seculari habitu degens vulnus inflixit—quem adhuc in hac vita superesse referebat—, ad testimonium malorum suorum adductum; cuius cruentatum et patens vulnus et sanguis ipse, propria voce clamans inproperabat et inputabat ei crudele effusi sanguinis crimen. Et sic cumulatis et conputatis sceleribus, antiqui hostes adfirmabant: eum, reum peccatorem, iuris eorum et condicionis indubitanter fuisse.

---

81 hefiestu] *distorted by burning: a pocket in the vellum, now closed by the special mounting of the burnt leaves, covers what I conjecture to be the upper part of* f *and the whole of* i. *Note that the reading assumes the ligature* ﬅ *which occurs nowhere else in the tract.*

stælde] s *certain from the remains of the top: but unless there is unusual distortion of the burnt edges,* stælde, *which suits the Latin 'inputabat', and may be construed with the following* (*conjectural*) on hine, *does not fit the remains very well.*

83 meniu synna on hine] *for the restoration cf. l. 47 above, and l. 43.*

84 hira gewealdes and hira hlytes] *for the restoration cf. l. 147 f. below.*

§ 6. '"⟨*Þa*⟩ ladedon me min þæt lyttla mægen þa þe ic earma and unm⟨*eodumlic*⟩e . . . re gedyde:—Sum cwæð: 'Ic eom fæsten þe he his lichaman on aclænsode wið ðam yfelan geornissum.' Sum cwæð: 'Ic eom hluttor gebéd þæt he geat in Drihtnes gesihðe.' Sum cwæð: 'Ic eom untrumra þegnung, þa he mildelice siocum gedyde.' Sum cwæð: 'Ic eom sealmsang þone he Gode gedyde to bote his unnyttra worda'": and swa him cegde anra gehwilc þæra mægna, and wæs hine beladigende wið his synnum; †and þas þe þe wæron eac miccligende þa engellican gastas, "and me wæron þas mægnu bescyldigende þa þe her trymedon;† and me wæron þa mægnu miccle maran geþuht þonne ic æfre wende þæt ic hig on minum mægne gefremman mihte."

§ 7. 'And he sæde eac þæt he geseage on þissum nioðeran middanearde fyrene seaðas, and þa wæron swiðe egeslice úp blæstende; and he geseah fleogan ingemang þam fyrenen lege þa earman gastas, þa wæron on sweartra fugela ónlicnissum; and hig wæron híofigende and wépende and gristbitigende mid menniscre stefne

6. 'E contra autem—dixit—excussantes me, clamitabant parve virtutes animae, quas ego miser indigne et inperfecte peregi. Quaedam dixit: "*Ego sum oboedientia, quam senioribus spiritalibus exhibuit*"; *quaedam*: "Ego sum ieiunium, quo corpus suum contra desiderium carnis pugnans castigavit"; alia: "Ego oratio pura, quam effundebat in conspectu Domini"; alia: "Ego sum obsequium infirmorum, quod clementer egrotantibus exhibuit"; quaedam: "Ego sum psalmus, quem pro otioso sermone satisfaciens Deo cecinit." Et sic unaqueque virtus contra emulum suum peccatum excussando me clamitabat. Et has illi inmensae claritatis angelici spiritus magnificando defendentes me adfirmabant. Et istae virtutes universae valde mactae et multo maiores et excellentiores esse mihi videbantur, quam umquam viribus meis digne perpetrate fuissent.'

7. Inter ea referebat, se, quasi in inferioribus, in hoc mundo vidisse igneos puteos horrendam eructantes flammam plurimos; et, erumpente tetra terribilis flamma ignis, volitasse et miserorum hominum spiritus in similitudine nigrarum avium per flammam plorantes et ululantes et verbis et voce humana stridentes et lugentes propria merita et praesens supplicium;

85–86 and . . . gedyde] *after* unm *indistinct remains of two letters; then a hole, after which* e *is clear and two more letters unclear; then a further gap, at the end of which stands* re (*possibly* ne), *with traces of an accent which may indicate a preceding long vowel. Between* unm *and* gedyde *the space would be enough for 20 to 25 letters in all.*

ll. 92–94. *The MS. is clear, and the corruption appears to be deep-rooted.*

hiora agene †fyrhtu†, and þæt andwearde wite; and hig gesæton hwilum lythwon on þæra seaða ofrum, and hig fiollon eft æfre heofigende in þa seaðas. Þa cwæð him án to of þam halgan englum: "Þeos lyttle rést getacnað þæt ælmihtig Drihten syleð þissum sawlum celnisse and reste æfter þam toweardan domes dæge."

§ 8. 'And se man gehyrde under þam seaðum, in þære nioðeran helle, swiðe egeslic gránung and swiðe micelne wóp þara hio-
f. 145 *a* figendra sawla. Þa ⟨*cwæð hi*⟩m tó an þæra engla: "Þeos granung | and þes wop þe þu her gehyrest in þisse nioðeran helle, þæt syndon þa sawla þe hiom næfre to ne cymð Godes seo árfæste miltse; ac hio sceall cwylmian se eca leg."

§ 9. 'And he þær geseah eac on sume stowe swiðe wundorlicre fægernisse, and þær blissode swiðe fægera sawla menigu: þa laðedon hig hine þæt he come to hiora gefean, gif him alyfed wære. Þa com þanon swiðe micel sweg, and se wæs on swiðe micelre swetnysse: þis þonne wæs þæra eadigra gasta oroð. Þeos stow þonne wæs be þan þa englas him sædan þæt hit wæs se mæra niorxnawang.

§ 10. 'And he þær geseah fyren éa, sio wæs gefylled mid weallende †wite†, and hio wæs eall inneweard byrnende, and hio wæs on wunderlicre fyrhtu; and þ⟨*ær wæ*⟩s an treow ofer þa éa on brycge

consedisse paululum herentes in marginibus puteorum; et iterum heiulantes cecidisse in puteos. Et unus ex angelis dixit: 'Parvissima haec requies indicat, quia omnipotens Deus in die futuri iudicii his animabus refrigerium supplicii et requiem perpetuam praestiturus est.'

8. Sub illis autem puteis, *adhuc in inferioribus et in imo profundo*, quasi in inferno inferiori, audivit horrendum et tremendum *et dictu difficilem* gemitum et fletum lugentium animarum. Et dixit ei angelus: 'Murmur et fletus, quem in inferioribus audis, illarum est animarum, ad quas numquam pia miseratio Domini perveniet; sed aeterna illas flamma sine fine cruciabit.'

9. Vidit quoque mire amoenitatis locum, in quo pulcherrimorum hominum gloriosa multitudo miro laetabatur gaudio; qui eum invitabant, ut ad eorum gaudia, si ei licitum fuisset, cum eis gavisurus veniret. Et inde mirae dulcedinis fraglantia veniebat; quia beatorum alitus fuit ibi congaudentium spirituum. Quem locum sancti angeli adfirmabant famosum esse Dei paradisum.

10. Nec non et igneum piceumque flumen, bulliens et ardens, mirae formidinis *et teterrimae visionis* cernebat. Super quod lignum pontis vice

---

102 fyrhtu] *read* wyrhtu. 121 wite] *read* pice.

onlicnysse. Þonne efstan þa halgan sawla t⟨*o þære*⟩ bricge fram þam gemote þe hig æt wæron, and hig gyrndon þæt hig oferforen þa éa. Þonne ferdon hig sume swiðe ánrædlice ofer þa bricge. And sume hig wurdon aslidene of þam triowe, þæt hig befeollan in þa tintregan éa: sume hig befiollan in fotes deopnesse; sume mid ealne lichaman; sume oð ða cneowu; sume oð ðone middel; sume oð ða helan: þonne symble wæs þara sawla æghwilc biorhtre þonne hio ær wæs, syððan hio eft coman up of þære picenan éa. Þa cwæð an engel to him bi þam feallendum sawlum: "Þis syndon þa sawla þe æfter hinsiðe sumere arfæstre clænsunge bihofiað, and Godes miltsunge, þæt hig syn him wyrðe to bringenne."

§ 11. 'And he sæde þæt he þær gesege scinende weallas, þa wæron on micelre biorhtnesse and on wundorlicre lengu and on órmættre heannesse. Þa cwaedon þa halgan englas: "Þis is sio halige and sio mǽrlice ceaster Hierusalem, in þære gefægniað symble þa eadigan sawla and þa halgan gastas." And þonne þa sawla coman ofer þa éa, þe ic ǽr big sæde, þonne efstan hig eallum mægne wið ðissa wealla. He þonne sæde þæt hig wæron swiðe beorhte scinende, and he sæde þæt him wurde for þisse micclan beorhtnesse his eagena gesihð forstynted, þæt he nænig þinga locian ne mihte on þa beorhnesse.

positum erat. Ad quod sanctae gloriosaeque animae ab illo secedentes conventu properabant, desiderio alterius ripae transire cupientes. Et quaedam non titubantes constanter transiebant. Quaedam vero labefactae de ligno cadebant in Tartareum flumen; et aliae tinguebantur pene, quasi toto corpore mersae; aliae autem ex parte quadam, veluti quedam usque ad genua, quaedam usque ad medium, quaedam vero usque ad ascellas. Et tamen unaquaeque cadentium multo clarior speciosiorque de flumine in alteram ascendebat ripam, quam prius in piceum bulliens cecidisset flumen. Et unus ex beatis angelis de illis cadentibus animabus dixit: 'Hae sunt animae, quae post exitum mortalis vitae, *quibusdam levibus vitiis non omnino ad purum abolitis*, aliqua pia miserentis Dei castigatione indigebant, ut Deo dignae offerantur.'

11. Et citra illud flumen speculatur muros fulgentes clarissimi splendoris, stupendae longitudinis et altitudinis inmensae. Et sanctos angelos dixisse: 'Haec est enim illa sancta et inclita civitas, caelestis Hierusalem, in qua istae perpetualiter sanctae gaudebunt animae.' Illas itaque animas et istius gloriosae civitatis muros, ad quam post transitum fluminis festinabant, tam magna inmensi luminis claritate et fulgore splendentes esse dixit, ut, reverberatis oculorum pupillis, pro nimio splendore in eos nullatenus aspicere potuisset.

§ 12. 'Sæde eac þæt þær cumen wære sumes mannes sawul to þam gemote se wearð dead in abboddomes þegnunge, and sio wæs swiðe wlitig gesegen. Þa gegripon þa deoflu þa sawle, and hig sædon þæt hio wære hiora hlytes and hiora anwealdes. Þa andswarode him án of þam halgan englum and cwæð: "Ic eow nu gecyðe hraðe, ge earman gastas, þæt þios sawul ⟨*ne bið eow*⟩res gewealdes."
f. 145 *b* Þa mid þy þe þis | gecweden wæs, þa com þær færlice micel heap swiðe hwittra sawla, and þus wæron cweðende: "Þes abbod wæs ure ealdor, and us ealle he gestrynde Gode mid his lare, and he bið alysed for þissum weorðe, and he ne bið eowres anwealdes." Þa gefuhton þa englas wið ðam deoflum, and þa englas þa geeoden on þa deoflu þæt hig generedon þa sawle of þara ⟨a⟩werigdra gasta anwealde. Þa þreade se halga engel þa deoflu, and cwæð: "Wite ge nu þæt ge genamon þas sawle buton rihte: gewitað ge nu, earman gastas, †nu† in þæt ece fyr." And þa se engel þis gecweden hæfde, þa ahofan þa awyrigdan deoflu swiðe ormætlicne hiaf, and hig wurpon hig sylfe mid cwealmlicre flihte on þa byrne⟨*nde*⟩ s⟨*ea*⟩ðas, and hig coman eft æfter lyttlum fæce in þæt gemot, and hig flito⟨*n bi*⟩ manna sawla gewyrhtum.

12. Narravit quoque, ad illum conventum inter alias venisse cuiusdam hominis animam, qui in abbatis officio defunctus est; quae speciosa nimis et formosa esse visa est. Quam maligni spiritus rapientes contendebant sortis eorum et condicionis fuisse. Respondit ergo unus ex choro angelorum dicens: 'Ostendam vobis cito, miserrimi spiritus, quia vestrae potestatis anima illa probatur non esse.' Et his dictis, repente intervenit magna choors candidarum animarum, quae dicebant: 'Senior et doctor noster fuit iste, et nos omnes suo magisterio lucratus est Deo; et hoc pretio redemptus est, et vestri iuris non esse dinoscitur,' et quasi cum angelis contra daemones pugnam inirent. Et adminiculo angelorum eripientes illam animam de potestate malignorum spirituum liberaverunt. Et tum increpans angelus daemones dixit: 'Scitote modo et intellegite, quod animam istam sine iure rapuistis; et discedite, miserrimi spiritus, in ignem aeternum'—cum vero hoc dixisset angelus, ilico maligni spiritus levaverunt fletum et ululatum magnum; *in momento et quasi in ictu oculi* pernici volatu iactabant se in supradictos puteos ignis ardentis; et post modicum intervallum emersi certantes in illo conventu iterum de animarum meritis disputabant.

---

155 awerigdra] *initial* a *added much later above the line.*
158 nu] *delete, unless it is an error for* inn *adv.*

§ 13. 'And hig fliton éac bi þara manna gewyrhtum þe in þissum life mislice lifiað. And he sæde eac, on þa tid þe he wæs buton lichaman, þæt he mihte sceawian þa men þa þe wæron mid synnum besmitene, and eac þá þe wæron mid halgum mægnum Gode þeowigende and mid árfæstnyssum hæfdon ælmihtigne God†. And he geseah þæt þa Godes men wæron symble †biscyldende† fram þam englum, and þa englas wæron to him geþeodde mid sibbe and mid lufu. And he sæde bi þam mannum þe wæron gefylde mid manfullum synnum, þæt þær wæron symble deoflu to þam geþeodde; and he sægde þonne se man syngode, oððe on worde oððe on dæde, þæt þa deoflu þæt singallice sædon þam wyrrestan deoflum, and þæt hig hit brohtan mid hleahtre in hira midnesse. And he sæde þonne se man fírnode þæt þa deoflu brohtan ælce synne onsundran þam oðrum deoflum to gewitnesse; and he sæde þæt se diofol semninga þa synne gelærde þone man, and þæt he hig eft semninga gecydde þam deoflum.

§ 14. 'And he sæde þæt he geseage grindan her on worulde án mægden on ánre cweorne. Þa gesioh hio licgan oþres mægdnes lorh wið híg, swiðe fægre awrittenne, mid fagum flese. Þa forstæl hio hine. Þa wæron þa deoflu sona gefylled mid swiðe ormætlice

13. Et diversorum merita hominum in hac vita commorantium dicebat se illo in tempore speculari potuisse. Et illos, *qui sceleribus obnoxii non fuerunt et* qui sanctis virtutibus freti propitium omnipotentem Deum habuisse noscebantur, ab angelis semper tutos ac defensos et eis caritate et propinquitate coniunctos fuisse. Illis vero, qui nefandis criminibus *et maculate vitae sordibus* polluti fuerunt, adversarium spiritum adsidue sociatum *et semper ad scelera suadentem* fuisse; et, quandocumque verbo vel facto peccaverint, hoc iugiter quasi ad laetitiam et gaudium aliis nequissimis spiritibus in medium proferens manifestavit. Et quando homo peccavit, *nequaquam* malignus spiritus *sustinuit moram faciens expectando, donec iterum peccaret*; *sed* singillatim unumquodque vitium ad notitiam aliorum spirituum offerebat. Et subito apud hominem peccata suasit et ilico apud daemones perpetrata demonstravit.

14. Inter ea narravit, se vidisse puellam quandam in hac terrena vita molantem in mola. Quae vidit iuxta se iacentem alterius novam colum sculptura variatam; et pulchra ei visa fuit, et furata est illam. Tunc, quasi ingenti gaudio repleti, quinque teterrimi spiritus hoc furtum aliis in illo

167 God] *a following word = 'propitium' omitted in MS.*: (*?*) gemiltsod(ne).

168 biscyldende] *read* biscyldede.

gefean, and þær urnon sona fif þa wyrrestan deofla and sædon þa stalu to scylde in þara oðra deofla gemote, and hig wregdon þa stale to scylde, and sædon þæt þæt mæden wære fyrenfull. And sæde eac þæt he þær gesege sumes ealdes preostes sawle on micelre unrotnesse sé wæs lyttle ær dead, and þam he þegnade ⟨*þonne he*⟩ f. 146*a* læg on his feorhadle, "and he me | þa bæd þa he wæs sweltende þæt ic bæde his ⟨*broðor þæt he*⟩ fríode ⟨*sum*⟩ mænnen for hine þæt wæs hiom bæm g⟨*emæne*". *Þa abead*⟩ he hit him; ac his lices broðor for his gitsunge agæ⟨*lde þa be*⟩ne and nolde hig gefyllen. Þa wæs his sawul on þære hextan sworetunge, ⟨*and wæ*⟩s wregende hire þone ungetriowan broðer, and hio hefiglice hine ⟨*þrea*⟩de.

§ 15 (= 16). 'And þa þis wæs eall þuss gespecen and gesceawod, þa bibudon þa eadigan englas þæt his sawul ahwyrfde eft buton yldinge to his lichaman; and he þa gecydde eall þæt him þær ætéawed wæs gelyfedum mannum; and þam þe hit bismorodan, þonne forwyrnde he þám þære segene. And sumum wife he gerehte hire synne, sio wæs eardigende in feorþiode; and he hire gecydde þæt hio mihte geearnian, gif hio sylf wolde, þæt hire wære ælmihtig God miltsiend. And sumum mæssepreoste he gerehte ealle þas

referebant conventu testificantes, illam furti ream et peccatricem fuisse. Intulit quoque: 'Fratris cuiusdam, qui paulo ante defunctus est, animam tristem ibi videbam. Cui antea ipse in infirmitate exitus sui ministravi *et exsequia prebui*; qui mihi moriens precepit, ut fratri illius germano verbis illius testificans demandarem, ut ancillam quandam, quam in potestate communiter possederunt, pro anima eius manu mitteret. Sed germanus eius, avaritia impediente, petitionem eius non implevit. Et de hoc supra dicta anima per alta suspiria accussans fratrem infidelem et increpans graviter querebatur.'

15. *Et similiter testatus est de Ceolredo rege Mercionum, quem illo tamen tempore, quo haec visa sunt, in corpore fuisse non dubium est. Quem, ut dixit, videbat angelico quodam umbraculo contra impetum daemoniorum, quasi libri alicuius magni extensione et superpositione, defensum. Ipsi autem daemones anhelando rogabant angelos, ut, ablata defensione illa, ipsi permitterentur crudelitatis eorum voluntatem in eo exercere. Et inputabant ei horribilem ac nefandam multitudinem flagitiorum; et minantes dicebant, illum sub durissimis inferorum claustris claudendum et ibi, peccatis promerentibus, aeternis tormentis cruciandum esse. Tunc angeli solito tristiores facti dicebant: 'Pro dolor, quod homo peccator iste semet ipsum plus defendere non permittit; et ob ipsius propria merita nullum ei adiutorium possumus prebere.' Et aufere-*

190 abead] *remains of last letter favour* d.

gastlican gesihðe. Þæs mæssepreostes nama wæs Bogia, and se hine gelærde þæt he þa gesihðe mannum cydde. And he gecydde þam preoste þæt he wæs iú for manegum wintrum bigyrded for Godes lufan mid iserne gyrdelse, and næs him þæs nænig man gewita.

§ 16 (= 17). 'And he sæde þa he eft sceolde to his lichaman, þæt he þa nænigre oðru wiht swa swiðe onscunode on ealre þære gesihðe þe he geseah swa his agenne lichaman, ne him nán þing swa ladlic þuhte ne swa forsewenlic: and he næfre gestanc hiardran fúlnes þonne him þuhte þæt se lichama stunce, buton þam deoflum and þam byrnendum fyre þe he þær geseah. And him þa wæs biboden þæt he hwyrfde to his lichaman in dǽgred, and ǽr he eode of his lichaman æt þam forman háncrede.'

bant superpositi tutaminis defensionem. Tunc daemones gaudentes et exultantes, de universis mundi partibus congregati maiori multitudine, quam omnium animantium in saeculo fieri aestimaret, diversis eum tormentis inaestimabiliter fatigantes lacerabant.

16. Tum demum beati angeli praecipiebant ei, qui haec omnia extra corpus suum raptus spiritali contemplatione vidit et audivit, ut sine mora ad proprium rediret corpus et universa, quae illi ostensa fuerunt, credentibus *et intentione divina interrogantibus* manifestare non dubitaret, insultantibus autem narrare denegaret; et ut cuidam mulieri, quae inde in longinqua regione habitabat, eius perpetrata peccata per ordinem exponeret et ei intimaret, quod omnipotentem Deum potuisset per satisfactionem repropitiari sibi, si voluisset; et ut cuidam presbitero nomine Beggan istas spiritales visiones cunctas exponeret et postea, quemadmodum ab illo instructus fieret, hominibus pronuntiaret: ***propria quippe peccata, quae illi ab spiritibus inmundis inputata fuerunt, confessa supra dicti presbiteri iudicio emendaret; et ad indicium angelici praecepti*** presbitero testificari, quia iam per plurimos annos zonam ferream circa lumbos, nullo hominum conscio, amore Domini cogente, habuerat.

17. Proprium corpus dicebat se, dum extra fuerat, tam valde perhorruisse, ut in omnibus illis visionibus nihil tam odibile, nihil tam despectum, nihil tam durum foetorem evaporans, exceptis daemonibus et igne flagrante, videret, quam proprium corpus. ***Et fratres eius conservos, quos intuitus est exsequias corporis sui clementer exhibere, ideo perhorruit, quia invisi corporis curam egerunt.*** Iussus tamen ab angelis primo diluculo redit ad corpus, qui primo gallicinio exiebat de corpore. ***Redivivo autem in corpore plena septimana nihil omnino corporalibus oculis videre potuit, sed oculi fisicis pleni, frequenter sanguine stillaverunt.***

18. ***Et postea de presbitero relegioso et peccatrice muliere, sicut ei ab angelis manifestatum est, ita illis profitentibus, verum esse probavit. Subsequens autem et citus scelerati regis exitus, quae de illo visa fuerunt vera esse, procul dubio probavit.***

19. *Multa alia et his similia referebat sibi ostensa fuisse, quae de memoria labefacta per ordinem recordari nullatenus potuisset. Et dicebat se post istas mirabiles visiones tam tenacem memoriae non fuisse, ut ante fuerat.*

20. *Haec autem te diligenter flagitante scripsi, quae tribus mecum relegiosis et valde venerabilibus fratribus in commune audientibus exposuit; qui mihi in hoc scripto adstipulatores fideles testes esse dinoscuntur.*

Vale; verae virgo vitae ut et vivas angelicae,
Recto rite et rumore regnes semper in aethere
Christum.

ADDENDUM: THE VERSES PREFIXED TO *GREGORY'S DIALOGUES*

THE existence of the correction noted at p. 202 above, and my interpretation of it, have been questioned.[1] As the point is important for literary history I shall labour it, beginning with a summary translation of the verses.

> The reader may find in me many good examples to help him to Heaven. 'Bishop W., poor servant' of God, 'ordered me to be written. The bishop who had this copy made which you hold in your hands and study, begs that you ask help for him of these saints whose memory it records'; and that God may forgive his sins, and grant rest in Heaven to him; 'and also to his lord who gave him the pattern copy', King Alfred, 'who is the best treasure-giver' he ever heard of among earthly kings.

Here *ðas bysene* is translated 'the pattern copy' as if it were *ða bysene*. Unless a vague use is allowed, the rendering 'this' troubles all the interpretations to be discussed.

The writer is the bishop himself, because nobody else would call him *þeow ond þearfa*. The alliteration proves that his name began with *W*. The tense used shows that King Alfred was alive when he wrote; and the choice of alliterative verse for a prefatory note in which the book itself speaks, as well as some forms that survive in this early-eleventh-century copy, e.g. *geliefeð*, *biesene*, *hiora*, *resðe*, *selesða*, are naturally explained in a composition dating from Alfred's reign, though *io* and *sð* might be considerably later.[2]

There is no doubt that in the manuscript the letters *tan* of *Wulfstan* stand on an erasure; they are in a blacker ink than the text, and in a different, apparently later hand. To guard against the possibility of personal illusion, I have obtained confirmation of these points from Mr. Neil Ker, whose experience of Anglo-Saxon

[1] See e.g. E. Dobbie *The Anglo-Saxon Minor Poems*, 1942, apparatus p. 112, and Introduction p. cxvi f.

[2] Cf. Wynflæd's will in Miss D. Whitelock's *Anglo-Saxon Wills*, 1930, p. 10 ff. and p. 109.

manuscripts is now unequalled. Ultra-violet rays do not reveal the original letters, because the erasure has been made by scratching deeply when the ink was dry.

What did the scribe write or intend to write? The inquiry is limited because in the lists of bishops only two names, *Wulfsige* and *Wulfstan*, begin with *Wulfs*, and there are no other Anglo-Saxon men's names beginning with those letters.

If we try *Wulfsige* first, his name fits the space of two or three erased letters, and accounts for the deep mark of erasure where the tail of *ʒ* would fall (none of the last three letters of *Wulfstan* would go below the line). Wulfsige was one of Alfred's bishops, and Alfred sent him the translation of Gregory's other book, the *Pastoralis* (see p. 145 above). Nothing in the verses is inconsistent with his authorship of them. We know from the end of Alfred's Prose Preface to the *Pastoral Care* that he expected books he sent to his bishops to be multiplied.

The alternative is that the scribe intended to write *Wulfstan* and bungled the end of it. But he wrote, probably at Worcester, in or soon after the period (1002–23) when Wulfstan the sermon-writer was bishop there. Wulfstan was a leading author and statesman of his day. How came the scribe to miswrite his name, on which it is not easy to go wrong? If by some chance he mechanically jumbled the last three letters, writing e.g. *Wulfsant*, why did he not himself correct it at once? These objections might be set aside if *Wulfstan* were a possible reading. But it makes nonsense. The lists of bishops are well preserved, and there is none of that name in or near Alfred's reign. The verses are not in the style of Wulfstan the sermon-writer.

Thus the evidence is that the original reading of the manuscript was *Wulfsige*, and that later a reader corrected it deliberately but erroneously to *Wulfstan*. He may have thought, or even known, that Bishop Wulfstan the sermon-writer ordered this particular copy of the *Dialogues* to be made.

When Keller proposed to read *Wærferð* for *Wulfstan*, he was unaware of the correction in the manuscript. He suggested that a Worcester scribe, copying the text in the bishopric of St. Wulfstan (1062–95), unconsciously substituted *Wulfstan* (*bisceop*) for *Wær-*

ferð (*bisceop*). This date seems to me much too late for both the handwriting and the language of the first two books in Otho C I. And is it credible that such a substitution would be made in two stages, of which the second—the corrector's substitution of *tan*—was certainly deliberate? If *Wærferð* and no other name fitted the context, that objection and the absence of manuscript support might be overcome. Wærferth was bishop of Worcester in Alfred's time; nobody challenges Asser's statement (ch. 77) that he translated the *Dialogues* 'imperio regis'; and Alfred's preface says the translation was for the King's personal use. Then the one thing we should expect Wærferth to say in a preface is that he translated the book: the verb *awendan* 'translate' alliterates temptingly with his name. The writer of this preface almost pointedly avoids any such claim.

Keller tried to meet the difficulty. With Wülker he denied that *bysen* could mean 'pattern book', overlooking the clear examples of that sense in Alfred and Ælfric. He translated 'his beahgifan þe him ðas bysene forgeaf' by 'seinem Ringgeber, der ihm diesen Auftrag gab': 'his lord who gave him this commission'. Now English *bysen* means either 'example' or 'exemplar', not 'commission'. The etymological sense 'command' or the like is recorded only from *Genesis B*, where recent editors suggest influence of Old Saxon *anbusan* 'command' corresponding to Gothic *anabusns*; but as all four examples in *Genesis B* alliterate with *b*, they may point to an unrecorded Old Saxon form without prefix corresponding to OE. *bysen*. Besides, *forgiefan* in the sense 'give (a command)' is not Old English. Keller's translation is unacceptable; and even if it could be accepted, it creates a new difficulty: there is no previous reference in the verses to any royal commission or command; so that both the name *Wærferð* and the information that supports his authorship of the verses have to be imported into them.

Keller's final interpretation is uncertain, for though he did not withdraw his first rendering, he later noticed the parallel of Alfred's Verse Preface to the *Pastoral Care* and allowed that *bysen* could mean either a 'pattern copy' for the Anglo-Saxon text, as I have rendered it, or a copy of Gregory's Latin text.[1] This last meaning

[1] Op. cit. p. 93 n.

is unexampled, but not impossible. It is possible, too, that Alfred gave Wærferth a copy of the Latin, though the Worcester library is not likely to have been without the most popular reading-book of the time. But even with this more defensible rendering, the verses do not say that their author translated the book. Alfred's own prefaces are all explicit in that essential. If Wærferth's name had manuscript authority one would hesitate to remove it, but the case for introducing it is weak.

Two possible objections to the reading *Wulfsige* deserve attention. First, why should the descendant of a copy of the *Dialogues* prepared by order of the bishop of Sherborne, reach Worcester, the home of the translation? It is not certain that Worcester had preserved its own copies throughout the tenth century, though it is likely. There were, however, special circumstances. When Oswald, who was not trained at Worcester, became its bishop in 961, the community was very small, as J. A. Robinson has shown in *St. Oswald and the Church of Worcester*. The Benedictine Reform ensured an increase of numbers and of reading, so that more books had to be supplied. Oswald did not suddenly reform St. Peter's, Worcester. He began with a separate community of monks at Westbury; then raised the new foundation of Ramsey; and, as a third stage, brought monks and a dean from Ramsey to Worcester. In this process books from outside might be expected to reach Worcester; and there is a close parallel: the early-eleventh-century Worcester book CCCC 12, a copy of Alfred's *Pastoral Care*, is not derived from MS. Hatton 20, which Alfred sent to Worcester and which certainly remained there, but is textually related to MS. Tiberius B XI, which was almost certainly a Winchester book.[1]

Apart from these special conditions, the movement of books from place to place must be reckoned common, not exceptional, in England of the late tenth and early eleventh centuries. Books tended to stay in one place when they were stillborn, or obsolete, or when the place was isolated. But the only way of disseminating texts, and one way of securing extra copies, was to send them from one place to another. This movement greatly complicates the task

[1] See above, p. 142.

of a historian of textual transmission, or of schools of handwriting and illumination; yet he must accept it, grateful for the compensating assurance that the chronology of development is not likely to vary much from place to place; and he must reject the convenient assumption that, unless the contrary can be proved in a particular instance, styles and types of text were strictly localized. It is easy to be influenced too much by the localization of a manuscript. So Keller and Hecht have given authority to the view that the revision of *Gregory's Dialogues* found in the late-eleventh-century MS. Hatton 76 (H) was made at Worcester simply because the manuscript, which is certainly not an original, was a Worcester book. That fact does no more than indicate a possibility. And because Otho C I (O) was also a Worcester book, Hecht elaborates in insignificant details its agreements with H against MS. CCCC 322 (C), and only touches on the important agreements of C, H against O.[1]

[1] Edition, II, p. 30 ff. Agreements of C, H against O, such as may be found in the apparatus, e.g. at I, p. 96 f., are seldom decisive when taken alone. But in O the verses under discussion are followed by a few lines of prose which are not in C, H: 'Here the first flow of the clean and pure stream begins to well up and pour forth through the holy breast of our father and teacher, the apostolic pope St. Gregory', &c. This is certainly part of Wærferth's text because it is echoed at the beginnings of Books ii, iii, iv in C; and H, which does not go beyond Book ii, has a corresponding passage at the beginning of that book. So C and H derive from a MS. which was defective at the beginning, where they also agree against O in preserving Alfred's preface. Then Hecht's diagrams of MS. relations (II, p. 35) are radically wrong in making C one branch and O, H another, unless O has been restored at this place from another MS. tradition. In that case the diagrams might still be radically wrong, and would certainly need an important correction: for then the main texts of O, C, H (if each is basically all of a piece throughout the first two books) would derive from one MS. which was imperfect at the beginning; so that all would represent one branch of the tradition. I cannot re-examine a very complicated problem, but note: (i) Alfred's preface could not be identified as belonging to the *Dialogues* if it were found as a detached scrap. Yet its position in C, H cannot easily be accounted for by physical mutilation of a common ancestor. (ii) A future editor should print O. Though its text is often imperfect as the result of fire-damage, and it has careless or perverse errors like the 'emendation' *hearpan* 'harp' for *apan* 'ape' at 62/15 and 62/23, yet it retains many good readings which probably represent the original, as well as archaic forms which have disappeared

The other objection is clearly put by Professor Dobbie: 'the scribe might carelessly have substituted a name which was familiar to him for a less familiar name [*Wulfstan* for *Wærferð*], but that anyone should have deliberately altered an older manuscript in this way [*Wulfsige* to *Wulfstan*] is hard to believe.'[1] The belief that Anglo-Saxon texts were not altered deliberately in readings of substance lies behind the practice of many recent editors. Combined with another—that Anglo-Saxon scribes usually copied accurately—it allows a critic to work back confidently from one late manuscript to a much older original. Add the view that *Beowulf*, for instance, has been transmitted in writing from its first composition, and the late manuscript may be treated as substantially what the poet wrote centuries earlier.[2]

Yet these are assumptions, not established truths or reasonable probabilities. They tend to make textual criticism easy by requiring all those who were concerned with the transmission of literature in a remote age to act uniformly in the way convenient to us. For most poetical texts it is impossible to prove or disprove them, because there is only one late manuscript; and no vernacular prose is recorded before Alfred's reign. But the few verse passages for which two manuscripts are available provide evidence of deliberate as well as careless variation;[3] the vicissitudes of the popular Latin text translated in *Wonders of the East* do not encourage belief in

from C and H. [When this was printing, I came upon P. N. U. Harting's important article in *Neophilologus* xxii (1937), p. 281 ff., which establishes the value of MS. O.]

[1] Op. cit. p. cxvii

[2] Critics who assume mechanical transcription throughout transmission necessarily emphasize mechanical errors, especially confusion of similar letter-forms, as the cause of deviation from the original. But if a vernacular poem like *Beowulf* was written down in the late seventh or early eighth century, and copied repeatedly until the surviving MS. was made at the end of the tenth century, it passed through handwritings different from the Southern book-hands of the tenth century, and very likely through some of the more cursive scripts that are poorly represented in extant early books and documents. In that case the possibilities of letter-confusion become too complicated to be of much help in textual criticism. It should be noted that the doctrine of uniform mechanical copying leaves no place for some methods of sifting variants, e.g. the delicate argument of *lectio difficilior*, which depend on intelligent variation.

[3] Above, p. 34.

accurate transmission;[1] the reviser of the *Dialogues* (MS. Hatton 76) had no scruples about altering the words of King Alfred's preface; and somebody deliberately produced the wrong reading *Wulfstan*. If analogies are admissible, in Middle English and other Western vernaculars there is plenty of evidence that medieval texts that were popular over long periods were subject to deliberate changes, made with the intention of explaining, correcting, expanding, abridging, or modernizing them.

The assumption that written Anglo-Saxon texts were not deliberately changed during transmission undoubtedly simplifies the task of criticism. To discard it means admitting many doubts, some of which cannot be resolved. Yet the working hypotheses of an historical study should be in themselves probable.

[1] Above, p. 74 ff.

12

THE AUTHENTICITY OF CERTAIN TEXTS IN LAMBARD'S *ARCHAIONOMIA* 1568[1]

I

. . . FOR the English text of Athelstan's *Ordinance*, Lambard's *Archaionomia* of 1568 is the sole authority. For *I Athelstan* Lambard has an English text which is entirely independent of that of the known manuscripts. It is assumed here, as elsewhere, that he had manuscript sources which are now lost. Of course some manuscript material has disappeared in modern times. I have, for instance, a script facsimile made by Richard Taylor in 1811 from a late-twelfth-century binding-leaf which was then in the possession of 'Mr Stevenson, printer, of Norwich': it contained the Old English text of *II Edgar*, and *III Edgar* as far as the word *he* in § 6, without the interpolations of the Harleian and Corpus manuscripts; and apparently no editor has come upon it. But the disappearance of a manuscript from one of the collections accessible to antiquaries in Lambard's time is uncommon enough to be matter for inquiry.

To begin with, the double text of *I Athelstan* is puzzling. It is not unusual to find more than one recension of a single Old English text, but nowhere else does a series of laws appear in two quite independent Old English drafts; and it is not easy to see how two such drafts came to be produced and promulgated. Liebermann does not consider the problem from this side, and his analysis of the relations of the versions (I. xxxiii, III 96–98) is not altogether clear: but his conclusion seems to be that Lambard's Old English texts of *I Athelstan* and the *Ordinance* derive directly from a lost manuscript of the early twelfth century, that this manuscript was once part of CCCC MS. 383, and that the Latin text of the *Quadripartitus* was translated from its archetype.

That Lambard's texts of *I Athelstan* and *Ordinance* have a single

[1] From a review in *Modern Language Review* xviii (1923), p. 100 ff., of F. L. Attenborough *The Laws of the Earliest English Kings*, 1922.

source appears to be certain, for they are distinguished from the other texts of the *Archaionomia* by an extraordinary neglect of the rules of Old English accidence and syntax, and by a diffused caninity of expression. But it is hard to believe that this source was a part of CCCC MS. 383: the positive evidence adduced for the identification is valueless; and as Lambard prints other parts of the manuscript with tolerable accuracy, it is not obvious why he or his printer should have produced from it the remarkable jargon of *I Athelstan* and the *Ordinance*.

It must be granted that Lambard was habitually careless about accidence. Throughout his book final *-e* is added or omitted almost at random, and there is a fair sprinkling of bad forms and misprints. But it would be hard to find anywhere else in the *Archaionomia* such a riot of inflexions in so short a space; for example: *ðurh ealle mine rice*; *mines agenes æhtes* gen. sg. (the only example of *æht* masc. cited in Bosworth–Toller *Suppl.*); *to ðam tide*; *ðæs beheafdunges* gen. sg. (where editors retain the misprint *ðær* for *ðæs*); *án earm Engliscmon* (acc.) *gif ge him habbaþ*, &c. These are not the forms or spellings of a twelfth-century manuscript, and if Lambard used such a manuscript his text could only be explained as the result of exceptional, deliberate, and unintelligent archaism. Even then it is not easy to see why he should change a presumable twelfth-century **to ðere tide* into *to ðam tide*.

The syntax is stranger still. The distinction of strong and weak adjectives, and of the indicative and subjunctive moods in the present tense, long survived the twelfth century; but here they have no place; for example: 'ge ðæs libbendes yrfes ge ðæs gearlices westmes'; 'ða heofonlica ðinga . . . 7 ða ecelic (acc.)'; 'ic bebeode . . . þæt hi . . . gesyllaþ . . .'; 'ic nylle þæt ge me hwæt mid woh begytaþ'; 'ic wille þæt ge fedaþ', &c. In 'warniaþ eow . . . ðæs Drihtenes eorres', the verb *warnian* is used with the genitive, which is the Old English construction of *wyrnan*; and *gebyrian* is twice construed with the simple infinitive: '. . . eallum ðe hio gehyrsumian gebyraþ' and 'nu ge gehyraþ . . . hwæt us fulfremian gebyraþ'. It cannot be supposed that a printer changed his copy in this manner, and Lambard was not in the habit of perverting his manuscripts so thoroughly.

Then there are disconcerting oddities of expression: *on þæs Drihtænes nama* 'in the name of *the* Lord'; *to ðam Drihten* 'to *the* Lord'; *ðæs Drihtenes eorres* 'the wrath of *the* Lord'. The article is commonly used in Old English with *Hælend* but not with *Drihten.* Longer specimens are: 'Ic wille þæt ge fedaþ ealle wæga án earm Engliscmon, gif ge him habbaþ, oþþe oþerne gefindaþ' = 'volo ut pascatis omni via pauperem unum Anglicum indigentem, si sit [t]ibi, vel alium inveniatis' (*Quadripartitus*); 'under þæs bisceopes gewitnesse, on ðæs rice it sie' = 'sub testimonio episcopi in cuius episcopatu sit' (*Quadripartitus*); and, finally, 'án sconc spices oþþe án rám weorþe .iiii. peningas, 7 scrud for twelf monþa ælc gear', 'a *leg of bacon*, or a *ram worth 4 pence*, and clothing *for* twelve months' = 'una perna, vel unus aries qui valeat quattuor denarios, . . . ad vestimentum duodecim mensium unoquoque anno'.

This is too great a strain on our faith. Lambard's ancient manuscript is a ghost, despite the pedigree Liebermann has prepared for it: and Lambard's texts of *I Athelstan* and the *Ordinance* are translations of the *Quadripartitus* into Elizabethan Anglo-Saxon. Hence the modernity of the constructions, and the sudden freedom from the grammatical restraints imposed by an old manuscript; hence, too, some half-Elizabethan spellings, like *gereafa* for *gerēfa* (4 times out of 5), which does not appear elsewhere in *Archaionomia.*

Let us now examine some difficulties in the text from this standpoint. In *I Athelstan* § 5 the use of the word *geornian* is so unnatural that Liebermann (iii. 98) thinks it was suggested by *geunnan* of the other version; but it is the natural translation of *cupire* in *Quadripartitus.* In *Ordinance* § 2 occurs the *ἅπαξ oferhealdan* 'to neglect', which is recorded in Bosworth–Toller and in *O.E.D.* s.v. *Overhold*: it is a mechanical rendering of *supertenere* in the *Quadripartitus*, and *supertenere* elsewhere renders OE. *forhealdan*, which probably stood in the lost Old English text of the *Ordinance*. *Án sconc spices* stands alone among Bosworth–Toller's examples of *sconc* and *spīc*, and in *O.E.D.* s.v. *Shank* the passage requires a special paragraph for the meaning, as well as an etymological note on the form. This is not surprising; for *perna* of *Quadripartitus* is the regular equivalent of OE. *flicce* 'flitch', and there can be no doubt that *flicce* stood in the lost OE. *Ordinance*. But the Elizabethan translator did not know this. He understood by *perna* what we now call a 'ham', and yet 'ham' in the modern sense of 'a cured leg of pork' was neither Old English nor Elizabethan, and 'gammon' was plainly not a native word. So he decided to give a paraphrase, and having come across *sconca* 'leg', produced the monstrosity *án sconc spices*! It does not seem to have occurred to him or to his editors that the choice between 'a leg of bacon' and 'a ram' was a strange one: the *án earm Engliscmon* required food and not breeding-stock; and since *aries* in the *Quadripartitus* elsewhere renders *weðer*, we may be confident that the lost OE. *Ordinance* specified *.i. weðer*, not *án rám*. The spuriousness of Lambard's text is thus confirmed: and even the plausible *siblac* = *hostias pacificas* (*I Ath.* § 2) must be expunged from the dictionaries.

The barbarous 'Old English' helps to identify the Latin manuscript of the *Quadripartitus* that the translator used. It was certainly one of the 'London' group, with near affinities to Liebermann's *K* (Cott. MS. Claudius D II) and *Or.* (Oriel College MS. 46), both of the early fourteenth century. Note, for instance, in *I Ath.* § 5: *Quadripartitus* 'quid Deo precupiam et quid complere debeatis': but *K*, *Or.* 'precipiam . . . debeamus', which is closer to Lambard's *hwæt Drihtene us* bebeod ⁊ *hwæt* us *fulfremian gebyraþ*; or again, in *Ord.* (Prologue): *Quadripartitus* 'si sit ibi'; but *K*, *Or.* 'si sit tibi' = Lambard *gif ge him habbaþ*. In one place *K* alone gives a corresponding text, and it is certainly corrupt: *I Ath.* § 3: *Quadripartitus* 'Recolendum quoque nobis est, quam terribiliter in libris positum est'; *K* '. . . *quod* terribiliter in *hiis* [so others of the London group] libris . . .': Lambard *We moton eac ðæs ðencan*, ðe *egeslic on* ðissum *bocum is gewriten*. Use of *K* would also explain the failure to translate *I Ath.* § 4, which is made unintelligible by *K*'s reading *chericete* for *cyricsceatta*. But account must be taken of *Ord.* § 1 where *K* has *witadeðeow*: Lambard (correctly) *witeðeowne*; and of *Ord.* (Prologue) where *K* has 'omni villa': the rest 'omni via': Lambard *ealle wæga*. It must be assumed either that the translator used a Latin manuscript now lost which was very close to *K*, or—what is more likely—that he followed a transcript of *K* which had been collated with another manuscript for at least two awkward readings.

If Lambard was the translator, he must have had his tongue in his cheek when he wrote in the Preface: 'Jam vero ne quis domi nostræ has natas esse leges arbitretur, plane suscipio atque profiteor, magna fide et religione ex vetustissimis . . . exemplaribus fuisse desumpta.' But there is evidence of his good faith. In 1567, the year before the Preface was written, Laurence Nowell gave him an Anglo-Saxon dictionary in manuscript, which is now Bodleian MS. Selden supra 63. It is significant that none of the rarities of the spurious laws is in Nowell's word-list; but among the later additions—made apparently by Lambard's hand—appear the following: (under *Sibbe*) '*Siblac*. hostia pacifica'; (after '*Sceanca*, the legges, see Scanca') '7 *Sconc*. idem, opinor. *Sconc spices*. a gamon of Bacon. *perna* Lat.' This is not the language of a forger contemplating his own handiwork. It rather suggests that Lambard received the texts from some friend and printed them without a doubt of their authenticity. Now in his Preface he writes: 'Obtulit mihi superiori anno [i.e. 1567] Laurentius Noelus, . . . qui me (quicunque in hoc genere sim) efficit, priscas Anglorum leges, antiquissima Saxonum lingua, et literis conscriptas, atque a me (quoniam ei tum erat trans mare eundum) ut Latinas facerem, ac pervulgarem vehementer flagitavit.' These words might refer to the loan of an old manuscript; but it is more likely that Nowell sent a transcript of the Laws in the imitative Anglo-Saxon script that scholars of the time used in making copies, whether for private use or for the printer. The spurious passages might easily creep into such a transcript: for if Nowell copied from a manuscript like CCCC 383, or Cotton Otho B XI, which begin Athelstan's Laws with *II Athelstan*, reference to a manuscript of the *Quadripartitus* would at once disclose the gap; and what more natural to an Elizabethan antiquary than to fill it as best he could, not with intent to deceive but simply to complete his collection of Old English texts? Once embedded in the transcript the fictitious laws might be forgotten by their author; there would be nothing in the script to reveal them to Lambard; and even when the true text of *I Athelstan* came to his notice in the course of collation, he would hardly recognize its superior claims.

A thorough study of the whole body of Lambard's texts would probably throw more light on their origin. His section-headings particularly, unless they have manuscript support, should be regarded as adventitious until they are proved genuine.

[*I have thought it unnecessary to reprint Professor Liebermann's defence of his view, because his reasons are set out fully in the reply that follows. On one major issue the balance has since been tilted against him: Flower showed, in* Laurence Nowell and the Discovery of England in Tudor Times *(1936) p. 28 f., that when Nowell transcribed the Old English version of Bede's History from MS. Otho B XI into B.M. MS. Addit. 43703, he added pseudo-Anglo-Saxon renderings of sentences that are in the Latin original but not in any other manuscript of the English version.*]

II[1]

To the kindness of Professor Liebermann I owe a copy of the article[2] in which he defends the authenticity of Lambard's *I Athelstan* and *Athelstan's Charitable Ordinance* against my argument that they are both translations into Old English made in the sixteenth century from the Latin of *Quadripartitus*. If such a matter could be settled by weight of authority the balance must be heavily against me. But after studying Professor Liebermann's reply, and re-reading the materials so admirably presented in his *Gesetze der Angelsachsen*,[3] I am not convinced that these texts are authentic. For, no doubt because his space was short, he has omitted to deal with some of the evidence on which I relied most, so that his alternative explanations are not clear; and on some details selected for discussion he does not quite meet the points I hoped to make. On other details, again, his argument is rather that they are consistent with the views expressed in his *Gesetze* than that they are

[1] From *Modern Language Review* xx (1925), p. 253 ff.

[2] *Anglia Beiblatt*, July 1924, p. 214 ff.

[3] The texts of *I Ath.* and *Ord.* are given in vol. i, pp. 146–9. The commentary on them is in vol. iii, pp. 96–99. Professor Liebermann's collection of texts is so accurate and complete that for the purposes of the present discussion it is hardly necessary to go farther afield.

inconsistent with my contention; and it is to be expected that many of the facts would be explicable on either hypothesis, since both were devised to explain them.

In general, Lambard's texts of *I Ath.* and *Ord.* have four distinguishing features: (i) they are found in no extant manuscript, and apparently no manuscript was known to Wanley when he made his Catalogue in 1705; (ii) Lambard's *I Ath.* differs extraordinarily in drafting from the *I Ath.* of the extant manuscripts (no Old English manuscript of *Ord.* survives); (iii) Lambard's *I Ath.* and *Ord.* are both very close to the Latin text of *Quadripartitus* as it appears in the 'London' group of manuscripts; (iv) both are expressed in barbarous Old English.

I have tried to explain all four features by assuming that these texts were translated from the Latin of the 'London' text by Laurence Nowell in or about 1567. Professor Liebermann has explained the first by assuming that Lambard used an Old English manuscript since lost unaccountably;[1] the second by assuming that before 1100 there had been a recasting (*lq*)[2] of the text of the extant manuscripts; the third by assuming that *Quadripartitus* (or rather that early draft[3] of it which he believes to lie behind the

[1] In *Gesetze*, vol. i, p. xxxiii, col. 2, it is suggested that the lost MS. of *Ord.* was older than the lost MS. of *I Ath.* Later (vol. iii, p. 98) it is recognized that their textual history is the same.

[2] i.e. the lost common source of L(ambard's) Old English and of Q(*uadripartitus*). Professor Liebermann is not quite accurate when he says I have called *lq* a ghost. That statement was limited to *I Ath.* and *Ord.*, for which there could be no *lq* if, as I believe, there was no *l*—no authentic source for Lambard. Whether evidence exists to establish an *lq* for any other text is a separate question, of which only a small part concerns us: because the *lq* which is assumed in *Gesetze* for, e.g., *II Eadweard* is of a different character from the *lq* dealt with here.

[3] In his *Quadripartitus*, Halle 1892, §§ ix and x, Professor Liebermann has shown that the extant MSS. containing *Quadripartitus* (or excerpts from it) fall into several groups, of which no one derives from another. That each of these groups represents a separate draft or recension by the author of *Quadripartitus* (*Gesetze*, vol. iii, p. 309, § 3) is not so well established. To accept it for present purposes will narrow the issue, although it is a bar to the pressing home of nearly all arguments drawn from the Latin text. For instance, in *I Ath.* § 3, where the extant MSS. have 'Us is to ðencanne hu ondrislic hit on bocum gecweden is', most MSS. of *Quadripartitus* have the equivalent: 'Recolendum quoque nobis est

text of the 'London' group) was translated from this recasting, *lq*; and the fourth (in so far as he notices abnormality of language) by the activities of the 'recaster before 1100', of another assumed reviser in the early twelfth century, of Lambard, and of the printer.[1]

It is a complicated hypothesis, giving ample scope for explanation of details; and facts that are inconsistent with it are necessarily few. To note such facts very briefly was one of the aims of my previous article, and it would serve no purpose to cover the same ground again, because the hypothesis has been supplemented and guarded in Professor Liebermann's latest contribution. Dealing with the argument that the readings in *I Ath.* § 5 can hardly be explained except in the sequence: extant manuscripts *ic ann* . . . *ge sculon*: translated by *Q.* 'præcupiam[2] . . . debeatis': miscopied in some 'London' manuscripts 'precipiam . . . debeamus': translated in Lambard by ***bebeod***(*e*) . . . ***us*** . . . ***gebyraþ***, he acknowledges that Lambard probably knew a manuscript of the 'London' group.[3] Apparently he is disposed to admit the intervention of an Eliza-

quam terribiliter in libris positum est'. But MS. Claudius D II of the 'London' group (the clause is missing in the earlier Rylands MS.) has the bad reading, 'Recolendum nobis quoque est *quod* terribiliter in *hiis* libris positum est', which corresponds to Lambard's 'We moton eac ðæs ðencan *ðe* egeslic on *ðissum* bocum is gewriten'. On the one view, the bad readings in Claudius D II are corruptions of the correct Latin, and Lambard's text translates them. On the other, Lambard's type of text (*lq*) arose somehow out of the correct Old English; the bad readings in Claudius D II are due to translation from *lq* in an early edition of *Quadripartitus*; and they were removed by the translator himself from later editions. It must, then, be assumed that the author of *Quadripartitus* knew not only *lq* but also the better text of the extant MSS. from which he made random corrections. This necessary and important extension of the hypothesis seems to have escaped attention.

[1] See, e.g., *Gesetze*, vol. iii, p. 96; vol. i, p. 146, col. 3 n.; and vol. i, p. xxxiii, col. 2.

[2] Cf. classical 'praecupidus', and (*ge*)*unnon* rendered by 'cupiatis' in the same clause.

[3] 'Ich wusste nämlich dass L(ambar)d zwar nicht Q(uadripartitus), wohl aber eine Hs. von dem diesen abschreibenden Londoner Stadtjuristen gekannt hat, und fand zweimal, in Fehlern gegen das Original, das Latein in Lond. übereinstimmend mit L(ambar)d', &c. (*Beiblatt*, p. 215). Whether Lambard or Nowell is responsible is relatively unimportant, and so is the distinction between *Q.* and the 'London' Laws.

bethan scholar in this decisive place, while maintaining that the documents are in other respects genuine.

To meet this development I shall try to show: first, that it is not only exceptionally and for an isolated word that the intervention of an Elizabethan is needed; then, that my hypothesis explains all the details, so that further assumptions are unnecessary; and, lastly, that three other texts in Lambard, for which no manuscript source is known, are Elizabethan renderings made under the same circumstances. Incidentally I shall draw attention to some of the difficulties of Professor Liebermann's position.

I

To begin with a point of detail: in reply to the argument that in Lambard's *Ord.* the whole phrase *án sconc spices oþþe án rám weorþe IIII peningas* is spurious, Professor Liebermann refers to his Glossary (*Gesetze*, vol. ii, p. 635), where no light is cast on my difficulties. They are these: elsewhere in the Anglo-Saxon laws we have *sceap*, *weðer*, *ewu*, *lamb*, but nowhere else is a *ram* specified. It may reasonably be supposed that the economy of a flock in Athelstan's day was very much what it was in later times: there were ewes for breeding, milk, wool, and meat; rams for breeding and wool; wethers for meat and wool; and the number of rams would be small compared with the number of ewes and wethers. No doubt rams were sometimes eaten, and it may be that a ram was fair tender under an order requiring delivery of a 'sheep'. But is it likely that in providing for the monthly food of a pauper the king would specify a ram, the most unsuitable kind of meat for the recipient, and perhaps the most inconvenient for the supplier? Next, *án sconc spices* is a barbarism from whatever angle it is examined.[1] *Sconca* is not elsewhere used for the hindquarter in Old English, and phrases like 'leg of mutton', 'gammon of bacon', 'haunch of venison', which are not recorded in the Oxford Dictionary before the sixteenth century, can hardly be carried back to the eleventh or the twelfth century. Again, *weorþe IIII peningas* is good modern English—'worth 4 pence', but the

[1] The isolation of the phrase in the Oxford Dictionary s.v. *Shank*, 1. e, is significant.

Old English expression is regularly *IIII peninga* (gen. pl.) *weorþ*.[1] And, as the elements are bad severally, so is their meaning when they are taken together. For *án sconc spices* = 1 ram = 4*d*.[2] And a ham is roughly one-eighth of the cured meat of a pig. So 1 pig = 8 rams = 32*d*. But modern conditions suggest that two sheep would have about the same meat value as one pig; and luckily the contemporary *VI Athelstan* § 6 confirms this, giving the values 1 pig = 2 sheep = 10*d*. My explanation is that the lost *Ordinance* had *.i. flicce oþþe .i. weðer*: which was regularly translated in *Quadripartitus* 'una perna vel unus aries'.[3] Nowell, taking both words in their usual meanings, rendered 'aries' by *ram*; and, as he knew no Old English for 'a gammon of bacon', he paraphrased 'perna' with *án sconc spices*. Applying now the independent check afforded by the values, we get 1 flitch = ½ pig = 1 wether = 4*d*., which gives a true relative value and a reasonable money value for the pig and sheep in Athelstan's time. Defenders of the phrase can hardly decline the task of explaining the words and their meaning in combination; and those who concede that it is spurious, but think it is interpolated in a genuine text, must consider how this strange patchwork came to be produced.

But in fact these versions are all of a piece. The linguistic characters that make them suspect cannot be localized in an occasional word or phrase: they are uniformly diffused through the texts, and are essential to the expression. The word-stems are standard West Saxon of the late tenth and the eleventh century. The inflexions, where they occur, are full Old English inflexions, but they are barbarously misused. The syntax shows an occasional Latinism,[4]

[1] The abnormal construction occurs again in Lambard's *Að*, § 1 '... biþ weorþ syx ceorliscra manna aþas'. Its significance will appear later.

[2] That the alternatives are equivalent in value is common ground: see *Gesetze*, vol. ii, p. 641, s.v. *Schinken*.

[3] For 'perna' = *flicce* see Bosworth–Toller, *Suppl*., s.v. *flicce*. For 'aries' = *weðer*, cf. Ine § 70, 1, where the translation 'Widder' 'ram' is unsatisfactory.

[4] e.g. *Ord*. § 1; *Q*. 'sub testimonio'; Lambard *under gewitnesse*. Examples of the other peculiarities are given in the first part, p. 233 f. above. Of these, only three are questioned. Against the explanation of the ἅπαξ *oferhealdan* (normal *forhealdan*) as a literal rendering of *Q*. 'supertenere', Professor Liebermann calls attention to other compounds in which *for-* and

several Modern English features, and a complete disregard for such radical distinctions as that between strong and weak adjectives, which is still clear in Chaucer. At every turn there is conflict with the history of vocabulary, accidence, and syntax that has been built up from reliable texts. Now, if an Elizabethan antiquary tried to translate from *Q.*, having a good knowledge of Old English vocabulary and a special familiarity with the phrasing of the Laws, this is the sort of Old English he might be expected to produce; for neither from tradition nor by training could he know the niceties of the old language. But if these peculiarities derive from an old manuscript, where among the ample remains of the tenth, eleventh, and twelfth centuries are they to be paralleled in a passage of natural prose?[1] If they are due to Lambard's mutilation of an old manuscript, has he anywhere else in his collection of Laws mutilated to the same degree a manuscript which is still available for comparison? If the printer is responsible, why did he choose just here to falsify his copy? (The peculiarities on which I rely cannot be explained as typographical errors.[2]) And if Lambard him-

ofer- have similar force. This can only affect the decisiveness of the example taken by itself. As evidence that the spelling *gereafa* (4 times out of 5) is genuine, an undoubted example is quoted from the twelfth-century MS. Harley 55. My argument was not that an isolated example with *ea* is impossible in the twelfth century (when almost every conceivable spelling of the *e* sounds may occur), but rather that its exceptionally free use in *I Ath.* and *Ord.* suited well with an Elizabethan origin; for the spelling *rea-* is recorded in *O.E.D.* for the sixteenth and seventeenth centuries only. I agree, however, that this is not good evidence against authenticity. On the other hand, the use of the definite article with *Drihten* (Modern English '*the* Lord') is in no way paralleled by three instances in *Swerian* (*Gesetze*, vol. i, p. 396), where, as Professor Liebermann himself suggests, the article is a strong demonstrative = 'that' and is good Old English idiom. It was not pretended that the forms *ðæs Drihtenes*, &c., are due to the Latin: they are due to the Modern English in which Nowell thought when translating the Latin.

[1] Copies of interlinear glosses should not be cited, because they are different in kind. Nor will an assemblage of irregularities from various places make a parallel, because here irregularity is concentrated. Manipulation of Old English texts after the twelfth century and before 1550 need not be reckoned with.

[2] Lambard was certainly not particular about final *-e*, and his printer probably set no great store by it. So the addition or omission of *-e* should not be used as evidence.

self falsified the text, or allowed his printer to do so, what becomes of his high reputation as an editor, which Professor Liebermann objects to the relatively charitable suggestion that he mistook Nowell's translation for a transcript from an old manuscript?

There is another important consideration. We have two distinct versions of *I Ath.*, one in extant manuscripts and one in Lambard. If Lambard's text is an antiquarian rendering of *Quadripartitus* made by a person who had not the Old English of the manuscripts before him, the anomaly is explained. But if that explanation is rejected, the problem remains. It is unlikely that the original wording of a law would be wantonly changed, and the evidence of many late manuscripts shows that considerable variations are not very common, and are usually explicable as modernizations or attempts to clarify the expression. But if Lambard's text ultimately derives from that of the extant manuscripts, nothing less than complete rewriting will account for the difference; and accordingly the recasting *lq* is postulated in *Gesetze*.[1]

Yet no motive has been suggested that would explain such a recasting. Certainly it was not the desire to make the meaning clearer or to bring the wording up to date; for in what age could a person who had before him the straightforward manuscript text of *I Ath.* Pro., 'and eow bidde . . . þæt ge ærest of minum agenum góde agyfan þa teoþunga, ægþer ge on cwicum ceape ge on þæs geares eorð-wæstmum', think that Lambard's sorry stuff, 'ic . . . bebeode . . . þæt hi ærost mines (!) agenes (!) æhtes (!) ðam (!) teoþe (!) gesyllaþ (!), ge ðæs libbendes (!) yrfes ge ðæs gearlices (!) westmes', was more modern or more lucid? And if a motive for its production could be found, *lq* still does not help very much. As it is by definition the source of *Q.*, it must be dated before 1100:[2] and any linguistic peculiarities that are attributed to it must be paralleled from eleventh-century manuscripts, which in fact maintain the accidence, syntax, and vocabulary of West Saxon fairly well. It

[1] *Gesetze*, vol. iii, p. 96 ff. The possibility of derivation from two different copies promulgated in Athelstan's time is admitted (*Gesetze*, vol. i, p. xvi), but is subsequently neglected, with good reason.

[2] *Gesetze*, vol. iii, p. 96.

will not explain, for instance, the occurrence twice in Lambard's *I Ath.*,[1] and nowhere else in Old English, of the modern substantival use of *teoþa(n)* = 'tithe(s)', which is first recorded from an extant manuscript of the thirteenth century.

It will not even explain some larger discrepancies between Lambard's texts and the extant manuscripts. If we compare the Latin for one phrase from the passage just cited: Extant manuscripts 'þa teoþunga, ægþer ge *on* cwicum ceape ge *on* þæs geares *eorð*-wæstmum': *Q.* 'decimas utriusque *in* vivente captali et *in* ornotinis frugibus *terre*': Lambard 'ðam teoþe . . . ge ðæs libbendes yrfes ge ðæs gearlices westmes', it is plain that the text of the extant manuscripts without modification, and not Lambard's text, lay before the translator of *Q.*; so that *lq*, if it ever existed, showed no recasting in this phrase. Still another recaster of the beginning of the twelfth century must be assumed to account for the divergence of Lambard's text from *Q.*;[2] and one may well ask where in the twelfth-century manuscripts of Anglo-Saxon laws a sentence has been so completely rewritten without change of bulk, matter, or arrangement; and how such a complete rewriting could leave unbroken in other places the very close relation with *Q.* that is supposed to have been produced by the previous recaster; and why these particular texts were so singularly afflicted with revisers.

2

I shall now turn to the considerations which lead Professor Liebermann to conclude that the authenticity of the texts is unshaken. No doubt he has selected the chief difficulties that stand in the way of the opposite view; and it will be best to deal with them all in order, lest any strong point should escape.

(*a*) Since Lambard knew a number of Old English legal texts which are now lost, why may not his *I Ath.* and *Ord.* derive from a lost manuscript? Perhaps the readiest answer is that the whole question of Lambard's lost Old English manuscripts is uncertain,[3]

[1] Oxford Dict., s.v. *Tenth* B. 1b and *Tithe* B; Bosworth–Toller, s.v. *tēoþa* 2a.

[2] *Gesetze*, vol. iii, p. 96 ff.

[3] It would be a grave error of method if, as Professor Liebermann says, I had denied that Lambard used any lost MSS. without giving my reasons. In fact, the denial concerned only *I Ath.* and *Ord.*, and was based on

and as his *I Ath.* and *Ord.* have exceptional features in common, it is legitimate to consider them apart and on their own merits.

(*b*) What scholar in Elizabethan times would try to deceive his colleagues without any political motive? As it is explicit in my hypothesis that there was no intention to deceive,[1] we are at one here.

(*c*) Who had the necessary knowledge to produce such texts? Certainly Laurence Nowell, Lambard's teacher, and (beside Joscelin) the first Anglo-Saxon scholar of the time. That he had a good knowledge of the Old English vocabulary is proved by the manuscript Dictionary he sent to Lambard in 1567.[2] Extant transcripts[3] and Lambard's Preface show that he had worked specially on the Laws. The right words and phrases in *I Ath.* and *Ord.* are thus accounted for; and the deplorable grammar and syntax could not be above Nowell's powers.

(*d*) Why did he overlook the Old English of *I Ath.* in the extant MSS. CCCC 201 and Nero A 1?[4] After all, Nowell was a pioneer,

evidence given. The assumption that for other texts he used Old English MSS. since unaccountably lost requires investigation, which would be easier if somebody would state as a working hypothesis the number of lost MSS. assumed, their content, and probable dates. As matters stand, it is not clear whether 'Lambard benutzte ausser erhaltenen Hss. manche verlorene' (*Gesetze*, vol. i, p. xxxiii), and 'Lambard zu einer ganzen Anzahl anderer Gesetze Texte kannte, die seitdem verloren sind' (*Beiblatt*, p. 215) mean the same thing. After all, Lambard worked in the great age of collectors of Old English MSS., which, as a class, have never since lost in interest or value. He made no long researches. He says he referred chiefly to Archbishop Parker's library, which has been well preserved. And relatively unimportant books and transcripts of his own have been carefully handed down.

[1] Above, p. 236.

[2] Bodleian MS. Selden supra 63.

[3] At Messrs. Hodgson's sale on 19 June 1924, the lots from the Lambard collection included: 'No. 512 Leges Ethelberti Regis Saxonice etc., *in Lambarde's hand*, 54 pp., sm. 4to, 1572, and a Common-Place Book . . . [containing *inter alia*] Extracts from the Laws of Alfred (to Henry I), *in Nowell's hand*, &c.'

[4] According to *Gesetze*, vol. i, p. xxv, col. 2, both Nowell and Lambard did use this MS. But the supporting reference to Turk *Legal Code of Alfred the Great*, p. 13, is unsatisfactory. Turk says loosely that Nero A 1 'passed like many copies by Nowell and Lambard' into the Cotton collection. But he cannot mean 'like many transcripts *of it* by Nowell and Lambard', for there is no record of these transcripts in the Cotton collection.

working before there were any catalogues, reference books, or ordered national collections; and at a given moment he might not know that the Old English basis of the Latin text of *I Ath.* was to be found in two manuscripts. Lambard himself records none of the remarkable divergences of these manuscripts from his print of *I Ath.*

(*e*) Why did he not translate also such interesting texts as *III* and *IV Ath.*? If it is fair to turn an unanswerable question, and to account rather for what is on record, I suggest that Nowell was using a manuscript that contained *II Ath.*[1]—CCCC 383,[2] or Otho B XI, or a transcript of either—and that on collating the Latin text[3] in a manuscript of the 'London' group, he noticed *I Ath.* and *Ord.* immediately before *II Ath.* He filled the gap in his collection of Old English Laws, not from another manuscript (because there was none of *Ord.*, and he had neither of the two that contain *I Ath.*) but by translating the Latin back into Old English—a proceeding not so strange when the subject was in its infancy.[4] He would be interrupted by the original text of *II Ath.*; but I do not think that ended his experiment. He went on to translate the pieces imme-

[1] No extant MS. of *II Ath.* contains also *I Ath.*

[2] MS. CCCC 383 now contains only the beginning of *II Ath.* It is quite possible that the missing quire has been lost since Lambard's day, and that his text of *II Ath.* is drawn primarily from this MS. (see *Gesetze*, vol. iii, p. 99). It is also possible that his *V Ath.* comes from the Corpus MS.; and if it followed immediately on *II Ath.*, as it does in *Textus Roffensis*, the order of pieces in *Archaionomia* (see below, p. 252) would be conveniently explained. But the first clause of *V Ath.* refers clearly to *II Ath.*, so that Lambard may have established the order by internal evidence rather than by MS. authority.

[3] It was by studying texts which had Latin equivalents that the early scholars attained to a reading knowledge of Old English.

[4] It was natural enough that those who began the study of Old English should try to write it, just as they would try to write Latin or French; and some attempts by Lambard in the front of the Dictionary that Nowell sent him are interesting because they show the same mixture of knowledge and ignorance that appears in *I Ath.* and *Ord.*: e.g. (referring to the gift):

Mid hiht ic þolige L[*aurence*] *N*[*owell*]
Butan hiht ic ahnige W[*illiam*] *L*[*ambard*];

and the rendering of 'Invigila lampadi' by *Wæccaþ þine leohtfæt*, where the modern use of *watch* and the polite plural are written back into West Saxon.

diately following *II Ath.* in the 'London' manuscripts, viz. *Episcopus,*[1] *Norðleod,*[2] *Mirce,*[2] *Að,*[2] *Hadbot,*[3] omitting the first and fifth as of ecclesiastical and not secular interest: that is to say, Lambard's texts of *Norðleod, Mirce, Að* are also modern. Perhaps he had not inclination or opportunity to do more.

(*f*) That Lambard knew *Quadripartitus* is no part of my contention.[4] Nor is his reputation as an editor impugned by assuming that (as was common among scholars until very recently) he relied on transcripts supplied by friends, and particularly by Nowell. In the Preface to *Archaionomia* he says that Nowell sent him 'the ancient laws' in 1567, with a request that he should make a Latin translation. Nowell had evidently been working on the Laws and was interrupted by an enforced journey abroad. Lambard seems to have regarded the Latin translation as his primary business; he had only a year for the whole work, which would preclude any exhaustive study of the scattered manuscripts; and it is not surprising that he should pass as genuine what modern scholars find defensible.

For the points already discussed Professor Liebermann claims no more than that they are reasons for doubting. The heart of his argument lies in the details that follow.

(*g*) In *I Ath.* § 4, 1, Lambard has *heofonlica*: *eorþlicum*: *ecelic*: *hwilwendlicum,* which is a more natural order than *Q.* 'eterna: terrenis: celestia: caducis', though the sense is the same. Professor Liebermann thinks that this clause in Lambard's text is due to the 'reviser before 1100', and that *Q.* translates it, changing the order for the worse. But it is just as likely that Nowell, finding the clause in *Q.* (it is not in the Old English MSS.), would change the order in his translation.

(*h*) In *Ord.* Lambard has *án earm Engliscmon* = *Q.* 'pauperem unum Anglicum indigentem': i.e. there is no separate and unnecessary word

[1] *Gesetze*, vol. i, p. 477.

[2] For the texts see *Gesetze*, vol. i, pp. 458–64. Lambard has neither *Episcopus* nor *Hadbot* (*Gesetze*, vol. i, p. xxxiii, col. 2, l. 15 is a slip).

[3] *Gesetze*, vol. i, p. 465.

[4] By 'Quadripartitus' Professor Liebermann means the complete work. I use it to include those parts of the complete work that are incorporated in MSS. of the 'London' Laws, because they are the parts that matter in the present discussion. Unless he knew them, Lambard's remarks (in his Preface) on the Latin versions existing in 1568 are hard to explain.

to render 'indigentem'. It is difficult to see how anything can be deduced from this in favour of one view or the other.

(*i*) *þæt ge alysaþ* in *Ord.* § 1 is quoted as peculiarly idiomatic, with a reference to the special use of *þæt* illustrated in the Glossary to *Gesetze* s.v. *þæt* IV A 2. But this passage is rightly excluded from the Glossary, because the construction of *þæt* is normal: 'ic . . . gecyþe . . . þæt ic wille þæt ge fedaþ . . . and þæt ge alysaþ'. In fact the expression is unidiomatic, for OE. usage requires the subjunctives *feden . . . alysen.*

(*j*) In *Ord.* § 2 Lambard's (*on ða tun . . . ðe ðis*) *ungefremed wunie* is said to be 'feiner' than *Q.* '(in ipsa villa . . . ubi hoc) non fuerit executum'. But subjective tests are not reliable even if we could be sure that the author of *Q.* would express himself better than a cultured Elizabethan. In Modern English a thing can be said to 'remain undone'; but where in Old English is there a parallel to *ungefremed wunian* used of a thing to be done? If there is none, the indication is against authenticity.

(*k*) In *Ord.* Prol. Professor Liebermann thinks Lambard's *gif ge him habbaþ* more concrete than *Q.* 'si sit ibi', for which the MSS. nearest to Lambard's text have the scribal error 'si sit tibi'. The passage is crucial, but the question that matters is 'Which is translated from the other?' And it seems more likely that an antiquary, coming on 'si sit tibi' (and bound to make the best of it in a context that requires the plural) would produce the barbarous *gif ge him habbaþ*[1] than that the translator of *Q.* would find in an eleventh-century MS. *gif ge him habbaþ* and render it 'si sit ibi'.

(*l*) Ibid. *Godes ðeowa* = *Q.* 'Dei ministrorum'. But either is a literal translation of the other, so that the evidence is neutral.

(*m*) Ibid. 'das ursprüngliche *ealle wæga*' = *Q.* 'omnia via'. If *ealle wæga* were the Old English for 'always' as well as the literal equivalent of 'omni via', the evidence would be neutral. But as 'always' is *ealne weg*, *ealneg* in OE., *ealle wæga* cannot be original, and is best explained as an unidiomatic literal rendering of 'omni via'.

(*n*) In *Ord.* § 1 'under þæs bisceopes gewitnesse on ðæs rice it sie = *Q.* 'sub testimonio episcopi in cuius episcopatu sit'. It is argued that a translator would have written *bisceoprice* instead of *rice*, which occurs also in Ine's Laws. But Nowell certainly knew Ine's Laws; and after *bisceopes* the simple *rice* avoids a repetition. Besides, I doubt that the syntax of the whole phrase can be paralleled in natural Old English.

The next three places are said to refute with special clearness the contention that Lambard's text is based solely on *Q.*

[1] Based on the regular 'est tibi' = 'you have'.

(*o*) *I Ath.* Prol. Extant MSS. 'þæt ge ærest of minum agenum góde agyfan þa teoþunga' = Lambard 'þæt hi ærost mines agenes æhtes ðam teoþe gesyllaþ' = *Q.* 'ut in primis de meo proprio reddant Deo decimas'. The argument is that 'Deo' in *Q.* arises from misunderstanding of *gode* ('goods') of the extant MSS., and that while Lambard has nothing corresponding to the erroneous 'Deo', his *æhtes* 'property' is a substitute for the correct *gode*.

Let it be granted for the moment that 'Deo' is a wrong rendering of *gode*. It follows that the reading in the supposed source *lq* was *gode*, and that *æhtes* was substituted for it after 1100. The person who made this substitution did not know that OE. *æht* is fem., for he gave it the masculine and neuter genitive sing. *æhtes*;[1] and he did not know that the weak gen. sing. *agenan* should be used after the demonstrative *min*. Nowell might well be guilty of such grammar, but a parallel could scarcely be found in the early twelfth century, when our second recaster is supposed to have worked. It is just conceivable, as an oddity, late in the twelfth century (though the old stem-form *æht-* would be less likely then). So it would seem that to support the genuineness of the text we need a third reviser!

But is it so sure that *æhtes* has been substituted for *gode* in a context that is not really ambiguous? *Q.* 'de meo proprio' would naturally be rendered with the help of a noun, and in fact Lambard re-translates *mines agenes æhtes* by 'ex meo proprio'. So there is no reason why Nowell should not have produced *mines agenes æhtes* without reference to any text but *Q.* Nor is his omission to render 'Deo' by any separate word surprising: for what is expressed in 'decimas reddere Deo' is implied in 'pay tithes'.[2]

Thus the argument fails even on the assumption that 'Deo' in *Q.* is an error for *gode* of the MSS.; and that assumption is itself unnecessary because in the same clause *Q.* renders *of heora agenum gode* by 'de suo proprio', showing that he interpreted *gode* correctly; and because 'decimas reddere Deo' is a legitimate rendering of *agyfan þa teoþunga*.

(*p*) In *I Ath.* § 2 the extant MSS. have *Iacob se heahfæder*: *Q.* 'Iacob pater excelsus'; Lambard *Iacob se hiehfæder*. Since Nowell knew that Jacob was a patriarch, and knew (as his MS. dictionary shows) that the Old English for 'patriarch' was *heahfæder*, it is hard to see how else than by *Iacob se hiehfæder* he could render 'Iacob pater excelsus'.

[1] The only example in Bosworth–Toller, *Suppl.*, where it must in any event be deleted now that it is shown to be later than 1100.

[2] Similarly in *I Ath.* § 3, where the extant MSS. have 'gif we þa teoðunga Gode gelæstan nellað', *Q.* and Lambard have no separate rendering for *Gode*.

(*q*) In *I Ath.* Prol. the extant MSS. have *þæt ylce don* = *Q.* 'similiter facere' = Lambard *þæt ilce gedó*[*n*]. This would be telling if 'to do the same' were not a usual rendering of 'similiter facere', and *don þæt ilce* the obvious rendering of 'do the same'. Even less helpful is *I Ath.* § 5: extant MSS. *mid unrihte* = *Q.* 'iniuste' = Lambard *mid woh*. There is no reason why a recaster should change *mid unrihte* to *mid woh*;[1] but a translator who knew *V Ath.* or *III Eadgar* or *II Cnut* (all in *Archaionomia*) would know the phrase *mid wo*(*h*), which Lambard re-translates by 'iniuste' in this passage.

(*r*) In *I Ath.* Prol. the extant MSS. have *agyfan* = *Q.* 'reddant' = Lambard *gesyllaþ*; and Professor Liebermann rightly says that *agyfan* is the readier word. Then why should a recaster alter it to *gesyllaþ*? That Nowell with 'reddant' before him should hit upon the less satisfactory synonym need cause no difficulty.[2]

(*s*) In *I Ath.* Prol. *Q.* 'archiepiscopus' = extant MSS. *ærcebiscop* = Lambard *hehbisceop*. In *Ord. Q.* 'archiepiscopus' = Lambard *ærcebisceop* (there are no extant MSS.). Nowell knew both Old English words, for he has them in his MS. dictionary; and the variety of rendering, if pointless, is not improbable. On the alternative view an early recaster deliberately altered *ærcebisceop* to *hehbisceop* in the first passage and left it unchanged in the second. If the recasters could be shown to act on any rational plan, the case for their existence would be stronger.

The next group of passages is cited to show that some of the variations of Lambard's text from the extant manuscripts can be paralleled in twelfth-century manuscripts. Two of these parallels are from *Mirce* and *Norðleod*, the authenticity of which will be considered later. From the rest it will be enough to choose the three that are most interesting.

(*t*) *I Ath.* § 5. Extant MSS. *gestrynan . . . gestrynan* = *Q.* 'adquirere . . . conquirere' = Lambard *begytan . . . begytan*. It is true that in

[1] That *mid wo* is explained by a late gloss *unriht* in the Harleian MS. of *III Edgar* § 4 tells against substitution of *woh* for *unriht* in the twelfth century, but not against the use of *woh* by an antiquary in the sixteenth century. It is of some importance, in view of the limitation given at p. 242 n. 1 above, to note that *unriht* is not a fourteenth-century gloss (*Gesetze*, vol. i, p. 202, col. 2 n.), but belongs to the well-defined group of Worcester glosses made about 1200.

[2] He gives *gesyllan* in his MS. dictionary, and he may have thought it more distinctively Old English than any form of 'give'. It is noticeable that he prefers *biþ* and *sy* to *is*.

Alfred § 65 the twelfth-century MS. CCCC 383 has *begytan* for original *gestrynan*, and the explanation is simple. OE. *gestrynan* means both 'to beget (children)' and 'to acquire'; but the meaning 'acquire' disappears after the Conquest. OE. *begytan* means usually 'to acquire', and retains this sense up to Elizabethan times, alongside the modern sense 'to beget (children)', which first appears in late Old English. Hence substitution of *begytan* for *gestrynan* in the sense 'acquire' is to be expected from the twelfth century onwards; and *begytan*, not *gestrynan*, is the word that would be suggested to Nowell by the usage of his own time if he were rendering 'adquirere', 'conquirere'.

(*u*) *I Ath.* Prol. Extant MSS. *on cwicum ceape* = *Q.* 'in vivente captali' = Lambard *þæs libbendes yrfes*. It is suggested that the substitution of *libbende* for *cwicu* is supported by the alliterative phrase *ne libbende ne licgende* applied to goods in *II Cnut* § 24. But there *libbende* is original: no MS. has the variant *cwicu*. And it is by no means clear why anybody who had before him the alliterative formula *on cwicum ceape* (every word of which is common in Middle English) should replace it by *libbende yrfe*, a phrase otherwise unknown for the good reason that *yrfe* itself means 'livestock', 'cattle'. As Nowell's rendering of 'vivente captali' *libbende yrfe* is easily accounted for.

(*v*) *I Ath.* Prol. Extant MSS. *freondscipe* = *Q.* 'amicitia' = Lambard *lufu*: and similarly in *Ord.* § 1, *Q.* 'amicitia' = Lambard *lufu*. Professor Liebermann explains, not altogether convincingly, that the recaster, failing to appreciate the threat of withdrawal of the royal favour, altered *freondscipe* to *lufu*; and thinks that an Elizabethan would naturally render 'amicitia' by the original word *freondscipe*. But to speak of the king's 'friendship' for his subjects in a formal document would sound too familiar in the days of the Tudors. The right word for the feeling between king and subjects was 'love', and so Nowell naturally translated 'amicitia' by *lufu* in this context. It happens that in both places the phrase is 'for my love', which is common in Elizabethan English.

The other passages offer no difficulty. So the simple and precise solution—that Lambard's *I Ath.* and *Ord.* are translations made by Nowell in or before 1567 from the Latin of the 'London' text—satisfies all the conditions that have so far been mentioned. Professor Liebermann's complex solution meets some of the conditions, but I think it can only be accommodated to the rest by more and more elaboration, until it slips beyond the reach of proof or disproof. Yet it is perhaps the best hypothesis that can be framed on the basis that these two texts are authentic.

3

Before examining *Norðleod*, *Mirce*, and *Að* in detail, it is worth while to note how they fall in *Archaionomia*. Lambard's order is *I Ath.*, *Ord.*, *II Ath.*, *V Ath.*, *Norðleod*, *Mirce*, *Að*.[1] But the texts of his *II Ath.* and *V Ath.* stand apart from the rest because they agree very closely with extant manuscripts,[2] while the rest show many remarkable variants.

That Lambard's *Norðleod*, *Mirce*, *Að* form a homogeneous group is hardly disputable; and they have so much in common with his *I Ath.* and *Ord.* that they are explained in *Gesetze* by the same assumptions, viz. a lost *lq* before 1100, and a second recasting very little after 1100.[3] On the whole they read more like genuine texts; but the short sentences, and the retention or clear indication of technical terms in *Q.*, would make the task of an antiquarian translator easier.

It happens that the first and the last clause of the group are good specimens for closer study. Lambard's *Norðleod* § 1 reads . . . *se wære belympaþ to ðam mægþe ðæs cynecynnes and þæt cynebot to ðam landleod*. Here at once are three false genders: *mægþ*, *cynebot*, *landleod* are all feminine, yet the forms of the article used are unmistakably masculine or neuter. *Landleod* (*Q.* 'terrae nationi': extant MSS. *leodum*) occurs in the Anglo-Saxon Laws only in this place and in Lambard's *Mirce* § 4, where again it is made masculine. *Cynecynnes* makes its only appearance in the Laws here, and the phrase *ðam mægþe ðæs cynecynnes* 'the kindred of the royal kin' is not a plausible variant of *magum* 'kinsmen', which is the reading of

[1] This order, which is by no means inevitable, and is not found in any extant Old English MS., differs from that of the 'London' group only in the omission of *Episcopus* and *Hadbot*, and the insertion of *V Ath.* after *II Ath.* An explanation is suggested in 2 (*e*) above.

[2] In the side-note to *II Ath.* § 6, 2 *blisgeras*, Professor Liebermann finds evidence that Lambard had access to a lost MS. other than the one he prints (*Gesetze*, vol. iii, p. 100, col. 1). It runs ' "alias *beligeras*," quod sonat "accusatores falsos" '. But this incredible reading was not in the source of *Q.*, which preserves *blasieras*; and it is most likely an unhappy Elizabethan conjecture for the rare form *blisgeras* 'incendiaries'.

[3] As an alternative to the second recasting, a series of double readings in *lq* is suggested (*Gesetze*, vol. iii, p. 260, col. 1). This raises fresh difficulties.

extant manuscripts.[1] Then *belympaþ to* (*Q.* 'pertinet': extant MSS. *gebyreð*) is plural instead of singular, and the sense 'is payable to' goes a little beyond the recorded meanings. No wonder Professor Toller remarks that 'the passage seems very corrupt'.[2]

The texts of *Að* § 2 are worth setting out in full:

Eleventh-century MSS.	*Textus Roffensis (after 1120)*	*Q. (London MSS.)*	*Lambard*
Mæssepreostes að and worldþegnes is on Engla lage geteald efendire for ðam seofon cirichadan þe se preost þurh Godes gife geþéah þæt he hæfde.	Mæssepreostes að and woruldþegenes is on Engla lage geteald efendyre; *and* for þam seofon cyrichadan þe se *mæsse*preost þurh Godes gife geþeah þæt he hæfde, *he bið þegenrihtes wyrþe.*	Misse presbiteri et secularis thaini iusiurandum in Anglorum lege computatur eque carum; *et* pro septem ordinibus ecclesię, quo sacerdos per Dei donum ascendit ut haberet[ur], *thaini recto dignus est.*	Messepreostes and weoroldðegnes aþ on Engla laga *biþ gelic gedemod; and* for þam seofon *cyriclicum endebyrdnyssum, ðam* se preost *be* Godes gyfa *up astigeð, biþ he þæs ðegnes rihtes geweorþod.*

This is the order of the texts if Lambard's version is a translation of *Q.*, and it presents no difficulty. But we must consider the alternative view that Lambard's text derives from the extant manuscripts in the first two columns, and that *Q.* is translated from Lambard's version.

The equivalence of *Textus Roffensis* and *Q.* appears at a glance. *Textus Roffensis*, like the earlier manuscripts, has *efendyre* = *Q.* 'eque carum', and *þæt he hæfde* = *Q.* 'ut haberet', neither of which are in Lambard; but it also has an intrusive *and* in common with *Q.* and Lambard, as well as the phrase *he bið þegenrihtes wyrþe*, where *Q.* and Lambard have equivalents, though the eleventh-century manuscripts have not. Hence, if ever there was an *lq*—a common source of *Q.* and Lambard—in this place it must have been almost identical with *Textus Roffensis*, and divergences in Lambard must be ascribed to the second recaster.

Again, since *Textus Roffensis* was written after 1120, it is later than the supposed *lq*, and probably later than the supposed second recasting. Yet its idiom is sound and its vocabulary normal; and there is no reason to expect a lower standard in any part of Lambard's text that is of a like age.

Let us now examine the divergences of the fourth column. *Efendyre*, which is plain English and caused no difficulty to the compiler of *Textus Roffensis*, is replaced by *biþ gelic gedemod*, which never

[1] *Q.* has *cognationi*.

[2] *Suppl.*, s.v. *landleod*.

was English.[1] *Endebyrdnys* did not survive into Middle English, yet it is substituted for *hād* which did.[2] *Be* (*Godes gyfa*), for *þurh* of the manuscripts, is an anachronism that reflects the comparatively late usage '*by* God's grace'. The regular formula *þegenrihtes wyrþe* is replaced by *þæs ðegnes rihtes geweorþod*, which again is impossible English.[3] There remains *ðam . . . up astigeð*[4] for *geþeah* of the manuscripts, and its significance will be brought out by a table showing all the uses of *geþeon* in this group of texts:

	Norðleod § 7	*Norðleod* § 7, 1	*Norðleod* § 9	*Norðleod* § 10	*Norðleod* § 11	*Að* § 2
All MSS.	geþeo	geþeo	geþeo	geþeo	geþeoð	geþéah
Quadripartitus	promoveatur	assurgat	promoveatur	assequatur	assequatur	ascendit
Lambard	beo gewelegod	biþ gerysen	sie gewelegod	begytaþ	begyten	up astigeð

As the verb (*ge*)*þeon* 'to prosper', &c., outlasted the Middle English period, the obvious interpretation is that *geþeon* has been variously translated in the Latin of *Q.*, and mechanically re-translated by somebody who always missed the right word. Fortunately the other view—that *geþeon* was altered without reason in the Old English source of *Q.*—can be dealt with shortly: for Old English idiom permits neither *ne bið butan to healfhyda gerysen* nor *up astigeð ðam cyriclicum endebyrdnyssum*.

The evidence already produced seems to me decisive against authenticity. If it is accepted, the following words (besides those previously mentioned) should be deleted from the dictionaries:

[1] The false conjugation of *gedemod* is unimportant in comparison with the false idiom.

[2] Perhaps some of the words and phrases in Lambard's text derive from Ælfric's *Grammar*, in which Latin words stand side by side with their Old English equivalents. At least it is remarkable that in *Mirce* § 3, 1, where the MSS. have *gebyreð oðer swilc* (*to bote*) = *Q.* 'debet addi tantumdem', Lambard reads *biþ to ðissum genumen eft swa micle*. In Ælfric's *Grammar* (ed. Zupitza, p. 5, l. 14) occurs *to ðisum is genumen se grecisca y* (where *is genumen* seems to be due to the use of 'adsumere' in Latin grammars); and at p. 108, l. 11 we have: 'tantumdem, þæt is, eft swa mycel'.

[3] *Geweorþod* takes *mid*+instrumental or simple instrumental—never the genitive. This is the only instance in Bosworth–Toller, *Suppl.*, s.v. *geweorþian*.

[4] *Astiged* in the print. The present tense *astigeð* is awkward, and is much more likely as a rendering of *ascendit* than as a variant of *geþeah*.

Norðleod § 11 *sunsunu* (son's son) which Professor Liebermann has already rejected as a misreading; ibid. § 7, 1 the compound *healfhyd* (MSS. *to healfre hide*); and ibid. § 10 *ofergylden* adj. (MSS. *goldfæted*), where the participle *ofergylded* might have passed muster.

Some other difficulties find an easy solution. For instance, Lambard agrees with three manuscripts of the 'London' group in omitting the whole clause *Norðleod* § 12; and in *Mirce* § 2 he agrees with one manuscript of the same group in the absurd statement (resulting from transposition of M = milia) that 'the King's wergeld is equal to 6000 thegn's wergelds, i.e. 30 sceattas.'[1] The agreement is accounted for if Lambard's text is translated from a manuscript of the 'London' group that contained these errors.[2]

A more complicated problem, which has vexed the commentators,[3] is presented by *Norðleod* § 10:

Extant MSS.	*Q.*	*Lambard*
And þeah he [*sc.* ceorlisc man] geþeo þæt he hæbbe helm and byrnan and goldfæted sweord, gif he þæt land nafað, he bið ceorl swaþeah.	Et si assequatur ut habeat loricam et galeam et deauratum gladium, si terram non habeat, tamen est {siþcundes / ceorlus}.	and gif he begytaþ þæt hæbbe byrne and helm and ofergyldene sweord, ðeah ðe he land næbbe, he biþ siþcund.

Here *Q.* is a kind of middle term between the manuscripts and Lambard: in the manuscripts the sequence *And þeah . . . gif . . . ceorl swaþeah* fixes the true reading *ceorl*; in Lambard the sequence *gif . . . ðeah ðe . . . siþcund*[4] fixes the opposite meaning—that the

[1] i.e. about 30 pence. I have not compared the Rylands MS. Lat. 155 for all clauses, but some specimens of its readings elsewhere, which I owe to Professor Powicke, are enough to show that it is not the 'London' MS. Nowell used.

[2] The alternative explanation, along the lines indicated above, p. 238 n. 3, is very clumsy.

[3] See *Gesetze*, vol. iii, p. 261, col. 3 for the views of Maurer and Seebohm. Professor Liebermann assumes that *lq* contained both the readings *ceorl* and *siþcund*; that Lambard's immediate source preserved only *siþcund*, and that both were taken over into *Q*. How *siþcund* became confined to the 'London' MSS. is not explained; nor is it clear, as this view implies, that as early as 1100 the mere possession of 'helm, corslet, and gilded sword' was considered enough to raise a *ceorl* to thane's rank.

[4] *Siþcund* for *gesiþcund* is not recorded elsewhere in English. *Q.* regularly drops the prefix; and this again points to derivation of Lambard's text from *Q*.

ceorl by virtue of possessing arms rises to the rank of thane; in *Q.* the conjunctions *si ... si ... tamen* are ambiguous, and substitution of *siþcundes* for 'ceorlus' is enough to reverse the sense. But it must not be supposed that the reading *siþcundes* is scattered through the manuscripts of *Q.*: it is peculiar to the 'London' group, and to Lambard's text which is closely related to that group. A satisfactory explanation must account for this well-defined distribution of the bad reading. Now, as two out of three 'London' manuscripts record also the reading 'ceorlus', and all the other manuscripts of *Q.* have 'ceorlus' only, it is a fair presumption that *Q.* originally read 'ceorlus', agreeing with the Old English manuscripts. But it happens that the next clause of *Norðleod* gives the conditions under which a *ceorl*'s descendants may become *gesiðcundes cynnes* (*Q.* 'siþcunde generationis'). A late reader or copier of *Q.*, who felt that the conditions in *Norðleod* § 10 should lead to the same result, may well have written 'siþcund(es)' over 'ceorlus', and so reversed the meaning. Derivation of the 'London' manuscripts from this altered copy would explain their readings, and also explain why the other families of manuscripts show no trace of the variant 'siþcund(es)'. And if Lambard's text is translated from one of the 'London' manuscripts, it would naturally reproduce *siþcund(es)*, and render the ambiguous conjunctions of *Q.* by *gif ... ðeah ðe*, which accord with that reading.

One passage remains which causes some difficulty on my view. In *Norðleod* § 2 the only eleventh-century manuscript (CCCC 201) has 'Arces [for *Arcebisceopes*] and æþelinges wergild is xv þusend þrymsa'; *Textus Roffensis* omits *Arcebisceopes and*; *Q.* likewise has (all manuscripts) 'Comitis wergildum est xv milia þrimsa'; while Lambard reads: 'Ærcebisceopes and eorles wærgild biþ xv m. ðrimsa'. The pointless changes that a writer with the Old English text before him would hardly make—*eorles* for *æþelinges*, *biþ* for *is*, *m.* for *þusend*—favour the view that Lambard's text is translated from *Q.* But how are we to account for *Ærcebisceopes* which is not in *Q.*, and is in the earliest Old English manuscript? It is not really satisfactory to assume that *Arcebisceopes* stood in a common source of Lambard's text and *Q.*, because the nature of *Q.*'s source for this set of laws is indicated both by *Q.* itself and by *Textus Roffensis*, and neither includes the archbishop.[1] Of the two alternatives I have to suggest, neither is very convincing unless the evidence already discussed is brought into account. It is just possible that Lambard, who says he used the Parker Library, consulted MS. CCCC 201 there—although, to be strict, this explanation goes beyond my hypothesis. It is more likely that *ærcebisceopes* was inserted by Lambard or Nowell to fill an obvious gap in the scheme of wergilds given in *Norðleod*: king; [archbishop and] atheling; bishop and alderman; mass-thane and secular thane: for the information that the archbishop ranked for wergild with the highest nobles, immediately below the king and above the bishops, was available elsewhere. Such tampering with texts might be thought incredible; yet a passage from *Mirce* will show what early editors were capable of.

MSS.	*Q.*	*Lambard* (*1568*)	*Wheloc's edition of Lambard* (*1644*)
Ceorles wergild is on Myrcna lage CC scill'.	ceorles weregildum est in Mircenorum laga CC sol.	Ceorles weregyld on Mercna land biþ CC scill.	Ceorles weregyld is CC and VI and LX þrimsa; þæt biþ CC scill. on Mercna land.

Without any warning Wheloc has mixed into Lambard's clause the reading of *Textus Roffensis* in *Norðleod* § 6: and were not the first edition of *Archaionomia* available, we might be tempted to think that he had access to a lost manuscript. No doubt the same kind of

[1] In *Gesetze*, vol. iii, p. 261, col. 1 it is suggested that the common source for *Textus Roffensis*, Lambard, and *Q.* had the same error *arces* that appears in MS. CCCC 201; that the translator of *Q.* and the scribe of *Textus Roffensis* could not understand *arces* and therefore omitted it; and that the copyist of the MS. from which Lambard printed (ordinarily stupid beyond any of his kind) solved the difficulty and restored *arcebisceopes*. The implications of this hypothesis are formidable. From the table giving the descent of the MSS. at p. 256 of the same volume, it appears that at least four lost MSS. must have contained the error *arces*; so that besides the scribe of CCCC 201, at least four others failed to understand *arces* and copied it mechanically. The scribe of *Textus Roffensis* also failed to understand it, but, unlike the others, chose to omit it. The translator of *Q.* did the same. Yet the problem that these seven had to solve was of the simplest: the context cries out for the reading *arcebisceopes*, and change of the last letter of *arces* gives *arceƀ*, the normal abbreviation for *arcebisceop*(*es*) in the eleventh and twelfth centuries. Such a chain of unlikely happenings ought not to be assumed.

thing went on in the transcripts of Old English texts used by Elizabethan editors, and variants that are known only from their copies or prints should be scutinized very closely before they are attributed to lost manuscripts.

13

HUMFREY WANLEY[1]

HUMFREY WANLEY'S claim to greatness rests on his work as a palaeographer and a librarian—he was the author of a Catalogue of Anglo-Saxon Manuscripts,[2] and the first Keeper of the Harleian collection.

He was born in 1672 at Coventry, where his father Nathaniel was vicar of Trinity Church. The father was a man of literary tastes. He wrote poems palely reminiscent of Vaughan; but he was best known for his *Wonders of the Little World*—a discursive treatise on Mankind, which was still to be seen in private libraries in the nineteenth century: Browning took from it his story of the *Pied Piper*. Nathaniel died when his son was eight years old. His finances were embarrassed, and Humfrey was apprenticed to a woollen-draper of Coventry. It was a time when trade offered great opportunities, but the apprentice soon showed a bent for antiquities. At least as early as 1689, when he was seventeen, he began to keep neat notebooks of curious information. In 1692 his studies were given a decisive turn by a visit to Oxford, from which he came back an enthusiast for the Saxon tongue.

He borrowed Anglo-Saxon books from Charles King, who had been a friend of Francis Junius, and astonished the lender by proposing to abridge and copy out Somner's *Anglo-Saxon Dictionary*. The result may be seen in Harley MS. 3317, with the note that he

[1] A lecture in a series on Great Scholars, read at Oxford on 1 November 1935 at the invitation of Professor F. M. Powicke. Besides the article in *The Dictionary of National Biography*, I have used a good paper, 'Humfrey Wanley and his Diary', by W. R. Douthwaite, 1888. Professor D. C. Douglas's *English Scholars*, 1939, which contains a chapter on Wanley, and provides an excellent background, was not then available. Many letters from and to Wanley are preserved in Bodleian and British Museum collections: to these I have added references only when the matter was of some importance.

[2] *Antiquæ Literaturæ Septentrionalis Liber Alter seu Humphredi Wanleii Librorum Vett. Septentrionalium, qui in Angliæ Bibliothecis extant . . . Catalogus Historico-Criticus, Oxoniæ* 1705.

allowed himself till 14 January 1693 to do it. He finished four months ahead of programme. It is a first proof of three humble gifts which become precious when associated with genius: patience, ability to plan one's time, and a beautiful hand.

Why should a visit to Oxford in 1692 so fire a young man? The great Elizabethan names in Anglo-Saxon studies—Parker, Joscelin, Nowell, the Spelmans, Lisle—are mostly Cambridge names. The greatest seventeenth-century Saxonist was the Dutchman Francis Junius who left Oxford his manuscripts, his papers, his type, but hardly a living school. His Oxford friend Marshall, who was Rector of Lincoln College when Hickes was a tutor there, died in 1685; Dr. Fell, who backed so many new movements, in the next year.

Then towards the end of the century occurred one of those sudden blazes of enthusiasm by which a subject leaps ahead, and this time it is nearly all Oxford—Hickes, Nicolson, Tanner, Edmund Gibson, Thwaites, Christopher Rawlinson, William Elstob. All of them would acknowledge that George Hickes lighted the torch with his *Grammar* of Anglo-Saxon, Gothic, and Icelandic, published in 1689 when he was Dean of Worcester.

It is one of those works not intrinsically great which yet transform their subject. Hitherto Anglo-Saxon had been picked up painfully from vocabularies, manuscripts, and a few printed texts. Its grammatical forms had been neglected as a barbarous confusion. Hickes for the first time showed that, like Greek and Latin, it had an orderly grammatical structure. He not only made it easier to learn Anglo-Saxon, and laid the foundations of a more rigorous study, but gave the language a new dignity. To scholars like Gibson and Thwaites, Hickes's *Grammar* was a revelation, and Anglo-Saxon became the rage. It happened that among the books which King lent Wanley was this *Grammar*; and bound up with his abridgement of Somner's Lexicon are his transcripts of the Anglo-Saxon part, and of Hickes's very imperfect Appendix of Anglo-Saxon manuscripts. This last is the germ of Wanley's Catalogue.

He was now finding it hard to reconcile drapery with his studies. He inquires whether it is sinful to transcribe manuscripts of the

Gospels on Sunday—an apprentice's one free day. King advised him that a scholar could live only by taking orders, but he seems to have been disinclined. He tried for a clerkship at the College of Arms, but the gentleman in charge had nephews. He tried for a post in the Tower Records. By 1693 it looked as if he must compromise with business and join Mr. Pate, another draper at Coventry who was a man of some learning. But about this time his interest in manuscripts attracted the notice of William Lloyd, Bishop of Coventry, who encouraged Burnet in the writing of his *History of the Reformation* and was one of the Seven Bishops of 1688. Lloyd saw at once the value of Wanley's talents in a time of active historical study, and by 1694 we find him travelling to take copies in private collections, visiting Oxford again, and making himself useful to Dr. Charlett, the Master of University, a leading figure at Oxford who was then busied about the summary Catalogue of Manuscripts in British Collections that passes under the name of Bernard.[1]

In 1695 Lloyd arranged for him to enter St. Edmund Hall to assist the Principal, James Mill, in making the collations for his famous edition of the Greek Gospels which appeared in 1707. From this work he gained first-hand experience of Greek manuscripts. Next year Charlett gave him a room in his lodgings, and by his influence Wanley became assistant at a salary of £12 a year to Hyde, Bodley's Librarian.

I should guess that his first years at Oxford were the happiest of a not unhappy life. He was making friends with the best scholars, measuring his length with them, doing small services to them all. He was devilling for Charlett, who collected books and coins and had a finger in every pie. The collation of Greek and Latin manuscripts gave him the chance of travelling to see the best collections. Above all, he was in Bodley, then the greatest library in the kingdom, under an easy-going librarian who gladly let him do the work. In 1697 he made the Index to the Catalogue of Manuscripts in British Collections, a task which gave him a short view of all the manuscript material. In the same year he was employed by the Curators to buy Bernard's manuscripts and the best of his printed

[1] *Catalogi Librorum MSS. Angliæ et Hiberniæ*, Oxford 1697.

books. It was the most important Bodleian acquisition of that period, and Wanley at once showed his special aptitude for the business of book-buying.

All the while his head was full of learned projects. The power of busy men of his day to plan and execute great enterprises is something of a miracle to us, who have more tools and less courage. Think of the *Acta Sanctorum* undertaken by Bolland and his successors; of Ducange's *Glossary of Medieval Latin*, 1678; of Bayle's Dictionary, 1695; above all, of the great enterprises of the Benedictine Congregation of St. Maur.[1] In England in the historical field we have Wharton's *Anglia Sacra*, 1691; Tanner's *Notitia Monastica*, 1695; Rymer's *Foedera*, 1704; Madox's *Exchequer*, 1711; Wilkins's *Concilia*, 1727, all still valuable. It was not that the age was uncritical or lacked extreme sceptics. It was the age of Newton's *Principia* and Bentley's *Phalaris*. The possibility that ostensibly old documents were falsifications was in every scholar's mind. While Anglo-Saxon studies were flourishing at Oxford, the French Jesuit Hardouin was arguing that all the Anglo-Saxon manuscripts were forgeries, and the language itself a fraudulent invention. What men of this age had was an overplus of energy, optimism, and a pride in their country, or the particular institutions they belonged to, which is conducive to great works. When Bernard Montfaucon, with some forty stout volumes to his credit already, made the last communication of his plans to the French Academy, he proposed a further work on Monuments of the French Monarchy in three volumes folio, to be followed by a Greek dictionary. Two days later he died peacefully at the age of eighty-six.

So it was natural for a youngster to have great plans. Wanley aimed at a history of Printing, in which he was allowed to have a special competence; and a history of Paper-making, for which he collected specimens. An earlier ambition, which had considerable importance in his training, was a collection of all the Alphabets of

[1] For these, see *Histoire Littéraire de la Congrégation de St. Maur*, Paris 1770, p. 589, an indispensable book. The name of the author, Dom Tassin, appears at p. 721, where his own work as a member of the Congregation comes to be listed. He was the principal author of *Nouveau Traité de Diplomatique*, 1750–65, which summed up and handed on the foundational work on palaeography and diplomatic.

the world: materials towards it are in the beautifully written Bodleian MS. S.C. 33184. Another project which shows his care for detail was a collection—as portable specimens of writing—of all the scraps of manuscript to be found in old bindings: in a draft application to the Curators he promises to give them the whole collection ultimately if they will allow him to remove the scraps preserved in Bodleian bindings.

In 1697 Edmund Gibson, a scholar distinguished for his judgement, foreshadows something bigger in a letter to Thoresby:[1] 'A young gentleman in Oxford, Mr. Humphrey Wanley, is laying the foundation of a *Res Diplomatica*, for England particularly. He designs and draws admirably well; having, besides, an unaccountable skill in imitating any hand whatsoever.' Now we see the outside influence which gave Wanley's work its special direction. For *Res Diplomatica* is a direct reference to Mabillon's *De Re Diplomatica*, 1681, a majestic answer to the doubts of the Jesuit scholar Papebroch, which laid the foundations of diplomatic studies and gave them their name. In fact Wanley first trained his hand to facsimile by copying the plates of handwriting in Mabillon. He learnt more than pencraft from Mabillon's book: he saw that handwriting had an historical development; that the study not merely of documents in the narrow sense but of all kinds of manuscripts, their dates and provenance, was a science, and that in England at least it was all his own.

Hickes, deprived as a non-juror, was now living in Oxford, and planning the expansion of his *Grammar* of 1689 into a grand Thesaurus of Northern Languages and Literature. As early as the winter of 1696 Wanley offered his help to improve the Catalogue of Anglo-Saxon Manuscripts appended to the *Grammar* which he had transcribed in 1692. In the spring of 1699 he entered into an agreement to be responsible for the whole catalogue, and that autumn we find him at Cambridge examining the manuscripts there. He was fairly launched on the only one of his books that came to an end; for Hickes was not merely watchful over his health, warning him against compotations, and damp sheets, and colds ('libraries', he said, 'have been the death of many brave men,

[1] *Thoresby Correspondence* i, p. 305.

particularly the Bodleian'), but he held him remorselessly to his undertaking. That was what Wanley needed: his weakness lay in the range and depth of his interests—history, languages, charters, manuscripts, printed books, coins, medals, seals, pictures, music sacred and profane—he wanted to be expert in them all.

The beginning of his great work coincided with a time of disappointments. In 1698, with his flair for inside information, he wrote begging the Vice-Chancellor to bring all the University's influence to bear on Sir John Cotton, who was hesitating about the settlement of the Cotton Library. The Vice-Chancellor was annoyed. University funds were low, and, as Wanley said, 'money must not be wanting'. He particularly disliked the word 'feasible' which Wanley had used, perhaps because it sounded too much like action. Anyhow, he was snubbed. He still implored Charlett to do all he could. 'Mr. Pepys', he wrote, 'looks upon that Library as one of the jewels of the Crown of England, and declared to me that, though he is a Cambridge man, yet he had much rather the Library was carried to Oxford.' And again in 1701, when the Library's future was being settled by statute, he reminded Charlett 'that the University might have had it, had they thought fit to have used all their endeavours to procure it even then when I first wrote to the Vice-Chancellor about it'. If the Library had come to Oxford it would have escaped the fire of 1731, but the history of the British Museum would have been different.

His lack of a degree was another trouble. According to Hearne, this master of orderly method could make nothing of Logic. 'By God, Mr. Milles,' he said to the Vice-Principal of St. Edmund Hall, 'I do not nor cannot understand it.' He was still an undergraduate when in 1698 Hyde told him that he wanted to resign at a convenient time so that Wanley could succeed him as Bodley's Librarian. For that a degree was essential. He begged Charlett to help him towards the B.C.L., but Charlett treated him coldly, and was not softened by a disquisition on the unprinted works of Chrysostom. Hickes, who could move mountains, was baffled because Charlett would promise nothing. It may be that he was unwilling to emancipate an invaluable slave, but perhaps he was willing that Wanley's candidature should be barred; for the successful candidate was Hudson of University College, and Hudson had been instrumental in securing Charlett's election as Master there.

Still the luck ran against him. A suggested fellowship at the future Worcester College fell through. The great Bentley, who kept the Royal Library in disorder, regarded it as a preserve of Trinity, Cambridge. Wanley decided to propose marriage to a cousin on the calculation that she had £3,000, but she had won a big prize in a lottery, and looked for nothing below a knight. Then, too, Bodley's Curators tightened the rein, so that in 1700 Hickes had to make a special appeal to the Vice-Chancellor to get him leave to go to London and examine the Cotton manuscripts.

The Catalogue seemed like a millstone round his neck, and it is no wonder that he tried to escape by an alternative project, which he had thought of in 1697. The Benedictines had made famous literary journeys, notably Mabillon's *Iter Germanicum* 1685 and *Iter Italicum* 1687; and in 1700 Wanley proposed that he should visit the libraries of France, Italy, and Germany to view their manuscripts, collate important texts, take specimens of handwriting, find out what works bearing on English History were on the Continent, and buy books. It was a magnificent scheme, which might have produced extraordinary results; and at first Hickes was attracted. He saw Sir Hans Sloane, who said £100 a year could be raised. Then suddenly Hickes turned against it. Years later he said he was afraid England would lose a genius to France. Really, I think, he woke up to the fact that he would lose his Catalogue. In 1698 he had applied to Charlett, who led the Delegates of the Press at Oxford, for 'the liberty of the Press', i.e. leave to print at the University Press, which alone had the necessary types, provided the costs were paid; and he began printing the *Thesaurus* in that year, with Thwaites in charge and Elstob assisting.[1] By June 1700 he found his own part still growing under his hand, the subscribers were murmuring, and Wanley had produced no copy.

Hickes did not know how much work was involved. To find out

[1] For a detailed account of the printing of Hickes's *Thesaurus*, see J. A. W. Bennett in *English Studies* (Essays and Studies of the English Association), 1948, p. 28 ff.

whether they contained any Anglo-Saxon fragments or glosses Wanley had to examine practically all our Latin manuscripts written before 1200: at Cambridge alone he says he examined many scores to no purpose. And he made the perennial mistake of giving too much time to the collection of material, and leaving too little for preparation for the press. His early descriptions were far too full, as can be seen by comparing his elaborate materials on the Rushworth Gospels in Harleian MS. 5911 with the one leaf of his copy for the printer that survives (in Bodleian MS. Rawl. D. 377), and happens to deal with the same manuscript. Again, he was not merely cataloguing every item in a manuscript with its incipit and explicit: he collated texts, and in the first twenty-five pages of the printed Catalogue collations appear—in his Preface he says it was without his knowledge, by error of the Printer.[1] Besides, he was transcribing 'all manner of epistles, wills, covenants, notes, charms, verses, catalogues', which he was quick to exploit for their bearing on the history of manuscripts. Most of these materials had to be cut out; and even on the reduced scale the extent of the copy when it began to come in startled Hickes: 'we must study brevity', he wrote; and the next few years saw a long and merciless battery of the wretched cataloguer, Thwaites reiterating 'The Press stands', and Hickes harping on broken promises, feigned excuses, and failing subscribers.

In December 1700, after another rebuff from the Vice-Chancellor, Bodley finally lost a great librarian. Without consulting Charlett, Wanley accepted the Assistant Secretaryship of the newly founded Society for Promoting Christian Knowledge at £40 a year (that, by the way, was the salary of Bodley's Librarian), and in March 1701 he became its first paid Secretary at £70 a year.

[1] A note in my copy dated 28 Feb. 1717–18 reports Wanley as complaining that 'though he had sent down to Oxford a very correct copy writ very fair, he never received a proof sheet to correct, though he wrote several letters to Mr. Thwaites. At last, going down himself, he found very many errata, and asking for the copy, the printers told him that the original from which it was printed being not called for, they had used it for waste paper.' This cannot be true for more than a part of the Catalogue; but it is likely enough that in other parts, to avoid more delay, Wanley was not given the opportunity of seeing proofs in which his corrections had been made.

This post gave him six years' security, in which he saw his Catalogue published (1705) and cultivated important friendships in London. Charlett had introduced him to Pepys and Sir Hans Sloane (who was everybody's doctor and watched over Wanley's indifferent health); Hickes had commended him to Harley, then Speaker of the House of Commons, who accepted the dedication of the Catalogue. With their influence, his constant effort was to find another post in which he could be with manuscripts. He tried for the Keepership of the old State Paper Office; and for ten years after 1700 he had fluctuating hopes of becoming curator of the Cotton Collection. In 1703 he was one of a committee of three appointed to report on the state of the Cotton manuscripts, and this brought him into closer relations with Harley, the principal Trustee.[1] The draft reports by Wanley in Harleian MS. 7055 supply the curious information that many manuscripts were already damaged by fire and wet before the Cotton fire of 1731.

His relations with Harley became closer when he made friends with Sir Simonds d'Ewes, and found that he was willing to sell the splendid family collection of materials for English History. Harley in 1703 put the negotiations in his hands with the happiest results: the purchase for £500 raised Harley's library to the first rank, and Wanley was temporarily employed to put it in order.

He did not forget his duty as an officer of the S.P.C.K. He translated from the French Ostervald's *Grounds and Principles of the Christian Religion*, and in 1705, clear of his Catalogue, he began an edition of the Bible in Anglo-Saxon from all the fragments, verse and prose. It was to have illustrations from the manuscripts with specimens of the hands; and Hickes was to provide the translation of the 'Cædmon' poems.[2] But when his conduct as Secretary was attacked by private enemies, he vindicated himself and then resigned, weary of the work. That his vindication was complete appears from the Society's asking him to remain, voting him 20 guineas as a mark of esteem, and inviting him to name his successor.

It required courage for a man of thirty-four, now married, to

[1] See Lansdowne MS. 841, ff. 63, 65, 66.

[2] Bp. Nicolson's letter of 20 Aug. 1705 in MS. Harl. 3780.

give up a secure post with nothing in prospect. For the next few years Hickes says 'he lived meanly and precariously, writing like a hireling for his bread'. Yet in the winter of 1707 he and a few friends met in a tavern to found the Society of Antiquaries, and with the notes of its early meetings in Harleian MS. 7055 is a very interesting list of historical projects they considered, in which Wanley is put down for the unprinted English historians.

Then in 1708 Harley found him employment on the cataloguing of his manuscripts: his descriptions of the first 2,400 manuscripts are by far the best part of the Harleian Catalogue which appeared exactly 100 years later. Afterwards he became the established Keeper of the Harleian Library. Henceforward his literary projects—the last was a Life of Wolsey from all the manuscript sources[1]—slide into the background: his time is all Harley's; his energies are concentrated on building up the first private collection of that age. For the Harleian Library that Wanley knew contained not only most of the manuscripts that were sold to the nation in 1753, but the best of that collection of printed books which Dr. Johnson described when it was sold by auction as 'excelling any library that was ever yet offered to sale, in the value as well as the number of volumes it contains'.

Early in 1715 he was given apartments in Harley's house. This was the occasion for his beginning the Diary,[2] which is a library journal rather than a personal diary. It runs from March 1715 to June 1726 (Wanley died in July at the age of fifty-five), with a gap from July 1716 to January 1720. During the gap his correspondence also is scanty, and perhaps he was unsettled by the transfer to Wimpole, where Sir Christopher Wren built Harley a new library. Early in 1714 Wanley had drawn up a paper,[3] well worth printing, on its arrangements and furnishings; but the books were not moved in till 1719.

It would take me too far afield to give an adequate account of the Diary, which is a source of the first rank for the history of

[1] Letter to Charlett of 10 Nov. 1708 in Bodleian MS. Ballard 13; cf. his advice to Fiddes on the researches necessary (to Charlett, 9 April 1720).

[2] Lansdowne MSS. 771 and 772, with the informal notebook Lansdowne 677.

[3] In MS. Harl. 7055.

manuscripts and the book-trade. Reading it, one is impressed by the amount of time and pains a busy statesman like Harley gave to books and book-collecting: he was a real book-lover, not a mere purse on whom Wanley drew.

Wanley's resourcefulness in the quest is amazing. He watches book-owners for signs of failing health or failing fortunes. He plays on their generosity, ambition, vanity, or cupidity to gain his ends. He persuades them to present the desired book to My Lord, or if not, exchange it, or sell it cheap, or bequeath it, or at least leave a first option in their wills. He was a superb bargainer. Here is an entry from the Diary for July 1720 that marked the end of a long negotiation with his friend the Somerset Herald:

> Mr. Warburton came to me at the Genoa Arms and then took me to another tavern, and kept me up all the night thinking to muddle me and so to gain upon me with selling his MSS. But the contrary happened.

In fact he got the manuscripts, including the fine eighth-century prayer-book Harley 2965, for £100, and Warburton was so disordered by the frolic that he could not deliver them next day.

Every opportunity is turned to account. The Diary begins 'March 2nd—Present My Lord Harley; Myself. This being St. Chad's day'—and the day suggests a line of approach to Lichfield Cathedral for St. Chad's Gospels. Another day, Sir George Wheler came in apologetically to explain that a manuscript which Wanley had borrowed from Lincoln College and which had most awkwardly disappeared, had after all turned up among the papers of one of the Fellows. In his delight at being cleared of a doubt, Wanley remembers that Wheler is a canon of Durham, and gets himself invited there in the hope of securing some of the Cathedral manuscripts, 'which will be more useful to the world in my Lord's Library than in that remote corner of the Kingdom'.

The building up of the Harleian collection is the more remarkable because the days when collecting was easy were past. Those who had books to sell knew all the tricks of the trade. Printed books were especially dear owing to the competition of rich men like the Earl of Sunderland. Early English manuscripts were almost unobtainable. Even to Harley Lichfield was unresponsive; Durham was cold; the Duke of Devonshire pleaded that he had the Æthelwold Benedictional from a friend. And it must have been a sore disappointment to Wanley when in April 1725 Mr. Pownall of Lincoln left him two manuscripts, called for them two days later, and failed to keep his promise to come back. They were the eighth-century Blickling Psalter and the Blickling Homilies, both of which Lord Lothian sold lately in the United States.

There were still good things to be had on the Continent, though some of Harley's best manuscripts were innocently bought from Aymon, who stole them from the Bibliothèque Nationale. But buying abroad required an elaborate system of agents and intelligence, extending to obscure dragomen in the Levant. A specimen of Wanley's instructions to an agent going abroad may be seen in the Preface to the Harleian Catalogue of 1808.

I must leave the Diary, and the proof it gives of his ability in every detail of a librarian's unselfish profession, to say something of his character.

Hearne, with the opinions he reports, will serve as Devil's advocate. According to him Wanley very much wanted steadiness and judgement; he wanted both learning and probity and would never have either; he stole books and coins from Bodley and probably from the Cotton Collection; he was a vain coxcomb; a very great rogue; a perjured wretch; a most terrible drinker, and generally drunk when he wrote.

But Hearne is not a credible witness where his prejudices are engaged. If Wanley's Latinity was not of the purest, Matthew Prior's couplet

Whatever Socrates has said
Or Tully writ or Wanley read

expressed the general admiration of his learning and his prodigious memory. His honesty was incorruptible: to rob a library must have seemed sacrilege to a man whose lifelong passion was to preserve and augment them. While he was still a draper's apprentice at Coventry he gave the library there a manuscript copy of one of Leonard Aretine's translations from Aristotle, and later the printed books and manuscripts which his expertness enabled him to buy for himself at bargain prices were presented or resold with disinterested public spirit. He was magnanimous, though he sometimes had cause of grievance. His disposition was social: next to a library he enjoyed his tavern; Pope writes to him as a connoisseur of wine, and he was an authority on the latest songs. There was an unusual quality in his manner and talk that pleased distinguished men when he was obscure, and later made him welcome in the best company. Pepys found his conversation 'wonderfully delightful'. Harley enjoyed sitting and talking with him after dinner. The Countess liked him well enough to furnish his tea-table with a large silver teapot, and later a fine large silver tea-kettle, lamp, and stand.

But I have to show that he was a great scholar, not that he was learned and interesting.

Palaeography is essential to the progress of those historical studies whose chief material is old writings: it enables us not merely to read them, but to use them with understanding: unless we know when and where they were written, vagueness is inevitable. To medieval studies especially, palaeography is what epigraphy is to the classical historian—a principal means of precision.

Let us first see how matters stood in England before Wanley. Archbishop Parker, who was not only a great collector but a great reader of manuscripts, had a Homer (CCCC MS. 81) and a Cicero's Rhetoric (CCCC MS. 158) which he asserted were the property of Theodore, the seventh-century archbishop of Canterbury. When Wanley visited Cambridge he saw that the first was a fifteenth-century manuscript on paper (later he traced it to the fifteenth-century Theodore Gaza for whom it was written[1]) and the Cicero an ordinary humanistic copy of the same date. Pass on from Parker to Hickes, whose *Dissertatio Epistolaris* in the *Thesaurus* was to become the basic treatise on English diplomatic. In a letter of 1696 he says 'I know not if ever I saw a Saxon MS. written before the Conquest'—meaning that he had seen many Saxon manuscripts, but could form no judgement of their true

[1] See M. R. James *A Descriptive Catalogue of the MSS. in C.C.C. Cambridge* i, p. 166.

age. No wonder he wrote to Wanley 'I have learned more from you than ever I did from any man': that was in 1697 when Wanley was twenty-five and Hickes his senior by thirty years. One would not expect Greek palaeography, which is more difficult, to be in better state. According to Wanley, with whose dating modern palaeographers agree, Bentley on different occasions gave dates two hundred and four hundred years too early for the Greek Biblical MS. Royal I D II. That was the state of palaeography in England before Wanley.

Now let us look beyond England. The classic account of the development of palaeography, as laid down by Traube,[1] the master of the modern study, is briefly this: Mabillon, who dealt primarily with diplomatic—with documents rather than literary manuscripts—described the national hands of Europe—Saxon, Lombardic, &c.—as independent kinds of writing, introduced and prevailing by national conquest. Montfaucon, whose *Palaeographia Graeca* (1708) gave the name to the subject, made the next step forward because he showed the historical development of each Greek letter-form, and yet another step in his catalogue of the *Bibliotheca Coisliniana* (1715), where he assigned dates to undated Greek manuscripts. Then, from 1721 on, the Italian Maffei, aided by his rediscovery of the very early Verona manuscripts, taught that Mabillon's national hands were but varieties historically developed from Roman writing: that Latin palaeography was all one.

Montfaucon and Maffei made their own discoveries. But before them, here in Oxford, Wanley had made these advances on Mabillon, and expressed them in clear words and daily practice.

The dating of undated manuscripts was his practical aim from the beginning. His method was to find what he called 'dates', i.e. manuscripts or documents which could be fixed to a definite year or years by a congruence of evidence. By reference to these as standards he settled the approximate age of undated manuscripts. So in 1697 he writes 'The charters may determine the age of all the Saxon manuscripts', and plans to get them all lent to the

[1] *Zur Paläographie und Handschriftenkunde* (published after his death), Munich 1909, p. 35 ff. The editor adds a reference to Wanley's Catalogue as containing dates.

Bodleian so that as a first step he can find out by comparison which are original. In the same year he says that a tour of the European collections, when he would see everything with his own eyes, would enable him to adjust the age of all manuscripts written in capitals. In his Catalogue of 1705 the age of manuscripts is indicated when it can usefully be done;[1] and in the preface he says 'the chief thing one wants to know about a manuscript is its age' (*ætas quidem primaria res est*). There he gives a short account of his methods: in fact, at one time or another he applied all the methods of dating now in use that are applicable in his special field; and how well he understood their limitations may be seen in that part of his letter in the *Philosophical Transactions* of 1701 which deals with the difficulties of dating manuscripts. For English writing, except for very early manuscripts where the comparative materials are on the Continent, he was not surpassed in dating until Sir George Warner's day at the British Museum.

Again his early interest in alphabets, and his skill in facsimile, led him to anticipate Montfaucon's study of the historical development of letter-forms—so that to him Montfaucon's *Greek Palaeography* was a disappointing book.[2] He sometimes made his copies of relatively unimportant documents in the hand of the original.[3] A man who can reproduce the detail and spirit of any hand with

[1] Cf. the Preface to the Catalogue f. a[2] verso: 'Maxime curavi quo quisque codex tempore scriptus erat, dicere.' The forms he uses are, e.g. 'ante octingentos annos Ælfredo rege jubente scriptus' (Hatton 20); 'circa tempora Æthelstani regis' (Junius 27); 'ante septingentos annos' (Exeter Book); 'seculo decimo exeunte' (Junius 11); 'circa annum Dom. 1064 exaratus, ut fas est coniicere ex tabellis nonnullis, et ex scriptura codicis' (CCCC 391); 'paullo post Conquæstum Angliæ' (Laud E.19).

[2] 'As to his *Palaeographica*, excepting some few things I could have made as good a book from our English libraries and collections alone: in lieu whereof, I can assure you that they can both correct and supply him much farther than any man can imagine who hath not perused him diligently and also spent much time in our public libraries and private studies' (to Charlett, 19 Nov. 1715, in Bodleian MS. Ballard 13). This does less than justice to Montfaucon's pioneer synthesis.

[3] Writing of the Account of Thomas Hall for the bishopric of Lincoln, which had been accidentally burnt, he says 'I have a copy which I think is exact, for I wrote in it the very same hand with the original' (to Charlett, 16 Oct. 1694).

his pen must be unusually sensitive both to the standard elements and the slightest variations of letter-form; and here Wanley had an advantage in minute observation which may never be repeated in this age of photography; and an advantage in the recording of his observations which, I believe, no other palaeographer had before photography.

This aspect of his work would be better known had Hickes kept the promise made in his General Preface—that it would be followed by Wanley's specimens of handwriting in chronological order, to meet Wanley's criticism of the fewness and meaningless disorder of the plates that do appear. Still, the published plates give some taste of his art, though they were often done at great speed under pressure. While harrying Wanley for copy, Hickes, who usually borrowed the manuscripts, would bid him come round for half an hour with a pen and parchment, and Wanley *wrote* the specimens—he did not draw or trace them. The continuous specimens of the Exeter Book which he made in June 1701 are well worth examining;[1] and there is a good example of his dissection into alphabets at p. 3 of the Gothic Grammar.

Again before Maffei, but with no such early manuscripts to point the way as the unique Verona collection, he perceived the historical development of the national hands from the Roman. In 1697 he proposes to trace 'the Greek and Latin letters from the oldest monuments; the Irish, Saxon, etc. from the Latin; and particularly Saxon from the oldest times up to today'. In December 1702, and more tentatively only because he was writing to Edward Lloyd, who still believed in Druidic origins, he speaks of composing

> a complete book concerning the original and progress of writing . . . my present notion (and the more I consider it, the more reasons I have to confirm it) is that the English-Saxons, the Welsh and the Irish had their letters from one common fountain, that is from the Romans or from Rome. I am sensible of the remains of the Runic letters amongst the Saxons; and do believe that some knowledge of them might creep in amongst the British; but since it appears that even the Runic letters are derived from the Roman, that does not hinder the Saxon, Welsh and

[1] Plates IV, V, VI of *Grammatica Islandica*.

Irish letters coming from the Roman, as well as the ancient French, German, and Spanish.[1]

The Preface to his Catalogue covers the same ground; but here he adds a classification of the Roman hands imitated in early England which could hardly be bettered if account is taken of the gradations and mingling of styles found in manuscripts of Anglo-Saxon times. He makes three divisions: Capitals (*grandiores*, *vulgo unciales*, *literae*) for permanent books and documents; a rather smaller and rounder script easier for copyists; a third (to be seen in Bishop Waldhere's letter of 705) of minuscule letters for quick writing, which gave way to the second in England after about A.D. 800. From the second of these he derives the script used for Anglo-Saxon.[2]

In the derivation of runes from Latin he was also far ahead of his time. The true doctrine, the true palaeographical method is implicit everywhere in his work. When he stumbles, it is for lack of historical tools.

Nor was this genius buried and unfruitful. His special knowledge was available to any inquirer in an active period of historical studies. I pass over Hickes's great debt to him in his *Dissertatio Epistolaris* and elsewhere in the *Thesaurus*, for two particular instances.

The value of Smith's edition of Bede 1722 lies in his use of the famous Moore manuscript as the basis of the text. Smith owed his knowledge of its age and history to a long letter of Wanley's dated 28 August 1703[3] in which the manuscript is discussed in detail—

[1] Letter to Lloyd of 24 Dec. 1702 in MS. Ashmole 1817*b*, f. 199.

[2] The exact words of his summary classification (f. c 2) have some importance, because both Mabillon and Maffei made threefold classifications of Roman writing: 'Præterea, ut *Runis* suis sensim relictis, *Romanorum* characteres usurparunt *Anglo-Saxones*: sic manus, quæ in usu apud *Romanos* erant, in scribendo imitati sunt. Eæ autem trium generum fuerunt: nempe una, quæ in grandioribus vel uncialibus (ut vulgo loquuntur) literis exarata erat; altera modi parum minoris et rotundioris formæ, quæ scribentibus maius commoda erat; tertia, quæ prompte et cum festinatione scribentibus maxime commoda, ex minusculis constabat. In quibus omnibus scripturæ generibus, codices chartæque in *Anglia Saxonica*, quemadmodum in *Germania*, *Gallia*, *Hispania*, immo et in ipsa *Italia* scripti sunt.'

[3] In Bodley MS. S.C. 29726.

down to the name of the Scotch gentleman, Cuningham, who bought it at auction on the Continent and sold it to Bishop Moore. It was Wanley who first saw that the text of Cædmon's *Hymn* in this manuscript is one of the earliest monuments of our language. And had Smith followed the indications he gave in the same letter about MS. Tiberius C III, Plummer's discovery of the independent value of that tradition would have been anticipated.

Again, in the unfortunate controversy about the foundation of Oxford in which Camden became involved, the manuscript of Asser which was destroyed in the Cotton fire of 1731 was a primary witness. The early accounts of it are conflicting: but Wise, who edited it in 1722, quoted Wanley's opinion that it was written 'about 1000 or 1001'; and W. H. Stevenson in his splendid edition, knowing Wanley's methods, deduced from Wise's odd precision that the hand must have been like that of an extant Cotton charter dated 1001. Wanley's answer to Wise is extant in the Bodleian: he compares the manuscript with that very charter, and clears up other doubts.[1]

Besides, he had a marvellous eye for what was important to other scholars, and he did not wait to be asked for information. He knows that Lloyd will be interested in the Welsh of St. Chad's Gospels. He sees a plan of a monastery in the Eadwine Psalter and immediately thinks of Tanner. He tells Hickes as soon as he lights on the Beowulf manuscript, for Hickes replies (20 August 1700) 'I can find nothing yet of Beowulph'. In the best work of his time, his work is everywhere.

His direct influence extended far beyond his own time. The high-water mark of Anglo-Saxon studies reached in the *Thesaurus* in 1705 was not passed again for more than a century. But in the nineteenth century, and especially in its latter half, there was a new wave of enthusiasm. In England Oxford was again in the front of it. Sweet played a leading part in the theoretical advance; Napier was the most delicate of English Anglo-Saxon scholars; W. H. Stevenson the master of modern Anglo-Saxon diplomatic. Yet, with nearly all the material in England, the movement and its methods were largely in the hands of foreign scholars. Wanley had

[1] See above, p. 148 n.

missed so little that a worker in his study abroad could find from the Catalogue what texts remained unprinted, the extant manuscripts and their age, the very folios on which he must look. He could go straight to the places in a short vacation, or order transcripts or, later, photographs. So editors often kept the good rule of going to the manuscripts in the letter, not in the spirit. All that slow rummaging in manuscripts and commerce of manuscripts so characteristic of the earlier English tradition appeared to be unnecessary, except to a few scholars like Napier and Liebermann (I speak only of Anglo-Saxon studies) who worked on material which Wanley did not profess to cover completely. The rapidity, efficiency, and comparative sureness of the development would have been impossible without Wanley, whose Catalogue was and still remains the key to the Anglo-Saxon manuscripts. But there was a price to be paid for the saving of time and trouble. The greatness of his work, hurried and immature as it is in the Catalogue, produced a kind of atrophy of those very faculties and interests which he had outstandingly. He was so good an intermediary that the study of Anglo-Saxon tended to be cut off from the manuscript sources which should vitalize it; and another stage was reached in the divorce of philology from history which Professor Powicke deplored in the first of this series of lectures on Great Scholars; for palaeography touches history at every point.

Note A to p. 56

THE RELATIONSHIP OF ÆTHELRED'S CODES V AND VI

WHERE V Æthelred 15 has only the general direction: 'Let other feasts and fasts be kept carefully, as those keep them who keep them best', VI Æthelred 23 adds that the Ember fasts are to be kept according to Gregory's ordinance. Here we touch on the long-standing problem of the relationship between the two codes. In his *Gesetze der Angelsachsen*[1] Liebermann argues forcibly that both represent the decisions of one witan, held at Enham in 1008 with King Æthelred and archbishops Ælfheah and Wulfstan present. The date is derived from one copy of V Æthelred, and is confirmed by the plan for building a fleet (V 27) which the Chronicle notices under that year. The place, the season (Pentecost), and the leading persons present are named in Wulfstan's Latin record (L), which is closely related to VI Æthelred. Yet between V and VI Æthelred there are differences of substance, order, and phrasing which have led Miss Whitelock to doubt whether both are the decisions of a single witan.[2] The question has interesting implications for textual criticism: if they are variant versions of one code, their differences are to be explained by the usual processes of textual divergence—scribal error or unauthorized modification; but if they represent the results of two witans, a new draught of authority in VI Æthelred must be reckoned with.

Where experts in the laws disagree or are in doubt, it is rash for anyone less well equipped to intervene. But when new information becomes available about one detail of the problem, in this case the Ember fasts, it is sometimes helpful to inquire what conditions would best fit that detail. To give some context, I propose to examine the group of laws on Church dues, feasts, and fasts which, basing on II Edgar 3, 4, 5, appears in V Æthelred 11–20, VI Æthelred 16–25, 2 and the related L, VIII Æthelred 7–17; in the text here called D Cn.,[3] and in I Cnut 8–17, 3;

[1] iii, p. 167. K. Jost *Wulfstanstudien*, Bern 1950, p. 43 f. agrees with Liebermann in this point, regarding the variations of VI Æthelred as the result of a 'private' recension.

[2] *English Historical Review* lxiii (1948), p. 433 ff.

[3] Liebermann i, p. 252 f. According to Liebermann it is a mere compilation from VI Æthelred and I Cnut. According to Miss Whitelock *E.H.R.* art. cit. it is a set of laws prepared by Wulfstan at the beginning of Cnut's reign. Jost *Wulfstanstudien* p. 94 ff. supports Liebermann. *Adhuc sub judice lis est*, and a decision is not essential for the present purpose.

as well as in three texts printed in Napier's collection of sermons attributed to Wulfstan: item XXIII = XLIII agreeing usually with V Æthelred, item L with VI Æthelred, item LXI with VIII Æthelred.

The character of the manuscript evidence for these laws requires notice. All the primary manuscripts date from the eleventh century. The Worcester MS. CCCC 201 provides one of the three copies of V Æthelred, the only complete text of VIII Æthelred, and the only text of D Cn. The other two copies of V Æthelred and one copy of I Cnut are in Nero A I, probably a Worcester collection (Wanley), but with Canterbury connexions.[1] The other complete copy of I Cnut derives from the same defective text, and is in Harley 55, which may be a Worcester manuscript in this as in its earlier part. The text of VI Æthelred and the related Latin L appear together in Claudius A III, a collection of fragments mostly from Canterbury, though these two texts, if not the actual copy, certainly originated in Wulfstan's province.[2] These are very narrow channels of transmission if regard is had to the number of duplicates of any national code that would be required for the aldermen,[3] sheriffs, and bishops, and the many others that would be needed while the laws were in force. Besides, it is agreed or claimed by good authority that all these texts were inspired or drafted by one man, Wulfstan. So the possibilities of early collation and conflation are exceptional.

In the group of laws selected there are three differences of content:

(i) The payment of churchscot at Martinmas (11 Nov.) is prescribed in VI Æthelred 18, 1, in L, in VIII Æthelred 11 and I Cnut 10; but not in any of the three manuscripts of V Æthelred or in Ð Cn. The practice is attested from Ine's day, so that there could be no good reason for omitting it in V Æthelred. It is in the derived 'sermon' XXIII = XLIII. Liebermann's explanation that the clause was dropped by scribal error from the archetype of the three extant manuscripts of V Æthelred is the natural one, and all three represent one defective copy. The expectation that these legal codes would show a high standard of scribal accuracy is disappointed; and there is more evidence of the same trend. The copy in MS. CCCC 201 also omits the preceding clause on Peter's Pence. An omission in the text of VIII Æthelred 12, 1 makes *leohtgescot* due only at Candlemas, 'let him who will contribute oftener', where V and VI Æthelred and I Cnut make it due three times a year. It is incredible that

[1] See Liebermann i, p. xxv.

[2] N. R. Ker, in *Studies in Medieval History presented to F. M. Powicke*, 1948, p. 71 n., identifies an annotating hand in Claudius A III as one that appears in several other MSS. connected with Archbishop Wulfstan.

[3] Cf. IV Edgar 15, 1: 'Let many copies be made from this, and sent to Alderman Ælfhere and Alderman Æthelwine, who are to distribute it everywhere, so that this ordinance may be known both to poor and rich.'

national rules affecting every parishioner could be suddenly changed and as suddenly restored; and Sermon LXI, which follows VIII Æthelred closely, has three dates, Christmas, Candlemas, and Easter, followed by *do oftor se ðe wille*: this is the true text, except that Christmas is a local variant of All Saints (1 Nov.) which is usually the third occasion. In I Cnut 12, both manuscripts require *leohtgescot* to be paid thrice a year, but specify only two dates, omitting Candlemas.[1] Ælfric kept a close watch on his scribes. Dunstan in his old age at Canterbury spent the early hours of the morning correcting errors in manuscripts.[2] But in the eleventh-century scriptoria which produced these codes there can have been no regular checking of the scribe's work. Careless omission of whole clauses is always a possibility.

(ii) The three manuscripts of V Æthelred 16, with D Cn. and I Cnut 12, prescribe for 'all England' the feast of Edward the Martyr (18 March), which is not in VI Æthelred or L or the relevant 'sermons'. There is no obvious reason why Wulfstan should omit this clause from his record L. Every member of the witan that approved it would remember it. Besides, he speaks with indignation of King Edward's murder in his sermon *ad Anglos* of 1014, though he does not call him saint or martyr. On the view that VI Æthelred and L are the result of a second witan, it is necessary to explain why Edward was nationally honoured in V Æthelred, deprived in VI Æthelred, and restored in I Cnut. Liebermann[3] supposes that the clause was struck out of VI Æthelred and L at Canterbury because Edward was regarded as the enemy of monachism. This motive is unlikely. If the hostility were general, a witan at which the leaders of the Church were monks would not have honoured Edward. On Liebermann's view, Ælfheah, archbishop of Canterbury, was one of them; and according to Canterbury tradition, their great saint Dunstan secured the throne for Edward.[4] Then again, it would be a senseless act. To erase a saint's name from a calendar, official or private, has a practical purpose; but a law of England is not altered by striking it out of some copies. There is another

[1] Lambard completes the text with a barbarous translation from *Consiliatio Cnuti*; cf. p. 232 ff. above; and for other examples see Miss D. Whitelock *English Historical Review* lvi (1941), p. 19 ff. All the Latin versions give the three occasions.

[2] *Memorials of St. Dunstan*, ed. Stubbs, p. 49.

[3] iii, p. 171.

[4] Adelard (before 1011) in *Memorials*, ed. Stubbs, p. 61; Osbern, p. 114. Little is known about the early history of Edward's cult outside of Shaftesbury. It was a delicate question in Æthelred's early years because he was murdered by supporters of Æthelred. For light on Æthelred's attitude in 1001 see Stenton *Anglo-Saxon England*, p. 368 n. If the late MSS. can be trusted in this point, Adelard calls him saint and martyr in the passage of his letter to Abp. Ælfheah cited above.

possibility. It has been mentioned that the three manuscripts of V Æthelred derive from one defective copy, and the law relating to Edward may have been interpolated in that copy: i.e. it may be the decision of a later witan. A detail of phrasing favours this view. Certain introductory formulae were regarded as variable. Thus the earlier copy of V Æthelred in Nero A I five times uses the formula: 'and ures hlafordes gerædnes and his witena is (þæt)', which is suited to Æthelred's lifetime; where the later copy in the same manuscript regularly substitutes: 'and witena gerædnes is (þæt)', which is the formula of VI Æthelred, independent of change of king, and suited to a collection of laws. The clause appointing Edward's feast reads: 'and sancte Eadweardes mæssedæg witan habbað gecoren (þæt)'. This is a well-established use, but it appears in this clause in V Æthelred (all MSS.), D Cn., and I Cnut, and nowhere else in the body of these texts. If the clause is interpolated in V Æthelred, then L and VI Æthelred may be a true record of the witan of 1008.

(iii) Of the Anglo-Saxon codes, only the associated VI Æthelred and L (followed here by D Cn.) specify the practice ordered by Gregory for the Ember fasts. That the later VIII Æthelred 16 and I Cnut 14, 1 agree with V Æthelred in giving only a general direction, tells against Gregory's rule being the addition of a witan later than that of 1008. We know that the issue was controversial. If, as seems probable, Winchester Cathedral was already among those who had adopted the Continental use, it is unlikely that the witan of 1008, called in a crisis, would stir up trouble by insisting on the English practice: Æthelred was at home in Winchester, and Ælfheah had previously been bishop there. Must we then suppose that Wulfstan misrepresented the decision of that witan? There is an alternative. When the question of the Ember fasts was discussed, prudent legislators might well conclude that there was much to be said on both sides, and leave the archbishops, each in his own province, to deal with this matter of detail as they thought best. Then if L is the Latin record that would guide his own higher clergy, and VI Æthelred the Anglo-Saxon text which all his clergy were to know and make known, Archbishop Wulfstan could fairly include with the witan's decisions his own ruling that the Gregorian practice was the 'best'. It was probably uncontroversial in his province, which was then more old-fashioned and less open to Continental influence than the South.

So this sample group of laws would be best explained if V Æthelred, in its original form, represents the laws approved for the English by the witan of 1008, whose chief draughtsman was Wulfstan; while L and VI Æthelred, at different levels, are promulgations of the same laws to clergymen by Wulfstan in his capacity as archbishop, with some explanations for their guidance, and some modifications of detail, not of policy, which he was authorized by the witan to make in his own province of

York. A cursory look at the circumstances and the complete texts should show whether this suggestion is worth consideration, and incidentally bring out the complexities of the problem.

The witan of 1008 met when a great new Danish invasion was expected. It had to deal first with ecclesiastical matters and second with defence: 'de catholice cultu religionis recuperando, deque etiam rei statu publice reparando vel consulendo', says Wulfstan, who held that good morals and a healthy Church were the first essentials for the safety and recovery of the country. Its decisions begin with a call for national unity: 'One God, one Church, one King.'[1] But the unity of England and its defence against a Danish invasion depended on the loyalty of the Danelaw—Anglo-Scandinavian eastern England from the Thames to the Tees, where conditions and customs were very different from those of the Southern and Mercian English. An assembly making laws for all England at that time had a choice of methods. It might decide to overrule local differences: this would cause dissension. Or it might detail and authorize respectable variant practices: this would waste time and perhaps confuse the law. Or, in the search for common ground on which everybody could agree, it might issue a set of laws drafted in such general terms that they had little practical effect. Or, where a specific provision was unavoidable, it might choose what was acceptable to a large part of the country, presumably the English part, and leave adjustments to conditions elsewhere to be made in special promulgations of the code. The suggestion is that the last two methods were followed by the witan of 1008, and that Wulfstan was authorized to make necessary modifications. He was the witan's principal adviser on ecclesiastical law and knew its intentions thoroughly. It was a factor in his great influence that he could speak for the Danelaw and was in touch with feeling there through his clergy. And as archbishop of York he had wide administrative powers.

V Æthelred fits in very well. Most of its provisions, viz. 1–27 and the closing 32–34, are drafted in such general terms that they would be acceptable to any Christian community in England at that time. They are mainly good resolutions, precepts, and exhortations. Penalties, on which there are likely to be differences of personal and local opinion, form a large part of the laws of the great law-making kings from Æthelberht onwards: here they are confined to the small group of clauses 28–31. In Edgar's codes earlier and in Cnut's codes later, differences between the laws of the English and the laws of the Danes in England are often mentioned: in V Æthelred they are only twice implied. According to V 30, a plotter against the king's life may defend himself by a threefold ordeal *on Engla lage*, which indicates some difference *on Dena lage*; and

[1] V Æth. pro.

by V 31 those who openly defy the laws of Christ or the king must pay 'swa wer, swa wite, swa lahslite, aa be ðam þe seo dæd sy'. Here *lahslite* refers to a system of fines peculiar to the Danelaw. But the words are a set formula: they occur in the so-called 'Laws of Edward and Guthrum' which Miss Whitelock[1] has shown to be contemporary with, perhaps a little earlier than V Æthelred; and a draughtsman who had ready to hand just the kind of comprehensive formula he sought throughout V Æthelred, would hardly strike out *swa lahslite* in order to make his penalty clauses uniform in application. Nothing forbids the belief that V Æthelred, in its original form, represents the text read over to the witan of 1008 for final approval, and issued through the king's officials to aldermen, sheriffs, and bishops.

Wulfstan tells us what L is: 'Haec itaque legalia statuta . . . in nostro conventu sinodali a rege (Æþelredo) magnopere edicta, cuncti tunc temporis optimates se observaturos fideliter spondebant; idcircoque ego (Wulfstanus) . . . Eboracensium archiepiscopus eadem ad sequentium memoriam, necnon et ad praesentium vel futurorum salutem, litteris infixi.' It was written after the assembly (*tunc temporis*); but because the authority of such a record depends on its being made while memory is fresh, I think it was a matter of months, not years after, and that *Quodam tempore* (*contigit*) at the beginning means 'on a recent memorable occasion'. L contains source material, explanations, argument, and circumstantial detail which would naturally be excluded from a code of laws. It begins with the discussions of the bishops, and goes on to deal with the various grades of clergy. This is logical and suitable in a document for ecclesiastics, and it may represent the order of the witan's discussions; but V Æthelred takes these clauses (V 4–9, 2) later, putting before them provisions limiting capital punishment and forbidding the sale of innocent men into slavery abroad, which are more important for laymen. If this group of clauses is transposed bodily, the order of V Æthelred and L (VI Æthelred follows L) is the same throughout, which is good evidence that we are dealing with one and the same code. There is a still stronger reason for taking the witan of 1008 and the witan of Enham to be the same. In L, Wulfstan has plenty of opportunity for explanation: he tells us, for instance, that the curiously prominent clauses about monks who had left their monasteries[2] were sponsored by the archbishops—perhaps because there was some question of the authority of bishops over abbots in this matter. It is hard to believe he would give no hint that in these clauses, and in practically all the others reported in L, the witan was simply re-enacting the decisions of another witan which met a year or so earlier.

[1] *English Historical Review* lvi (1941), p. 1 ff.

[2] V 5–6, 1 = VI 3–3, 2.

L is in language and content a learned record, such as Wulfstan might send to the king, to the archbishop of Canterbury, and to the bishops and higher clergy of his own province. Jost's[1] detailed study has thrown light on its sources, and has confirmed that VI Æthelred was in the main produced by working over V Æthelred with reference to L. Then if Wulfstan compiled VI Æthelred, there is reason to believe that he is responsible for any divergence from V Æthelred in which VI and L agree. (i) Notable additions to the extant text of V in both VI and L are § 34 which gives the penalty for damaging the king's ships, and § 39 which gives the penalty for violating a nun dedicated to God or ravishing[2] a (dedicated) widow. The second is an unusual clause introduced apparently because there was some special circumstance that drew attention to the crime or the penalty; but, except for Wulfstan's account of L, there is nothing to show whether it was originally part of V Æthelred or was added by Wulfstan. The first was probably part of the code passed by the witan. It fits neatly into the small group of clauses which state a penalty. Then again, it is directed against negligence resulting in *corruptela vel fractura*: an assembly concerned with the supply of ships, meeting at Pentecost (mid-May in 1008), would have reports of damage arising from neglect during the winter lay-up, because it would appear at the Easter refitting. (ii) Both V and VI Æthelred sometimes enter into details which seem out of keeping with the broad, general character of the code, though they may have been inserted by the witan in the course of discussion. L omits several of these, no doubt because Wulfstan regarded them as unimportant, viz. V 12, 1 = VI 21 which settles who is to have *sawlsceatt* when a person is buried outside of his own parish; V 14, 1 = VI 22, 3 where the fast of Philip and James (1 May) is not insisted on because the period from Easter to Pentecost was free of compulsory fasts,[3] as a balance to the long Lenten fast; and V 20 = VI 25, 2 which defers the settlement of payments that happen to fall due on holy days. (iii) But L and VI agree in omitting V 28 which fixes the heavy penalty of 120 shillings for leaving the *fyrd* when the king is not with it. This clause fits into its context, and may have been omitted in L because it was difficult or inexpedient to fix a penalty for this offence in the Danelaw. (iv) V 3 = VI 10 urges restraint in the application of the death penalty; but V 28 and 29 name it for the offence of leaving the *fyrd* in which the king is, or of coming near the king after being excommunicated. VI 35 and 36 and L omit the death penalty for both offences.

[1] Op. cit. p. 13 ff.

[2] For *vi opprimere* in this sense, see the Vulgate Gen. xxxiv. 2. If VI Æth. is Wulfstan's work, *nydnæman* must translate it, and it can have the same sense. Liebermann's interpretation 'forced marriage', '*Raubehe*', introduces a different kind of crime.

[3] Cf. I Cnut 16, 1.

Again, the change may have been politic as well as merciful in the Danelaw.

It cannot be chance that the important differences in (i), (iii), (iv) all concern the small group of clauses V 28–31 = VI 34–39 that give penalties, on which differences between Southern England and the Danelaw are to be expected. As each clause came before the witan for discussion, these differences would appear, and at that time not only Wulfstan but the king's officers in the Danelaw could be authorized to apply specified alternative penalties. Most of the offences in this part of the code are secular, not ecclesiastical, and therefore not within the normal administrative discretion of an archbishop. Certainly the changes were intended to be authoritative and effective.

L is a learned record, and VI Æthelred is intended for another audience. (*a*) This is clear in § 10 on capital punishment, where L cites three Biblical texts, and in their place VI quotes *et dimitte nobis debita nostra*, &c.[1] from the Lord's Prayer, which would come home to the humblest parish priest and, when translated, to every parishioner. (*b*) VI begins with a reference to the opening exhortation (*frumræd*) of the bishops, and goes on to the various grades of religious in the order of L. (*c*) It shows the influence of the sermon style in matter as well as in phrasing: thus, when dealing with capital punishment it calls for wise moderation in § 10, 2 which is based on earlier Anglo-Saxon texts[2] and expressed in Wulfstan's characteristic manner. (*d*) Neither V nor L has anything corresponding to VI 5, 2, a lament that some priests have two or more concubines: this is intended to reach priests, not their congregations. (*e*) Where V 10 forbids illicit marriages to all Christians, VI 12, developing brief indications in L, defines the prohibited marriages in a way that would help both priests and laymen. (*f*) There are other helpful rulings or clarifications: V 22, 1 orders everybody to prepare for the sacrament *oft and gelome* = L *creberrime*; but VI 27, 1 has a practical rule that was later adopted in I Cnut 19: they must do so at least three times a year. V 29 punishes *ænig amansumad man* = L *quisquam de excommunicatis* who comes near the king; VI 36 has the specific 'gif morðwyrhtan oððe mansworan oððe æbære manslagan . . . '. In VI 22, 3 added words make it clear that the fast of Philip and James is not forbidden to those who wish to keep it. (*g*) In one place the elucidation is itself vague. V 26, 1 is an exhortation to consider ways of improving security (*frið*); L adds that robbery is to be punished *multimodis penis* (short of death?); VI 32 explains 'as is most satisfactory to the householder (*bonda*) and most unpleasant to the robbers'.[3] The Norse words

[1] Adopted in II Cnut 2*a*.

[2] Jost op. cit. p. 38 n.

[3] Adopted in II Cnut 8. This addition in VI, with those noted in

bonda, and *cyric-ren* 'sacrilege' added in VI 28, 3, point to circulation in the Anglo-Scandinavian part of England. (*h*) The two clauses in V which indicate a different penalty in the Danelaw are modified: VI 37 has words that Liebermann[1] thinks were in the original text of V Æthelred, viz. 'and on Dena lage be þam þe heora lagu sy', after *on Ængla lage*; and in VI 38 *swa lahslite* is dropped, probably, as Liebermann suggests, by a Southern copyist, for Worcester as well as Canterbury was outside the Danelaw. (*i*) Unlike V and L, VI Æthelred contains little new that is legally important. After V 10, 1 which suggests the subject, VI 14 on church-sanctuary and the protection given by the king's hand is added; but it is derived from the contemporary 'Edward and Guthrum', § 1. That VI Æthelred is the borrower appears from another added clause: VI 6 (cf. V 1) ends with the rejection of heathen practices: L specifies various kinds of sorcery and idolatry: 'incantatores, magos, phithonicos et veneficos necne idolorum cultores'; but VI 7, using 'Edward and Guthrum' 11, takes over serious crimes that are not peculiar to heathens. (*j*) The added VI 32, 2 on true weights and measures[2] is suggested by the reference to coinage in L, and is not new in Anglo-Saxon laws (see, e.g., III Edgar 8, 1). The topic had already been touched on in V 24 = VI 28, 2; but the repetition in VI 32, 2 may be due to the special responsibility of parish priests for weights and measures: cf. *Episcopus* 12 'let every measure in his parish and every weight be fixed very exactly by his [the priest's] ruling, and if there should be any dispute, let the bishop settle it'.[3] (*k*) The penalty for violating a dedicated nun or widow in L is loss of all property; in VI 39 'gebete þæt deope for Gode and worolde' is substituted. It is not clear that any change of the secular penalty is intended, but certain that the Church's doctrine of the saving virtue of penitence is added in VI.[4]

The divergences of VI Æthelred from V and L afford no evidence that it was composed much later than L. On the whole, they favour the suggestion that the document is an exposition of the laws in V Æthelred and L for parish priests in the province of York, so that they could know the laws themselves and make them known to their congregations. It was intended to be authoritative and effective, and is not, as Jost suggests, a private recension in which Wulfstan brought the laws approved by the witan of 1008 nearer to his own wishes. Its influence on later laws, especially Cnut's, excludes the view that it had a very limited local or personal application.

(*d*), (*e*), (*i*), (*j*), is witnessed by the nearly contemporary Sermon L in Napier's *Wulfstan* p. 266 ff., of which VI Æthelred is a principal source.

[1] *Gesetze* iii, p. 170. [2] Adopted in II Cnut 9.

[3] Liebermann i, p. 479.

[4] Cf. Cnut's letter to his regents and people, § 17 (*Gesetze* i, p. 274), on the penalties for taking a nun to wife.

The assumption has been made throughout that in Æthelred's day laws were promulgated not only by public meetings in borough, shire, or hundred, but through the parish churches, i.e. by the authority of archbishops and bishops. Clearly that was the best way of publishing laws affecting the Church. But these were not sharply distinguished from secular laws. Breaches of both came before the same courts; bishops and aldermen were required to declare both in the shire moots,[1] and parish priests had a part in secular processes, sometimes by virtue of their office, as in oaths and ordeals, sometimes because of their education and local standing, as in the sale of goods.[2] So all new laws could be announced in parish churches with advantage, and the practice is confirmed by the number of contemporary sermons or fragments which deal with laws. How were new laws communicated to the parish priests? One way would be to send them official copies of the laws approved by the witan. But the archbishop or bishop might wish to add explanations or give practical advice, such as would be added nowadays in a covering letter. On the view that has been suggested, Wulfstan preferred to fuse this supplementary material into the text of the laws, a method which would be especially convenient for the less educated clergy. Thus a variant but authoritative text of the one code of laws would be circulated, and if it were sent directly or through bishops to all parishes in the province of York, the number of copies must be reckoned in hundreds.

Two contemporary texts, identical in most respects, were bound to interact, especially in a centre like Worcester, of which Wulfstan was still bishop, and which served as a link between North and South. As examples: the part of the text D Cn.[3] printed by Liebermann i, p. 252 f., is essentially a selection of clauses from VI Æthelred which has been collated for content with the defective text of V Æthelred, so that it omits the requirement that churchscot shall be paid at Martinmas and includes the festival of Edward the Martyr.[4] Again, in the Vatican leaf which preserves the beginning of X Æthelred, the king reminds his people of what was agreed at Enham, and repeats the first three clauses of V Æthelred. The text agrees with Liebermann's second copy of V Æthelred (G[2]), which in its first clause (and in other places not quoted in X Æthelred) has been conflated with VI. Evidently this conflated text was already in use in Æthelred's lifetime. So when later legislation follows these laws, we may expect readings that point to the use of mixed texts, not of sharply segregated forms of V Æthelred on the one hand or VI Æthelred on the other.

[1] III Edgar 5, 2.
[2] III Edmund 5.
[3] See above, p. 278 n. 3.
[4] See above, p. 280 f.

Note B to p. 77

LIBER MONSTRORUM AND ENGLISH HEROIC LEGEND

THE importance of the beginning of *Liber Monstrorum* for *Beowulf* studies has been explained by Miss Dorothy Whitelock, *The Audience of Beowulf*, 1951, p. 46 ff. If my arguments are accepted, its significance is enhanced, and there are far-reaching implications.

The death of Hygelac, king of the Geats, in the second decade of the sixth century, is the one verified and datable event in Old English epic remains (*Beowulf*, *Finn* fragment, *Waldere* fragments). The interest in the details of Geatish history shown in *Beowulf*, especially in the last part, where they are dragged into the story of the Dragon fight, is the more remarkable because the Geats were remote from England, and so obscure from the sixth to the tenth centuries that hardly anything else is recorded of them.

The current explanation is that these stories were brought to England by the latest Anglian settlers, and survived only in England.[1] Thus they serve to support the view, now almost canonical, that from the sixth to the tenth century English heroic legend was insulated from Continental Germanic influences.

Yet recent historians have emphasized Anglo-Saxon contacts with their Continental neighbours.[2] Frisians, whom Müllenhoff[3] thought of as intermediaries in the early diffusion of epic legends, were still manning English ships in Alfred's day.[4] The missionary enterprises of Wilfrid, Willibrord, and Boniface, beginning in the late seventh century and prospering in the eighth, established contact with Germanic peoples from the North Sea to Bavaria: if it could be supposed that all the missionaries were too austere to be interested in secular stories which passed as history, their attendants, messengers, and the ships' crews that carried them must still be reckoned with. A natural trade route ensured com-

[1] See e.g. A. Brandl *Geschichte der altenglischen Literatur*, 1908, p. 12 ff.; H. M. Chadwick *The Heroic Age*, 1912, p. 51 f.; R. W. Chambers *Beowulf: An Introduction*, 1921, p. 102 f.; W. W. Lawrence *Beowulf and Epic Tradition*, 1928, p. 255 ff. See, however, Miss Whitelock's objections, op. cit. p. 46.

[2] Notably W. Levison *England and the Continent in the Eighth Century*, 1946, with its critically selected references.

[3] *Beovulf*, 1889, p. 104 ff.

[4] *Anglo-Saxon Chronicle*, under 897.

munications with Flanders.[1] There were many liens with the empire of Charlemagne, who thought it worth while to collect the vernacular traditions of the Franks,[2] and had close relations with other subject and independent Germanic peoples. Especially in his dealings with Offa we hear something about the foreign travels of laymen—merchants, pilgrims, merchants pretending to be pilgrims, political refugees like Queen Eadburh and the future King Ecgberht. Old Saxons borrowed the story of Cædmon's inspiration,[3] and gave England *Genesis B*. Scandinavian raids began late in the eighth century, but we are not justified in excluding the possibility of friendly intercourse before that date, still less in assuming that in the following period of Scandinavian attacks and settlement, relations with the English were always and everywhere hostile. If we add to these considerations the value attaching to new or different stories in an age when they were the chief kind of entertainment, and the qualifications of the ideal *scop*—far-travelled like Widsith, ready like Deor to produce apt illustrations from a wide repertory—then the supposed insulation of English heroic story from the sixth century onwards is a thing to wonder at rather than a probability to be assumed in the absence of precise evidence to the contrary.

From the nature of the case such evidence is rare. But the *Liber Monstrorum* supplies it at a key point, if it is an English compilation. Near the beginning it reads:

> De Hyglaco[4] Getarum rege:—Et sunt mirae magnitudinis ut rex Higlacus qui imperavit Getis et a Francis occisus est; quem equus a duodecimo anno portare non potuit; cuius ossa in Rheni fluminis insula, ubi in Oceanum prorumpit, reservata sunt et de longinquo venientibus pro miraculo ostenduntur.

This is evidence that information about Hygelac reached England from across the North Sea. What is told about his stature and weight does not derive from *Beowulf* or the known Frankish historians, but follows naturally from the inspection of his bones, and is exactly what is relevant to the author's purpose. It is evidence, too, that when the author wrote, Hygelac's bones were still shown to travellers on an island near the mouth of the Rhine, a district well known to English travellers and missionaries from Wilfrid's time onwards. At that place there was a

[1] See Levison op. cit. p. 167 f. for early traces of English relations with the churches of Flanders, which were continuous throughout the Anglo-Saxon period.

[2] Einhard *Vita* c. 29.

[3] See the *Præfatio in librum antiquum lingua Saxonica conscriptum*, ed. Sievers, *Heliand*, 1878, p. 4.

[4] *Hyglac* is the form in *Liber Vitae*, and is to be expected in Northumbria; see Sievers, Paul and Braune's *Beiträge* x (1885), p. 463 f.

special reason why stories of the Geatish king and the expedition that resulted in his bones being left among the Frisians should be preserved or invented, just as pious stories clustered round the tombs of saints.

Hence the importance of the date of *Liber Monstrorum*. The later it is placed, the more disturbing to the prevailing view its testimony is. Even if it could be carried back to the seventh century (with *Mirabilia* earlier still), it would prove that information about Hygelac the Geat reached England long after the Anglo-Saxon settlement was complete. Nobody, I think, will contend that this text belongs to the sixth century.

Note C to p. 97

THE ARRANGEMENT OF THE EXETER BOOK

THE arrangement, which presented unusual difficulties to a compiler, deserves closer examination. As there is evidence that leaves have been lost before the fragment of *Azarias*, the first part contains all the longer poems, and they are all religious: *Christ I* (*Advent*), *Christ II* (*Ascension*), *Christ III* (*Judgement*), *Guthlac A*, *Guthlac B*, *Azarias*, *Phoenix*, *Juliana*. Their incipits are regularly distinguished by a line of bold capitals with a preceding space. Some arrangement by subject is apparent in the first five; but it is external: for instance, *Azarias* comes between *Guthlac B* and *Phoenix*, which are closely related in style.

Shorter didactic poems, mostly religious, follow on folios 76*b*–100*a*. Three of these are irregularly distinguished by the line of bold capitals and a preceding space, viz. *Gifts of Men* f. 78*a*, *Widsith* f. 84*b*, *Soul and Body* f. 98*a* (the second heading follows *Amen* at the end of the preceding poem, the third follows *Finit* at the end of the Bestiary group). In this part the order of poems is unpredictable; for instance, *Wanderer*, which to us seems close to *Seafarer* in tone and style, is separated from it by two pieces of very different character, *Gifts of Men* and *Precepts*.

Still shorter secular poems, including all the known Old English Riddles, are the main content of the rest of the manuscript. But the Riddle collection is broken at f. 123*a* by *Husband's Message* and *Ruin*, and more glaringly at 115*a* by *Wife's Complaint* and a group of religious pieces—three longer: *Judgement Day*, *Prayer* (*Resignation*), *Descent into Hell*; and four shorter: *Alms*, *Pharaoh* (a kind of riddle), *Paternoster*, and *Maxims* fragments. These seven pieces look like a patch of collected material that was not digested into the general plan. It is salutary to think that had the compiler distributed them so that *The Descent into Hell* came between *Advent* and *Ascension*, it would almost certainly have been claimed as part of the supposed longer work '*Christ*', which even then would lack a *Passion*.

Alongside or among the Riddles, the Exeter Book contains all the extant secular lyrics or elegies. Superficially there are similarities between the two kinds: some of the Riddles are descriptive, as *Ruin* is; many begin in the first person, like *Wife's Complaint*; several contain runic puzzles, as does *Husband's Message*. But one might have hoped for some sign that the Riddles and the elegies were drawn from separate sources. There is none; and if the compiler had found these elegies together, it is barely credible that he would have taken the trouble to scatter them. One detail of their arrangement is perhaps significant: *Deor* (which the scribe has distinguished exceptionally by capitals at the beginning of each stanza) and the old 'First Riddle' come together at f. 100. These are the two Old English poems with refrains, and it is likely enough that they were transcribed from the same source.

Note D to p. 124

THE AUTHORSHIP OF THE VERSE TRANSLATION OF BOETHIUS'S METRA

THE question of the poetic dialect, and especially its vocabulary, would be clearer if Alfred's authorship of the verse translation of the Metres could be established. The comprehensive earlier discussion is well summarized in R. Wülker's *Grundriss zur Geschichte der ags. Litteratur*, Leipzig 1885, p. 414 ff.; and new arguments have been adduced by Sievers (see Sedgefield's edition p. xxxv); by E. Krämer in his edition, *Bonner Beiträge* viii, 1902; and by R. Jordan *Eigentümlichkeiten* p. 67 n. Sedgefield p. xxxvi ff. and G. P. Krapp *The Paris Psalter and the Meters of Boethius*, New York 1933, p. xlv ff. are content to recapitulate and to throw the onus of proof on those who deny Alfred's authorship. It is generally agreed that he made the prose translation, or rather paraphrase, of both the Proses and the Metres;[1] that the Anglo-Saxon verse Metres were produced by simply turning this prose into metre; and that the result has no merit as poetry.

That Boethius's Latin was not consulted afresh for the verse is no objection to Alfred's authorship. He was not a scholar or even well grounded in Latin. William of Malmesbury, who used sources that are now lost, says that Asser prepared the way for the translation of *De Consolatione* by making a simplified Latin version: 'librum Boetii . . . planioribus verbis elucidavit . . . iussu regis . . . ut levius ab eodem in Anglicum transferretur sermonem.'[2] If so, there were two intermediaries between Boethius and the verse paraphrase.

Nor does the poverty of the verse tell against Alfred. There is no reason to think that he had poetic abilities or much previous experience in verse composition; and to reproduce the original successfully required both in an exceptional degree, because the subject-matter lay outside the range of traditional Anglo-Saxon verse.

The arguments that have been drawn from the content or the language of the translation are no more conclusive. Jordan, for instance, finds it significant that the verse has twice *gedrefnesse* 'trouble', which he identifies as an Anglian abstract formation, where the corresponding

[1] The earliest external evidence that Alfred paraphrased *De Consolatione* is his kinsman Æthelweard's statement in the later tenth century; but nothing more can safely be deduced from Æthelweard's artificially obscure Latin.

[2] *Gesta Pontificum* p. 177; cf. *Gesta Regum* i, p. 131.

prose has *gedrefednesse*. The word does not belong to the old poetic vocabulary, but the first form is metrically convenient, the second intractable. Alfred, whose wife was Mercian, who asked the Mercian Wærferth to translate Gregory's *Dialogues* for his personal use, and whose other English literary helpers were Mercians too, is as likely as anybody to make use of such an alternative form to help out his verse. However inconvenient it may be to give him up as the touchstone of pure West Saxon, in fact his literary language was peculiarly subject to Mercian influence. This influence is likely to have effects in verse, where technical difficulties encouraged the borrowing of alternative forms that were easily intelligible. But in prose, too, abnormal forms may be adopted for special reasons: in Alfred's prose works Jost[1] found *nænig* only once, in Wulfstan's account of his Baltic voyage; but it occurs near the end of Alfred's Will, where the West Saxon prose equivalent *nan* had already been used twice in the same sentence.

Really the issue depends on the evidence of the two proems, both of which attribute the verse to Alfred. To understand their claims to authority, some consideration of the two surviving manuscripts is necessary. The twelfth-century MS. Bodley 180 (= B) contains the Prose Proem and the prose paraphrase of Boethius's Proses and Metres. In the mid-tenth-century MS. Otho A vi (= C), now fire-damaged but restorable in essentials from Junius's transcript and collations, the prose and verse proems are followed by the same paraphrase of the Proses, but metrical renderings of most of the Metres are substituted for the corresponding prose renderings of B.[2] From this evidence it has been inferred that Alfred first issued his paraphrase all in prose (as in B) without proem; and that later he, or somebody else, versified the Metres, substituted this verse at the appropriate places, and provided the prose and verse proems which refer to it.[3] On this view any doubts of Alfred's authorship of the verse must attach to the whole of the Prose Proem as well as to the Verse Proem. But it is a possible rather than an inevitable explanation. So long as Alfred began by making a version all in prose

[1] *Wulfstanstudien* p. 159. Its occurrence in the Prologue to Ine's laws, ed. Liebermann i, p. 88, is evidence that *nænig* was general Old English in earlier times.

[2] Metres i, 6, ii, 2, iv, 7 remain in prose, possibly because they were not identifiable as verse in Asser's simplified Latin draft. The arrangement of C is not easy to visualize from Sedgefield's edition, and his text of the prose common to B and C is a composite, not a critical text. Thus at 32/27 he reads *gegyrewod* with B, where C and the still earlier Napier fragment have the correct *geārod* 'endowed'; and at 33/5 he reads *þe on þisse worulde is* with C, where B and the Napier fragment are almost certainly right in omitting *þisse*.

[3] Sedgefield Introd. p. xxxix f., accepting Leicht's interpretation.

(which is natural enough, even if he intended from the outset to versify the Metres), a text of the B-type would exist in manuscript, and it might be preserved by later copies even if Alfred himself published only the final C-type, with one proem (the Prose) or with both. Again, if Alfred versified the Metres and composed the Prose Proem, all the extant materials would be together in the same scriptorium, and the Prose Proem may have been copied into the archetype of B at that stage.

The two proems are very early evidence of the attribution to Alfred, for MS. Otho A VI was written about the middle of the tenth century, when many who knew Alfred were still living. The Verse Proem is the less explicit, and as the information it contains could be derived from the Prose Proem, attention may be concentrated on the latter. Literally translated, it runs:

> 'King Alfred was the translator of this book, and turned it from Latin into English, as it is now done. *Sometimes he put word for word, sometimes sense for sense, according as he could interpret it* most clearly and *with fullest meaning*, despite *the various and manifold worldly troubles* that often harassed him in mind and body. These troubles are very hard for us to number which in his days came upon the kingdom he had taken in hand. And yet, *when he had learned this book*, and turned it from Latin into English prose, he then made it into verse, as it is now done. And now he begs and in God's name beseeches each of those whom it pleases to read this book, to pray for him, and not to blame him if he [the reader] understands it more rightly than he [the translator] could: because every man, *according to the capacity of his mind* and the time available, must speak what he speaks and do what he does.'

This is evidence different in kind from Ælfric's casual attribution of the Old English Bede to Alfred.[1] If the whole proem is a falsification, it is a very elaborate one. The fabricator must have taken pains to borrow the italicized phrases in the first part from Alfred's Prose Preface to the *Pastoral Care*; and the italicized phrase near the end from Alfred's prose translation of Boethius 145/6 ff., 147/14 ff. These parallels are in the Proses, not in the Metres. There too Alfred thrice uses *æmetta* 'free or undisturbed time' (Bosworth-Toller otherwise records it only twice from the *Pastoral Care* and once from the OE. Bede); and the pattern of the last clause appears at 112/19 f.: 'wyrce hwa þæt ðæt he wyrce, oððe do þæt ðæt he do'. The composer must have had, besides, a keen sense of Alfred's difficulties, which is not hidden by the coldness and detachment of the third personal form. And surely the request for prayers, and for a charitable attitude to any defects in the work, is beyond the art of

[1] *Catholic Homilies* ed. Thorpe ii, p. 116 f.

a forger in the early tenth century? No reason has been suggested why so much care should have been taken, in Alfred's lifetime or soon after, to give verisimilitude to a fictitious preface. The Prose Proem has an unmistakable dignity. The insistent 'now . . . now . . . now' suggests that it was composed as soon as the work on Boethius was finished; and, curiously enough, Alfred uses 'now' freely in his Will and the Prose Preface to the *Pastoral Care*. This proem must, I think, be in the main what it professes to be, the preface Alfred wrote for his translation of *De Consolatione*.

The authenticity of parts of it, including the claim that Alfred made the verse, may still be doubted. Certainly the sentence: 'These troubles are very hard for us to number (*ða bisgu us sint swiðe earfoðrimu*) which in his days came upon the kingdom he had taken in hand' reads like the comment of a later writer. The effect of remoteness inherent in the indirect statement must be discounted. In a preface composed by Alfred in his last years, nobody would doubt the genuineness of the sentence: 'It is very hard to recount the troubles which in my time came upon the kingdom I had taken in hand.' But the indirect form is broken by *us*, which invites suspicion. Three possibilities suggest themselves. The whole sentence may be an early interpolation, though there is no special reason why anybody but Alfred should add this reflection: to write a sentence into a book requires some pains and therefore some motive. Or the troublesome *us* may have been added by a reader: yet it is supported by both manuscripts which are in other respects independent, and such a neat way of removing the difficulty is not altogether convincing. Or, after all, Alfred may have composed the sentence. Direct speech breaks in on the artificial indirect in other Anglo-Saxon texts, though I have not noticed a place in which Alfred uses *we*, *us* to mean simply *I*, *me*. But suppose the thought occurred to him that if it was hard for him it was hard for others too, some of whom had supported him through these troubles, to recount them all? The indirect 'ða bisgu *him* sint swiðe earfoðrimu' might seem to give a false emphasis, and he might compromise on the half-impersonal *us*, sharing the difficulty with his readers. In all the circumstances, I prefer this last possibility. Those who maintain that the whole Prose Proem is the work of a clever and painstaking forger must explain why he slipped so unnecessarily into writing *us*.

The sentence that claims the verse for Alfred follows immediately. It repeats the phrase 'as it is now done' to echo the opening sentence, and gives the information, which modern critics confirm, that the verse was made from the prose translation. This would be known to the versifier, whether Alfred or another, but not to anybody who was relying on vague tradition or conjecture. And again, what motive could another author have, at any date that can reasonably be assigned to the proem, for attributing his own work to the King? In those days English books were few, and there were men still alive who knew what Alfred had done.

For these reasons I take the whole of the Prose Proem to be genuine. If so, the verse Metres are a full specimen of the language used by King Alfred in verse in his last years (895–9). A main component is the 'poetic dialect' of the earlier poems, without which Anglo-Saxon alliterative verse is hardly possible. It appears in the general structure of the lines: in phrases like *findan on ferhðe*, *ginfæsta gifa*, *heardra henða*, *meca ecgum*, *mine gefræge*, *ofer Metodes est*; in the many synonyms for 'men', 'man', 'warrior', e.g. *elde* pl., *firas*, *foldbuende*, *sundbuende*, *rinc*, *gumrinc*, *magurinc*, *scealc*, *secg*, *sceotend*, *wigend*, *lindwigend*; in the compound variants for sea: *egorstream*, *eargeblond*, *fifelstream*, *hronmere*, *laguflod*, *merestream*; in uncontracted forms of the present indicative singular and the weak past participle, e.g. *ymbhwearfest*, *swinceð*, *getyhted*. None of these are found in the corresponding prose, and they are structural in the verse. If, then, some poetical words appear which survive in Anglian prose, e.g. *worn* 'multitude' in alliteration, or *sigora* gen. pl. 'victories' where *sige* of the prose would not make metre, they should be ascribed to the traditional poetic dialect, not to an Anglian strain in the versifier or to fresh borrowing from Mercian.

There is besides a strong blend of contemporary West Saxon prose which is alien to the earlier poetry. It is definite in the use of alternative forms like contracted *cymð*, *gesælð*, *geendebyrd*, when they fit the metre, but perceptible everywhere in the prosy and often feeble expression, which allows such a line as

gif þæt nære, þonne hio wære [fordrugod].

In judging the result, it must be remembered that Alfred was a prose-writer, whose natural prose would be both diluted and distorted by the effort to make verse. Besides, he was versifying, as faithfully as he could, his own prose paraphrase: it was far removed from the high style of the earlier poetry, and it proffered lame verses like xxv. 26

ðonne meaht ðu gesion þæt he bið swiðe gelic.

Above all, the subject-matter of *De Consolatione* was strange to alliterative verse, and therefore almost impossible to express in the traditional vocabulary and phrasing. Had Alfred chosen a series of battle-pieces instead of a course of philosophical instruction, he would probably have come nearer the usage of the earlier verse, and been better thought of as a poet.

Note E to p. 184

THE ORDER OF ÆLFRIC'S EARLY BOOKS

In his edition of Ælfric's *De Temporibus Anni*, E.E.T.S. (1942), p. xlix ff., Professor Henel raises new doubts and makes new suggestions about the order of Ælfric's early books. He adopts the reasonable view that *De Temporibus* was composed after the *Catholic Homilies* and before the *Grammar*. He then turns to meet 'a serious objection', first made by Miss C. L. White:[1] it is agreed that Ælfric's first two books are the two volumes of *Catholic Homilies*; it has been generally assumed that the *Grammar* is his third book, the fourth being the *Lives of Saints*: 'so there would be no room for *De Temporibus Anni* before the *Lives*.'

He fails to notice that this objection is based on an indiscriminate use of the terms 'work' and 'book'. The two volumes of *Catholic Homilies* are one work, but Ælfric calls them 'two books'. The *Grammar* is one work and in the prefaces he calls it *iste libellus, þeos lytle boc, þeos boc*. *De Temporibus* is a work but not a book; he calls it *an lytel cwyde* 'a short discourse', which is not to be reckoned a sermon (*spell*). Hence *De Temporibus* stands outside Ælfric's numbering of his early books. It was certainly issued after the *Catholic Homilies*, but Ælfric's statements would allow it to come either before or after the *Grammar*.

Having noted the relative smallness of *De Temporibus* as a possible answer to the objection, Professor Henel goes on to propose an alternative answer: that the *Lives of Saints* are not Ælfric's fourth book, but the fourth book of his translations from sacred sources; so that neither *De Temporibus* nor the *Grammar* is in the count. We are then left without a third book of translations from sacred sources. He suggests that Ælfric's share in the Old English *Heptateuch*, defined as '*Genesis* i–xxiv and *Numeri* xiii–xxvi, perhaps more', is this third book, which falls between the *Grammar* and the *Lives of Saints*.

I confess to some bewilderment at the number of problems raised and left unexplained by this suggested alternative answer to an objection which is really groundless. But it serves a useful purpose by challenging the assumption that Ælfric thinks of the *Grammar* as his third book when he speaks of the *Lives* as *quartus liber*.

It will help the discussion to quote the Latin *Preface* to the *Lives*:[2]

'This book also (*hunc quoque codicem*) I have translated from the

[1] *Ælfric*, Boston 1898, p. 54 n.

[2] Skeat's translation, with one necessary adjustment which does not affect its impartiality in this argument.

Latin into the usual English speech, desiring to profit others. . . . For I call to mind that in two former books (*in duobus anterioribus libris*) I have set forth the passions or lives of those saints whom that illustrious nation celebrates by honouring their festival,[1] and it has [now] pleased me to set forth, in this book, the passions as well as the lives of those saints whom not the vulgar, but the monks, honour by special services. I do not promise, however, to write more in this tongue, because it is not fitting that more should be translated into our language, lest peradventure the pearls of Christ be had in disrespect. And therefore I hold my peace as to the book called *Vitae Patrum*, wherein are contained many subtle points which ought not to be laid open to the laity, nor indeed are we ourselves quite able to fathom them. . . . Nor am I able, in this translation, to render everything word for word, but I have at any rate carefully endeavoured to give exact sense for sense, just as I find it in the holy writing (*in sancta scriptura*). . . . Let it not be considered as a fault in me that I turn sacred narrative (*divinam scripturam*) into our own tongue, since the request of many of the faithful shall clear me in this matter, particularly that of the governor Æthelwerd, and of my friend Æthelmer, who most highly honour my translations by their perusal of them; nevertheless I have resolved at last to desist from such labour after completing the fourth book, that I may not be regarded as tedious (*decrevi modo quiescere post quartum librum a tali studio, ne superfluus iudicer*).'

The beginning of the English preface is also relevant:

'Ælfric humbly greets Alderman Æthelweard; and I tell thee, beloved, that I have now collected in this book the passions of the saints which I have had occasion to turn into English; because thou, beloved, above all, and Æthelmær, have asked me for such writings, and received them from my hands, to strengthen your faith with narratives which hitherto you had not in your own language. Thou knowest, beloved, that in the two previous books (*on þam twam ærrum bocum*) we translated the passions and lives of the saints whom the [whole] English nation honours with festivals. Now it has seemed good to us to write this book about the passions and lives of the saints whom monks among themselves honour in their offices.'

Here *sancta scriptura, divina scriptura*, are used to include the lives of saints, and do not, as might be supposed, point to translations from the Bible.[2] The references to 'the two earlier books' and 'the fourth book'

[1] This is the definition of the content of the two volumes of *Catholic Homilies*.

[2] Similarly, in the Latin preface to the first volume of *Catholic Homilies*, where exposition of Bible texts bulks larger, he writes: 'transtulimus

imply that contemporary readers would be in no doubt about the identity of the 'third book', which is not mentioned. Presumably its contents were not like those of the books under discussion, and this condition would suit the *Grammar* better than a collection of translations from the Bible. But did Ælfric at any time issue such a collection?

We may rule out a collection in the precise form suggested by Professor Henel—'portions of the Old Testament: *Genesis* i–xxiv and *Numeri* xiii–xxvi; perhaps more'—as inconsistent with Ælfric's orderly mind. It was one thing to translate *Genesis* i–xxiv for Æthelweard, who already had the rest in a version by a different translator, and quite another to issue such fragments as the 'third book' of a series in which the first, second, and fourth books are carefully planned. The same objection would apply to the *Genesis* fragment taken alone. It would be less effective against a translation of the whole Pentateuch.

But there is no evidence that Ælfric translated the whole Pentateuch. Apart from a doubt about the correct text, the statement in his letter to Sigweard[1] is obscure, because he does not distinguish translation of the words of the Bible from expository sermons. Critics seem to be agreed that the extant Old English version of the Pentateuch contains little of his work. Nor is there evidence that he issued a volume containing translations of the Pentateuch by other hands, let alone that he thought of it as his own third book. He objects to the work of other authors being mingled with his own.[2] The Preface to his *Genesis* fragment makes it doubtful that, if a volume of translations from the Bible were part of his plan of instruction, he would choose the Old Testament. Besides, his books that are certainly early—*Catholic Homilies I*, *Catholic Homilies II*, *Grammar*, *Lives of Saints*—have each their Latin and English prefaces, and one would expect any intervening book to be similarly equipped. But no preface to the Pentateuch[3] (or Hexateuch) survives, and evidently the compiler of the extant Old English version did not know of one, since he used Ælfric's inappropriate English preface to the first part of *Genesis*.

By comparison, the case for regarding the *Grammar* as the implied 'third book' is strong. It has Latin and English prefaces. Its English preface is evidence that it was, in fact, Ælfric's third book: 'I Ælfric decided to turn this little book on grammar, called [in Latin] "Grammatica", into the English language, after I had translated the two books

hunc codicem ex libris Latinorum, scilicet sanctae scripturae'. 'Adapt' is nearer than 'translate' to Ælfric's sense of *transferre* and *awendan*.

[1] Ed. S. J. Crawford, *The Heptateuch*, E.E.T.S. (1922), p. 31 *On ealre ðare fare* of the later MS. is easier to construe than *on ealre þare racu* of MS. Laud Misc. 509.

[2] See p. 167 above.

[3] Ælfric's term is 'the five books that Moses wrote'; so it is unlikely that he would describe a collection of or from them as one book.

containing eighty sermons [i.e. *Catholic Homilies* I and II], because grammar is the key that unlocks the meaning of books', &c. It is a necessary part of his plan of instruction: first the two books of *Catholic Homilies*, each providing a year's course of sermons for the feast-days that were nationally kept, to meet the needs of the parishes; then *De Temporibus*, a supplement, primarily for the use of priests, on the universe and the elements of chronology; then the *Grammar* to enlarge the number of those who could read Latin; then the *Lives of Saints* to make available in a wider circle certain cults and exemplary legends that had been confined to the monasteries. It was a plan for education in the vernacular comparable to Alfred's plan a century earlier, but more systematic and concentrated on the advancement of religion.

To object that the *Grammar* was insignificant in comparison with the *Catholic Homilies* and the *Lives* is to mistake its contemporary importance. It was then something new—the first Latin grammar in any vernacular. It was original, too, in its aim of providing an introduction to both languages (*sum angyn to ægðrum gereorde*), for I believe Ælfric was the first writer to commend and to practise the study of English grammar and style by the methods applicable to Latin. Although he modestly addresses this book to the young, he does not underestimate its part in his general plan: it is to provide, as the English preface shows, for the future of learning and religion:

> 'Whence shall wise teachers come among God's people, unless they learn while they are young? And how can the faith be propagated, if sacred doctrine and its teachers decay? Therefore God's ministers and monks should take warning now, lest in our day sacred doctrine should lose its fervour and decay; as happened in England only a few years ago, so that no English priest could compose or thoroughly interpret a letter in Latin, until Archbishop Dunstan and Bishop Æthelwold restored learning in the monasteries.'

The practical success of the *Grammar* justified his expectations, for no other book in Anglo-Saxon approaches it in the number of copies that survive. Positive evidence is needed to dispossess it of its natural place as the third book implied in Ælfric's description of the *Lives of Saints* as *quartus liber*.

INDEX I. MANUSCRIPTS NOTICED

OXFORD

VERCELLI

VARIOUS

INDEX II. VERSES DISCUSSED OR EMENDED

INDEX III. WORDS AND FORMS

† *indicates rejection of the word, form, or usage.*

INDEX IV. GENERAL

Some scattered matter is summarized under HANDWRITING, SCRIBES, TEXTUAL CRITICISM, OLD ENGLISH STUDIES. *Works whose authorship is reasonably certain are entered under their authors. The figures I, II, III refer to the special indexes.*

OTHER TITLES IN THIS HARDBACK REPRINT PROGRAMME FROM SANDPIPER BOOKS LTD (LONDON) AND POWELLS BOOKS (CHICAGO)

ISBN 0–19–	Author	Title
8143567	ALFÖLDI A.	The Conversion of Constantine and Pagan Rome
6286409	ANDERSON George K.	The Literature of the Anglo-Saxons
8228813	BARTLETT & MacKAY	Medieval Frontier Societies
8111010	BETHURUM Dorothy	Homilies of Wulfstan
8114222	BROOKS Kenneth R.	Andreas and the Fates of the Apostles
8203543	BULL Marcus	Knightly Piety & Lay Response to the First Crusade
8216785	BUTLER Alfred J.	Arab Conquest of Egypt
8148348	CAMPBELL J.B.	The Emperor and the Roman Army 31 BC to 235 AD
826643X	CHADWICK Henry	Priscillian of Avila
826447X	CHADWICK Henry	Boethius
8219393	COWDREY H.E.J.	The Age of Abbot Desiderius
8148992	DAVIES M.	Sophocles: Trachiniae
825301X	DOWNER L.	Leges Henrici Primi
8154372	FAULKNER R.O.	The Ancient Egyptian Pyramid Texts
8221541	FLANAGAN Marie Therese	Irish Society, Anglo-Norman Settlers, Angevin Kingship
8143109	FRAENKEL Edward	Horace
8201540	GOLDBERG P.J.P.	Women, Work and Life Cycle in a Medieval Economy
8140215	GOTTSCHALK H.B.	Heraclides of Pontus
8266162	HANSON R.P.C.	Saint Patrick
8224354	HARRISS G.L.	King, Parliament and Public Finance in Medieval England to 1369
8581114	HEATH Sir Thomas	Aristarchus of Samos
8140444	HOLLIS A.S.	Callimachus: Hecale
8212968	HOLLISTER C. Warren	Anglo-Saxon Military Institutions
8223129	HURNARD Naomi	The King's Pardon for Homicide – before AD 1307
8140401	HUTCHINSON G.O.	Hellenistic Poetry
8142560	JONES A.H.M.	The Greek City
8218354	JONES Michael	Ducal Brittany 1364–1399
8271484	KNOX & PELCZYNSKI	Hegel's Political Writings
8225253	LE PATOUREL John	The Norman Empire
8212720	LENNARD Reginald	Rural England 1086–1135
8212321	LEVISON W.	England and the Continent in the 8th century
8148224	LIEBESCHUETZ J.H.W.G.	Continuity and Change in Roman Religion
8141378	LOBEL Edgar & PAGE Sir Denys	Poetarum Lesbiorum Fragmenta
8241445	LUKASIEWICZ, Jan	Aristotle's Syllogistic
8152442	MAAS P. & TRYPANIS C.A .	Sancti Romani Melodi Cantica
8148178	MATTHEWS John	Western Aristocracies and Imperial Court AD 364–425
8223447	McFARLANE K.B.	Lancastrian Kings and Lollard Knights
8226578	McFARLANE K.B.	The Nobility of Later Medieval England
8148100	MEIGGS Russell	Roman Ostia
8148402	MEIGGS Russell	Trees and Timber in the Ancient Mediterranean World
8142641	MILLER J. Innes	The Spice Trade of the Roman Empire
8147813	MOORHEAD John	Theoderic in Italy
8264259	MOORMAN John	A History of the Franciscan Order
8116020	OWEN A.L.	The Famous Druids
8131445	PALMER, L.R.	The Interpretation of Mycenaean Greek Texts
8143427	PFEIFFER R.	History of Classical Scholarship (vol 1)
8111649	PHEIFER J.D.	Old English Glosses in the Epinal-Erfurt Glossary
8142277	PICKARD-CAMBRIDGE A.W.	Dithyramb Tragedy and Comedy
8269765	PLATER & WHITE	Grammar of the Vulgate
8213891	PLUMMER Charles	Lives of Irish Saints (2 vols)
820695X	POWICKE Michael	Military Obligation in Medieval England
8269684	POWICKE Sir Maurice	Stephen Langton
821460X	POWICKE Sir Maurice	The Christian Life in the Middle Ages
8225369	PRAWER Joshua	Crusader Institutions
8225571	PRAWER Joshua	The History of The Jews in the Latin Kingdom of Jerusalem
8143249	RABY F.J.E.	A History of Christian Latin Poetry
8143257	RABY F.J.E.	A History of Secular Latin Poetry in the Middle Ages (2 vols)
8214316	RASHDALL & POWICKE	The Universities of Europe in the Middle Ages (3 vols)
8148380	RICKMAN Geoffrey	The Corn Supply of Ancient Rome
8141076	ROSS Sir David	Aristotle: Metaphysics (2 vols)
8141092	ROSS Sir David	Aristotle: Physics
8264178	RUNCIMAN Sir Steven	The Eastern Schism
814833X	SALMON J.B.	Wealthy Corinth
8171587	SALZMAN L.F.	Building in England Down to 1540
8218362	SAYERS Jane E.	Papal Judges Delegate in the Province of Canterbury 1198–1254
8221657	SCHEIN Sylvia	Fideles Crucis

8148135	SHERWIN WHITE A.N.	The Roman Citizenship
8113927	SISAM, Kenneth	Studies in the History of Old English Literature
8642040	SOUTER Alexander	A Glossary of Later Latin to 600 AD
8222254	SOUTHERN R.W.	Eadmer: Life of St. Anselm
8251408	SQUIBB G.	The High Court of Chivalry
8212011	STEVENSON & WHITELOCK	Asser's Life of King Alfred
8212011	SWEET Henry	A Second Anglo-Saxon Reader—Archaic and Dialectical
8148259	SYME Sir Ronald	History in Ovid
8143273	SYME Sir Ronald	Tacitus (2 vols)
8200951	THOMPSON Sally	Women Religious
8201745	WALKER Simon	The Lancastrian Affinity 1361–1399
8161115	WELLESZ Egon	A History of Byzantine Music and Hymnography
8140185	WEST M.L.	Greek Metre
8141696	WEST M.L.	Hesiod: Theogony
8148542	WEST M.L.	The Orphic Poems
8140053	WEST M.L.	Hesiod: Works & Days
8152663	WEST M.L.	Iambi et Elegi Graeci
822799X	WHITBY M. & M.	The History of Theophylact Simocatta
8206186	WILLIAMSON, E.W.	Letters of Osbert of Clare
8114877	WOOLF Rosemary	The English Religious Lyric in the Middle Ages
8119224	WRIGHT Joseph	Grammar of the Gothic Language